Parties and Politics at the Mughal Court 1707–1740

Parties and Politics
at the
Mughal Court
1707–1740

SATISH CHANDRA

OXFORD
UNIVERSITY PRESS

OXFORD
UNIVERSITY PRESS

YMCA Library Building, Jai Singh Road, New Delhi 110 001

Oxford University Press is a department of the University of Oxford. It furthers the University's objective of excellence in research, scholarship, and education by publishing worldwide in

Oxford New York
Auckland Bangkok Buenos Aires Cape Town Chennai
Dar es Salaam Delhi Hong Kong Istanbul Karachi Kolkata
Kuala Lumpur Madrid Melbourne Mexico City Mumbai Nairobi
Sao Paulo Shanghai Singapore Taipei Tokyo Toronto

and an associated company in Berlin

First published 1959
By People's Publishing House
Fourth Edition 2002
By Oxford University Press, New Delhi

ISBN 0 19 565444 7

Typeset in Pratap (Baskerville) in 10.5/12
by Excellent Laser Typesetters, Pitampura, Delhi 110 034
Printed in India at Pauls Press, New Delhi 110 020
Published by Manzar Khan, Oxford University Press
YMCA Library Building, Jai Singh Road, New Delhi 110 001

Dedicated with love and gratitude
To my father
Dr (Sir) SITA RAM

DIACRITICAL MARKS

ḥ	ح
ṣ	ص
s̤	ث
ṭ	ط
ẓ	ض
z̤	ظ
z̲	ذ
‘	ع
’	و

Vowels

ā	long	a	short
ī	long	i	short
ū	long	u	short

Contents

Preface to the Fourth Edition **xi**
Preface to the Third Edition **xxii**
Preface to the Second Edition **xxiii**
Preface to the First Edition **xxiv**
Abbreviations **xxvii**
Introduction **1**
The Dominant Classes in Medieval Indian Society 3
The Zamindars 3
Assignees of Land Revenue—Jagirdars and Others 7
The Organization, Character and Composition of the Nobility 11
Stresses Operating on the Nobility 19
Political Problems 19
Crisis of the Jagirdari System 29
Note on Khāliṣah and Zamindars 34
Note on the Crisis of the Jagirdari System 35
I Beginning of the Party Struggle at the Court **40**
Groups at the Court 40
The Civil War 49
Marāthā and Rajput Affairs 57
II Conciliation or Coercion? **60**
Bahādur Shāh 60
The Rajput Question 67
The Deccan Problem 79
The Sikh Uprising 89

Death of Mun'im Khān: Beginning of the Struggle for Wizārāt 92
General Policy and Administration 94

III Zu'lfiqār Khān Struggles for Wizārat **101**
The Problem of Wizārat 101
Zu'lfiqār Khān and the League of the Three Princes 104
Zu'lfiqār Khān as *Wazīr*—His Power and Position 107
General Policy and Administration of Zu'lfiqār Khān 113
Defeat and Downfall of Jahāndār Shah and Zu'lfiqār Khān 122

IV The Saiyid Brothers Struggle for 'New' Wizārat (i) **126**
Antecedents and Early Careers of the Saiyid Brothers 126
Early Relations of Farrukh Siyar and the Saiyid Brothers 129
Position and General Policy of the Saiyids after the Accession of Farrukh Siyar 135
The First Trial of Strength—Its Causes and Consequences 142

V The Saiyid Brothers Struggle for 'New' Wizārat (ii) **155**
Position of 'Abdullāh Khān 155
The Recall of Jai Singh, and the Outbreak of the Jat War 160
Deepening of the Political Crisis at the Court 164
The Saiyid-Marāthā Pact 168
Events Leading to the Deposition of Farrukh Siyar 171

VI The Saiyid 'New' Wizārat **181**
Powers and Position of the Saiyids 181
Early Revolts against the Saiyids 183
Political Problems of the Saiyids 186
The Revolt of Niẕām-ul-Mulk and the Downfall of the Saiyids 192

VII Niẕām-ul-Mulk and the End of the Struggle for Wizārat **205**
The Wizārat of M. Amīn Khān 205

Arrival of Niẓām-ul-Mulk and his Early Difficulties 207
Niẓām-ul-Mulk's Scheme of Reforms, and his Departure for the Deccan 211
Jat and Rajput Affairs 214

VIII The Marāthā Advance Towards North India (1725–31) **221**
General Features 221
The Marāthās and Their Policy of Expansion 224
The Marāthās and Niẓām-ul-Mulk 228
The Marāthā Advance into Malwa and Gujarāt 231
The North Indian Reaction 235

IX Conquest of Malwa and Bundelkhand (1732–42) **254**
The Progress of Marāthā Armies 254
The 'Peace' and the 'War' Parties at the Court 258
The Peace Negotiations of 1736 262
The Marāthā Raid into the Dū'āb 266
The Battle of Bhopal 268
Final Ceding of Malwa and Bundelkhand 273

Appendix A: Was There an Imperial Campaign in the Year 1735–6? 276

X Mughal Politics and Nādir Shāh **278**
The Northwest and the Mughals 278
Racial Groups and Party Politics at the Court (1728–37) 280
Invasion of Nādir Shāh and the Attitude of the Nobles 283

Concluding Remarks **293**

Appendix B: Document to Illustrate the Early Relations of the Saiyids and the Rajputs 305

Appendix C: Documents Concerning the Early Relations of the Rajputs and the Marāthās 307

Select Bibliography **311**

Chronology **321**

Index **331**

Preface to the Fourth Edition

This book when first printed in 1959, was designed to shift discussion on the fall of the Mughal empire from the acts of omission and commission of individuals, especially Aurangzīb, to the larger social, economic, and institutional-cum-administrative processes. It was hoped that this would also help in placing religion in a broader socio-political and economic context, and not seen as almost the sole motivating factor in history during Medieval times. It is difficult to say to what extent these objectives have been attained.

Another purpose of the study was to re-examine the role of the eighteenth century, specially its first half, which, till then, had been dismissed as a period of growing anarchy, decline of character, and cultural stagnation.

Following the present work, there have been many more studies in which discussion on some of the issues that had been raised here were carried further. Thus, the character, composition, and role of the Mughal nobility; the structure and composition of the rural society with special reference to the landed elements; the growth of the economy including the agrarian economy and its impact on the primary producer, the peasant; the role of opposition and dissident movements and elements, such as the Marāthās, the Rājpūts, the Jats, the Afghāns, and the Sikhs have been subjected to critical and scholarly study by a number of historians. I have written elsewhere on some of these.[1] It is not my purpose here to

1 *The Eighteenth Century in India: Its Economy and the Role of the Marathas, the Jats, the Sikhs and the Afghans*, Calcutta, 1986, rev. ed., 1991.

review these various works except in so far as they have a bearing on some of the major issues raised in the present study.

There has been a good deal of discussion on the crisis of the *jāgīrdārī* system in the context of a discussion on the factors leading to the downfall of the Mughal empire. I have added a note on the subject in the present work, and have also written on the subject separately.[2]

I had argued that the basic problem facing the Mughals was that the available social surplus was insufficient to defray the cost of administration, pay for wars of one type or another, and to give the ruling class a standard of life in keeping with its expectations.[3] I had linked the problem to the continuous expansion of the ruling class, price rise etc. one the one hand, and, on the other, to 'a deep seated social crisis which had resulted in limited expansion of agriculture and also limited rapid expansion of industry and trade (both of which were) based on the introduction of new technology, and the removal of all barriers hindering that expansion'.[4]

In recent studies there has been a tendency to look upon the *jāgīrdārī* crisis merely as a financial-cum-administrative crisis rather than treating it simultaneously as a manifestation of a deep-seated social crisis. Athar Ali has provided a great deal of statistical information on the expansion and composition of the Mughal nobility under Jahangīr and Shāh Jahān, as also under Aurangzīb. He has shown that between 1595 and 1656–7, the number of *manṣabdārs* holding ranks of 500 *ẕāt* and above increased 4.2 times. During Aurangzīb's reign the number of *manṣabdārs* holding rank of 1,000 *ẕāt* and above (figures below that are very hard to get) increased much more slowly—from 486 between 1658–78 to 575 between 1679–1707 i.e. an increase of only 16.25 per cent.[5] While Athar Ali notes that these figures are incomplete, he argues plausibly for a slowdown of the increase of ranks under Aurangzīb. However, the *jāgīrdārī* crisis continued to grow during the period. J. F. Richards has argued against it, pointing out that the incorporation of Bījāpur and Golconda increased the resources of the Mughals by 24 per cent,

2 'Review of the Crisis of the Jagirdari System' in *Medieval Indian Society, Jagirdari Crisis and the Village*, New Delhi, 1982, pp. 61–75.

3 *Parties and Politics*, 1959, xlvi.

4 Ibid., xlix.

5 Athar Ali, *The Mughal Nobility under Aurangzeb*, 2nd ed., Delhi, 1997, 9–11; *Apparatus of Empire*, 1985, xiii–xvii.

with the *manṣab* ranks increasing only to that extent. In support of his contention that there was no *jāgīrdārī* crisis as such, J. F. Richards cited documents from the Deccan from the 'Ināyat Jung Collection showing large areas under *pāi bāqī*, i.e. areas yet to be assigned as jāgīr.[6]

J. F. Richards' contention that there was no *jāgīrdārī* crisis has been refuted by a number of scholars and needs hardly to be gone into in detail here. It is clear that the graphic accounts of the suffering of the nobility, especially the *khānazāds*, i.e. sons and descendants of old nobles, due to lack of *jāgīrs*, or delays in granting them, cited by contemporary observers such as Khāfī Khān and Bhīmsen cannot be set aside on the basis of *jama'* figures or stray documents. A careful study of the Mughal documents of the Deccan, especially the mass of documents in the 'Ināyat Jung Collection, has yet to made. Even a cursory study of these documents show numerous complaints about lack of *pāi bāqī* and that due to *be-jāgīrī* (lack of *jāgīrs*) people were dying everyday. These complaints seem to be particularly numerous after R.Y.40, 1696–7.[7] Athar Ali has also drawn attention to a document of the year A.H. 1117, 1706 relating to Hyderbadi Karnātaka, contained in *Selected Documents of Aurangzeb's Reign* (ed., Yusuf Husain Khan) showing that the area under *khāliṣah* accounted for only 6 per cent of the *jama'*, the *pāi bāqī* accounted for 20 per cent of which 16 per cent was in the hands of *polygārs*, thus leaving very small areas for assignment.[8]

However, even this does not provide us a clear picture of the situation. A recent study of the 'Ināyat Jung documents shows that there was a large amount of *pāi bāqī* in the Ḥaiderābādi and Bījāpur areas which were called *mulk-i-jadīd* or new areas.[9] In a statement

6 J. F. Richards, *Mughal Administration in Golconda*, Oxford, 1975, 158, 306–9.

7 See S. M. Azizuddin Husain, 'Scarcity of *pai baqi* Lands During Aurangzeb's Reign in the Light of Inayat Jung Collection Documents', *Procs. I.H.C.*, xxxlx, 1978, 426–30.

8 Athar Ali, *The Mughal Nobility under Aurangzeb, 1997*, 2nd ed., xxi–xxii.

9 'Problems of the Deccan Administration in the last Decade of Aurangzīb's Reign—based on Explorations in the 'Ināyat Jung Collection' of the National Archives, Zakir Husain, (paper presented to the I.H.C Session, Calcutta (lxi), 2001, in 'Papers from the Aligarh Historians Society', ed. Irfan Habib, 54–66 (mimeo).

addressed to Aurangzīb it is stated that 'In the *mulk-i-jadīd* Bījāpur and Ḥaiderābād the *pāi bāqī* is considerable, since owing to its low income the (claimants) representatives do not accept (*jāgīrs*) from it in accordance with the *jama'*....'[10]

The background to this situation is clear from the documents. The *mulk-i-qadīm* or the old country was the area in the Deccan conquered upto the time of Shāh Jahān, i.e. Khāndesh, Ahmadnagar, and Berār while *mulk-i-jadīd* or the new country included the areas conquered by Aurangzīb which comprised Bījāpur and Ḥaiderabād including the Karnataka, and parts of Daultabad and Bidar provinces.[11] Large parts of the *mulk-i-jadīd* were disturbed and unsettled, and were called *ghair-'amlī*. This was particularly so in the Karnataka where the *polygārs* were very powerful, and no settlement had been made with them so that military force was the only means of compelling them to pay. The position was better in the old Ḥaiderabād state, but the situation in Bījāpur had deteriorated due to Marāthā depredations.[12]

Faced with the unceasing demands for war, provisioning of forts, cost of artillery and payment for the soldiers, Aurangzīb tried to increase the *Khāliṣah* by incorporating into it the more productive areas, and to assign *jāgīrs* to the nobles serving in the Deccan in the less productive, *ghair-'amlī* areas. This was resisted by the nobles because of the yield being far below the *jama'*—in some cases even of two months.[13] The *manṣabdārs* were afraid that in this situation they would not be able to present a sufficient quota for inspection (*dāgh*), and their *jāgīrs* would be confiscated.

This was the reason why large areas remained under *pāi bāqī*. Far from showing that the existence of large *pāi-bāqī* implied that there was no shortage of *jāgīrs*, it indicated a growing crisis in the functioning of the *jāgīrdārī* system.

How did Aurangzīb himself see this developing crisis? Perhaps the situation was too complex for a uniform approach. Thus, he does reluctantly agree to reduction (*takhfīf*) of *jama'* of the *jāgīrs* in the new areas, but also remarks: 'The disorderly, useless

10 'Ināyat Jung Collection—hereafter I.J.C.—1/0/0 (old 1/14/129, not dated).

11 I.J.C. 146/12–167 and 178.

12 J. F. Richards, *Golconda loc.cit.*, 111–34.

13 C. I/40/10–27 dt. 25 *Sha'bān* 40 R.Y., 19 March 1697; Zakir Husain, *loc.cit.*, 56–60.

Decannis should be confined to the *mulk-i-jadīd*, and to the (old areas) with reduction (only) and only, thereafter in other areas.'[14]

But in general Aurangzīb does not seem to have been conscious of a growing *jāgīrdārī* crisis. His constant refrain was that there was no shortage of *jāgīrs*—pointing perhaps to the large *pāi bāqī* which was unacceptable to the nobles. He ordered that expenditure should match with income, and asked for *khāliṣah* to be expanded to meet the expenditure—'but not at the expense of (*jāgīrs* assigned for meeting) pay claims of the army'![15] He insisted on old rules and regulations (*ẓābṭah wa dastūr*) being implemented, although the situation was vastly different, with many Marāthās (probably a euphemism for Deccanis) continuing, in connivance with revenue officials, to hold their *jāgīrs* even without any contingents.[16]

Thus, it seems that Aurangzīb was living in an unreal world of his own, increasingly losing touch with harsh reality. That the *jāgīrdārī* system was becoming dysfunctional has been hinted at indirectly by Bhīmsen. He points out that because of the smallness of the forces of the *manṣabdārs* and the *faujdārs*, the *zamindars* had become strong, and that in this situation 'it was difficult for a *dām* or *darham* to reach the *jāgīrdār*'.[17] Bhīmsen has underlined the social basis of the *jāgīrdārī* system. The *jāgīrdārī* system implied delegating to the *jāgīrdārs* the responsibility of collecting state dues from the *zamindars* who were numerous, armed with their own bastions (*garhis*) and clan/caste followers among the cultivators. The symbiotic and contradictory relationship between the state and the *zamindars* has been brought out by Nurul Hasan and we hardly need to dwell on it here.[18] The *zamindars* in the Deccan might have been reconciled to Mughal rule, and were willing to aid them in the tasks of revenue assessment and collection if the *jāgīrdārī* system had worked reasonably well and Mughal rule had

14 L.J.C.—1/0/0–486. A separate order says '...newly enrolled Decannis, without contingents should receive most of their *ẕāt* pay claim in the New Territory (*mulk-i-jadīd*)'.

15 Zakir Husain, *loc.cit.*,

16 I.J.C. 1/45/11–12.

17 Bhīmsen, *Nuskha-i-Dilkasha*, ff. 139a–b.

18 S. Nurul Hasan, 'Zamindars under the Mughals' in *Land Control and Social Structure in Indian History* (ed.) F. E. Frykenburg, Madison, 1969, 18–31.

stabilized, for which a settlement with the Marāthās was necessary. By the time this had been done under the successors of Aurangzīb, the roving Marāthā bands had become too powerful to be contained, and the Imperial authority had been weakened due to factionalism, civil wars, etc. This led to the further accentuation of the *jāgīrdārī* crisis which, in turn, reacted on the Imperial authority.

It has been argued in the present work that the growing factionalism in the nobility was based on struggle for power, on the one hand, and, on the other, struggle for the possession of productive *jāgīrs*, the ethnic form being, at best, an outer cover which could be departed from at any time according to need and convenience.

The *jāgīrdārī* crisis grew apace during the first half of the eighteenth century. Some of the manifestations were: (i) growing factionalism in the nobility; (ii) distancing of the *khānazāds* from the monarchy; (iii) growth of the *ijāra* system; (iv) growing dysfunctionality of the Mughal military system based on cavalry contingents led by nobles; and (v) modification of the *jāgīr* system, with a tendency of both *jāgīrs* and offices to become hereditary.

The old hierarchical society, and the *jāgīrdārī* system which was based on it, were at odds with the rising social forces. The impact of this on the *jāgīrdārī* crisis during the eighteenth century, and its impact on the rise of a new class of *zamindars* who were more assertive, and not prepared to accept the role assigned to them by Mughal administrators, needs to be studied concretely.

Recent studies on the nature of rural society in eastern Rajasthan show that there was a process of growing segmentation of rural society, largely in response to a growing market-oriented money economy. Mughal agrarian policies also tended to favour the emergence of a class of rich cultivators who had the necessary physical and monetary resources to expand and improve cultivation.[19] The emergence of this class of cultivators with sizeable human and physical resources, including land, at their disposal,

19 See present author's 'Role of the Local Community, the Zamindars and the State in Providing Capital Inputs for the Growth and Expansion of Cultivation' in *Medieval India: Society etc.*, 166–83. Also, Nurul Hasan *et al.* 'The Pattern of Agrarian Production in the Territories of Amber (C. 1650–1750) in *Procs. I.H.C.*, xxvii, 1966, 245–64.

and dominating the village community, often on a caste basis, consisted of what were broadly designated *khud-kāsht* or resident owner-cultivators. These sections formed, for some time, what I have called 'a tripod' with the *zamindar*s and the state forming the other two legs. I have argued this was the basis of rural stability in north India during the first half of the seventeenth century. We are still not clear about the factors leading to the break-up of this tripod in the upper Gangetic doab and the Punjab during the second half of the seventeenth century. Thus, some of the *khud-kāsht*, such as the Jats of western Uttar Pradesh and Punjab moved towards opposition to the Mughal state. Maybe the slow pace of development, the unwillingness/inability of the Mughal state to involve these rising elements more closely in the tasks of administration, and reluctance to accord to these non-elite elements a higher status than was normative in an essentially hierarchical society may explain it. We have mentioned elsewhere that the rise of the Marāthā movement in opposition to the Mughals was based not merely on a lure for plunder but also a bid to raise social status.[20] Recent studies show that many of the great Marāthā military leaders of the eighteenth century and prominent military figures did not belong to old *deshmukh* families, but came from the lower elements aspiring to raise their social status.[21]

Under different circumstances, these development–oriented rich peasants could have played the same role in India as the squirearchy in England. However, during the eighteenth century, we see some of the rich peasants emerging as *ijāredār*s or *mahājans*.[22]

As far as the 'rich firms' of bankers is concerned, there is little evidence to support the thesis that they turned against the Mughal rulers, and aided in the dissolution of the empire. However, once a regional ruler had emerged and stabilized his position, these 'firms' were prepared to play a role in transmitting money or

20 See Satish Chandra's 'Social Background to the Rise of the Maratha Movement during the Seventeenth Century' in *Medieval India*, 139–46.

21 Stewart Gordan, *The Marathas*, CUP, 1993, 108. '(Except for three families) the rest of Shahu's elite were leaders of successful, largely independent bands.' Many of them had been village head-men or petty deshmukhs.

22 Dilbagh Singh, *The State, Landlord and Peasants in Rajasthan during the 18th Century*, Delhi, 1990, 130–7; S. P. Gupta, the *Agrarian System of Eastern Rajasthan*, Delhi, 1986, 225–32.

providing loans, as in the case of the Marwaris who migrated to Poona, or the Marwaris such as Jagat Seth, and the Armenian Khwāja Wājid at Murshidabad in Bengal. Some bankers took lands on *ijāra* as security for the money they had advanced.[23] But by far and large, the traders and bankers did not try to purchase land or become *zamindar*s, the Burdhwan *raj* set up by a *khatri* trader being an exception.

The distancing of the *khānazāds*, which consisted largely of the Īrānī and Tūrānī nobility, from the monarchy was a consequence of the growing crisis of the *jāgīrdārī* system during the eighteenth century. These elements, which considered the Mughal monarchy as a racial institution, were reconciled to the induction of Hindus, Hindustanis and Afghāns into the nobility only as long as it provided stability to the state and gave further opportunities of territorial expansion. There was growing resentment among them at the refusal of Aurangzīb to give *manṣab*s and *jāgīr*s to *khānazāds* following the large-scale induction of Deccanis and Marāthās. Under Aurangzīb's successors, their demand was the removal from service of 'ignoble', 'incompetent' people, who were identified as Hindus, Kashmiris, Hindustanis, as also men from the Dīwāni and Khān Sāmāni offices, where these elements predominated. Failing to get their way, these *khānazāds* were the sections which took the lead in setting up new principalities or *riyāsat*s. Interestingly, in these *riyāsats,* while the form of the *jāgīrdārī* system was preserved outwardly, the *jāgīr*s ceased to be transferable, and became hereditary *de facto*. Thus, *jāgīr-i-watan* became the norm.[24] This put a virtual stop not only to the induction of competent people from the lower orders, but also a stoppage of patronage to the stream of immigrants from abroad. One benefit of this was the closer identification with or absorption of the existing Īrānīs and Tūrānīs into the Indian social order. However, there is no evidence to show that the new class of hereditary *jāgīrdār*s looked after the interests of the cultivators, or acted as improving landlords, which Bernier would have us believe would have been the result if the transfer of *jāgīr*s had not existed. (Bernier remarks were *not* directed against frequency of transfers, but transferability as such of *jāgīr*s.)

23 *Ibid.*
24 Muzaffar Alam, *The Crisis of Mughal North India,* OUP, 1986, 124–6.

It has been pointed out that the Mughals became increasingly more backward during the seventeenth century in the field of military technology and methods of warfare. Thus, their field artillery remained poor as compared to the Europeans, and they were very slow to adopt the quick firing flint-lock gun and the use of infantry. It has been further suggested that it was in some sense due to the 'rigidity' of the *manṣabdārī* system and the vested interests of the *jāgīrdār*s because infantry forces would have had to be centrally recruited and paid.

It may be readily conceded that growing technological backwardness had serious consequences for the Indians when later the Marāthās, and successor states, such as Bengal, Awadh, Hyderabad etc. had to contend with technologically superior forces led by the French and the British. But this technological backwardness had little to do with struggle against the Marāthās who emerged as the chief challengers of the Mughals during the first half of the eighteenth century. The Marāthās depended upon lightly armed cavalrymen living on the countryside, who conducted a mobile mode of warfare. Superior artillery, or infantry armed with superior, quick-firing guns would hardly have been effective against them. As it was, even in its weakened condition, Mughal artillery was powerful enough to deter Baji Rao from attacking the Niẓām's fortified position as late as 1738 at Bhopal.

The military and technological challenge faced by the Mughals should, perhaps, be seen in a different perspective. We have during the eighteenth century the rise of a new class of aggressive, military-minded *zamindar*s, some belonging to the old Rājpūt families, a few to lower class adventurers, and a few to the Afghāns and Jats etc. Contemporary writers use various adjectives to describe this new class of aggressive *zamindar*s, but they emphasize their 'daring' and 'presumptousness' in challenging Imperial officials. Thus, in 1722, 'Aẕamatullah Khān, the *faujdār* of Moradabad, was almost defeated by the Afghans who used 'bows and muskets'.[25] Even earlier, the Afghāns were said to be in the employ of local *zamindar*s of ṣūbah Agra and Allahabad and creating disturbances.[26] The Jats with 200 of their musketeers,

25 *Iqbāl Nāma,* ed, S. H. Askari, Patna, 1953, p. 85.
26 *Akhbārāt 8 Rabī' I* R.Y. III (1127)/14.3.1715; 4 *Ẕīq'ad* R.Y.IV (1128/10.1716.

riding on their horses 'which were swift-moving like the wind' attacked the Imperialists at Ḥasanpur while fighting against 'Abdullāh Khān Bārahā.[27] Even more significant was the case of Bhagwant Adārū, the *zamindar* of Kora-Jahānabād, who defeated and killed Jān Niṣar Khān, the *faujdār* of the area. The *wazīr*, Qamaruddīn Khān, failed to suppress him and had to call in the *ṣubahdār*, Burhān-ul-Mulk Sāadat Khān, to help.[28]

In all these cases, we are told that the *zamindars*, proud of the size and strength of their armies, attacked with 'bows and muskets', while Bhagwant Adārū used 'cannons and muskets'.[29] In other words, the wide dispersal of muskets and even cannons had resulted in the loss of the military edge against the *zamindars* which the imperialists had enjoyed earlier. Orders to local *faujdārs* to prevent locksmiths from manufacturing guns had little effect.

Thus, the struggle between centripetal and centrifugal forces had reached a new phase. Had the *jāgīrdārī* system based on cavalrymen become redundant in this situation? Was a new type of regional centralization needed to cope with this situation? Larger and more efficient forces, that needed more money, were also required. These are problems which had to be faced by the successor states of the Mughals. But they do not concern us here.

Thus, the working of the *jāgīrdārī* system has to be seen in the wider socio-cultural context. The *jāgīrdārī* system was designed to cope with a social–political situation that was rapidly changing during the eighteenth century. While the system worked it was able to keep in check the centrifugal forces represented by the *zamindars*, and promoted a centralized polity.

The linking of the crisis of the *jāgīrdārī* system with a deepening social crisis and increased factionalism in the ruling classes leading to a break-up of a central polity still remains at the core of the Mughal crisis of empire. To that extent, the main thesis put forward in this work still remains valid.

27 Shiv Dās, *Shāhnāma*, ed. S. H. Askari, Patna, 1980, p. 139; The Ruhelas were the first to use on a large scale infantry armed with muskets in field battles. Thus, in 1749, the Ruhelas had 5,000 matchlockmen concealed in bushes who defeated the army of the Bangash chief, Qā'im Khān, *Khazānah-i 'Āmrah*, p. 30

28 W. Irvine, *Later Mughals* ii, 277; Muzaffar Alam, *Crisis of Empire*, 315.

29 *Iqbalnāma*, 130.

I am happy that the Oxford University Press is bringing out a new edition of this book which has been out of print for some time. In the preface to the new edition, I have tried to carry forward the debate on the crisis of the *jāgīrdārī* system.

New Delhi
May 2001

SATISH CHANDRA

Preface to the Third Edition

I am glad that the People's Publishing House is bringing out a paperback of *Parties and Politics* which has been out of print for a long time.

I have resisted the temptation of tampering with the original text except adding a supplementary note on the Crisis of the Jāgīrdārī System. I hope this would be useful to students of Medieval Indian History.

New Delhi
17 September 1979

SATISH CHANDRA

Preface to the Second Edition

A good deal of fresh material, mostly of documentary character, has become available since the publication of this book in 1959 and a number of useful monographs and theses have been written. I have not, however, undertaken a large-scale revision of the book. My justification for not doing so are two—most of the documentary material has not yet been even classified and indexed. A proper assessment of the fresh material has, therefore, yet to be made. Secondly, how far should an historian revise what he had written earlier? If I was to rewrite now the book I had written earlier, it might be a different book! I have, therefore, left the text unchanged, but have incorporated, in an addendum, all such points which have either to be defended or modified in the light of fresh evidence or where fresh light is shed on particular aspects.

I am grateful to students and to many friends and well wishers who received the book with kindness and at whose insistence the book is being re-printed. I am grateful to the Centre for Advanced Studies, Department of History, Aligarh Muslim University, for having accorded permission for bringing out a second edition. My thanks are due to the People's Publishing House for having brought the book out by the photo-offset method.

SATISH CHANDRA

Jawaharlal Nehru University
New Delhi
1972

Preface to the First Edition

The study of the important institutions of the Medieval period has been attracting increasingly the attention of the students of Medieval Indian history. The nobility as an institution played a very important role in the growth, organization, administrative structure, social and cultural life, and ultimately, the downfall of the Mughal empire. Without a proper study of the character, organization, composition and role of the nobility at various periods, our understanding of many aspects of the Mughal empire, and of the forces which ultimately led to its disintegration, must remain incomplete. In the present work, an attempt has been made to study the role of the nobility in the downfall of the Mughal empire, with special reference to the position of various ethnic and religious groups in the nobility after the death of Aurangzīb, the basis of the rise and struggle of parties at the court, and the impact of this struggle, of the rise of the Marāthās, Jats and other indigenous elements, and of developments in the field of administration. The study has been terminated at 1740, as the Mughal empire no longer commanded an all-India importance after that date, and because the developments in the subsequent period do not reveal any basically new features as far as the history of the Mughal empire is concerned.

A careful study of the political history of the period has been made by Sir William Irvine in his valuable work the *Later Mughals.* However, Irvine did not concern himself with the working of the institutions, or the study of the problem of the nobility during this period. A great deal of fresh material, too, has become available since the appearance of Irvine's work. The mass of the *Jaipur Akhbārāt* which are unusually full upto the year 1719, and the records in the *Peshwa Daftar* and the other Marathi records have now become available to the historian of the period. These records are of a unique type. They not only supply absolutely reliable chronology and throw fresh light on a number of important political episodes, but enable us to study in detail the shifting alliances and affiliations of individual nobles and the various political groupings of the times, and to follow many of the highly secret and confidential negotiations between them. Much of this information, by its very nature, could not be available to the chroniclers of the period. The political history of the period has been studied afresh in the light of the these valuable records, since they throw considerable light on the rise of parties and their politics. A number of works, such as the letters of Qutb-ul-Mulk 'Abdullāh Khān (*Bālmukand Nāmah*), the *Iqbālnāmah* etc. which were not known or not available to Irvine have also been utilized for the first time. Advantage has also been taken of a number of useful monographs dealing with local history, or the lives of some of the eminent nobles of the time, e.g., *Niẓām-ul-Mulk Aṣaf Jāh* by Dr Y. Husain, *Malwa in Transition* by Maharajkumar Dr R. Sinh, *Peshwa Baji Rao I and Maratha Expansion* by Dr V. G. Dighe, *The First Two Nawabs of Awadh* by Dr A. L. Srivastava, etc.

My grateful thanks are due, first and foremost, to Dr R. P. Tripathi who, as the Professor of History at the Allahabad University, inspired me to devote myself to the study of history, and without whose invaluable guidance and advice, this work could never have been completed. I am also deeply grateful to Dr Banarsi Prasad Saksena for his kind help at various times, and to Dr S. Nurul Hasan, Director of Historical Research, Aligarh University, who gave valuable suggestions to me in revising my work and preparing it for publication. Mr S. H. Askari, Patna College, Bihar, was kind enough to bring to my notice some very useful material, including the rare manuscript, *Bālmukand Nāmah.* I am beholden to the (late) Sir Jadunath Sarkar and to Maharajkumar Dr Raghubir Sinh for having allowed me full facilities for the use of their libraries. I am also grateful to the authorities of the Bankipur Library, Patna; the Rampur Library; the National Library and the Asiatic Society of Bengal, Calcutta; the Aligarh University Library, etc. for giving me facilities for work in their libraries.

Lastly, I must thank my younger colleagues, especially Messrs Athar Ali, Noman Ahmad Siddiqi and Iqtidar Alam in helping me correct the proofs, check up references, and in preparing the Index. I am also thankful to my various other friends and well-wishers who have given me help, advice and suggestions at various times.

Aligarh
1959

SATISH CHANDRA

Abbreviations

Aḥkām	*Aḥkām-i-'Ālamgīrī*, edited by Sarkar
Aḥwāl	*Aḥwāl-ul-Khawāqīn* by M. Qāsim Aurangābādī
Anand	Anand Ram 'Mukhliṣ' *Safarnāmah*
Āshūb	M. Bakhsh, *Tārīkh-i-Shahādat-i-Farrukh Siyar wa Julūs-i-M. Shāhī*
Bāl.	*Bālmukand Nāmah*
Bayān	*Bayān-i-Wāqi'* by 'Abdul Karīm Kāshmīrī
B.N.	*Bahādūr Shāh Nāmah* by Ni'mat Khān 'Ālī' (Dānishmand Khān)
Dil.	*Nuskhah-i-Dilkasha* by Bhimsen
Harcharan	*Chahār Gulzār-i-Shujā'ī*
Hadīqat	*Hadīqat-ul-'Ālam* by Mīr 'Ālam
Ījād	M. Aḥsan Ījād, *T. Farrukh Siyar*
Iqbāl	*Iqbālnāmah*, prob. Shiv Dās
Īrādat	*Tazkirah* or *Tārīkh-i-Mubāraki*
Irvine	*Later Mughals*
Jahān-Kushā	*Jahān-Kushā-i-Nādirī* by Mirza M. Mahdī
J.R.	*Jaipur Records*
K.K.	Khāfī Khān, *Muntakhab-ul-Lubāb*
Kāmwar	*Tazkirat-us-Salāṭīn-i-Chaghtā* by M. Hādī Kāmwar Khān
Khujastah	*Khujastah Kalām*, ed. by Sahib Rai
Khush-ḥāl	*Nādir-uz-Zamānī*
Khazīnah	*Khazīnah-i-Āmirah* by Ghulām 'Alī 'Āzād'
M.A.	*Ma'āṣir-i-'Ālamgīrī* by Sāqī Musta'id Khān

Mir'āt	*Mir'āt-i-Aḥmadī* by M. 'Alī Khān
M.M.	Mirza Muḥammad, *'Ibrat-Nāmah*
M.U.	*Ma'āṣir-ul-Umarā* by Shāhnawāz Khān
Qāsim	Qāsim Lāhorī, *'Ibratnāmah*
Riyāẓ	*Riyāẓ-us-Salātīn* by Ghulām Husain
Ruqa'āt	*Ruqa'āt-i-'Ināyat Khānī* by 'Ināyat Khān
Raqā'im	*Raqā'im-i-Karā'im*
Shiv Dās	*Shāhnāmah-i-Munawwar-Kalām*
Siyar	*Siyar-ul-Muta'akhkhirīn* by Ghulām Ḥusain
T. Hindī	*Tārīkh-i-Hindī* by Rustam 'Alī Shāhabādī
T. Muẓ	*Tārīkh-i-Muẓaffarī* by M. 'Alī Khān Ansārī
Wārid	*Mir'āt-i-Wāridāt* or *Tārīkh-i-Muḥammad Shāhī* by M. Shafī Wārid Tehrānī
Yaḥyā	*Tazkirat-ul-Mulūk*

JOURNALS

B.I.S.M.	*Bharat Itihas Sanshodhak Mandal Journal*
J.A.S.B.	*Journal of the Asiatic Society of Bengal*
J.I.H.	*Journal of Indian History*
J.U.P.H.S.	*Journal of the U.P. Historical Society*
I.C.	*Islamic Culture*
I.H.C.	*Indian History Congress Proceedings*
I.H.R.C.	*Indian Historical Records Commission Proceedings*
M.I.Q.	*Medieval India Quarterly*

Introduction

The eighteenth century in India saw far-reaching changes in political organization, social institutions, and economic life and condition. The Mughal empire which had given a sense of unity to the country for a century and a half, and led to progressive developments in many different fields, disintegrated rapidly. The Marāthā bid to establish a hegemony in the entire country failed, and the British merchant-adventurers succeeded in laying the foundations of an empire of a new type. In order to understand the historical processes which lay behind these developments, it is necessary to analyse in detail the social, economic and political forces working in the seventeenth and eighteenth century India as well as in the rest of Asia and the Western world. Till a systematic study of these aspects is made, our understanding of such important events as the disintegration of the Mughal empire, the failure of the Marāthās to establish a unified empire, and of the process of development in diverse cultural fields must remain tentative and incomplete.

The organization of the nobility was one of the most important institutions devised by the Mughal emperors. The functioning of the administrative system, the due discharge of political and military obligations by the state, the maintenance of social standards, in fact, the existence of the Mughal empire itself depended, in a very large measure, on the proper working of this institution. The necessity of a more detailed study of the rise, organization, internal composition and evolution of the nobility of the Mughals, and of its impact on Mughal policies and institutions has been felt increasingly by all serious students of Medieval history. In the present work, an attempt has been made to study the role of the Mughal nobility in the empire between the death of Aurangzīb and the invasion of Nādir Shāh; the position of ethnic, regional and religious groups within the nobility; the impact of these groups upon the parties and politics at the court, and the attitude of different sections towards internal elements like the Jats and Marāthās, and external foes like Nādir Shāh. The Mughal nobility ceases to play a dominant role in shaping the politics of the country after the invasion of Nādir Shāh, rulers of 'independent' principalities and the Marāthā *sardars* occupying a larger part of the stage. During the period from the invasion of Nādir Shāh to the third battle of Panipat (1761), scarcely any new political issues are introduced. The advance of the Marāthās towards the heart of the empire, the Afghān invasions from the northwest, the exploitation of ethnic and group rivalries at the court by powerful individuals and their bid to seize the reins of authority at the centre—all these are the continuation, and to some extent, the repetition of the problems of the earlier period. For this reason, and due to the practical difficulty of dealing adequately with the voluminous source-material and of tracing the complex currents and cross-currents of the period in a single work, the present study has been terminated with the invasion of Nādir Shāh (1739).

The Mughal nobility in its institutionalized form was the outcome of a long process of historical evolution the roots of which may be traced back to political and economic developments in West Asia under Islam, the peculiar socio-economic condition of India which rendered a strong political authority necessary, the experience of the Turkish sultans in India, the Turko-Mongol traditions which the Mughal rulers brought with them into the country, and, finally, the political genius of Akbar and the circumstances attending his reign. It is beyond the scope of the present work to attempt to trace even in outline this complex process of development. The nobility played an extremely important role in the establishment, expansion and consolidation of the Mughal empire during the latter half of the sixteenth and the first half of the seventeenth century. But the successful working of this institution posed a number of difficult economic and administrative problems. Apparently, no lasting solution of these could be devised, and by the end of the seventeenth century the nobility was face to face with a crisis which took the shape of an acute scarcity of *jāgīrs*. Basically, the crisis was born out of the inability of agricultural and industrial production to cope with the increasing requirements of the ruling class. Akbar, and later Jahāngīr and Shāh Jahān, had to face this problem. By the time Aurangzīb came to the throne, a serious situation already existed. It was further aggravated by the numerous wars of Aurangzīb—particularly in the Deccan, and the extended conflict with the Jats, Marāthās, Rājpūts, Sikhs etc. Although Aurangzīb tried a number of devices to solve the political and military problems, he could not achieve any lasting success, and bequeathed to his successors a tangled and difficult situation.

In order to understand the nature of the problems facing the empire after the death of Aurangzīb, it is necessary to analyse briefly the character and composition of the ruling classes, their relations with the king and with the various social and political elements inside the country, their social and cultural outlook, and their inner tensions and problems.

The Dominant Classes in Medieval Indian Society

The Zamindars

In Medieval Indian society, the elements which were economically and politically dominant may be said to constitute two broad classes—one the various rajas and chiefs as well as hereditary 'landlords', called by early writers *rāis* and *thākurs*, for whom the generic word '*zamindār*' is used in later Persian authorities; and second, the assignees of revenue called *iqṭā'dārs*, and later, *jāgīrdārs*. The common feature of both these social classes was that they lived largely by the appropriation of the social surplus produced by the peasant, though there were important differences in the mode of the appropriation of this surplus.

The position of the *zamindars* was, in practice if not strictly in theory, a hereditary one, and many of them had been in possession of their estates for a considerable time before the arrival of the Turks in India. For practical purposes, and in order to stabilize their position quickly, the early Turkish conquerors allowed most of them to continue in their previous situations on condition of their recognizing the Turkish political authority, and paying revenue in various forms for the lands in their possession. They were also under a general obligation to render a variety of other services including military service, and aiding the local authorities whenever called upon to do so.

Inspite of their willingness to 'compromise' with the *zamindars*, the Turkish, and later the Mughal rulers found the problem of establishing a satisfactory relationship with the *zamindars* of various categories one of the most difficult and complex problems they were called upon to tackle.

The *zamindars* were ever-willing to take advantage of the internal and external difficulties of the new rulers, or any weakness on the part of the central or local government, to withhold revenue and to encroach on land belonging to others.[1] Frequently, they acted as local tyrants, extorting as much as possible from the cultivators within their sphere of authority. The peasant was basically in a position of dependence upon the *zamindar*, and had generally to pay large levies apart from a more or less fixed share of the produce. Not only the peasant, but even the merchants passing through the territories of a *zamindar* were generally required to pay tolls and cesses which substantially increased the cost of the transit of goods.[2]

The Turkish and Mughal rulers attempted, in their own interests, to create conditions in which greater security of life and property might prevail, to stabilize and standardize currency and prices and weights and measures, to develop the means of

1 *Cf.* the remarks of Barani (Sir Syed's, ed.) 180; also instructions to *ṣūbahdārs, Ā'īn* (N. K., 1983) i, 195–6; Sarkar, *Mughal Adm.*, 57–60, 127. The author of the *Ājnāpatra*, a 17th century political treatise, declares: 'They (the *zamindars*) are not inclined to live on whatever they posseses, or to act always loyally towards the King. All the time they want to acquire new possessions bit by bit and to become strong, and after becoming strong to seize (land and power) forcibly from some and to create enmities and depredations against others.' (As quoted in *I.H.C.*, V 405).

See also Āshūb, 152; *M. U.* ii, 826.

2 M. Tughlaq abolished the non-*shara'ī* taxes, as also the duties on foreign goods coming to India overland. (Ibn Baṭṭūṭah, Def. et Sang, ed., iii 288). Firūz takes credit for abolishing 52 illegal cesses (*Futūḥāt*). Sher Shah, Akbar, Aurangzīb etc. repeatedly issued instructions forbidding the levying of illegal cesses, and specially road-dues (*rāhdārī*). This demonstrates the persistence of such dues. (See Moreland, *India at the Death of Akbar*, 46–50. Sarkar, *Aurangzeb* iii, 85).

communications, and to limit the power of the various local elements, specially the *zamindars*, by stringent military measures. To the extent that they were successful in doing so, the peasants and the merchants benefited. The process of political and administrative consolidation implied a dimunition in the power and authority of the *zamindars*, although some of the measures indirectly benefited them also. The attempt of the state to ascertain the real productivity of the soil, to abolish all but the 'sanctioned' cesses, and the restriction of the right of coinage etc. were resented by many of the *zamindars* as measures which affected their political and economic interests. The stronger *zamindars* also chafed at the check imposed by the state on their encroachment upon the territories of their neighbours. Hence, they attempted in various ways to slow down, and if possible, even to reverse the process of political integration. This tussle—now open, now concealed—between the *zamindars* and the central authority was a constant feature of Medieval Indian society, and powerfully influenced the development of many institutions. In areas such as Rajputana and Bundelkhand, tribal and clan institutions still had considerable vitality and dominated social consciousness. The *zamindars* and the local rajas in these areas were leaders of their tribe or clan, and an attempt to curtail their rights and prerogatives was likely to provoke the opposition of the entire clan brotherhood. In other areas too, the *zamindar* was often a tribal or clan chief, and any encroachment upon his customary rights was often regarded as an encroachment upon the tribal way of life. Thus, apart from the Rājpūts, the Jāts, Gūjars, Afghāns etc. had also preserved their tribal institutions in a greater or lesser degree.

The struggle for land (or rather, the social surplus which it produced) was thus a cardinal feature of medieval society, and gave rise to a multiplicity of social, economic and political problems. The Turkish and the Mughal rulers attempted to restrict the power of the *zamindars* in various ways. Large holdings were sought to be broken up, sometimes by interposing men of different communities in areas dominated by one community. Or, *zamindars* who were considered to be disaffected or disloyal were replaced.[3] Simultaneously, a strong machinery of government was sought to be built at the provincial, *sarkār* and *pargana* level. In Akbar's time,

3 Thus, see *Manual* quoted by Sarkar, *Mughal Adm.*, 64.

the highest service was thrown open to all, and even some *zamindars* were appointed *manṣabdārs*. Thus, the outlook of the *zamindars* was sought to be changed. Nevertheless, the *zamindars* as a class continued to pose a serious problem for the administration. In central India and Rajputana, in the mountainous areas, and in the Deccan as a whole, they continued to form a very powerful and numerous group. As the empire expanded over these areas, it had to tackle and solve the problems posed by this powerfully entrenched group: the solutions, or their absence, reacted, in turn, on other institutions and state policies.

Regional and linguistic sentiments were also sometimes brought into play. Amīr Khusrau had noted and commented upon the popularity of the regional languages as early as 1317 when he wrote: 'There is at this time in every province a language peculiar to itself, and not borrowed from any other—Sindhi, Lahori, Kashmiri, Kubarī (Dogri of the Jammu area?), Dhūr Samundarī (Kannarese of Mysore), Tilangi (Telugu), Gujar (Gujarati), Ma'bari (Tamil), Gauri (N. Bengal), Bengal, Awadh, and Delhi and its environs. These languages...have from ancient times applied in every way to the common purposes of life.'[4]

While some regional languages have not been noted, Amīr Khusrau's observation draws attention to a remarkable development in early Medieval India, viz. the growth of the modern regional languages. The sentiment of regional loyalty was bound to be strengthened by this development. Many other factors contributed to the further development of this sentiment. In many of the small principalities which were set up following the break up of the Tughlaq empire, regional languages and culture found patronage.[5] The Bhakti movement which developed apace in various areas used the regional languages for the propagation of the new ideas, and attempted to promote social solidarity by lowering the barriers of caste, and encouraging feasts, fairs etc.

Akbar seems to have taken into account the growth of regional sentiments in drawing up his provincial boundaries. Many of the provinces coincided, broadly, with linguistic and traditional

4 *Nūh Sipihr* (I.R.A. Series), xxxi, 178–80; Elliot iii, 562. The *A'in* (iii, 45, Nawal Kishore, ed.) enumerates similar divisions.

5 Thus, see D. C. Sen, *Hist. of Bengali Lit.*, 9–15, for growth of Bengali under Muslim kings of Bengal, *Hist. of Marathi Lit.* by R. Ranade for Marathi in Deccan states etc.

divisions,[6] although administrative convenience was probably the dominant consideration. In these provinces, the local elements were, to some extent, associated with the task of administration, while some of the governors interested themselves in the promotion of local culture.

The *zamindar* class appears to have exercised a considerable influence on the growth of regional sentiments.[7] The inter-play of the various factors mentioned above, and the utilization of the sentiments of regional loyalty by *zamindar*s in some areas, created an extremely difficult situation, to cope with which the maximum of internal cohesion and elasticity of policy and approach were necessary. These, in turn, depended upon a number of factors: the capabilities of the monarch, the vigour, efficiency and morale of the nobility and the army, the continued support of broad sections of the population etc.

Assignees of Land Revenue—Jāgīrdārs and Others

Turkish rule resulted in the introduction in north India of a new social class called the *iqṭā'dār*s, and later, the *jāgīrdār*s. The word 'nobility' is often applied to these sections, though a more correct word would be *jāgīrdār*s, since the 'nobility' may also be held to include the indigenous aristocracy, i.e. the *zamindar*s, and many others such as the *Shaikhzādā*s, or the holders of *milk* or *in'ām* or *madadd-ima'āsh* who were not directly in the service of the King.

For the purposes of administration and revenue-collection, the Turkish conquerors parcelled out the country into tracts called *iqṭā's* over which they appointed *iqṭā'dār*s (also called *muqṭi'*). The *iqṭā'dār* was expected to collect the state dues, and to defray the sanctioned expenses including his personal expenses out of the income. The position of the *jāgīrdār* who came later was essentially the same. From the income of the *jāgīr* he was expected to maintain a fixed contingent for the service of the king, and also to meet his own expenses. However, the *jāgīr* was essentially the assignment of revenue, and did not primarily involve any administrative charge.

6 Jahangir noted in his *Memoirs* 'it is agreed that the boundary of a country is the place upto which people speak the language of that country' (*Tuzuik*, 298).

7 See p. 29 below.

The fundamental difference between the position of a *zamindar* and that of a *jāgīrdār* thus was that the position of the latter was not a hereditary one, and the *jāgīr* could not devolve from father to son, though a monarch might reward good services by taking a *jāgīrdar's* son into royal services and conferring a *jāgīr* upon him. But the son would be expected to justify his selection by service. A *jāgīr* lasted only as long as a person continued to serve the King. Moreover, it was frequently changed from one place to another in order to prevent the growth of local associations on the part of an individual holder. The grant of *jāgīr* was, in fact, only a means of payment for royal service. It did not confer any rights in land or claim to a hereditary territorial position. A *jāgīrdār* could realize his dues directly from the peasants through village head-men, or in other ways from the *zamindar*s.[8] But it should be kept in mind that a *jāgiir* was not necessarily an assignment on land revenue: it was any kind of fixed revenue including customs dues.

Thus, the *jāgīrdār*s were entirely an official class. They were dependent for their promotion and advancement, and even for their economic existence, on the will of the king. While this created more favourable conditions for the establishment of royal absolutism, such a development was not reactionary in the peculiar condition of Medieval Indian society, since it aided the process of integration which could only proceed under a powerful king.[9]

Apart from being instruments of political integration, the *jāgīrdār*s also became the instruments of a new agrarian policy which was gradually evolved by the Turkish sultans, and further developed by Sher Shah and the Mughal kings, as political conditions stabilized, and as they gained experience of administrative and revenue affairs. The policy was aimed at augmenting the resources of the state by improving and expanding cultivation through measures such as the provision of better facilities of irrigation, the substitution of lower grade crops by higher grade (generally cash) crops, and by a system of crop rotation. The officers were expected to

8 Lands held by the *jāgīrdār*s and by the *zamindar*s did not form two separate categories. See *Waqāi'Sarkār* Ajmir, Aligarh Univ. Ms. 88 *et passim.; Nigār Nāmah-i-Munshī,* Aligarh Univ. Ms.

9 *Cf.* the remarks of Bernier, 65. Bernier fails to understand the Medieval Indian reality, and argues that the absence of a hereditary landed aristocracy made for despotism and arbitrariness by the kings, and oppression by the *jāgīrdār*s who had no local interests.

take steps to bring virgin land under cultivation. Peasants were encouraged by means of remission of revenue for breaking up uncultivated soil, loans (*taqāvī*) were advanced for the purchase of seed-grains etc. and for restarting production—especially in the wake of natural calamities like floods, drought etc.[10] While none of these measures were new, their cumulative effect when applied on a large scale by an efficient and carefully supervised administrative machinery was by no means negligible. Moreover, the *jāgīrdārs* were made to realize that unless they developed and extended cultivation in their respective charges, they would be hard put to it to make the two ends meet, or at any rate, to live comfortably.[11]

Although the *jāgīrdārs* formed an entirely official group which was technically open to all, in practice they were an elite group strongly wedded to the principle of nobility of birth. Thus, absence of a noble lineage was considered a disqualification for royal service, and especially for high office. Extravagant respect was paid to those supposedly connected by blood to some royal family, or to some famous Shaikhs, or to the Prophet himself.

Like the *zamindars*, the *jāgīrdārs* also regarded land as the main source of wealth and power. In normal times, a *jāgīr* was preferred to cash stipends. Cash stipends frequently involved inordinate delays in payment, and it could be hoped that given a good *jāgīr* in a settled area, the actual realization would be greater than its face value. The manoeuvering for productive and easily manageable (*sair ḥāṣil*) *jāgīrs* was one of the important pre-occupations of the nobles and their agents at the court.

Inspite of differing in many respects from the *zamindars* in their political and economic outlook, the *jāgīrdārs* could not rise above their feudal environment.[12] Rather, their deep-seated aspiration

10 See specially Tripathi, *Some Aspects of Muslim Adm.*, 277–337, for the evolution of this policy from the time of M. Tughlaq to Akbar. Subsequent Mughal sovereigns continued to lay great stress on agricultural improvement. See Jahangir *Tuzuk*, 7 in particular *farmān* of Aurangzīb to Rāsikh Das Krori (translated by Sarkar, *Mughal Adm.*, 214–24).

11 *Cf.* the controversy between Shāh Jahān and Prince Aurangzīb regarding the financial demands of the latter as the Viceroy of the Deccan, and Shāh Jahān's reply. (*Aurangzeb* i, 183–8).

12 The word 'feudal' has been used in the generic sense of indicating a society dominated by landed elements, i.e. by those who derive their income

continued to be to set up as a full-fledged feudal class, and to convert their *jāgīrs* into hereditary estates. This aspect came to the surface in times of stress or when a weak monarch ascended the throne. Thus, the nobility played a dual or a dialetical role, being a factor of integration at one time, and of disintegration at another.

Apart from the *zamindars* and *jāgīrdārs*, there was another more or less numerous class in Medieval Indian society which also lived by appropriating the social surplus produced by the peasant. This included various village officials who were generally hereditary. These stood midway between the cultivator and the *zamindar*, partaking of some of the characteristics of both. Apart from these, there were various petty assignees of land-revenue such as the holders of *waqf, in'ām, milk, madadd-i-ma'āsh* etc. In practice, though not in theory, their positions also tended to be hereditary and they appear to have become somewhat like petty *zamindars*. Though not very important politically, the large body of petty assignees formed a lower stratum to the nobility, and served as a recruiting ground for the latter. It also served as a link between the ruling classes and the masses. Many of these assignees settled down in the neighbourhood of their assignments in small towns or *qaṣbahs* which became a meeting ground for the culture which the Turkish rulers brought with them, and Indian culture in its local aspect.

The power and importance of the *zamindars* and *jāgīrdars* rested not only on the financial and military resources at their disposal, but also on the fact that there were no other social forces to challenge their position. The peasantry, because of the peculiar organization of the village economy, was immersed in narrow

---

primarily from the surplus produced by the peasant. Although there are many differences between Indian and European feudalism, this feature might be considered as common to both.

Cf. Kosminski's definition of feudalism as:

(a) A special type of landed property which was directly linked with the exercise of over-lordship over the basic producers of society, the peasants, though of course with considerable variation in the degree to which that over-lordship might be exercised.

(b) A special type of class of basic producers with a special connection with the land—which remained, however, the property of the ruling class of feudal lords.

(*Studies in the Agrarian Hist. of England,* Oxford, 1956, p. VI). See also W. C. Smith, *Modern Islam in India,* 337.

routine, unable to view the community as a whole and aloof from the affairs of the government. The pattern of the village economy in which local needs tended to be met by and large by local production, also limited the development of the industrial and commercial sections, and made them largely dependent on the patronage of the monarchs and the *jāgīrdārs* and *zamindars*. Although the expansion of trade and industry following the political integration of northern India led to the growth of the mercantile and business community—specially during the seventeenth century,[13] the contribution of trade and industry to the total wealth of the country could not compare favourably with land-revenue. Thus, the business community could not develop to the point where it could play a significant political role.

THE ORGANIZATION, CHARACTER AND COMPOSITION OF THE NOBILITY

Before the time of Akbar, the nobility lacked definite organization. During the Sulṭanat period, the territorial nobility or *zamindars* were excluded from the list, and hence, the Hindus had little to do with the nobility. Humayūn made an elaborate classification. He divided the court into three sections, and each section into twelve grades.[14] In this way, a definite order of precedence was established within each section. However, it is not clear to what extent this order of precedence was actually followed and whether there were any definite privileges associated with the various grades.

While the famous *manṣabdārī* system which Akbar instituted was not entirely new, *manṣabs* having been awarded even by some of the earlier rulers, Akbar gave the system a definite order and form, and introduced a number of new elements in it. He classified the nobles into grades depending on the numbers of *sawārs* to be maintained by them, the lowest rank being 10, and the highest

13 There is plenty of evidence about the growth of urban communities during the sixteenth and seventeenth centuries. See in particular Palsaert, *Jahangir's India* (Moreland), 7, 46; Fitch, *The First Englishman in India* (Locke) 180; Thevenot, *Travels* (Sen), 44–6, 96 *et passim.*

Cf. W. C. Smith's article 'The Mughal Empire and the Middle Class' (*Islamic Cul.* (1944), 349–63).

14 Khwandamīr, *Qānūn-i-Humāyūnī*, 132–3, Ishwari Prasad, *Humayun* (1955), 53–6.

5,000. However, the *manṣab* soon became merely an index of rank, status and salary, unrelated to the number of *sawārs* to be maintained. Generally those holding the *manṣab* of 1,000 and above were classified as *amīrs*, though sometimes *manṣabdārs* of 500 and below were also included in the category of *amīrs*. A number of modern writers have used the word *amīr* for all categories of *manṣabdārs*. But it seems clear that the contemporary writers generally used the word *amīr* only for the higher *manṣabdārs*, the small *manṣabdārs* and the *zamindars* being treated as separate groups.

The number of grades could be increased or varied by a process of sub-division. Thus, the upper limit was raised to 7,000 in the later years of Akbar's reign, and subsequently ranks of even 8,000 were granted. Further sub-divisions were made by the introduction of separate *ẕāt* and *sawār* ranks, and by the introduction of *dū-aspah sih-aspah* categories etc. The crux of the system was the fixing of a definite salary for each *manṣab* and for the number of *sawārs*. Out of this salary, the holder was required to meet his personal expenses and also to maintain a definite number of horsemen and a transport corps of camels, carts etc. The salary could be either in cash, or in the form of a *jāgīr* or partly in cash and partly in *jāgīr*.

The introduction of the idea of definite salaries subtly changed the nature of the nobility. The nobles now came to be regarded as the paid servants of the king. Thus, a further step was taken in the bureaucratization of the nobility. However, it would be misleading to draw a parallel between the nobility of the Mughals and modern paid bureaucracy. The emoluments enjoyed by the nobles, especially in the upper echelons, were very high. They tended to dominate not only in the political but in the economic field as well; they retained the characteristics of a ruling class while acquiring some of a civil service.

The *manṣabdārī* system not only established a definite order of precedence among the nobles, but led to the gradual evolution of definite conventions regarding pay, promotion, privileges etc. Offices at the court or in the provinces often carried extra allowances, or well-recognized perquisites. Or, the king might grant additional allowances as a special mark of favour, and to meet local exigencies. Besides this, there were other honours such as titles, the use of kettle-drums and banners etc. which the king used as rewards for service and as a mark of favour. These honours were greatly valued by the nobles, and there was often a keen contest for them.

Like most ruling groups, the nobility of the Mughals was to some extent self-perpetuating, so that the son of a nobleman found it easier to enter the service of the king than an outsider. But it was not a closed corporation. The Mughal emperors regarded nobility of birth as an important qualification, but merit and learning were even more important, and men of humble origin could and did rise to the highest offices. Even writers, professional artists, and lower administrative officials were sometimes granted *manṣab*s. Apart from the Rājpūts, a small number of *zamindār*s belonging to different areas such as the Bundelas, hill Rajas, Jats etc. also found admission to the ranks of the *manṣabdār*s. Generally speaking, all entrants, irrespective of their ancestry, had to work their way up from the lower grades, promotion depending mainly on merit. It was thus very different from a typical tribal or territorial aristocracy (i.e. the *zamindar*s), and the hereditary feudal nobility of Medieval Europe where the son automatically succeeded the father in his titles, rank, possessions and sometimes even the office.[15]

The Mughals never showed much predilection for ethnic, national or clan exclusiveness. The nobility of Bābar and Humāyūn included Īrānīs, Tūrānīs, Uzbeks and even Afghāns—though the latter two were considered the chief enemies of the Mughals. Indian nobles, i.e. those who were the descendents of earlier immigrants from West and Central Asia, or were Indian converts to Islam, seem also to have found employment at the Mughal court from the very beginning. At first, the nobles had little sense of loyalty to the Timurid dynasty, and hardly any common traditions or sense of common purpose. Some of the more ambitious among them dreamt of displacing the Timurids, and rose in rebellion. Akbar's essential humanism and generosity, high sense of purpose and personal magnetism, coupled with his unfailing success in the field of battle gradually won the devotion and loyalty of the nobility and created a definite tradition. But Akbar was not satisfied with this. By means of the *manṣabdārī* system he sought to weld the various heterogenous elements into an organized and harmonious whole, so that the nobility could become an efficient and

15 The hereditary *rajas* were given a *manṣab* on succession to the *gaddī*. Further promotions had to be earned.

dependable instrument of the royal will. Akbar seems to have desired that the various ethnic, national and religious groups in the nobility should be so balanced that the king did not become dependent on any one section, and enjoyed the maximum freedom of action. Akbar's alliance with the Rājpūts was prompted in good measure by a desire on his part to counter-balance the power of a section of the old nobles in whose loyalty he did not have full confidence. However, the alliance gave the Rājpūts opportunities for distinction and advancement which they could scarcely have secured otherwise. The alliance with the Rājpūts was maintained and even sought to be extended by Jahāngīr and Shāh Jahān, and came to be regarded as one of the corner-stones of Mughal policy. The Rājpūts had formed the ruling class of northern India before the advent of the Turks. Apart from forming the ruling dynasties in Rājpūtānā, large numbers of Rājpūt *zamindars* were scattered all over north India. The importance of an alliance with the Rājpūts was thus far greater than that of an adjustment with some locally influential Rajas. It constituted a long and significant step towards the evolution of a composite ruling class consisting of both Muslims and non-Muslims.

The principle of balancing the various ethnic and regional groups was also sought to be applied by Akbar to the contingents that the *manṣabdārs* were required to maintain. In the initial phase, the contingents of a large number of the *manṣabdārs* consisted of tribal levies, or their clansmen and fellow country-men. Gradually, definite rules and conventions were developed regarding the composition of a noble's contingent. While some Mughals and most Rājpūt nobles continued to maintain contingents exclusively of Mughals or Rājpūts, mixed contingents seem to have gradually become the usual feature.[16] Thus, the forces making for tribal, national and sectarian exclusiveness were dealt a blow.

The reputation of the Mughal emperors as generous patrons of learning and administrative talent, and of their being remarkably free from narrow racial or sectarian prejudices attracted to their court able and ambitious men from many countries. Most of these men came from the neighbouring countries of Īrān, Tūrān and Afghānistān, though a few came from more distant lands like Turkey, Egypt, Abyssinia and even Arabia. Some of the

16 *Cf.* Irvine, *Army of the Indian Mughals*, 206.

new-comers were remarkably able people, and rose to occupy the highest offices in the state. There can be little doubt that the influx of these men broadened the field from which the Mughal emperors could choose men for the royal service. However, it would be misleading to over-emphasize the position of these new-comers in the administrative service, or to imagine that they were considered indispensable in any way. The Mughal emperors, as has been emphasized earlier, were deeply attached to the aristocratic principle, and when a representative of some noble family of Īrān or Tūrān, or someone who had held high office in a neighbouring kingdom came to the court—sometimes in consequence of a political upheaval, or to flee from personal or sectarian persecution—they welcomed him and appointed him to a suitable *manṣab.* Similar consideration was extended to ancient families among Indian Muslims and Rājpūts. But further promotion generally depended largely on merit, although individual connexions, intrigue etc. inevitably played a part,.

No systematic study has been made as yet of the position of the different ethnic, national (or regional) and religious groups in the nobility of the Mughals at various periods. Some modern writers have divided the nobility into 'foreigners' and 'Indians', identifying the former with the Mughals, and the latter with Hindustanis and the Rājpūts. But such a division seems to be of doubtful validity for the seventeenth century. The word Mughal was loosely used to denote those who had recently come to the country form Īrān and Tūrān.[17] However, the Mughals were not the representatives of any foreign power which had its economic and political interests outside the country. Once they joined the emperor's service, they made India their home, and hardly kept any contact with the land of their birth. One of the conditions of service was that they should bring their wives and children to the country. Since service generally lasted till death, there was no question of returning to the country of their birth after retirement. Large numbers of the

17 The Mughals spoke Persian with an accent, and were also generally more fair-skinned than the Indians. For this reason, many Indians took Kashmiri wives, so that their children might pass off as Mughals. (See Bernier, p. 404).

Cf. also the remark of Bernier (p. 212) that the Mughal *umarā* were 'adventurers who entice one another to the Court.' Bernier generally paints in an unfavourable light many of the Mughal institutions which he failed to understand. His remarks on these matters have therefore to be treated with caution.

so-called Īrānīs and Tūrānīs had lived in the country for one generation or more.[18] They were thus wholly different from the English civil servant in India. Culturally, too, the Mughal nobles did not form any distinctive group. Like the other immigrants at the Mughal court, they rapidly adopted the language and the manners and customs prevalent at the court. They married in the country, and assimilated the culture which had been gradually developed at the Mughal court and was widely prevalent among the upper and to some extent even among the lower classes all over northern India, and which had also influenced many parts of south India. The policy of the Mughal emperors was to give respect and honour to the Mughal nobles and to all deserving immigrants, but to resist their claims to a superior or dominating position. Likewise, the 'Arabs, Rūmīs, Uzbeks etc. who came to the country also rapidly assimilated the culture of the Mughal court. However, some of the new-comers assumed at times an arrogant attitude, and adopted an air of superiority in relation to things Indian and to the other sections among the nobles. The Mughal nobles prided themselves as belonging to the original home of the emperors, and claimed by implication a special status. The 'Arabs, Rūmīs etc. also claimed a privileged status.[19]

Contemporary writers recognized the existence of numerous sub-regions in India, these being geographical and also, to some extent, cultural units. Thus, reference is made to Gujarāti, Kashmiri, Deccani and Hindustani nobles. In most of these regions, there were a number of clearly recognizable communities or clans in existence which are often mentioned as separate entities. Thus, the term Deccani included Afghāns, Marāthās, Ḥabshis etc. living in the Deccan. The term Gujarāti included the Afghāns as well as native converts living in Gujarāt. However, regional consciousness was not sufficiently developed to overcome the particularism of different clans, and of communal or ethnic groups. Hence, contemporary writers designate nobles by the regions from which they originally came or in which they settled down, as well as by their ethnic or clan group. Regional consciousness seems to have been more developed in some areas such as Bengal, Gujarāt and parts of the Deccan, and less developed in northwest India. The

18 Thus, see Aurangzīb's remark about Irānīs 'whether born in *wilāyat* or in Hindustan.' (*Aḥkām,* 39).

19 *Cf.* the remarks in *Khazīna'-i-'Āmira,* 186.

Mughals, Afghāns, (as also the Jats) etc. living in this area continued to be designated separately, while the word Hindustani tended to be used in the sense of the other Muslims settlers or converts belonging to modern UP, Punjab, and Rajasthan. But it would not be correct to imagine that these various groups had separate interests of their own or formed distinct entities, a good deal of co-mingling of blood having taken place, and many of the Mughal and Afghān immigrants having largely identified themselves with those who had lived in the country for generations or were converts.

The terms applied to the various sections in the nobility are thus somewhat misleading. One cause of the confusion of terms apparently was that the earlier tribal or clan concepts were gradually giving place to a territorial or regional (though not yet a national) concept, the process being in different stages of development in different areas.

By the second half of the seventeenth century, the only group among the Indian Muslims which retained the tribal-clan structure to any considerable degree were the Afghāns. The abiding weakness of the Afghāns was their lack of tribal unity, so that it was impossible for them to make a united stand against the highly organized armies of the Mughal emperors. However, the Afghāns continued to be a restless element which could create difficulties at the local level. They were found ever willing to throw in their lot with local rebels or to support ambitious adventurers. The policy of the Mughals was to be wary of the Afghāns, but not to deny them *manṣabs* or employment. Large numbers of Afghāns gradually found employment in the Mughal armed forces. But Afghān nobles remained few in numbers. Afghān nobles wielded considerable power at the Bijāpur and Golkonda courts. With the annexation of Bijāpur and Golkonda, many of these Afghāns lost their pre-eminent positions, and hence, felt somewhat dissatisfied. However, there was nothing like an Afghān party at the court. Culturally, too, the Afghāns did not form a separate group, hardly any differences remaining between them and the others on this score.

The Rājpūts who formed a regional as well as a tribal-clan group had shown themselves even less capable than the Afghāns of overcoming their tribal-clan disunity. Nor did they have the advantage of numbers. But their traditional position as rulers and leaders of Hindu society gave them a social status which Akbar was quick to recognize. As a special mark of confidence, the Rājpūts were deputed to guard the royal *ḥaram*, a position which they continued to enjoy throughout the seventeenth and the eighteenth centuries. The Rājpūts were also valued as doughty warriors. The actual number of Rājpūts in the nobility was never large, but gifted individuals like Mān Singh, Jai Singh and Jaswant Singh rose to the highest ranks, giving to the Rājpūts an importance and lustre far greater than what they might have otherwise attained. The Bundelas, like the Rājpūts, also were a tribal-clan cum regional group. But for various historical reasons, they could not attain a position comparable to that of the Rājpūts till well into the eighteenth century.

As the empire expanded towards the Deccan, many Marāthās also entered the royal service. The problem of assigning to the Marāthās a position which would accord with their aspirations and importance and which would not, at the same time, upset the internal balance in the nobility or unduly strain the resources of the empire, proved a difficult one, and became a factor in the organization and growth of a movement in Mahārāshtra aimed at regional independence. There may have been some dissatisfaction in some other regions also at the status and position accorded to local elements in the nobility of the Mughals. In a big country like India, with a considerable sense of particularism in different areas, and with sub-regional languages and cultures, the existence of such sentiments would be easy to understand. Nevertheless, no strong movements aimed at regional independence developed, with the exception of Mahārāshtra and partially the Punjab, till political developments and socio-economic factors had shattered the fabric of the empire, and led individual nobles to nurse the ambition of carving out separate principalities for themselves.

Religious and sectarian differences also affected the nobles. Thus, among the Muslims there were Shī'ahs and Sunnīs. Sectarian controversy and bitterness between the two sometimes ran fairly high. Shī'ahs were often identified with Īrānīs, there being a widespread belief that most of the Īrānī nobles were secretly Shī'ahs.[20] However, it is difficult to test the validity of this assumption, there being many Sunnīs among the Īrānīs also. Aurangzīb disliked Shī'ism strongly, and we are also told that for

20 *Cf. Tavernier* (ii, 177): '. . .they (i.e. the Persians) themselves to please the King and advance their own fortunes, made no scruple about conforming themselves externally to the cult and customs of the Sunnīs.' See also *Aḥkām*, 70.

this reason he harboured a deep-seated distrust of the Īrānī nobles. However, this allegation is of doubtful validity, for Aurangzīb accorded some of the highest and most important offices to nobles of Īrānī extraction.[21] The Īrānīs were supposed to be very intelligent and good administrators, just as the Hindustanis were supposed to be brave to the point of foolhardiness, the Mughals firm and resilient.[22]

Relations between the Hindu and Muslim nobles seem to have been cordial on the whole, though most of the Hindus adhered strictly to caste restrictions regarding dining and inter-marrying etc.

The nobility of the Mughals, although it suffered from a number of internal weaknesses, was on a broad view, a remarkable institution which welded into a homogenous and harmonious whole, men belonging to different regions and tribes, speaking different languages and professing different religions, and with differing cultural traditions. The Mughals succeeded in imbuing the nobles with a sense of common purpose and loyalty to the reigning dynasty, in imparting to them a distinctive cultural outlook, and in creating traditions of high efficiency and endeavour in administration. It was, thus, a definite factor in securing for a century and a half a remarkable degree of unity and good government in the country.

During the later part of the seventeenth and in the early part of the eighteenth century, stresses were placed on the nobility which, combined with its internal weaknesses, led to growing factionalism in the nobility and disrupted the empire. We must now turn our attention to a rapid survey of these developments.

Stresses Operating on the Nobility

Political Problems

Among the first to come in conflict with the Mughal state during the time of Aurangzīb were the Jats who rose in rebellion near

21 Although Aurangzīb disliked the Shī'ah tenets, and on occasions even referred to the Shī'ahs as '*rāfizīs*' and '*gul-i-biyābānī*', he did not apparently allow his public judgement to be clouded by these considerations. Also, see p. 45 below.

22 *Aḥkām*, 8, 39, 52. For Aurangzīb's remarks regarding the Deccanis, see *Aḥkām*, 31. Many of these opinions, it is obvious, represent the prejudices of some of the sections at the Mughal court.

Mathura in 1669. The uprising rapidly spread to the neighbouring districts and at its height there were more than 20,000 men, mostly Jat peasants, under arms. The hastily constituted peasant levies put up a desperate resistance and won a number of initial successes against the Imperial forces. At last, Aurangzīb himself marched against the Jats at the head of a large army and defeated them after heavy fighting. It is said that 4,000 Mughal soldiers also fell on the field. Mopping up operations continued for more than a year.[23]

The Jat uprising is generally ascribed to the oppression of local *faujdārs* and religious persecution. About the former there can be little doubt. The *faujdār* of Mathura, 'Abd-un-Nabī, amassed a fortune of 30 lakhs by illegal exactions.[24] The question of religious persecution is not so clear. A temple at Agra was reported destroyed in 1661–2, but the famous temple of Vishwanath built by Bir Singh Deva Bundela was not destroyed till *after* the uprising.[25]

Sporadic trouble continued. In 1686, there was a second uprising of the Jats. This time, the Jats were better organized, and it was not till 1691 that the Kachchhwāhā chief, Bishan Singh, succeeded in crushing the uprising. As the Jat rebellion progressed, it became less a peasant uprising and more a movement of local chiefs against rival *zamindars* and for the acquisition of plunder. Although a Jat state could not be set up in the time of Aurangzīb, the growth of the power of the Jat chiefs prepared the ground for such a development later on.

The growing mood of resistance and defiance was also demonstrated by the *Satnāmi* uprising in 1672. Though described by the author of the *Ma'āṣir-i 'Ālamgīrī* as 'a gang of bloody, miserable rebels, goldsmiths, carpenters, sweepers, tanners and other ignoble being',[26] the *Satnāmis* were mostly peasants who formed a religious brotherhood. They did not observe distinctions of caste and rank, and followed a strict puritanical code of conduct. They

23 *M.A.*, 92–4, *Aurangzeb* iii, 335–6.

24 *M.A.*, 83.

25 *Aurangzeb* iii, 291.

26 *M.A.*, 114–15. See also W. C, Smith's article, 'Lower Class Rising in the Mughal Empire,' *Islamic Culture* 1946, pp. 21–40. The author fails to note the role of the landed classes in many of the uprisings, and the resulting contradictions in the movements.

made no difference between Hindu and Muslim.[27] Once again, local officials failed to cope with the situation. Aurangzīb marched at the head of an army, and with the help of the Rājpūt Rajas and local *zamindars*, crushed the *Satnāmis*.

The clash between Aurangzīb and the Sikhs began in 1675 with the execution of Guru Tegh Bahadur. There had been occasional conflicts between the Mughals and the Sikhs since the time of Jahāngīr. But these had not resulted in any definite breach between the Sikhs and the Mughals. The early relations of Aurangzīb with the Guru had been quite normal, the only distracting factor being the struggle for succession in the Guru's own family. The final cause of the rupture is not clear. According to Sikh tradition itself, it was due to the intrigues of the Guru's rival, Ram Rai, who charged him with temporal ambitions (the Guru was called '*Sachcha padshah*'), and the Guru's protest against the forcible conversion of Hindus in Kashmir.[28] But some later writers mention another cause, viz. that the Guru had allied himself with a Muslim *faqīr*, Hāfiz Ādam, a follower of Shaikh Aḥmad Sirhindī, and that the two were laying waste the whole province of the Punjab.[29]

Under the leadership of Guru Govind, the Sikh uprising developed into an attempt to set up a Sikh state in the Punjab hills. This led to a clash with the hill Rajas and provided the background for the establishment (about 1699) of the *Khalsa* or military brotherhood. While the *Khalsa* was to be an instrument of resistance to oppression of all kinds, it implied at the same time the goal of founding a state ruled over by the Guru. The step was opposed by a section of Sikhs who wished to adhere to the basically non-political and universal character of the early movement, and who also disliked the establishment of a new *pahul* or ritual by the guru which abolished caste and identified the gurudom with the *Khalsa*.[30]

By themselves, neither the Jat uprisings nor the Sikh attempt to found an independent state, were sufficiently serious to pose a real danger to the Mughal empire. But they exemplified a growing spirit of resistance and assertiveness by various sections and communities. These movements adversely affected the Imperial prestige and were apparently regarded by Aurangzīb as part and

27 See Tara Chand, *Influence of Islam*, 192–4.
28 See I. B. Bannerjee, *Evolution of the Khalsa* ii, 55–62.
29 *Siyar*, 401. See also Cunningham, *History of the Sikhs*, 64.
30 *Cf.* I. B. Bannerjee, *loc. cit.* ii, 120–2.

parcel of Hindu disaffection against the state, although the Rājpūts and the hill Rajas of the Punjab, as also the bulk of the peasantry in the Indo-Gangetic plains had remained aloof from them. Hence, they tended to accentuate the general spirit of animosity and discord between sections of the Hindu and Muslim communities.

The breach with the Rathor and Sishodia Rājpūts following the death of Jaswant Singh in 1679 was of far greater immediate concern to Aurangzīb than either the Jat or the Sikh uprisings.

The exact motives of Aurangzīb in the dispute are not quite clear. It has been suggested that he wanted to punish the Rājpūts for the support given by Jai Singh and Jaswant Singh to Dārā in 1656. But such a course does not accord with Aurangzīb's treatment of these two chiefs or other supporters of Dārā during the intervening years. Nor does Aurangzīb seem to have desired the annexation of Jaswant's state. A more plausible view seems to be that Aurangzīb simply desired greater control over the internal affairs of the state and, perhaps, over the Rājpūts as a whole. The Emperor's march to Jodhpur seems to have been inspired by the fear of local complications by the relations of Jaswant Singh.[31]

A detailed critique of Aurangzīb's Rājpūt policy is hardly relevant to our purposes. That it was fraught with grave dangers and promised few tangible returns seems undeniable. This Rājpūts had not shown themselves disloyal, and the unsympathetic treatment meted out to the descendants of an old and distinguished chief was bound to cause serious disquiet to the other. Aurangzīb had thus embarked upon a dangerous policy, and when the Rājpūt chiefs defied his authority by fleeing from the court with the son of Jaswant Singh, he decided to go the whole hog and to try and crush Rājpūt resistance to his plans. Hence, Inder Singh was deposed and Jodhpur taken under direct Imperial control.[32] The war against the Rathors soon expanded into a war against the Sishodias of Mewar.

31 Ishwardas (Add. 23, 884, f. 75a). 'At the death of the Maharaja every Rājpūt in Mārwār out of the proud ambition of asserting his leadership got ready to create disturbance and mischief.'

Also, see Note at end of Chapter.

32 *M.A.*, 179, *Dil.*, 165. (For recent reviews of the Marwar War, based on new sources, see M. Athar Ali, 'Causes of the Rathor Rebellion of 1679', I.H.C., xxiii, 1961, pp. 135–41; Satish Chandra, Introduction to *Jodhpur Hukumat ri Bahi*, (eds) S. Chandra, R. Sinh, G. D. Sharma, Meenakshi, Delhi, 1976, vii–xv.)

Although an agreement with the Sishodias was patched up in 1680 and, at the same time, the promise of restoring Ajit Singh to *manṣab* and *raj* when he came of age was reiterated,[33] hostilities with the Rathors continued. In 1698, an agreement was concluded with Ajit Singh restoring him to the *gaddi*, but Jodhpur city remained under the control of the Imperialists as a guarantee of good behaviour on his part. This did not satisfy Ajit Singh who did not adhere to the treaty and kept Rājpūtānā in a disturbed condition.

The Rathor uprising should not be regarded as constituting a breach between the Mughal Emperor and the Rājpūts as such, for the Kachchhwāhās, Hārās etc. continued to serve the Mughal empire. Nor was the material damage to the Mughal empire very large. Its importance lay rather in as much as it constituted a definite setback to the attempt to establish a composite ruling class consisting of various elements among the Muslims and the Hindus in the country. It thus strengthened the forces of separatism among the Hindus and the Muslims. In the second place, the absence of a powerful Rājpūt section in the nobility ultimately made negotiations with the Marāthās more difficult. It also led to the diversion of resources at a critical time and emboldened others like the Jats and Sikhs to continue to defy Mughal authority.[34]

The power and influence of the Marāthās had steadily grown in the politics of the Deccan states during the seventeenth century, and already in the time of Shāh Jahān, Shāhjī Bhonsle had carved out a semi-independent principality for himself, first around Poona, and then at Bangalore. The early efforts of Shivaji, the son of a neglected wife of Shāhjī, were directed towards recovering his father's *jāgīr* in Poona. His growing ambitions, and the manifest inability of the Bijāpur government to curb his activities, brought him into clash with the Mughals who were reluctant to see a new state arise on their southern border and were suspicious of the plundering proclivities of Shivaji. A tussle with the mighty Mughal empire faced Shivaji with a difficult choice—whether to strike out for independence or to come to terms with it. In 1665, when Jai Singh hemmed in Shivaji at Purandar and occupied most of his

33 *Aurangzeb* V, 269.

34 The Bundela conflict was very largely a struggle between rival claimants to the *gaddī* of Orchha, and never assumed the dimensions of a popular struggle even to the extent the Rājpūt uprising did.

forts, Shivaji agreed to a treaty by which out of the 35 forts then in his possession yielding an annual income of five lakh *huns* in the former Nizāmshāhī kingdom, he was to be left with 12 forts yielding one lakh *huns*, (i.e. five lakh rupees), and was allotted *tāluqahs* yielding nine lakh *huns*—four lakhs in the Bijāpuri Tal-Konkan and five lakhs in Bālāghāt. The latter was in anticipation of a joint campaign against Bijāpur. In return for these, Shivaji was to pay 40 lakh *huns* in instalments of three lakhs each year, be loyal and obedient to the Mughal government, refrain from plundering the imperial dominions, and perform service in the Deccan whenever called upon to do so. His son, Shambhāji, was accorded a *manṣab* of 5,000, and accompanied by Netāji, the trusted lieutenant of Shivaji, was to attend on the *ṣūbahdār* of the Deccan.[35]

Thus, Shivaji was given autonomy within an area which, if the Bījāpur campaign proved successful, would actually yield him an income greater than what he had enjoyed before. He was also exempted from personal service (except in the Deccan)—a privilege extended only to the Rana of Mewar, the most illustrious and the oldest ruling house in Rājpūtānā.* The *manṣab* granted to Shivaji's son was also not a low one, being equal to that held by the Rana of Mewar. But it was not likely to satisfy Shivaji since similar ranks had already been granted to a number of Marāthā chiefs regarded by Shivaji as inferior to him in status and power.[36]

The treaty of Purandar might have formed the basis of a lasting settlement between the Mughals and Shivaji. But the failure of Jai Singh's campaign against Bījāpur completely changed the situation. Shivaji was left with an income of only one lakh *huns*, and for the realization of even this he had to reckon with the hostility of Bījāpur. It was obvious that the Marāthā alliance could only be preserved if Aurangzīb relinquished hold of most of Shivaji's forts, or compensated him somewhere else.

* This is correct only partially. Rana Rāj Singh had been raised to the rank of 6,000/6,000 (1,000 *du-aspah sih-aspah*) by Aurangzīb after the battle of Sāmūgarh. (Aurangzib's *farmān* reproduced in *Vir Vinod* ii, 425–32). But 5,000 had remained the *manṣab* of all the earlier Ranas, as also of the immediate successors of Rana Rāj Singh.

35 Sarkar, *House of Shivaji*, 117–18.

36 *Ibid.*, 113. In 1630, when Shāhjī had joined the Mughals, he had also been granted the rank of 5,000. (Lahori, *Pādshāhnāmah* i, 328.)

No fresh approach was made by Aurangzīb to Shivaji between 1666 and 1675. In 1675, Bahādur Khān, the Viceroy of the Deccan, offered a rank of 6,000 to Shambhāji, the son of Shivaji, and asked Shivaji to surrender 17 forts only, as against the 23 secured by Jai Singh.[37] Evidently, the Mughals still regarded the treaty of Purandar as the basis for negotiations with Shivaji. But Shivaji's power and aspirations had grown considerably in the meantime, and he was in no mood to accept such trifling concessions which showed the small value attached by the Mughals to a Marāthā alliance.

Meanwhile, a fresh source of friction between the Mughals and the Marāthās made its appearance. This was Shivaji's practice of levying *chauth* and *sardeshmukhi* from Mughal territories. Though *chauth* and *sardeshmukhi* were traditional imposts, Shivaji was probably the first leader of consequence to use them systematically as a means of gathering the sinews of war against his enemies. *Chauth* did not, at first, imply any claim to a privileged political position in the Deccan, but was in the nature of a war-tax. It constituted, however, a challenge to the Mughal capacity to safeguard their territories from external plunder, and thus compromised their sovereignty. At the same time, the manner of enforcing the claim was a menace to the trade and industry of the entire area, and threatened to disrupt the vital link between the rich and industrious west coast and the populous centres of north India. The claim for *sardeshmukhi* rested on the legal fiction that Shivaji was the chief *Deshmukh* of the Deccan. It was enforced in the same manner as the claim for *chauth*.[38]

Thus, the main differences between Shivaji and the Mughals centred around the territory and *manṣab* which was to be granted to Shivaji, and later, around the claim for *chauth* and *sardeshmukhi*. For strategic and economic reasons, the Mughals were unwilling to see a powerful Marāthā state arise on their southern border, on the flank of the vital trade route to the west coast. Financial stringency made it impossible to satisfy the ambitions of Shivaji except at the expense of the Deccan states. But for a variety of reasons, Aurangzīb was not prepared or unable to make a

37 *Aurangzeb* V, 222–3.

38 For the controversy regarding the nature and origin of *chauth* and *sardeshmukhi*, see Ranade, *Rise of the Maratha Power*, 219–38; Sen, *Maratha Adm.* 97–9; Sardesai, *New Hist.* ii, 51–2; Balkrishna, *Nature of Sardeshmukhi*, *I.H.C.*, 1939, 1189–93.

concerted move against the Deccan states till 1676. By the time, Shivaji's ambitions had soared higher, and he had become convinced of the advantages of playing a lone hand rather than of serving the Mughals. Personal factors also played a part. Aurangzīb had a deep-seated distrust of Shivaji which the various 'exploits' of the latter had done nothing to allay. He failed, at the same time, to understand the nature of the forces represented by Shivaji, and hence, grossly under-estimated the real power of the Marāṭhās, and the worth of an alliance with them for the rapid conquest and consolidation of the Deccan.

Aurangzīb went to the Deccan in 1681, ostensibly in pursuit of Prince Akbar. But the threat from the side of the Prince soon passed, and the Emperor's main pre-occupation became the conquest of Bījāpur and Golkonda. There is insufficient evidence to support the view that Aurangzīb determined, at this stage, upon the total destruction of the Marāṭhā state. The capture of Shambhāji was an unexpected piece of good luck for Aurangzīb. Although Shambhāji was treated as a rebel for the sin of helping Prince Akbar, and was executed, the treatment accorded to Shambhā's son, Shāhū, suggests that Aurangzīb contemplated the recognition of his title to Shivaji's *gaddi* when he came of age. Shāhū was granted the *manṣab* of 7,000 which had also been conferred on Shambhāji in 1678, accorded the title of Raja, and lodged inside the *gulāl-bār*, and not inside fortress-prisons like the deposed rulers of Bījāpur and Golkonda. Decent allowances were fixed upon him, and when he was 12 years old, Aurangzīb married him to two girls of respectable Marāṭhā families, and presented him with the sword of Shivaji which had been captured with Shambhāji in 1689.[39]

Between 1689 and 1698, Aurangzīb concentrated his efforts upon taking possession of the rich and fertile tract extending upto Jinji. He was apparently convinced that once the Mughal hold on this area had been effectively established, the Marāṭhās would either come to their senses and accept his terms, or they would be surrounded and crushed.

With Mughal territory extended upto the Karnātak, Rajārām bottled up in Jinji, and the Marāṭhā state shattered, the situation

39 *Raqā'im* 23b, *M.A.*, 332, 433, 482. *Cf.* Sardesai, *New Hist.* i, 331.
The *gulāl-bār* was a large enclosure near the special apartments of the Emperor, the doors of which were made very strong, and secured with locks and keys. (See *Ā'īn* i, 27).

seemed to be overwhelmingly in favour of Aurangzīb. But Aurangzīb had not reckoned with the national spirit of the Marāthās which now came into play. The Marāthā resistance revived from about 1695, and after Rājārām's return from Jinji in 1698, the Mughals had to suffer a number of reverses. Rājārām parcelled out the Mughal territories among Marāthā *sardars*, and asked them to levy their own contributions. The extended communications of the Mughals were highly vulnerable to the quick-moving Marāthā bands. The local officials often deemed it more profitable to make private deals with the Marāthās than to offer them serious resistance.[40] To cope with this situation, Aurangzīb constituted powerful cavalry units supported by artillery under Z̲u'lfiqār Khān, Chīn Qulīch Khān, and others. But the heavier armaments, lack of local support, and ignorance of local topography made the Mughals often helpless against the Marāthās in a war of movement. In desperation, Aurangzīb entered upon the futile expedient of trying to conquer the various Marāthā forts one by one. But the situation was now vastly different from 1664, and Jai Singh's success against Shivaji could not be repeated. The only alternative before Aurangzīb was to attempt negotiations.

Meanwhile, the war had inflicted extensive damage upon the Marāthās too, and in 1695 and 1698, they had attempted to open negotiations with the Mughals, but in vain.[41]

In 1700, on the death of Rājārām, his widow, Tārā Bāi, proposed peace to Aurangzīb, offering to maintain a contingent of 5,000 troops for Imperial service, and to cede seven forts in return for the recognition of her son, Shivaji II, as the King of the Marāthās, the grant to him of the rank of 7,000, and the right of collecting *sardeshmukhi* in the Deccan. Thus, Tārā Bāi dropped the claim for independence as also for *chauth*. We are told that Aurangzīb rejected these terms, demanding the ceding of all forts.[42] The motives of Aurangzīb can only be guessed. He may have felt some hesitation in bypassing the claims of Shāhū, or he may have

40 See *Dil.*, 140a–b.

41 *Dil.*, 122a-b, *Aurangzeb* V, 105, 131.

42 *Aurangzeb* V, 136, *Akhbārāt*, 12 March 1700.

K. K. (ii, 626, 782) states that Tārā Bāi asked for 9 per cent as *sardeshmukhi*, but 'for the honour of Islam and other reasons, Aurangzīb rejected the proposal.' This event is placed 'towards the end of Aurangzīb's reign', but presumably refers to the negotiations of 1700.

seen in these terms a sign of weakness, and believed that the Marāthās would come round completely to his point of view if he showed patience and firmness a little longer.

In 1703, negotiations were opened with Dhānā Jādav through Prince Kām Bakhsh for the release of Shāhū 'on certain terms'. Shāhū was transferred to Kām Bakhsh's camp, and invitations were drawn up for no less than 70 Marāthā *sardars* to come and see him after which they were to be conducted to the Imperial presence, and admitted into Imperial service. In other words, Aurangzīb wanted the Marāthā *sardars* to tender allegiance and accept Shāhū as their ruler. What concessions he offered in return is not known. According to some later historians, he was prepared to grant *sardeshmukhi* over the six *ṣūbahs* of the Deccan, in addition, apparently, to the *swarājya* of Shivaji, i.e. the territories which Shivaji controlled at the time of his death. We are told that the documents granting *sardeshmukhi* were actually drawn up and handed over to Aḥsan Khān to be delivered to the Marāthās. But 'the plan did not please Aurangzīb who prudently felt misgivings as to the craftiness of the Marāthās and was apprehensive that if they assembled forty or fifty thousand horse near the royal camp, they might by pretence carry off Raja Shahu and Prince Kām Bakhsh to their hills of difficult access'.[43] Hence, the negotiations were broken off.

43 K. K., 520, *M.A.*, 473. *T. Ibrāhīm Khān* (Rampur Ms., Elliot viii, 259), states: 'Towards the close of His Majesty's life time, a truce was concluded with the Marāthās on these terms, *viz.* that 9 per cent (Elliot says 3 per cent, but the original reads—'*har sad az maḥṣūl-i-mulkī nah rupiah*') of the revenues drawn from the Imperial dominions in the Dakhin should be allotted to them by way of *sardeshmukhi*; and accordingly Aḥsan Khān commonly known as Mīr Malik set out from the threshhold of royalty with the documents confirming this grant to the Marāthās in order that after the treaty had been duly ratified, he might bring the chiefs of that tribe to the court of the Monarch of the World. However, before he had time to deliver these documents in their custody a royal mandate was issued, directing him to return and bring back the papers in question with him.'

Ibrāhīm Khān is supported by the *Khazīnā'-i-'Āmira* (p. 41) which says 9 per cent was agreed to. Khāfī Khān (p. 520), though in agreement with Ibrāhīm Khān with regard to the events, does not make any mention of the grant of *sardeshmukhi* by Aurangzīb.

Duff (i, 445), followed by Ranade, (p. 226), says that Aurangzīb was, for a time, prepared to grant ten per cent as *sardeshmukhi*. The event is, however, wrongly place in 1705, and no authority is cited.

A final effort for peace, in 1706, through the mediation of Ẕu'lfiqār Khān was equally fruitless.[44]

The rise in Mahārāshtra of a powerful movement aimed at regional independence created for the Mughals a problem which was not purely regional in its implications. A successful defiance of the Mughal authority by the Marāthās not only militated against the principle of an all-India Timurid monarchy but it also upset the delicate alliance of the Muslims and Hindus in the nobility. On the other hand, it was difficult to adjust the ambitions of the various Marāthā *sardars* in the existing framework of the nobility, particularly as the *jāgīrdārī* system on which the institution of the nobility rested was already in a state of deep crisis.

Crisis of the Jāgīrdārī System

The political problems of Aurangzīb were accompanied by a deepening crisis of the *jāgīrdārī* system which accentuated and, in turn, was accentuated by the political crisis.

The Mughals evolved a number of administrative devises to ensure the proper functioning of the *manṣabdārī* system. These administrative devises, while valuable in themselves, could not, however, help them to overcome the basic problem, viz. that the available social surplus was insufficient to defray the cost of administration, pay for wars of one type or another, and to give the ruling class a standard of life in keeping with its expectations. It would appear that in India as in a number of western countries during this period, there was a decline in the value of

---

Manucci (iii, 498–9) states that Aurangzīb tried to sow dissension among the Mārathās by releasing Shāhū, granting him *chauth* (of the Deccan) and leaving Kām Bakhsh as the governor of Bijapur, Golkonda and the two Carnatics and himself retiring to Delhi.

No Persian or Marathi authority supports Manucci who, in general, is a very unreliable authority, especially where political affairs are concerned. K. & Parasnis (ii, 111–12), and S. G. Sardesai (*New History*, 356) assert that 'towards the end of his life Aurangzīb had consented to grant to the Maratha Government Chauth and Sardeshmukhi and the restoration of Shivaji's Kingdom (*Swarajya*)'. This view is apparently based on Manucci and, as such, is untenable.

44 *Dil.*, ff. 154b, 155a, *M.A.*, 511.

money.[45] Among other things, it led to a rise in the cost of administration. Simultaneously, the expectations and the cost of living of the ruling class tended to rise. The Mughal monarchs themselves set the pace by incurring large expenditure on all kinds of pomp and show, as well as on the patronage of the various arts and crafts. While this gave employment to large numbers of artists and artisans, and stimulated some types of industry and trade, it did not solve the basic difficulty which remained one of agricultural production. Then, as now, agricultural production formed the backbone of the Indian economy, and, ultimately, a stable growth of income could only be based on a rise in the value and volume of agricultural production. A rise in the requirements of the ruling class without a corresponding rise in agricultural production resulted directly or indirectly in the growth of economic pressure on the producing classes. As has been mentioned earlier, the Mughal emperors laid great emphasis on the promotion of agriculture. Expansion of agriculture, as well as the improvement of irrigation facilities, the introduction of high grade crops, provision of seeds, *taqāvī* in times of distress, etc. formed an important branch of state activity, and officials were instructed to exhort, and if necessary to compel the individual peasants to cultivate as much land as possible. While there is evidence of a continual expansion of the cultivated area during the seventeenth century, signs of a crisis of the *jāgīrdārī* system became visible during the latter years of Jahāngīr's reign. *Ẕāt* and *sawār* ranks had long ceased to indicate the total number of horsemen or horses actually maintained. Shāh Jahān re-fixed the salaries and made it a rule that not more than one-third of the number indicated by the *sawār* rank was to be actually maintained by a noble: generally, the contingent was less than even one-third. Salaries were scaled down proportionately by

45 According to Hodiwala (*Historical Studies in Mughal Numismatics*, 245–52), the gold *muhar* appreciated considerably in terms of the rupee between the time the *Āīn* was composed at the end of the 17th century.

The decline in the purchasing power of the rupee is also reflected in the rise in he price of food-grains and ghee. [*Cf. M.A.*, 98, for prices at Agra in 1670 when harvest had been exceptionally favourable, with those in the *Ā'īn* (N. K. i, 38 *et seq.*)]. Allowing for the difference in the weight of the *man*, the prices of wheat, gram, and ghee in 1670 were 2½ to 3 times higher than at the beginning of the century. The rise in the price of sugar and indigo was even greater, as indicated by the prices given in the *English Factory Records.*

the practice of paying salaries for only ten, eight, six or even four months in the year. The majority of nobles apparently received salaries for six to eight months only.[46] Thus, appearances were preserved, while reality was sought to be faced by spreading the available resources more widely. But Shāh Jahān's reforms should not be understood to imply any reduction in the net salaries of the nobles after setting off the cost of maintenance of the troopers. Rather, in actual practice the net incomes were perhaps higher. Shāh Jahān's court was reputed to be the most splendid in the world and many nobles accumulated vast fortunes.

The reforms of Shāh Jahān mitigated but could not solve the financial crisis. Resources could not keep pace with growing expenses, and when at the end of the thirteenth year of his reign, Aurangzīb reviewed the position, he was faced with a revenue-deficit.[47] Despite economies in expenditure, emphasis on simplicity, the imposition of fresh taxes, and constant injunctions to his nobles to extend and improve cultivation,[48] Aurangzīb failed to solve the financial crisis.

Struggle for *jāgīr*s and employment at the court tended to re-inforce the latent spirit of racial and religious exclusiveness, and to the raising of slogans for the exclusion of the Hindus from the nobility. At the same time, the pressure for solving the internal crisis at the expense of the Deccan states grew. But much of the Deccan was itself a deficit area. In any case, misgovernment and internecine warfare among factions and groups had reduced it to a state where no quick yields could be expected. There was the further problem of satisfying local aspirants, and of finding the basis for a satisfactory settlement with the Marāthās.

The final annexation of Bījāpur and Golkonda was actuated by political rather than financial considerations. The growing power of the Marāthās posed a problem that could no longer be ignored. The results seem to have borne out all the fears which had made Aurangzīb hold back from undertaking a forward policy in the Deccan during the first two decades of his reign. The military operation proved long and expensive, and gold had to be freely

46 See Aziz, *Manṣabdārī System*, 52–3.

47 *M.A.*, 99–100.

48 Thus, see Aurangzīb's *farmān* to Muḥammad Hāshim, Dīwān of Gujarāt (Translated by Sarkar, *Mughal Adm.*, 198–214), Manucci iii, 253.

expended to buy over Deccani nobles. For purposes of political expediency, large numbers of Deccani nobles had to be given *manṣabs* and employment. In the best of times it would have been difficult to satisfy the aspirations of all the new entrants. Unsettled conditions in the Deccan and north India and Marāthā depredations made the task doubly difficult. As it was, the Deccani nobles were dissatisfied at the 'low' ranks accorded to them.[49] Almost every noble desired a *jāgīr* in northern India or in the settled parts of the country, and exerted his influence to that end. This placed the officials of the revenue department in an extremely difficult situation. As 'Ināyatullah Khān, the *dīwān-i-tan-o-khālisa* and a great personal favourite with Aurangzīb, complained, 'the contingents of the officers who are daily passed in review before your Majesty are unlimited (in number) while the land available for granting as *jāgīrs* is limited (in area). How can a limited figure be made equal to an unlimited one?'[50]

The result was that there were inordinate delays in the grant of *jāgīrs*, and when finally granted they yielded only a fraction of the sanctioned emoluments.[51] The efforts of the *jāgīrdārs* to realize the full value of their *jāgīrs* seem to have made themselves felt in a number of areas, especially in the marginal areas such as those around Agra, or on the borders of Rājpūtānā and parts of the Deccan where agriculture had never yielded a very large surplus. The flight of peasants from land[52] was the first symptom of this growing crisis which later on spilled into violence and desperate armed uprisings.

The uncertainty of income from the *jāgīrs* also demoralized the administration. Many nobles practically ceased maintaining contingents or kept a far smaller contingent than was required. Many

49 *Aurangzeb* V, 68.

50 *Aḥkām*, 57. We are told that the number of *manṣabdārs* had increased from 8,000 in 1659 to 14,556 in 1690 (Wāris, *Bādshāhnāmah*, 70; *Zawābit-i-'Ālamgīrī* (Or. 1641) f. 15a; Sharma, *Religious Policy*, 133). Out of these, 7,657 nobles were on cash (*naqdī*) salaries, while only 6,899 held *jāgīrs*, i.e. less than half of the total.

51 Thus, see K.K., 602–3. See *Raqā'im*, ff. 6b–7a for Aurangzīb's efforts to check inflation of revenue artificially in Gujarāt.

See *Akhbārāt*, 11 *Rajab* yr. 39, 5 February 1696 for the imprisonment of noble who refused to serve without a *jāgīr*.

52 See Bernier, 225–26. *Raqā'im*, 24a–b.

others in the Deccan came to a private arrangement with the Marāthās for the division of the state dues, instead of resisting their encroachments. Others—especially those in the lower grades, began to prefer cash salaries to *jāgīrs*, or to farm out their *jāgīrs* to various middle-men.[53]

Thus, by the end of Aurangzīb's reign, the *jāgīrdārī* system had reached a state of acute crisis, presaging a complete breakdown, or a new series of reforms which would remove the worst abuses and to give official sanction to things which could not be changed. It is necessary to bear in mind, however, that the problem of the *jāgīrdārī* system was, at root, a social problem which no mere economies in expenditures and administrative devises for expanding cultivation could solve. What was really required was the rapid expansion of industry and trade, based on the introduction of new technology and the removal of all barriers hindering that expansion. These barriers, in the ultimate resort, were the barriers of the existing social order which encompassed trade and industry in too narrow a sphere. Hence, a basic improvement in the situation was beyond the competence of any one king.

☆ ☆ ☆

From the foregoing review, it should be apparent that at the end of Aurangzīb's reign, the Mughal empire was faced with a serious situation. The financial position had grown steadily worse and, as a result of this and a number of other developments, the crisis of the *jāgīrdārī* system had reached a stage when the entire *manṣabdārī* system was threatened with collapse. The spirit of obscurantism and revivalism had grown both among the Muslims and Hindus: the efforts to create a composite ruling class had suffered a setback and separatist forces had been strengthened. The rebellions of the Jats, Sikhs, etc., the breach with the Rāthors, and the pro-longed conflict with the Marāthās had damaged Imperial prestige, and encouraged the forces of opposition in all quarters. Ambitious men were attempting to gather strength in their hands in order to strike out on their own, should the situation

53 Thus, see *Akhbārāt*, 24 *Jam* II Yr. 38, 29 January 1695 for leasing out of *jāgīrs* to merchants by nobles in Kashmīr. *Cf.* also the remarks of Khāfī Khān (ii, 88–9, 565) about the state of the administration under Aurangzīb.

warrant it. Thus, the general atmosphere was one of expectancy and uncertainty.

However, in spite of many defects of policy and a number of personal shortcomings on Aurangzīb's part, the Mughal empire was still a powerful and vigorous military and administrative machinery. The Mughal army might fail against the elusive and highly mobile bands of Marāthās in the mountainous regions of the Deccan. Marāthā forts might be difficult to capture and still more difficult to retain. But in the plains of northern India and the vast plateau extending upto the Karnatak, the Mughal artillery was still master of the field. Thirty or 40 years after Aurangzīb's death, when the Mughal artillery had declined considerably in strength and efficiency, the Marāthās could still not face it in the field of battle.[54] Continuous anarchy, war and the depredations of the Marāthās may have depleted the population of the Deccan and brought its trade, industry and agriculture to a virtual standstill. But in northern India which was the heart of the empire and was of decisive economic and political importance in the country, the Mughal administration still retained much of its vigour. In fact, the administration at the district level proved amazingly tenacious and a good deal of it survived and found its way indirectly into the British administration.

Politically, despite the military reverses and the mistakes of Aurangzīb, the Mughal dynasty still retained a powerful hold on the mind and imagination of the people.[55]

It is against this entire background that the history of India in the eighteenth century and the parties and politics at the Mughal court have to be viewed.

Note on Khāliṣah and Zamindars

In the case of the states of many autonomous or semi-autonomous *zamindars* and rajas, the Mughal government neither interfered with local administration nor did it fix the revenue demand on the

54 *Cf.* Bernier who has a rather low opinion of the morale, discipline and organization of the Mughal armies (p. 55) but considers the 'stirrup-artillery' to be 'extremely well-appointed' (pp. 217–18).

55 *Cf.* Spears, *Twilight of the Moghuls* (p. 9): 'there was for his (the Emperor's) authority something of the reverence and spirit of acceptance which exists in Britain for the parliament.'

basis of a detailed assessment. It fixed a lump-sum tribute called *peshkash* which was generally to be deposited in the *khāliṣah* treasury (though it appears that sometime this tribute could also be assigned to a *manṣabdār* as part of his *tankhwah-i-jāgīr*.[56] Or, it might be assigned to the raja himself as *watan jāgīr*).

However, the phrase '*dar khāliṣah ẕabt namūdah*' (taking a state into *khāliṣah*) is used either in the sense of depriving a raja of his *watan jāgīr* or dispossessing him of his *zamindarī*. The use of the word annexation in the context of removing a raja from his hereditary domain is, therefore, misleading.

In the case of Aurangzīb's action in Mārwār on the death of Jaswant Singh, the words 'bringing the state under *khāliṣah*' have been used in the specific sense of taking over the administration and the revenue-collection from the members of the ruling branch of the house. After some time, the state was handed over to Inder Singh, the grandson of Amar Singh who was the brother of Jaswant Singh. It seems that in many cases of disputed succession where the Emperor for any reason could not or did not decide whom to recognize as the raja, or on account of dissatisfaction with the conduct of a raja wanted to remove him, he appointed imperial officers to administer that territory and collect revenue till such time as he had decided whom to recognize as the raja. Thus, taking over the state of a raja under *khāliṣah* was somewhat similar to the administration of states under Courts of Words.

Note on the Crisis of the Jāgīrdārī System

Outwardly the *jāgīrdārī* crisis appeared to be an administrative and economic crisis, but from a deeper study, it must be viewed in the context of the economic and social relations in medieval India, specifically the agrarian relations, and the administrative superstructure that was reared on the basis of these relations.

Both caste and the structure of rural society played a significant role in the attempt of the Turkish and Mughal rulers to control and utilize the *zamindars* for collecting land revenue from their tracts (*ta'lluqa*). The owner–cultivators—called *khud-kāshta* in 17th–18th century Persian revenue documents, formed a privileged group in

56 For example, the territory of the raja of Nagarkot was assigned in *jāgīr* to Birbal to whom the raja was required to pay a substantial amount (*Akbarnāma* iii, pp. 36–7).

village society with well-recognized hereditary rights and duties.[57] Dominating a village or a group of villages in a region, the *khud-kāshta* often belonged to one caste or clan. The Jats in north-western India, and the Marāthās in western India may be considered examples. Local officials (*muqaddam, kulkarnī, patel* etc.) and intermediary zamindars were often drawn from the same sections i.e. the *khud-kāshta* or the land-owners. The Sulṭans and later, in a more systematic manner, the Mughals tried to establish direct relations with the land-owners in order to determine the productivity, nature of crops etc., and on that basis to fix and thereby limit the perquisites of the *zamindars*.[58] The growth of pargana administration also tended to limit the local power of the *zamindars*.

The growth of central authority and prestige, and the Mughal emphasis on justice, which broadly implied not permitting one group of people to encroach on the duties of another,[59] gradually created a situation in which the cultivators began to look to the central government rather than to the local *zamindar* or chieftain for protection, and the redressal of their grievances if they reached beyond a certain point. This triangle between the central government, the *zamindars* and the dominant section of the cultivators i.e. *khud-kāshta* provided a kind of balance which was the basis of Mughal stability. It lasted as long as the *zamindars* and the cultivators looked to the central government for support and redressal of grievances rather than joining hands to resist and fight it. It also provided the essential social basis of the Mughal *jāgīrdārī* system which, unlike the *iqṭā'adārī* system, divested the grantee of administrative responsibility over the area assigned to him as *jāgīr*. The *faujdār* who was the *lynchpin* of the Mughal administrative system, had the dual responsibility of making available military

57 See Satish Chandra, 'Some Aspects of Indian Village Society in Northern India during the 18th Century: The Position and Role of the *khud-kasht* and *pahi-kasht*' *Indian Historical Review*, Vol. 1, No. 1, 1974, 51–64.

58 See S. Nurul Hasan, 'The Position of the Zamindar in the Mughal Empire', in R. E. Frykenberg (ed.), *Land Control and Social Structure in Indian History* (Madison, 1969), 18–31.

59 *Ā'in* Blochman, p. 4: See also the views of the contemporary poet, Suradasa, for whose this was the basis of social stability (Savitri Chandra, 'Two Aspects of Hindu Social Life and Thought as Reflected in the Works of Tulsidasa', *Journal of Economic and Social History of the Orient*, Vol. XIX, pt. I, 1976, 48–60.

support to the *jārgīrdār* or his agent, where necessary, in collecting the land-revenue due, and also in providing a channel of redress against the exactions of the *jāgīrdār* and his agents. The *wāqia'-navīs* was meant to watch over both the *jāgīrdār* and the *faujdār*. This system of checks and balance, rising up to the provincial and central levels, was an essential feature of the Mughal administrative system and was designed as a safeguard against abuse of power and authority in a fundamentally feudal setup.

By the very nature of medieval Indian society, the delicate social balance outlined above was liable to be upset on a number of counts, such as serious struggle for power at the centre, disaffection in the nobility etc. At the local and regional levels, augmentation of the power of the *zamindar*s, directly or indirectly, could also have far-reaching consequences.

The first signs of a social and economic crisis in the Mughal empire appeared in the shape of a financial and administrative crisis, viz., a growing gap between the assessed land revenue (*jama'*) and the realization (*ḥāṣil*). The introduction of the rule of one-third/one-fourth and the month scales (*māhwār*) by Shāh Jahān on a regular basis was aimed at reducing the emoluments and the obligations of the *manṣabdār*s in order to bridge the gap in the revenue-resources available to the empire for distribution as jāgīrs. Under Shāh Jahān, a *manṣabdār* rarely had a jāgīr of more than eight months, or less four months. Due to the operation of the month-scale, the number of *sawārs* and remounts available to a *manṣabdār* declined, and hence his ability to collect from the land-holders the share of the land-revenue which was due to him. This set up a vicious circle which proved difficult to break. The fundamental reason for this was the inability and unwillingness of the Mughals to change the existing social relations, especially the agrarian relations. The *khud-kāshta* who had large land holding often belonged to a higher or 'middle castes', while a growing number of landless peasants or peasants with dwarf holdings belonged to the low castes. The latter were not permitted or provided the means of bringing under cultivation and acquiring proprietory rights over large tracts of cultivable wasteland.[60] Thus

60 Satish Chandra, 'Some Institutional Factors in Providing Capital Inputs for the Improvement and Expansion of Cultivation in Medieval India', *Indian Historical Review*, Vol. III, No. 1, July 1976, 83–98.

the Mughal government depended largely on the *zamindars* and dominant land-owning castes in the village for agricultural growth and expansion.

The theory that frequent transfer of *jāgīrdārs* during Aurangzīb's reign became a major factor in the exactions of the peasantry and the breakdown of the *jāgīrdāri* system also needs careful consideration. Bhīmsen remarks that a *manṣabdār* was uncertain whether he would remain in the *jāgīr* the following year due to exactions of the royal *mutaṣaddīs* and the practice of taking a large *qabẓ* (security money) from the *āmils* and that this was ruinous for the peasants.[61] Possibly, Bhīmsen who was himself a small *manṣabdār*, has generalized the experience of small *manṣabdārs* who were at the mercy of the royal *mutaṣaddīs.* Transfer does not seem to have been so common among the bigger *manṣabdārs* to whom more than three-fourths of the revenue yielding territories were assigned.[62] Moreover, the bigger *manṣabdārs* had generally to collect land revenue from *zamindars* who could not easily be coerced to pay more. The transfer of these *jāgīrdārs* would thus not have much effect on the cultivators.

It would appear that the position of the *zamindars* as a class had tended to become stronger during the seventeenth century, on account of the Mughal policy of integrating the *zamindars* with the machinery of administration to realize land revenue from the cultivators, and to also give them a guaranteed portion of the produce by including it in the *jama'*. Even the policy of extending and improving cultivation depended largely on the cooperation of the *zamindars*. As a result, the Mughal administration, especially at the local level, began to be identified more closely with the *zamindars*, thus alienating the land-holders who looked to the ruler for protection against oppression.

From a careful reading of Bhīmsen's account, it would appear that while the rise of the Marāthās, the weakening of the position of the *jāgīrdārs*, and the inability of the Mughals to successfully introduce in the Deccan their carefully balanced system of

61 Bhīmsen, *Nuskhah-i-Dilkasha,* f. 139a.

62 A. Jan Qaisar, 'Distribution of the Revenue Resources of Mughal Empire among the Nobility', *Procs. I.H.R.* XXVII, 1965, 240. The figures refer to the twentieth year of Shāh Jahān's reign, and include *manṣabdārs* holding ranks of 500 *ẕāt* and above.

administration adversely effected the peasantry and deprived the Mughal state of their support and goodwill, it had the opposite effect on the *zamindars*, Bhīmsen says: 'The province given to the *manṣabdārs* in *tankhah* cannot be governed because of the smallness of their force (*jamia't*). The *zamindars* too have assumed strength, joined the Marāthās, enlisted armies and laid the hands of oppression on the country. When such is the position of the *zamindars*, it is difficult for a *dām* or *darham* to reach the *jāgīrdārs*.'

From the middle of the seventeenth century, if not earlier, the Mughals were unable to sustain and further strengthen the social balance which had enabled the Mughal central government to stand forth as the champion of the cultivators, and on this basis, isolate the *zamindars* and reduce their perquisites. This was not confined to the Deccan but extended to the north, as shown by the Jat and other rebellions. The growing social imbalance was accompanied by an administrative crisis, the two acting and reacting on each other. It were these processes which may be considered the essential basis of the crisis of the *jāgīrdārī* system.

CHAPTER I

Beginning of the Party Struggle at the Court[1]

Groups at the Court

Towards the end of Aurangzīb's reign, and by the beginning of the eighteenth century, two groups of nobles came to the forefront at the court. These groups played an important part at the Mughal court for the next four decades. Hence, the character and composition of these groups, and the antecedents, outlook and political affiliations of the leading characters in the two groups deserve careful examination.

The leading figures in the first group were the *wazīr-ul-mamālik* Asad Khān, and his son Z̲u'lfiqār Khān who had become *bakhshī-ul-mamālik* in 1702. Asad Khān belonged to a well-known family of Īrān, his grandfather Z̲u'lfiqār Khān being the *bēglar bēgī* of Shīrwān in the time of Shāh 'Abbās I. After the execution of Z̲u'lfiqār Khān by Shāh 'Abbās on some suspicion in 1600–1, the family had to face hard times, and Asad Khān's father Khānlar (entitled Z̲u'lfiqār Khān Qarāmānlū), migrated to India towards the end of Jahāngīr's reign. He was shown great kindness by Shāh Jahān, married to the daughter of Ṣādiq Khān, the brother-in-law of Yamīn-ud-Daulah Āṣaf Khān and raised ultimately to the rank of 3,000. Towards the end of Shāh Jahān's reign, he retired on account of paralysis, and settled down at Patna.[1]

1 *Tārikh–i-'Ālam Ārā'i* 'Abbās by Iskandar Munshī 570, *M.U.* ii, 85–9.

Muḥammad Ibrāhīm, entitled Aṣad Khān, was the eldest son of Zu'lfiqār Khān Qarāmānlū by Ṣādiq Khān's daughter, and was apparently born in 1055 H, 1625–6. He was a great favourite with Shāh Jahān and married the daughter of Āṣaf Khān. In 1654, he received the title of Asad Khān, and was made *ākhtah bēgī* (Master of the Horses), and soon afterwards, the second *bakhshī*. It is not necessary for our purposes to examine the subsequent career of Asad Khān in detail. Suffice it to say that he was a great favourite with Aurangzīb also, and continued to serve under him as the second *bakhshī*. In 1661, he was raised to the rank of 4,000/2,000. In 1669, when the *wazīr*, Ja'far Khān died, no one was appointed to succeed him, Asad Khān being nominated the *nā'ib wazīr*. The following year, he was also nominated as the chief *bakhshī* in succession to Lashkar Khān deceased, and combined this post with that of the *nā'ib wazīr* till 1673. In 1676, he was promoted to the post of the *wazīr*, and formally invested with the jewelled ink-pot of the office.[2] Subsequently, he was appointed to the Deccan at the head of a large army, and later served in the Rājpūt campaign. He took an active part in the siege of Bījāpur, and was rewarded with the *masnad* of *wizārat*.[3] Next year, following the capture of Golkonda, he was raised to the rank of 7,000/7,000.

Thus, by 1676, Asad Khān had attained a pre-eminent position which he continued to hold during the remaining 31 years of Aurangzīb's reign—one of the longest spells of office enjoyed by any *wazīr*. His rank and position, noble lineage and relationship with the royal family ensured him the highest respect from all quarters. Aurangzīb, we are told, had a very high regard for his capacities and capabilities, though it is difficult to estimate the influence he exercised as *wazīr* in shaping Aurangzīb's policies.[4] Towards the end of Aurangzīb's reign, Asad Khān was, for some time, placed in charge of the base camp at Islāmpurī, being

2 *M.A.*, 152, M.U. ii, 311.

3 *M.A.*, 281, M.U. ii, 311–12. This implied that Asad Khān was permitted to sit on a *masnad* in the royal presence which was deemed a very high honour. The date for this event was found in the chronogram—'*Zēbā shudah masnad-i-wizārat*' (1097). Beveridge (*M.U.* i, 270) has wrongly taken this to mean that he was appointed *wazīr* at the time.

4 For Aurangzīb's recommendation of Asad Khān to his sons, see *Aḥkām*, 11.

considered too old and infirm for active campaigning. Later, he accompanied Aurangzīb during the sieges of Kondānā. Rājgarh and Wāgangīra.

Z̲u'lfiqār Khān, the son of Asad Khān was born in 1649, and received his first *manṣab* in 1660 when he was only eleven years old, In 1677, he was married to the daughter of Amir ul-Umarā Shā'istah Khān, who was the maternal uncle of Emperor Aurangzīb, and awarded the title of I'tiqād Khān. As I'tiqād Khān, he made his mark in 1689 by the capture of Rāhērī (Rājgarh)—an extremely strong fort in which the treasures and families of Shambhājī and Rājārām were lodged. As a reward, he was raised to the rank of 3,000/2,000, and granted his ancestral title of Z̲u'lfiqār Khān. After this, he was sent against the fort of Panhālā.[5]

The real career of Z̲u'lfiqār Khān may, however, be said to commence with his nomination in 1690 to the command of an army for the capture of Jinjī. It was an important assignment, for Rājārām, the successor of Shambhājī, had taken shelter there and made it the rallying centre of the Marāthās. With Jinjī in his hands and Rājārām captured, Aurangzīb hoped to bring the Marāthā campaign to a virtual end, the task of establishing law and order in the rest of Mahārāshtra not being considered so difficult a task thereafter. But Z̲u'lfiqār Khān found himself faced with tremendous difficulties. Jinjī was an extremely strong fortress, and his forces were really not adequate for the task assigned to him. Communications and supplies were difficult to maintain in the face of Marāthā activities, the lack of support by the local population and chiefs,[6] and the fact that many of the Deccani nobles assigned to Z̲u'lfiqār Khān were disaffected and did not have their heart in the enterprise.[7] With the arrival of Santājī Ghorpāde and Dhānājī Jādav in the Karnātak in 1692, the situation became all the more difficult. Z̲u'lfiqār Khān found himself hard-pressed, and Asad Khān and Prince Kām Bakhsh were ordered to go to his help. However, the latter's intrigues caused further confusion, and necessitated his arrest, and a temporary abandonment of the siege.[8] It was not till 1698 that Z̲u'lfiqār Khān captured Jinjī, and

5 *M.A.*, 332–3, *M.U.* ii, 94.
6 Sarkar, *Aurangzeb* V, 94–6.
7 Sarkar, *Aurangzeb* V, 68, 74.
8 For details, see *Aurangzeb* V, 78–85.

even then the chief prize, Rājārām, escaped him. Aurangzīb was far from pleased at this, but rewarded Z̲u'lfiqār Kh̲ān with a rise of 1,000 *sawārs*, bringing his *manṣab* to 5,000/5,000.[9]

The Jinjī period marks an important phase in the life of Z̲u'lfiqār Kh̲ān, for it was apparently during this period that he gathered a group of devoted followers, and formed many associations with the Deccani nobles. According to some contemporary observers, he even began to nurse the ambition of independence in the Deccan.[10] The political views of Z̲u'lfiqār Kh̲ān also began to develop during this period. In 1697, he forwarded to Aurangzīb a proposal from Rājārām for a settlement, but Aurangzīb would not hear of it.[11]

After the fall of Jinjī, Z̲u'lfiqār Kh̲ān was, at first, deputed to deal with the Marāthā general, Dhānājī Jādhav, in the Konkan, and then given a roving commission to deal with the Marāthā bands wherever they might be. Z̲u'lfiqār Kh̲ān failed to inflict much damage on Dhānājī due to the rapid movements of the latter, but he won frequent successes against the other Marāthā chiefs, and earned a name for himself as one of the most successful generals. In 1702, he succeeded Bahramand Kh̲ān deceased as the *mīr bakhshī.* In 1705, when Aurangzīb was hard pressed at Wāgangīra, Z̲u'lfiqār Kh̲ān was summoned with all his generals. His arrival turned the tide of battle and the fort fell soon afterwards. But as Aurangzīb suspected Z̲u'lfiqār Kh̲ān and his lieutenant, Dalpat

9 *M.A.*, 392, *M.U.* ii, 97. Irvine ii, 9 is not correct in stating that the title of *Nuṣrat Jang* was conferred on him at the same time. He was accorded this title in the 39th regnal year (1696–7) when he was also raised to the *manṣab* of 5,000/4,000. Earlier, in Jan. 1692, he had been made 4,000/2,500 for the capture of Trinomālee (*M.A.*, 345).

10 François Martin, the founder of Pondicherry, who was in constant touch with the court of Jinjī, 'frequently in his letters and Memoirs expressed the opinion that Zulfiqar Khan had, during the course and particularly at the end of the siege of Jinjī, an understanding with Rajaram; in expectation of the death of the very old Aurangzeb and the civil wars that would fatally follow among his sons, he had conceived the ambition of carving out for himself an independent principality, and with that object he wanted to placate (manage) the Marathas' (Kaeppelin, 295 n, quoted in *Aurangzeb* V, 101).

Manucci (iii, 271) says the same thing, and Bhimsen, who was in Zu'lfiqār's camp, also hints at it (*Dil.*, 125a, 106a).

11 *Dil.*, 122b, *Aurangzeb* V, 105.

Rao, of colluding in the escape of Pidiā Nāyak, he was given insignificant rewards.[12] However, he was raised soon afterwards to the rank of 6,000/6,000.[13]

A significant step taken by Aurangzīb in 1706 was the transfer of Shāhū to Z̲u'lfiqār Khān's army for the purpose of negotiating a settlement with the Marāthās. This was a tacit recognition of the political importance attained by Z̲u'lfiqār Khān, as also his special relations with the Marāthās. From this time, if not earlier, Z̲u'lfiqār Khān seems to have taken a close personal interest in Shāhū. He wrote conciliatory letters to the Marāthās, inviting them to join Shāhū, but the Marāthā *sardars* were too suspicious Mughal policy for any positive response on their part.[14]

Thus, by the time Aurangzīb died, Asad Khān and Z̲u'lfiqār Khān occupied the two leading posts at the court—those of *wazīr* and *mīr bakshī* with the ranks of 7,000 and 6,000 respectively, and had acquired tremendous prestige and influence. Z̲u'lfiqār Khān was one of the most successful generals of the time and was considered a rising star. Among the chief supporters of Z̲u'lfiqār Khān may be mentioned Dā'ūd Khān Pannī, Rao Dalpat Bundela, and Rao Rām Singh Hāṛā. All the three were renowned warriors, and had served in the Karnātak for a long time under Z̲u'lfiqār Khān. Rao Rām Singh, the Hāṛā chief, had succeeded to the *gaddi* of Kotah in 1692–3 at the instance of Z̲u'lfiqār Khān and had served under him since then. In 1706 Z̲u'lfiqār Khān had also secured for him the *zamindari* of Bundi in place of Budh Singh who had been displaced.[15] Rao Dalpat Bundela, who had entered service in 1668, was assigned to Jinjī in 1690 and served with Z̲u'lfiqār Khān thereafter.[16]

Dā'ūd Khān Pannī was the son of Khiẓr Khān, a merchant who had risen to the position of one of the leading *sardars* of Bījāpur.

12 *Dil.*, 153b, *M.U.* (ii, 98–9) ascribes it, however to the envy aroused in Aurangzīb's breast by the universal praise of Z̲u'lfiqār Khān. 'As Emperor Aurangzīb was disposed to be malicious and uncharitable, he to spite Z̲u'lfiqār Khān granted increased allowances to the Tūrānī officials, and to him he only granted a sword and robe of honour, and deputed him to capture certain forts and to chastise the Marāthās'.

13 *B.N.*, 103, *M.U.* ii, 99.

14 *Dil.* ii, 154b–155a. *M.A.*, 511, *Aurangzeb* V, 207.

15 *M.A.*, 514, *M.U.* ii, 323.

16 *M.U.* ii, 317–23.

After the assassination of Khizr Khān at the hands of the Deccani party in 1677, Dā'ūd Khān had entered the Imperical service along with his brother, Sulaimān Khān, and was attached to his uncle, Ranmast Khān, who later acquired great fame and was awarded the title of Bahādur Khān. Later, he was attached to Z̲u'lfiqār Khān, and made his mark by his exploits during the siege of Jinjī. When Z̲u'lfiqār Khān was recalled to the court after the capture of Jinjī, Dā'ūd Khān was made his deputy in the *faujdārī* of Ḥaiderābādī-Karnātak and two years later, in 1701, the *faujdārī* of Bījāpurī-Karnātak was added to it. In 1704, he was made the deputy for Prince Kām Bakhsh who was the *ṣūbahdār* of Ḥaiderābād, and raised to the rank of 6,000/6,000.[17]

Dā'ūd Khān had many connections among the Deccani nobles, and was reputed to be a very wealthy man. It was said, too, that he held, rather unorthodox opinions, and that he was very favourably inclined towards the Hindus.[18]

It should be obvious from the foregoing account that the group consisting of Asad Khān, Z̲u'lfiqār Khān and his adherents was a very powerful and influential group. The combined *manṣabs* of its leading figures came to 24,500 *z̲āt* and 24,000 *sawār.*[19] It is also obvious that the group was not a racial one. Asad Khān and Z̲u'lfiqār Khān, although proud of their Persian descent, had been born in India, and by the time Aurangzīb died had been in the country for more than three-quarters of a century. The group was essentially a family-cum-personal group, and was held together by family loyalties and the personal relations of its adherants with Z̲u'lfiqār Khān. The group had no clearly defined politics at the

17 *M.A.*, 439, 483; *M.U.* ii, 63–5. He was removed from the *nā'ib* governorship of Ḥaiderabād in 1705 and sent to assist Z̲u'lfiqār Khān in the siege of Wāgangīra (*M.A.*, 494).

18 He had a Hindu wife, and was said to keep in his house an idol which he worshipped (see K.K., 884, 964; *Mir'āt* i, 403).

19 This was made up as follows:

	Z̲āt	*Sawār*
Asad Khān	7,000	7,000
Z̲u'lfiqār Khān	6,000	6,000
Dā'ūd Khān	6,000	6,000
Dalpat Bundela	3,000	3,000
Rām Singh	2,500	2,000
	24,500	24,000

time, but we have already noted Z̲u'lfiqār Khān's interest in Shāhū and his efforts to secure a settlement with the Marāthās. His close association with the Bundela and the Hāṛā Rājpūt chiefs was also not without significance.

The second group at the court consisted of Ghāzī-ud-Dīn Fīrūz Jang, his sons Chīn Qulīch Khān (later Niẓām-ul-Mulk) and Ḥāmid Khān Bahādur, and his cousin. Muḥammad Amīn Khān.[20] Fīrūz Jang's father, Khwājah 'Ābid, had come to India towards the end of Shāh Jahān's reign and joined Aurangzīb in the Deccan just as he was starting for northern India to contest the throne. The father of Khwājah 'Ābid, 'Ālam Shaikh, was a well known man of letters in Bukhārā and traced his descent from the famous saint Shaikh Shihāb-ud-Dīn Suhrawardī. Khwājah 'Ābid took part in the expeditions against Dārā, Shuja', and Jaswant Singh, and was rewarded with the post of *Ṣadr-i-Kul*. Later, he was appointed the Governor of Ajmer and then of Multan. In the sixteenth year of the reign (1674–5), he came under a shadow and was sent on pilgrimage to Mecca. He was restored to the post of *ṣadr-i-kul* in 1680–1, and was subsequently made the Governor of Bīdar. He died of a gun-shot wound at the siege of Golkonda in 1687. His *manṣab* at the time was 5,000.[21]

Ghāzī-ud-Dīn Khān (Mīr Shihā-ud-Dīn) came to India in 1079–80 H., 1668–9, and made his mark in the Rājpūt war when at great personal risk he brought the Emperor news of Ḥasan 'Alī Khān's column in the Arāvalī ranges. He served against the Marāthās with distinction, and was awarded the titles of Ghāzī-ud-Din Khān and Fīrūz Jang. In 1685, he received the fish standard (*māhī marātib*) for bringing provision to A'ẓam at the siege of Bījāpur. He was given the main credit for its capture and raised to the rank of 7,000/7,000. Next year, he added fresh laurels to his crown by the capture of Adonī. The same year he was blinded in an epidemic of bubonic plague at Ḥaiderābād[22] but continued in the service. In 1698, he was appointed the Governor of Berar, a post which he continued to hold during the rest of Aurangzīb's reign. From 1700

20 References to the careers of these nobles are as follows: Fīrūz Jang *M.U.* ii, 872; Niẓām-ul-Mulk iii, 837, 875; M. Amīn Khān i, 346; Ḥāmid K. iii, 765.
21 *M.U.* iii, 837, 875.
22 The plague raged for two months and carried off about a lakh of people. It chiefly affected the eyes, ears and speech (*M.A.*, 317–19).

to 1702, he was also in charge of the base camp at Islāmpurī, and was commissioned to chase Nīmājī in Malwa and Berār. He inflicted a crushing defeat on Nīmājī and was rewarded with the title of *Sipah Sālār.* He kept a large park of artillery as may be gauged from a typical incident. In 1701, on his way back from Bahādurpur, Aurangzīb passed near the camp of Ghāzī-ud-Dīn, and, as was his custom, held a review of the Khān's troops. The Khān's army covered four measured *kos* and included a splendid park of artillery. After inspecting them, Aurangzīb confiscated a good part of the artillery, and wrote a letter of reproof to Prince Bīdār Bakht, saying 'You with double allowances have no such establishment of guns as Fīrūz Jang has. He has all the things that he should have, or rather, that he should not have'.[23]

Chīn Qulīch Khān was born in 1082 H./1671, presumably at Agra. He participated in the early campaigns of his father, including that of Adonī, and was then commissioned to chastise the Marāthās. In 1699, he was raised to the *manṣab* of 3,500/3,000, and the following year, he was made the Governor of Bījāpur and the *faujdār* of Til-Konkan, A'ẓamnagar and Belgaum and raised to 4,000/4,000. He took an active part in the capture of Wāgangīra in 1705, and was rewarded with the rank of 5,000/5,000. We are told that after the capture of Wāgangīra, Chīn Qulīch acquired great influence with the Emperor who, it is said, consulted him on all important matters of state.[24] Chīn Qulīch's half-brother, Ḥāmid Khān Bahādur, and brother, Raḥim-ud-Dīn Khān, also served under Fīrūz Jang. In 1707, they held the *manṣabs* of 2,500/1,500 and 1,500/600 respectively.[25]

Chīn Qulīch's second cousin, M. Amīn Khān came to India in 1687, after the execution of his father by the *Khan* of Bukhārā. He was appointed to the *manṣab* of 2,000/1,000 and, in course of time, acquired a reputation as a brave and intrepid warrior. At first, he served under Fīrūz Jang. In 1698, he was called to the court and made the *Ṣadr.* It is said that Aurangzīb took this step with the deliberate intention of counter-balancing the Īrānīs, since he had grown suspicious of the power of the leading (Īrānī) family, that of Asad Khān and Z̲u'lfiqār Khān.[26] This appears doubtful however,

23 *M.A.*, 468, *M.U.* ii, 875–6.
24 *M.A.*, 474, 481, 496, 515, Y. H. Khān, *Aṣaf Jāh.*, 42.
25 *M.A.*, 481, *M.U.* iii, 766.
26 *M.U.* i, 347.

Aurangzīb had, at first, chosen Khwājah 'Abdullāh to succeed as the *Ṣadr*, but the Khwājah died at Aḥmadnagar before he could set out for the court. Aurangzīb then appointed M. Amīn Khān as the Ṣadr. He was considered well-qualified for the post on account of his descent from Shaikh Shihāb-ud-Dīn Suhrawardī, and because his uncle, Khwājah 'Abid, had held the post of *Ṣadr* during the early years of Aurangzīb's reign. As a matter of fact, little evidence can be found to support the popular belief that Aurangzīb discriminated against nobles of Persian extraction on the ground of their Shī'ite faith, although it is true that he made no secret of his personal dislike of the Shī'ite doctrines. Thus, many of his leading officials were of Īrānī extraction and, presumably, followed the Shī'ite faith. Soon after his appointment as the *Ṣadr*, M. Amīn Khān submitted a petition making a request for the post of one of the *bakhshīs*, on the ground that 'both the *bakhshīships* have been conferred on heretical demon-eating Shī'ahs', and that his appointment would be the 'means of strengthening the (Sunni) faith and snatching away employment from accursed misbelievers'. Aurangzīb sternly rejected the petition.[27] The fact that Ẕu'lfiqār Khān was appointed the *mīr bakhshī* in 1702 also tends to disprove the suggestion that Aurangzīb entertained doubts regarding the loyalty of this family to the throne.

With numerous other influential connections, and highly respected on account of its noble and saintly lineage, this group of nobles which we may call the 'Chīn' group occupied a position of great power and importance. The combined *manṣabs* of the leading adherents of the group came to 20,000 *ẕāt*, 15,600 *sawār*.[28] In actual

27 *Aḥkām*, 39.

Aurangzīb wrote across the petition, 'What connection have earthly affairs with religion? and what right have administrative works to meddle with bigotry? For you is your religion for me is mine. If this rule (suggested by you) were established it would be my duty to extirpate all (Hindu) Rajas and their followers'.

28 This was made up as follows:

	Ẕāt	*Sawār*
Ghāzī-ud-Din Fīrūz Jang	7,000	7,000
Chīn Qulīch Khān	5,000	5,000
M. Amīn Khān	4,000	1,500
Ḥāmid Khān	2,500	1,500
Raḥim-ud-Dīn Khān	1,500	600
	20,000	15,600

power and influence it was, however, definitely inferior to the group of Asad Khān, Ẕu'lfiqār Khān etc. In character, it was essentially a racial-cum-family group. Both Fīrūz Jang and M. Amīn Khān had themselves come to India from Tūrān. They were always ready to extend patronage to their compatriots from Tūrān so that Tūrānians formed a large part of their following.[29] Chīn Qulīch Khān and Ḥāmid Khān also were generous patrons of the Tūrānīs. This gave the group greater cohesiveness than the group of Asad Khān, Ẕu'lfiqār Khān etc. But the strained relations between Fīrūz Jang and Chīn Qulīch Khān,[30] and the blindness of the former were a serious drawback for this group.

Between these two groups of nobles there was, from the beginning, a sense of rivalry and competition for royal favour. In particular, the two younger men, Ẕu'lfiqār Khān and Chīn Qulīch Khān, had a keen sense of personal rivalry and did not get on well with each other.[31] While such rivalry was by no means unusual and must not be exaggerated, the ambitions of these two remarkable personalities, and their efforts to clear their way to supreme power constituted a fixed point in Mughal court politics for more than a quarter of a century, and powerfully influenced other developments during this period.

The Civil War

A civil war among the princes usually provided the nobles an opportunity for securing concessions of various types from the rival contestants. It also constituted a period of difficult decisions for individual nobles: failure to back the winning candidate might result in a serious setback to their careers. The sons of Aurangzīb—Mu'aẕẕam, A'ẕam and Kām Bakhsh—had been exerting themselves since a long time to win adherents among the nobles in anticipation of the civil war that would inevitably follow the death of Aurangzīb. The elder brother, Mu'aẕẕam, had been imprisoned by Aurangzīb in 1687, and after his release in 1695, had been sent away to Kabul as the governor.[32] Kām Bakhsh was learned and

29 *M.U.* iii, 169.

30 Irādat, 52.

31 *Ḥadīqa*, 55, *M.A.*, 439.

32 For the early life of the Princes, see Sarkar, *Aurangzeb's Reign*, 46–129. The eldest son, Muḥammad Sulṭān, was born in 1639 of his Hindu wife,

judicious but he was fickle-minded. A'ẓam had succeeded in winning the support of the leading nobles at the court. In particular, he had won over Asad Khān and Ẕu'lfiqār Khān to his side.[33] At the court, A'ẓam Shāh and Kām Bakhsh frequently quarrelled among themselves, and A'ẓam, presuming upon the men and resources at his disposal, sought opportunities for a show-down with Kām Bakhsh. In order to save the life of Kām Bakhṣh and to prevent an outbreak of war between the two brothers while he was still alive, in February 1707 Aurangzīb appointed Kām Bakhsh the *ṣūbahdār* of Bījāpur and gave him leave to depart. Kām Bakhsh was presented with all the trappings of royalty, and permitted to beat his drums from the door of the royal enclosure—a privilege reserved for kings. Earlier, Aḥsan Khān had been appointed his c̄hief *Bakhshī* and asked to look after him. M. Amīn Khān was also instructed to join him. M. A'ẓam was ordered to march to his *ṣūbah* of Malwa, and he left very much chagrined.[34]

A will alleged to have been found under Aurangzīb's pillow after his death provided for the partition of the empire, assigning Bījāpur and Haiderābād to Kām Bakhsh. It is possible that in sending Kām Bakhsh to take charge of Bījāpur. Aurangzīb was also motivated by the desire of giving effect to this scheme, hoping that with the support of some of the leading nobles, Kām Bakhsh, who was the favourite of his old age, would be able to defend himself against his rivals. But perhaps Aurangzīb was concerned more with holding the balance even between his sons so that none

---

Nawāb Bāi. He was imprisoned in 1659 for deserting to Shuja', and died in prison in 1676.

The fourth son, Muḥammad Akbar, was born in 1657 of his principal wife, Dilrās Bānū Begum. He rebelled in 1681, and died in Persia in 1704.

Of the surviving sons, Muhammad Mu'aẓẓam was born of Nawāb Bāi in 1643, A'ẓam of Dilrās Bānū Begum in 1653, and Kām Bakhṣh of Udaipuri Maḥal in 1670.

33 K.K., 547. Ẕu'lfiqār Khān had been granted the *māhī marātib* (fish standard) at the request of A'ẓam 'though it was a rule not to give it to a noble below the rank of 6,000'. He had also been made *sipah sālār* at A'ẓam's request (*Ruq'āt* vi, Irādat, 14, *M.U.* i, 310).

34 *M.A.*, 520, K.K. ii, 547–8, *Dil.*, 158. According to the Jaipur *wakīl's* report (*J.R.* 26 Ẕīqa'dah yr. 51, 26 February 1707), it seems that A'ẓam claimed the entire Deccan for himself (*tamām Dakin az-mā-ast*) and left for Malwa very much displeased.

of them might accuse him of favouritism in the same way as he had accused his father of favouritism towards Dārā. But Aurangzīb's hope of attaching M. Amīn Khān to Kām Bakhsh could not be realized. For Kām Bakhsh had travelled only a couple of stages from Aḥmadnagar when news was received of Aurangzīb's death, and immediately M. Amīn turned back to join A'ẓam.

When Aurangzīb died at Aḥmadnagar on 3 March 1707, A'ẓam had barely gone two stages from the Imperial Camp. He hurried back and took possession of the royal effects. All the nobles who were present at the court, including the *wazīr,* Asad Khān, declared for him. Z̲u'lfiqār Khān, the *mīr bakshī,* who was on a roving mission to chase the Marāthās, hurried back from the Tungbhadrā Dū'āb with Rām Singh Hāṛā, Dalpat Bundela and Tarbiyat Khān *mīr ātish* and joined A'ẓam near Aurangābād.[35]

With the support of the most powerful nobles in the empire, and with the royal stores, a park of artillery and the veterans of the Deccan wars at his disposal, A'ẓam was popularly regarded as being in a very favourable position for winning the civil war. But his advantages were more apparent than real. Many of the high grandees were unwilling to face the hazards of a civil war and were half-hearted in A'ẓam's cause, or openly declined to accompany him. Thus, the powerful 'Chīn group' did not evince any desire to take part in the forthcoming struggle. After proclaiming himself the Emperor, A'ẓam, in order to conciliate this important group, had conferred the rank of 6,000/6,000 on M. Amīn Khān, and that of 7,000/7,000 and the title of Khān-i-Daurān on Chīn Qulīch Khān. The latter was also made the Governor of Burhānpur (Khāndesh) in place of Najābat Khān, and directed to send a deputy to his charge, remaining at the court himself. But Chīn Qulīich proceeded only a stage or two beyond Aurangābād, and quitted the camp on the pretext that his presence was required in his province.[36]

Fīrūz Jang remained at Daulatābād and made no move to join A'ẓam. Z̲u'lfiqār Khān proposed to A'ẓam that he should march *via* Daulatābād in order to compel Fīrūz Jang to join him. But A'ẓam was unwilling to leave the direct road to Agra, and gave a

35 *Akhbārāt,* Z̲u'lfiqār Khān joined on 29 *Z̲ilḥijjah,* 2 April 1707.

36 *Akhbārāt,* 10, 25 *Z̲ilḥijjah,* 14 March, 29 March 1707, K.K., 572, *Dil.,* 158b. 162a. Kāmwar mentions the rank of 5,000.

haughty answer that his opponent was not a Dārā Shikoḥ, and his personal troops (*wālā-shāhīs*) were sufficient to deal with him.[37] In reality, A'ẓam was greatly annoyed at the refusal of Fīrūz Jang and Chīn Qulīch Khān to march with him, but thought it discreet to dissumulate, and thinking that it was 'safer to leave Fīrūz Jang behind as a friend than as a foe', conferred the title of *sipah sālār* upon him, and made him the Governor of Aurangābād and the Viceroy of the Deccan. He was awarded an elephant and other presents which were all entrusted to Chīn Qulīch Khān to be forwarded to him. Manṣūr Khān, *dārōghah-i-tōpkhānah-i-dakin*, was asked to look after Aurangābād till Fīrūz Jang's arrival.[38]

M. Amīn Khān, too, did not proceed a stage or two beyond Burhānpur. He plundered the rear of the army when it was passing through the rocky defiles of Dā'ūdnagar, and returned to Burhānpur. Many of the soldiers raised in the Deccan also deserted. M. Amīn then joined Chīn Qulīch Khān at Aurangābād where they took possession of several districts.[39]

Not only Fīrūz Jang and Chīn Qulīch Khān, but even Asad Khān and Ẕu'lfiqār Khān were not keen to leave the Deccan and to accompany A'ẓam Shāh, and tried their best to persuade the latter to leave them in the Deccan by pointing to the activities of the Marāthās.

The half-heartedness of these and other nobles is ascribed by Irādat Khān to the insane pride of A'ẓam which made him despise the advice of others, his *Shī'ite* inclinations, and his parsimoniousness in giving increments and promotions.[41] But Irādat Khān's charges do not seem to be well founded. As another contemporary author, Khāfī Khān, observes, 'in fact, he (A'ẓam) had not the money to

37 *M.U.* iii, 877.

38 *Akhbārāt*, 4 *Muḥarram*, 29 March, K.K., 572, Qāsim, *Ẕafar-Nāmah-i-Bahādur Shāh*, 10.

Y. H. Khān (*Āṣaf Jāh*, 35) states that Fīrūz Jang was put in charge of Burhānpur, which is not correct.

39 K.K., 572. A'ẓam declined several offers to pursue him and contended himself with sending *farmāns* to Fīrūz Jang and Chīn Qulīch about the matter.

40 *Dil.*, 162a, *A'ẓam-ul-Ḥarb*, 188–92, *Akhbārāt*, 27, Muḥ., 30 April, Kāmwar.

41 Irādat, 11–12, Kāmwar A'ẓam was suspected of *Shī'ite* tendencies ever since his illness in 1693 when he had come under the influence of an Imāmite *faqīr* (*Aurangzeb* V, 363). He had given up the prayers of Friday, and more than half his army was allegedly made up of *Shī'ites*.

be liberal with'.[42] The Deccan wars had been very costly. The Deccan was traditionally a deficit area, and because of Aurangzīb's reluctance to spend the hoarded treasures of Shāh Jahān, the pay of the army was sometimes three years in arrears towards the end of his reign, and the mainstay of the Emperor had come to be the revenues of Bengal. The little money that A'ẓam found in the royal treasury went to meet the arrears of the salaries to the soldiers.[43]

The bitter words and the ill-temper which A'ẓam occasionally showed no doubt alienated many of his followers. For if any noble spoke to A'ẓam on the question of money and promotions, 'he in his proud and haughty way, gave sharp answers that there was no real necessity in his army, but fear of the opposite party.'[44] However, the reluctance of the leaders of the two main groups at the court to participate in the civil war, their keenness to be left behind in the Deccan, their many connections with Deccan nobles, and the desertion of large numbers of Deccani soldiers with them suggest that the interests of both groups of nobles were already centred in the Deccan. This was a dangerous portent for the future since the Deccanis continued to regard northern India as an alien country, and the rule of the Mughals as alien rule. Hence, in case of weakness in the central authority, a move for the creation of an independent state or states in the Deccan was bound to gather momentum.

Many of A'ẓam's difficulties would have been solved if he could have reached and occupied Agra first, since it contained a good part of the hoarded treasure of Shāh Jahān. But 'there was not a single person who doubted that, comparing the distance of Peshawar with the difficulties in the way of A'ẓam Shāh, Shāh 'Ālam would arrive before him'.[45] A'ẓam might have gained control of Agra if

42 K.K., 531, 583.

43 Asad Khān reported to A'ẓam that the Treasury of the Stirrup (*khazānah-i-rikāb*) contained 52 lakhs in cash, and 53 lakhs in *ashrafis* of hundred *muhars* (i.e. gold), while about a crore was owing to the soldiers in salary. A'ẓam Shāh ordered this entire sum to be utilized to pay the soldiers 'so that he may be able to face God, and free himself of obligation to His late Majesty (Aurangzīb)' (Khush-hāl, 8–9).

44 K.K., 581, 583.

45 *Ibid.* Irvine i, 19 has misconstrued this passage and asserted just the opposite.

he had permitted his son, Bīdār Bakht, who was the Governor of Aḥmadābād, to march on Agra. But A'ẓam's mind had been poisoned against Bīdār Bakht by suggestions that Bīdār Bakht nursed the ambition of winning the throne for himself. A'ẓam therefore ordered the latter to wait in Malwa till his arrival from the Deccan. Bīdār Bakht waited for A'ẓam for a month and twenty days in Malwa. Meanwhile, the third son of Shāh 'Ālam, 'Aẓīm-ush-Shān, who had been recalled from Bihar by Aurangzīb just before his death, reached Agra. The commandant of the fort, Bāqī Khān, who was the father-in-law of Bīdār Bakht, refused to yield the fort till one of the contestants reached in person. Since the previous arrival of Shāh 'Ālam was a foregone conclusion, this practically secured Agra for him.

Muḥammad Mu'aẓẓam, entitled Shāh 'Ālam, was the Governor of Kabul and Lahore at the time of Aurangzīb's death. Besides this, the governorship of Multān was held by his eldest son, Jahāndār Shāh. Another son, 'Aẓīm-ush-Shān, was the Governor of Bengal and Bihar. With the resources of these provinces and the recruiting grounds of the Punjab and Afghanistan at his disposal, Shāh 'Ālam was in a strong position to contest the claim of A'ẓam, though the latter had nothing but contempt for him, and called him a '*baqqāl*' (shopkeeper) in derision. In tact, foresight and understanding also, Shāh 'Ālam was superior to A'ẓam. His exile from the court in far away Kabul had really been a blessing in disguise, for he had been able to win to his side a body of reliable supporters, and to drill his army by constant marches so that he acquired a horror of sleeping under the roof of a house—a habit which he retained even later in life. He had been lucky in securing, in 1703, the services of an obscure nobleman, Mun'im Khān, who was a very efficient man of business, and, as Shāh 'Ālam's agent, soon put his finances in order. At Shāh 'Ālam's recommendation, Mun'im Khān was made the *dīwān* of Kabul, and the *nā'ib ṣūbahdār* of Punjab, and raised to the rank of 1,500/1,000.[46]

In anticipation of a civil war, Mun'im Khān had exerted himself to gather a war chest for Shāh 'Ālam, and also silently collected camels and oxen to drag the cannons, and boats for crossing the rivers between Peshawar and Lahore.[47]

46 For the career of Mun'im Khān, see *M.U.* iii, 675 and Ch. ii, below.
47 Irādat, K.K., 573.

Shāh 'Ālam received the news of Aurangzīb's death at Jamrūd near Peshawar, on 20 March 1707. In view of Mun'im Khān's preparations, he was able to march rapidly on Lahore and from there to Delhi. Twenty-eight lakhs from the Lahore treasury, and thirty lakhs from the Delhi treasury helped him to pay his soldiers. Even then, we are told that many soldiers remained discontented and in acute want,[48] till Agra was reached on 12 June. Bāqī Khān, the commandant of the fort, submitted to Shāh 'Ālam, and presented to him the keys of the fort. Two crores were taken out by Shāh 'Ālam from the treasures of Shāh Jahān, and distributed among his followers.

When A'ẕam reached near Gwalior, he received the news of the occupation of Agra by his rival. Much agitated, he decided to leave the *wazīr*, Asad Khān, at Gwalior with the ladies and the unnecessary equipment and jewels and treasure, and to march on Agra at once.

The two contestants met at the plains of Jājū, near Sāmūgarh, on 18 June 1707. The forces of A'ẕam were definitely inferior to those of Shāh 'Ālam. We are told that A'ẕam had started with a force of 35,000 horse actual (*maujūdī*) which had swelled to 50,000 horse besides infantry by the time he reached Gwalior.[49] Shāh 'Ālam's force is placed by some authorities at as high a figure as 150,000 horse, but it may have been less.[50] Apart from the advantages which numbers and an ample treasury conferred, Shāh 'Ālam had also been able to stiffen his forces with heavy guns taken from the fort of Agra. On the other hand, A'ẕam had to leave most of his heavy artillery behind in the Deccan and at Gwalior in order to advance more quickly.[51] His army had also suffered greatly from the rigours of the march and the hot season.

Thus, by any reckoning, victory was beyond the grasp of A'ẕam Shāh. The battle of Jājū was essentially in the nature of a gamble on his part. He hoped to take the enemy by surprise, and to strike a decisive blow before Shāh 'Ālam had time to consolidate his position. For this reason, perhaps, he did not formulate any plan

48 Harcharan, 17.

49 K.K., 583. The muster before Jājū revealed a strength of 65,000 horse and 45,000 foot.

50 Valentyn, 276, *Dil.*, 164a.

51 *Dil.*, 162a. In a typical fashion, A'ẕam had loftily declared that fighting with artillery was not manly and that he would fight with swords only.

of action. Instead, he went boldly forward 'like a fierce lion dashes upon a flock of sheep'.[52]

A'ẓam gained an initial advantage in a brush with what he mistakenly thought was the main body of Shāh 'Ālam's force but was, in reality, only the advance-guard. As soon as the main force of Shāh 'Ālam joined battle, A'ẓam's position deteriorated. Shāh 'Ālam's artillery played havoc in his army. Many prominent nobles, and Prince Bīdār Bakht and his brother, Wālā Jāh, were killed. Z̲u'lfiqār also received a slight wound. Perceiving that the day was lost and that there was no hope of victory, he went up to A'ẓam Shāh and advised him to flee in order to live and fight another day.[53] But A'ẓam, probably with the fate of Dārā in his mind, refused to do so, and resolved to sell his life dearly. He continued to fight with a small force of 300–400 horsemen around him. Z̲u'lfiqār, accompanied by Ḥamīd-ud-Dīn Khān, went off to Gwalior, and his example was followed by many others. The end came when A'ẓam was struck by an arrow. Rustam Dil cut off his head, and carried it to Shāh 'Ālam.

Z̲u'lfiqār Khān's refusal to stand by the side of his royal master till the end has been adversely commented upon by a number of contemporary observers, some of whom go so far as to make his flight the chief cause of A'ẓam's defeat.[54] While this is certainly an exaggerated view, there can be little doubt that Z̲u'lfiqār Khān's conduct violated contemporary notions of loyalty, and earned for Z̲u'lfiqār Khān the reputation of being 'ambitious' and 'unreliable'.

The War of Succession served to weaken the empire further. About 10,000 men, and many brave and tried nobles, some of whom had won great reputation and experience against the

52 Irādat.

53 K.K., 596.

54 Thus, Dānishmand Khān and Bhīmsen take the view that 'If Nuṣrat Jang, as required by his loyalty, had joined actively with the other leaders in the attack, and had even for a little while held his own in the battle, all the difficulties which fell on A'ẓam Shāh would never have happened' (*B.N.*, *Dil.*, ff. 165).

Irvine (i., 30) follows Bhīmsen and declares: 'His (Z̲u'lfiqār's) flight determined the defeat of the army'.

But K.K., who is a most careful and balanced observer, gives a different account.

Marāthās were killed. Dalpat Bundela and Rām Singh Hāṛā, the lieutenants of Ẕu'lfiqār Khān, also perished on the battlefield. The two contestants, especially Shāh 'Ālam made lavish gifts and promises to the soldiers and nobles in order to win their support, and thus further worsened the already precarious financial position of the Empire.[55]

Marāthā and Rājpūt Affairs

We shall now take note of two steps of considerable historical importance taken by A'ẓam Shāh before his defeat. First of all, at Dūrāhā near the Narmada, Shāhū was allowed to escape. It is a controversial point whether he simply ran away, or his escape was connived at.[56] Some modern authors go so far as to assert that A'ẓam actually signed a treaty with Shāhū granting him the *chauth* and *sardeshmukhi* of the Deccan in addition to the *swarajya* of

55 K.K. (p. 576) says that of the 24 crores amassed by Shāh Jahān, 9 crores of rupees in cash besides vessels of gold and silver were found in the Agra fort, or, according to another account, 13 crores including *ashrafis* and rupees of 100 to 300 *tolas* weight specially made for presents, and the *ashrafis* of 12 *māshahs* and 13 *māshahs* of Akbar's reign.

Four crores were taken out of this by Shāh 'Ālam, 2 crores being distributed among the officers and men.

56 K.K. (p. 581) says that Ẕu'lfiqār persuaded A'ẓam Shāh to set Shāhū at liberty along with 50 others who were his friends and companions. K.K. is followed by *M.U.* (ii, 351) and, among modern historians, by Duff (i, 304), Irvine (ii, 162), Sardesai (*Riyasat* i, 2), Sinha (*Rise of the Peshwas*, xii), and Rajwade (*Patren Yādī* ii, 9).

An entry in the *Bahādur Shāh Nāmah* (d. 17 *Jamāda* II, 15 September 1707) states that 'Shāhū, who had run away out of the wickedness and villainy of his nature and had intentions of rebellion and disturbance, had been removed from his *manṣab* of 7,000 *ẕāt*, 7,000 *sawārs*. He expressed repentence and asked for mercy and was restored to his *manṣab*'.

A *wāqi'ah-nawīs's* report in the *Akhbārāt* (14 October 1707) also states that Shāhū had simply 'run away' (*farār-kardah*).

Bhīmsen, who was in Ẕu'lfiqār's camp, writes, however, that Shāhū escaped at A'ẓam's instance (*Dil.* ii, 162).

There is necessarily no conflict in the views of Bhīmsen and Khāfi Khān. Shāhū went with a fairly large retinue (pp. 50–70 according to K.K.), and no attempt was made to pursue him. It is clear that both A'ẓam and Ẕu'lfiqār connived at his escape.

Shivaji, and numerous other concessions.[57] Apart from the doubtful authenticity of the authority upon which this assertion is founded, there also seems little reason for these sweeping concessions to a captive prince who had hardly any independent support among the Marāthā*sardars*. On the other hand, the fact that no pursuit was undertaken and no orders regarding Shāhū issued to Imperial offices in the Deccan militates against the theory that Shāhū simply ran away. As a matter of fact, Shāhū gave out that he came armed with an Imperial *farmān*, and ceremoniously visited the tomb of Aurangzīb near Aḥmadnagar, and was not molested by the royal officers.[58]

57 Thus, Kincaid and Parasnis (ii, pp. 121–3) mention a treaty in which A'ẓam agreed to *chauth* and *sardeshmukhi* over the six *ṣūbahs* of the Deccan, and also that Shāhū should be made Governor of Gondwānā, Gujarāt, and Tanjore 'during good behaviour'.

This appears unlikely, Gondwānā and Tanjore never having been Mughal *ṣūbahs*.

A Maratha document entitled *Shiv Chhatrapatichi Bakhar* states:

'While camping at Burhanpur through the good offices of Aurangzeb's daughter who regarded Shahu as her son, he with his followers was set free and allowed to proceed to Deccan on the following understanding:

You should proceed to your kingdom. Take care of the same by putting down formentors of quarrels. You should remain loyal to the Emperor and should not harass the Emperor's territories. When we are satisfied that your behaviour towards us is satisfactory we shall on reaching Delhi and on our accession to the throne set free your wife and other females who are in our captivity and shall grant you your sardeshmukhi watan in the six subas of the Deccan, right to levy Chauthai in the said subas of which you are in enjoyment, Mahals in Balaghat forming part of Bijapur Kingdom, half of Daulatabad Mahals forming part of the patashaha territory bounded by Bhima and Ganga and farmans relating to these shall be given to you. All thanas, forts and fortifications included in this territory are given to you. For the present, a letter addressed to the Suba is given to you stating that your Kingdom should be given to you and you should be allowed to guard the same. Whatever territory in Karnatak, Gondvan, Gujrat, Tanjore belongs to you should be taken by you in your possession. Whenever the Emperor is in danger you should render help to him with your army and whatever orders are issued to you should be obeyed by you'.

(Quoted in Deccan History Cong. Proceedings, 247–8).

58 K.K., 583. Earlier, his followers had looted and set fire to the outskirts of Aurangābād.

Hence, the conclusion seems inevitable that Shāhū's escape was simply connived at. There was both policy and calculation behind it. His release would keep the Marāthās divided during A'ẓam's absence, and in the event of his establishing himself as the Marāthā ruler held out the prospect of an agreement with the Marāthās through him. According to Khāfī Khān, this step was taken at the instance of Z̲u'lfiqār Khān 'who was very intimate with Shāhū and had for long been interested in his affairs'.[59]

Next, at the instance of Z̲u'lfiqār, the *manṣabs* of 7,000/7,000, and the titles of Mirza Raja and Maharaja were conferred on Jai Singh and Ajit Singh respectively. Both the Rajas were asked to serve A'ẓam with large armies, Jai Singh actually joining Prince Bīdār Bakht in Malwa. Negotiations were also opened with the two rajas for the restoration of their homelands to them, and they were promised 'other favours undreamt of by their forefathers'.[60]

These two steps, although taken largely due to the exigencies of the civil war, represent a considerable departure from the policy of Aurangzīb. Perhaps, in the eyes of A'ẓam and Z̲u'lfiqār, the stern policy of Aurangzīb had proved a failure. Their actions presaged a new policy of concessions designed to bridge the gulf between the Rājpūts and Marāthās, and the Mughal empire. A'ẓam did not live to carry this policy to its logical conclusion. The task devolved upon Shāh 'Ālam who was called upon to find a solution to the vexed problems which faced the Empire.

59 K.K., 581. According to Marāthā tradition, at the capture of Raigarh, Z̲u'lfiqār had given an undertaking to Shāhū's mother, Yeshubai, that he would look after and protect Shāhū (K&P, *loc. cit.* ii, 111–12).

But no contemporary authority makes any reference to this.

60 *Akhbārāt*, 20 May 1707, *Wakīl's* reports d. 30th April and 24 May (Sitamau Collection—*Misc. Papers*, Vol. I, 97–101, 109–14; *Sarkar Collection*, Vol. XI, 117–23).

A'ẓam had made a secret treaty with the Rana of Udaipur to give him the rank of 7,000/7,000, excuse the supply of contingent, remit *jizyah* in Mewar if not in the whole of India, and cede many *parganas*, such as Phulya, Māndalgarh, Bidnūr, Ghiyāṣpur, Pardhān, Dūngarpur etc. which had been granted in lieu of the *manṣab* of 5,000, and subsequently re-attached (*V.V.* ii, 659–60). The pact shows A'ẓam's willingness to make far-reaching concessions to the Rājpūts to secure their help in the civil war.

CHAPTER II

Conciliation or Coercion?

BAHĀDUR SHĀH

After ascending the throne, Bahāhur Shāh (Shāh 'Ālam) was compelled to reckon with the problems which Aurangzīb had bequeathed to his successors—the worsening financial situation, the grave defects in the working of the *jāgīrdārī* system and the consequent demoralization in the nobility, the growth of ideological trends among the Hindus and the Muslims which tended to accentuate mutual differences and suspicions, the general problem of maintaining law and order especially in the Deccan where the Marāthās posed a serious challenge to the Mughals, the conflict with the Sikhs, the continued differences with the Rathors and the Sishodias, and the effect of all these upon the prestige of the monarchy and upon the nobility some of whose members saw in the difficulties of the monarchy an opportunity for self aggrandizement.

In facing these problems, Bahādur Shāh inclined towards a policy of cautious compromise and conciliation, both on account of his character and general outlook, and the concrete situation with which he was faced.

Bahādur Shāh did not share the puritancial outlook of his father, Aurangzīb, though he was of a deeply religious bent of mind and, we are told, never missed a chance of visiting a saint and conversing with him. Like some of his other brothers, he professed a belief in *Ṣūfī* doctrines, and was even suspected of *Shī'ite* inclinations.[1] He was born of a Hindu mother and, in accordance with the Mughāl tradition, also took a Hindu spouse,[2] but it would be difficult to say whether this modified his political and religious outlook in any way. Contemporary historians do not lend support to the view that the political policies of Bahādur Shāh were influenced in any considerable degree by his religious views. But with his elevation to the throne, the association of the monarchy with religious orthodoxy came to an end.

The political views of Bahādur Shāh during the period of his princehood are rather obscure. He held the post of Viceroy of the Deccan several times, but his policy and general conduct of affairs were considered weak and unsatisfactory by the Emperor who, for this reason, did not permit him to hold independent charge of the Deccan for any length of time.[3] During the final operations against Bījāpur and Golkonda, he was accused of colluding and conspiring with Abu'l Ḥasan, the King of Golkonda, and was placed in confinement by the Emperor. According to Khāfī Khān who wrote about forty years after these events, the prince considered the invasion of Golkonda a breach of faith and desired that 'war and peace should be dependent on his approval as heir-apparent and that so far as possible he should bind Abu'l Ḥasan to his interest'. For these reasons he had wanted to use his influence with the Emperor to obtain a pardon for Abu'l Ḥasan.[4]

Bahādur Shāh was not released from confinement till 1695. He was sent to northern India as the Governor of Agra, and was then appointed to Multan. In 1698, he was appointed the Governor of Kabul and specially charged with keeping watch on the Indo-Persian frontier. He was also nominated the Governor of Punjab in 1700. Thus, during an important phase of Aurangzīb's reign,

1 See K. K., 603, 661–81 for the assumption of the title 'Saiyid' by Bahādur Shāh, and the rioting over his attempt to add the word '*waṣī*' after the name of 'Alī in the Friday prayers.

2 Bahādur Shāh was born of Nawāb Bāi daughter of Raja Rājū of Rājaurī (Kashmir). In 1061H, 1661 he was married to the daughter of Raja Rūp Singh (*M.A.*, 37, K.K. ii, 123).

3 Bahādur Shāh was the Viceroy of the Deccan after the removal of Shāh'i stah Khān from 1667–72, and from 1678–80 (*M.A.*, 45, 57, 60–1 *et passim*). Throughout this period, the actual command of the field armies was entrusted to some prominent noble appointed directly by Aurangzīb.

4 K.K., 331–2.

Bahādur Shāh remained largely out of touch with Imperial affairs.

In the case of the Rājpūts, it appears that as early as 1681, Bahādur Shāh had concluded a secret treaty with the Rana of Mewār promising to abolish the *jizyah*, and to grant other favours to the Rājpūts in return for military support whenever he should enter into a contest for the throne with his brothers. It seems that pacts of a similar nature had been concluded by A'ẓam and Prince Akbar with the other Rājpūt chiefs.[5] While in the immediate context these pacts demonstrate the importance attached by all the princes to Rājpūt support, the division among the Rājpūts reduced the value of their friendship in the long run. The pacts ceased to have much force with the passage of time, and during the War of Succession, Bahādur Shāh received no help from any of the ruling chiefs of Rājpūtānā.

The circumstances mentioned above seem to be largely responsible for the fluidity of Bahādur Shāh's views on the Rājpūt and Marāthā problems. Hence, in the early stages, his policy was one of trial and error, and of cautiously groping his way towards compromise and settlement of the outstanding problems and disputes.

The first problem before Bahādur Shāh was to choose the leading office-bearers.

After his victory over A'ẓam, Bahādur Shāh had declared that he would not regard it as an offence for anyone to have helped A'ẓam Shāh, observing that if his own sons had been in the Deccan, they too would have been forced by circumstances to join A'ẓam. Hence, all those who submitted immediately were promised employment and restoration of the *manṣab*s held by them under Aurangzīb.[6] Letters of reassurance were sent to Asad Khān, Ẕu'lfiqār Khān and others at Gwalior, and they were invited to the court. Ghāzī-ud-Dīn Khān Fīrūz Jang, Chīn Qulīch Khān, Muḥammad Amīn Khān, and many others were summoned from the Deccan.[7]

The policy of not penalizing the adherents of a defeated rival was in keeping with the traditions of the Mughals in India, as well as in the best interests of the empire, and Bahādur Shāh

5 *V.V.* ii, 659–60.

6 Irādat Khān (78–80) gives the main credit for this policy to Mun'im Khān who represented to the Emperor that it was not possible to administer the realm without the help and co-operation of the old 'Ālamgīrī nobles.

7 K.K., 600, Kāmwar, 14.

personally. It enabled Bahādur Shāh to secure the adhesion of most of the old 'Ālamgīrī nobles, and to isolate Kām Bakhsh who maintained a precarious hold on Bījāpur and Ḥaiderābād. In fact, the war of succession was now regarded as virtually over, the defeat of Kām Bakhsh being considered only a matter of time.

The reconciliation of the pretensions and aspirations of the old 'Ālamgīrī nobles with the claims of his own immediate supporters formed the first serious test of statesmanship for Bahādur Shāh. In the alleged will and testament of Aurangzīb which Bahādur Shāh apparently regarded as genuine and which he had offered to accept on the eve of the battle of Jājū, a strong recommendation had been made to the princes to retain Asad Khān as the *wazīr*, no matter which one of them succeeded to the throne. On the strength of this recommendation, and on the basis of his long service and experience, family connections etc., Asad Khān claimed the *wizārat* for himself, and the post of the *mīr bakhshī* for his son, Z̲u'lfiqār Khān. His claims were supported by Prince Jahān Shāh, then his father's favourite, and allegedly even by some of the begums.[8]

Bahādur Shāh had little difficulty in accepting the claim on behalf of Z̲u'lfiqār Khān whom he raised to the rank of 7,000/7,000, and confirmed in his previous post of *mīr bakhshī*. But he had already promised the *wizārat* to his trusted follower and confidant, Mun'im Khān, whose services in securing the throne for him have been already noted. At the same time, Bahādur Shāh did not want to alienate two such capable and influential nobles as Asad Khān and Z̲u'lfiqār Khān.

A way out of the difficulty was sought by appointing Mun'im Khān as the *wazīr*, and reviving for Asad Khān the post of *wakīl-i-muṭlaq* which had not been conferred on anyone since the days of Āṣaf Khān in the reign of Shāh Jahān. Asad Khān accepted this proposal formally. But privately he submitted a petition claiming for the *wakīl-i-muṭlaq* all the privileges which had been enjoyed by Āṣaf Khān. These comprised the attendance of all the chief officials including the *wazīr* at his audience, the submission to him of all letters relating to the appointments, dismissals and transfer to the *ṣūbahdārs*, *faujdārs*, *dīwāns* etc. for his signature, and of all the office reports regarding the resumption or transfer of *jāgīrs*; the

8 Shākir, 63.

right to receive a copy of all the reports from the provinces sent by the *ṣūbahdārs*, *dīwāns*, news-reporters etc., and to keep in his possession the Great Seal which was fixed on all *farmāns*. In addition to these, he claimed other personal distinctions: the grant of the rank of 9,000/9,000, the *tōgh tuman*, the governorship of Lahore, the right to sit in the *Dīwān-i-'Ām*, permission to beat his drums after those of the royal princes etc.[9]

Bahādur Shāh was greatly vexed at these vaulting claims of Asad Khān. But out of a desire to conciliate him, he accepted all his demands, except the claim for a *manṣab* of 9,000/9,000 and the right to sit in the *Dīwān-i-'Ām*. These two privileges of Āṣaf Khān, it was explained, were due to his relationship with the Emperor. Hence, Asad Khān was granted the rank of 8,000/8,000 and the title of Āṣaf-ud-Daulah. Mun'im Khān was made the *wazīr* with the rank of 7,000/7,000 *dū-aspah sih-aspah*, one crore *dām in'ām*, and the title of Khān-i-Khānān and the (absentee) governorship of Agra. Two of his sons Mahābat Khān and Khān-i-Zamān, were granted the ranks of 5,000 and 4,000 respectively, Mahābat Khān being also appointed to the post of third *bakhshī*. Most of the other incumbents were confirmed in their previous offices.[10]

But this did not solve the difficulty. The older nobles were not happy at the sudden elevation of an obscure noble like Mun'im Khān to the *wizārat*. In particular, Asad Khān and Ẕu'lfiqāṟ Khān resented the loss of the *wazīr's* office. On the other hand, Mun'im Khān disliked the regulations which, at least formally, made him a subordinate of Asad Khān, so that 'on the day that Āṣaf-ud-Daulah acted as the *dīwān*, it became incumbent on Khān-i-Khānān to wait upon him as the other ministers did, and to obtain his signature to documents'. Since Mun'im Khān had no intention of sharing his powers with Asad Khān, 'whenever any ministerial business of importance arose, he did not communicate it to Āṣaf-ud-Daulah'.[11]

At length, an excuse was found to put the *wakīl-i-muṭlaq* out of the way. It was decided that as Asad Khān was fond of a life of comfort and pleasure and had reached an advanced age, he should

9 Kāmwar, 14, Qāsim, 17. The text of Asad Khān's petition to the Emperor and the latter's reply have been quoted in *T. Muẓ.* (pp. 157–62) and Shākir (66–8).

10 *B.N.*, 104–17, K.K., 626–7, Kāmwar, 14.

11 *B.N.*, 169, K.K., 601.

retire to Delhi and rest there in peace. In accordance with this decision, he was asked to escort Zīnat-un-Nisā Begum to Delhī, and placed in charge of the *ṣūbahs* of Lahore, Delhi and Ajmer. Zu'lfiqār Khān was made his father's deputy, but 'with the exception that the seal of Āṣaf-ud-Daulah was placed upon revenue and civil *parwānās* and *sanads* after the seal of the *wazīr*, he had no part in the administration of the government'.[12]

Shortly after this, Chīn Qulīch Khān and Muḥammad Amīn Khān arrived from the Deccan. Muḥammad Amīn Khān was granted the rank of 5,000/3,500 and, at first, confirmed in the post of *Ṣadr*, but soon afterwards he was replaced and appointed the *faujdār* of Moradabad and Sambhal. This was an important charge, for the *faujdārī* of Moradabad was equal in area to a province.[13] Chīn Qulīch Khān was promoted to the rank of 6,000/6,000, accorded the title of Khān-i-Daurān, and made the Governor of Awadh and the *faujdār* of Gorakhpur. We are told that he accepted the post 'with reluctance',[14] his heart still being in the Deccan, and resigned six weeks later. However, at Mun'im Khān's instance, he withdrew his resignation, and was raised to the rank of 7,000/7,000.[15]

Fīrūz Jang had been responsible for the disgrace and imprisonment of Bahādur Shāh at the siege of Golkonda in 1687, and was afraid to come to the court. As a special gesture to him, and at Mun'im Khān's instance, he was appointed the Governor of Gujarāt, and given permission to proceed to his charge without waiting upon the Emperor.[16] The presence in the Deccan of a rival claimant to the throne in the person of Kām Bakhsh was, perhaps, largely responsible for the adoption of such a conciliatory policy, for the countenance of Fīrūz Jang's refusal to attend the court was interpreted as a sign of weakness.[17]

12 K.K., 601–2, *B.N.*, 169–70. Asad Khān left for Delhi on 1 September 1707.

13 *Akhbārāt*, 17 August, 28 October, *B.N.*, 215, Kāmwar, 2.

14 *B.N.*, 219, 226, K.K., 689.

15 *B.N.*, 283, 287, 290, 316; M.M., 96 b; K.K., 679. *Akhbārāt* (entry dated 13, *Ẕīqa'dah*, 5 February 1708) simply say that he came to Delhi (from his charge), and was dismissed.

16 Irādat, 53.

17 Thus K.K. (p. 616) observes:

'Such was the feebleness of the new ministry and such was the contempt into which their administration had fallen that the new governor (Fīrūz Jang) set out (for Gujarāt) without leave and even without waiting on the Emperor.'

In the following years, Fīrūz Jang, Chīn Qulīch Khān and Muḥammad Amīn Khān do not seem to have exercised much influence on state policy. Some authors have ascribed this to the alleged ill-will of Mun'im Khān and Bahādur Shāh towards them.[18] It seems, however, that the real cause of the dissatisfaction of this group was a feeling of having received less than their deserts, and a lack of enthusiasm for the policy of 'concessions' to the Rājpūts, Marāthās etc. which had been adopted by Bahādur Shāh at the instance of Mun'im Khān and Ẕu'lfiqār Khān. For this reason, they felt themselves out of joint with the spirit and policy of the administration.[19]

The position of this group was further weakened by the death of Fīrūz Jang in 1710. At about the same time, Chīn Qulīch resigned his *manṣab* and post, and settled down to a retired life in Delhi.[20]

Thus, the two dominant figures on the scene remained Mun'im Khān, the *wazīr*, and Ẕu'lfiqār Khān, the *mīr bakhshī*. The party struggle at the court of Bahādur Shāh, revolved mainly around the struggle for power between these two personalities. The struggle was not only personal, but had political implications too. Ẕu'lfiqār Khān apparently favoured a policy of bold and far-reaching concession to the Rājpūts and the Marāthās with the object of healing the breach which had opened up between these sections and the empire. This was foreshadowed by his actions as the chief adviser of A'ẕam Shāh during the latter's march from the Deccan to contest the throne. Mun'im Khān was very close to Bahādur Shāh in character and general outlook. Like Bahādur Shāh, he had been deeply influenced by *Sūfī* ideas: he was even credited with having written a book on Sūfiism which earned the disapproval of orthodox circles.[21] He too, like Bahādur Shāh, was inclined towards a policy of compromise and conciliation. He had been partly instrumental

18 Thus, the author of the *M.U.* (iii, p. 667) states that it was on the adverse report of Muḥammad Amīn that Mun'im Khān had been reduced in rank by 590 *sawār* during the siege of Khelna in 1702, and had lost the office of the *Dārōghah-i-Filkhānah*, as also his *jāgīr*. *Cf. M.A.*, 462 which gives a somewhat different account.

19 *Safinah-i-Khushgū* (O.P.L.) f. 158b.

20 *Akhbārāt*, 8, *Zīqa'dah* Yr. 4, 6, February 1711, M.M., 99, K.K., 879.

21 The title of the book was '*Ilhāmāt-i-Mun'imī*'. According to Anand Ram *Mukhliṣ*, the real author of the book was the historian, Irādat Khān (see Hodiwala, 667).

in the adoption of a policy of generosity towards the old 'Ālamgīrī nobles who had espoused the cause of A'ẕam. However, being a noble who had newly risen to high position he lacked experience of political and administrative affairs, so that he was reluctant to make big departures from existing policies, or to undertake bold measures such as the situation required. His middle-of-the-road policy satisfied no one, and ultimately created conditions in which the various problems of the empire worsened, and the struggle of parties and individuals at the court was sharpened.

The Rājpūt Question

The problem which next engaged the attention of Bahādur Shāh was the Rājpūt question. During the civil war, both A'ẕam and Bahādur Shāh had bid for Rājpūt support. A'ẕam had granted to Ajit Singh and Jai Singh the titles of Maharaja and Mirza Raja, the ranks of 7,000/7,000, and the governorships of Gujarāt and Malwa respectively. Jai Singh had joined A'ẕam Shāh in Malwa, but deserted him during the battle of Jājū.[22] However, he received no favour from Bahādur Shāh who had been joined by Vijai Singh, the younger brother of Jai Singh. Ajit Singh joined neither side, and took advantage of the civil war to expel the Mughal commander from Jodhpur. He did not attend the court, or send the customary congratulations to Bahādur Shāh on his accession to the throne. In Jodhpur, he was said to be 'oppressing the Musalmans, forbidding the killing of cows, preventing the summons to prayer, razing the mosques which had been built after the destruction of idol-temples in the late reign, and repairing and building anew idol-temples'. The Rana of Udaipur and Raja Jai Singh were said to be acting in close cooperation with him.[23]

Hence, a war to punish Ajit Singh and to destroy this 'coalition' was decided upon, and on 9 October 1707, Mihrāb Khān was appointed the *faujdār* of Jodhpur. The emperor himself set out for Rājputānā on 10 November, marching by way of Amber and Ajmer.[24]

22 M.M., 56b, Khalīl (Buhar Ms.) 6. *A'ẕam-ul-Ḥarb* (331–4) says that he did this at the advice and instigation of his younger brother, Vijai Singh. But this seems unlikely, as relations between the two brothers were not good.
23 K.K., 606.
24 *B.N.*, 177, *Akhbārāt*.

Moving leisurely, the royal encampment reached Amber, the capital of Jai Singh, towards the end of January 1708. Bahādur Shāh directed that as there was a dispute for the Kachhwāhā throne between the two brothers, Jai Singh and Vijai Singh, the state 'should be confiscated to the Imperial establishment', that the name of the town should be changed to Islāmābad, and that a 'new' *faujdār* should be sent there in the person of Saiyid Aḥmad Sa'īd Khān Bārahā.[25] The Emperor camped in Amber for three days during which the town was deserted by the inhabitants. The *mutṣaddīs* proceeded to confiscate the goods of Jai Singh, but these were returned to him soon after, and the kingdom was conferred on Vijai Singh.[26]

The action taken by Bahādur Shāh was not a sudden one. Soon after the battle of Jājū, Jai Singh had been told that since there was a contention (*munāqayat*) between him and his younger brother Vijai Singh, Amber would be taken into *khāliṣah*, and thereafter bestowed upon Vijai Singh.[27] Even before leaving for Rajasthan, towards the end of August 1707, the *ṣubahdār* and the *dīwān* of Ajmer were ordered to take possession of Amber.[28]

Bahādur Shāh had no intention of establishing direct Mughal rule over Amber. He simply took advantage of a disputed succession to transfer the *gaddī* from one branch of the house which he distrusted to another. Jai Singh had sided with A'ẓam in the civil war. Moreover, he was suspected of colluding with Ajit Singh in his 'aggression' against Jodhpur.[29] Jai Singh's younger brother,

25 *B.N.*, 254–6, M.M., 56a, Kāmwar, 87b. *M.U.* ii, 500, *Bahādur Shāh Nāmah* (Stewart), 317, *Siyar,* 379, *Khulāsat-ul-Tawārīkh* of Kalyān Rāi (*J.B.O. R.S.* 1920) 20. See also Irvine i, 47–8.

According to *Akhbārāt,* 1 March 1708, the name of Amber was changed to Mominābād.

26 *B.N.*, 254, 279, 288; *M.U.* ii, 81, 500–1; M.M., 56a.

27 Letter of Jai Singh to the Rana dated 22 July, 25 August 1707 (O.S.) Bhīmsen, ff 169.

28 Rajasthan State Archives, No. 3002, 24 *Ramaẓān, R.Y.* i, 19 December 1707.

29 K.K., 605, *B.N.* (398) says 'Jai Singh had sided with Muḥammad A'ẓam and been a rebel and disturber. According to the laws of war and revenge, it would have been proper to execute him, but the Emperor out of the kindness of his nature (only) ordered that the *zamindari* of Amber should be confiscated from that infidel.'

Vijai Singh, on the other hand, had joined Bahādur Shāh at Kabul, and had rendered him good service at Jājū. But the state was not handed over to Vijai Singh at once. As was the usual procedure of the Mughals in such cases, it was first taken into Imperial custody or *khāliṣah,* so as to prevent local disturbances and to ensure a smooth change over.[30] As one contemporary writer says, 'Saiyid Ḥusain Khān Bārahā, *faujdār* of Mewat, was ordered to establish an Imperial *thāna* at Amber which was the seat of the Kachhwāhā rajas, till the men of the Raja (Jai Singh) had been expelled from it'.[31] However, even after the kingdom had been handed over to Vijai Singh, the capital of the state, Amber, continued to be garrisoned by the Imperial *faujdār.*[32]

Perhaps, the real reason for Bahādur Shāh keeping a hold on the cities and parganas of Jodhpur and Amber, and his even greater firmness with the Rajputs than Aurangzīb, was to demonstrate that he would maintain the general policies of Aurangzīb. In this way

30 The actual words used by *B.N.*, M.M. and *M.U.* are '*dar sarkār-i-Shāhī ẓabṭ namūdah*'. This seems to have been used as an equivalent for the commoner expression 'taken into *khāliṣah*'. (For a discussion of the significance of *khāliṣah* see 'Introduction' above). We have another instance from Farrukh Siyar's reign of the use of *khāliṣah* as a kind of Court of Wards. In 1715, when Jai Singh came to the court, Budh Singh was deprived of Bundi which was taken under *khāliṣah,* and then handed over to Bhim Singh (M.M. ff. 60).

31 M.M., 56a.

32 M.M., 56a, *B.N.*, 288. Vijai Singh accompanied Bahādur Shāh in the campaign against Kām Bakhsh. When Ajit Singh and Jai Singh fled from the royal camp, the title of *Mirza Raja* was conferred upon him—perhaps as a kind of reaffirmation of his appointment to the *gaddī* of Amber. He had been granted the *manṣab* of 3,000/2,000—which was also the *manṣab* of Jai Singh—on 18 November 1707. On 29 August 1707, he was given a further rise of 500 *ẕat* (*B.N.*, 268,448).

Tod (ii, 333) states that Vijai Singh was taken prisoner when Jai Singh retook Amber, and that after a long captivity, he was poisoned in 1729 for intriguing with the *wazīr,* Qamar-ud-Dīn K., and Budh Singh Hāṛā.

However, the *Akhbārāt* makes it clear that Vijai Singh was *not* a prisoner at least till the end of Bahādur Shāh's reign. He is mentioned as returning to the court after his marriage on 6 July 1710, and again on 6 December 1710, he was appointed to the army of Jahāndar Shāh, the eldest prince. He also took part in the siege of Sādhaurā (*Akhbārāt,* 14, 28 January 1712; Khush-ḥāl, 316). Earlier, on Amber being returned to Jai Singh, he had been granted Tonk and Bhusāwar in *jāgīr* (*Akhbārāt* 11, *Jamāda* II, 1122, 7 August 1710).

he may have wished to please and to win over the orthodox section, particularly the Ālamgīrī nobles, in his contest with Kām Bakhsh.

Bahādur Shāh's action in Amber closely resembles that of Aurangzīb in Jodhpur following the death of Jaswant Singh. His motives were probably similar, viz. a desire to gain greater control over Rājputānā and the trade routes passing through it. However, it was hardly likely that Bahādur Shāh would succeed where Aurangzīb had failed, and his action in Amber could only result in widening the breach with the Rājpūt rajas.

As Bahādur Shāh advanced beyond Amber, Rana Amar Singh of Udaipur averted a threatened invasion of his country by sending his brother, Bakht Singh, to wait on the new emperor with a letter of congratulations and, as *nazr*, one hundred gold coins, one thousand rupees, two horses with trappings mounted with gold, one elephant, nine swords etc. Even then, such were his apprehensions that he fled from his capital and sent his family, property etc. into the hills as the Imperial army reached near his territories. But the emperor graciously accepted his submission.

When Bahādur Shāh reached near Ajmer, peace offers were received from Ajit Singh, but they did not prove acceptable. Meanwhile, Mihrāb Khān, the *faujdār*-designate of Jodhpur, reached near Mertha, and after defeating an army under Ajit Singh, occupied the town.[33]

Farmāns were now sent to Durgadas and to Ajit Singh calling them to the court. Ajit Singh sent a reply professing submission, but entertaining doubts regarding the emperor's intentions. Hence, Khān-i-Zamān, the son of Mun'im Khān, was sent to Jodhpur along with Raja Budh Singh Hāṛā and Najābat Khān, to meet and reassure Ajit Singh.[34]

On 24 February, Ajit Singh formally surrendered to Bahādur Shāh at Mertha. He was graciously received, and restored to the *manṣab* of 3,500/3,000 which he had held during the previous reign, and was also granted the title of Maharaja, together with many other presents. Two of his sons were also granted *manṣab*s. At the same time, *Qāẓī* Qāẓī Khān and M. Ghauṣ *Muftī* were sent off 'to re-establish Islām in Jodhpur'.[35] In other words, the situation prevailing at the time of Aurangzīb's death was restored.

33 *B.N.*, See also Irvine i, 45–6.
34 *Akhbārāt*, 6 February, *B.N.*
35 *B.N.*, 316.

Some modern historians have charged Bahādur Shāh with 'treachery', and alleged that Mihrāb Khān was sent by 'stealth' to occupy Jodhpur and that 'Ajit burned with rage when he heard of it'.[36] However, Khāfī Khān explicitly states that Ajit humbly agreed 'that Khān-i-Zamān and *qāẓī-ul-quẓẓāt* Qāẓī Khān might come into Jodhpur to rebuild the mosques destroy the idol-temples, enforce the provisions of the Shari'at about the summons to prayer and the killing of cows, to appoint magistrates, and to commission officers to collect *jizyah*'. The author adds, 'This "request" was accepted and the sins of Ajit Singh were pardoned, and officials of justice like *qāẓīs* and *muftīs* as well as *imāms* and *mu'azzins* were sent to Jodhpur and neighbouring towns'.[37]

Thus, it seems to be wrong to allege any breach of treaty by Bahādur Shāh. But there can be little doubt that Ajit Singh was not reconciled to the loss of Jodhpur. According to the official history of the reign, 'Ajit Singh repeatedly petitioned for the restoration of Jodhpur, but because he harboured the intention of rebellion and disturbance in his heart, the Emperor, who comprehended all matters, did not grant his request'.[38]

Due to his distrust of the Rājpūts, and in order to vindicate Imperial prestige, Bahādur Shāh decided to keep hold of Jodhpur. *Jizyah* was also levied there.[39] Worse still, Ajit Singh and Jai Singh were kept in a state of semi-captivity in the Imperial camp

36 Tod ii, p. 905, V. Reu *Hist. of Jodhpur,* p. 295. *V.V.*, p. 834 says that Ajit was offered the *pargana* of Sojat but refused to accept it without Jodhpur.

37 K.K., 606–7.

38 *B.N.*, 398.

39 K.K., 606. Tod (i, p. 419) quotes from a Persian paper, stipulating a treaty between the Rana of Mewar and the emperor that 'the Jizyah shall be abolished—that it shall no longer be imposed on the Hindu nation: at all events that none of the Chagtai race sanction it in Mewar'.

Tod places this just before the death of Rana Amar Singh which, however, he wrongly assigns to the year 1716 (correct date, 10 December 1710). As *jizyah* was definitely abolished by the year 1713, such a pact could only have been signed by Bahādur Shāh, if at all, in 1708 or in 1710, when he was returning from the Deccan.

Keene (*Turks in India,* 184) who thinks that the agreement included the abandonment of cow-slaughter, *jizyah* and *ḍoli* (marriage with Rājpūt princesses) probably bases himself on Tod.

However, contemporary Persian sources do not lend support to Tod's account.

while the emperor marched to the south to deal with Kām Bakhsh. However, on 30 April 1708, when the royal camp arrived at Mahābalēshwar on the Narmada, the two rajas effected their escape. For the moment, Bahādur Shāh deemed the matter of Kām Bakhsh more important, and refrained from ordering a pursuit.[40]

This, in effect, constituted a breakdown of the Rājpūt policy so far pursued by Bahādur Shāh, apparently at the instance of Mun'im Khān. Mirzā Muḥammad, a contemporary writer, sharply criticizes Mun'im Khān, and denounces this policy as 'ill-conceived'. 'They (Ajit and Jai Singh) should have been given assurances and concessions', he opines. 'But the *wazīr*, Mun'im Khān, remained oblivious of this. Rather, he advised His Majesty that they should be put off with sweet words and empty promises, while their countries were to be handed over to the charge of Imperial officers, and that they should be induced to remain at the court in the hope of obtaining large *jāgirs* and their affairs prolonged till the action against Kām Bakhsh was over. Whatever was deemed suitable could then be done. In the meantime, Rājpūt resistance would have been crushed and their strength sapped.'[41]

After effecting their escape, Jai Singh and Ajit Singh proceeded to Udaipur, where they made an agreement with the Maharana for joint resistance to the Mughals. If the Rājpūt tradition be accepted, the Rājpūt rajas planned not only to recover their countries, but to expel the Mughal influence from Rājputāna completely, and even dreamt of bringing the entire Hindustan under their sway.[42]

The conference of the rajas at Udaipur lasted, between festivities, almost for a month. It is evident from contemporary records, that the meetings led to an agreement by which the Rana agreed to help Ajit Singh and Jai Singh in recovering their homelands. To fulfil this agreement a Mewār contingent of 7,000 troops, under the

40 M.M., 57a, Wārid, 152, Khush-ḥāl, 32.

41 M.M., 56b.

42 According to Rājpūt tradition, it was proposed at the conference that the Rana should be made the Emperor of Hindustan after turning out the Mughals from India, but Ajit Singh claimed the throne for himself, and so the matter was dropped (*V.V.* ii, 767).

K.K. (pp. 619–20) says that one Saif Khān had formed an agreement with the Rājpūts for the supply of 17,000–18,000 Rājpūt horsemen to Kām Bakhsh for making a sudden descent on Delhi while Bahādur Shāh was in the Deccan. But the proposal was rejected by Kām Bakhsh.

command of Shyāmal Dās and Mahā Sāhani Chatrabhuj, accompanied Ajit Singh and Jai Singh. It appears that this contingent was with-drawn after the expulsion of the Mughal *faujdārs* from Jodhpur and Amber, for the rana was finding it difficult to meet its expenses. Although Durga Das requested the Maharana for a contingent in order to lay siege to Sāmbhar, the Maharana did not accede to his request.[43]

The second part of the agreement related to the marriage of the rana's daughter, Chānd Kunwari, with Jai Singh which took place on *Asharh Badi* 2, 1765 V.S., 5 June 1708. Before the marriage, Jai Singh had to sign a document agreeing, among other things, that the rana's daughter would get precedence over all his other ranis and that the male issue from this union would succeed to the Amber *gaddi*.[44] This was the price which the rana extracted for helping Jai Singh in recovering his kingdom.

There is no reference to any agreement among the rajas for ousting the Mughals from Rajputana, much less from India; nor do the subsequent movements of the Rajas suggest any such intention on their part.

The Rana also had grievances against the Mughals owing to the *parganas* of Pur, Māndal and Bidnur having been sequestrated in lieu of *jizyah* in 1681. Subsequently, they were restored to him on condition that he would send a contingent of 1,000 *sawārs* to serve the emperor and pay a sum of rupees one lakh annually in lieu of *jizyah*. However, owing to the promised sum of rupees one lakh annually having fallen in arrears, the *parganas* were once again taken away. After the agreement of 1709, Sānwal Das and Jaswant Singh attacked Pur and Māndal, and ousted the Mughal *faujdār*, Firoz Khān, Jaswant Singh losing his life in the battle.[45]

The Maharana also intervened in the affairs of Rāmpurā. This small state which had acted as a buffer between Malwa and Mewār, had formerly been under the suzerainty of Mewār, but it had been separated from Mewār by Akbar. As the power of Mewār revived, the Ranas attempted to regain their control over it. The forces of the Maharana attacked Rāmpurā, but were unsuccessful.[46]

43 R. S. A., Shyamal Das Collection.

44 *Kapaldwara* Doc., R. S. A. No. 14060 dt. *Jeth Badi* 15, 1765 V.S., 20 May 1708.

45 *Vir Vinod* ii, 665–72, 752–8; Ojha, *Udaipur*, 899, 910.

46 R. Sinh, *Malwa in Transition*, 48–52, 117.

It will thus be seen that each of the Rājpūt rajas had his own personal grievance against the Mughals.

After dispersing, Ajit Singh attacked and occupied Jodhpur, and Jai Singh recovered Amber. They then over-ran the Mughal outposts in Hindaun and Bayānā.

When the news of this Rājpūt outbreak reached the Emperor, he ordered Asad Khān, the *wakīl-i-muṭlaq,* to march from Delhi to Agra, and to take steps to repress the disturbance. A number of well-known warriors and generals, including Chīn Qulīch (Khān-i-Daurān) the *ṣūbahdār* of Awadh, Khān-i-Jahān, the *ṣūbahdār* of Allahaḅad, and M. Amīn Khān the *faujdār* of Moradabad were appointed to help him. But these nobles never marched. Instead, Asad Khān and Z̲u'lfiqār Khān, who did not apparently agree with Mun'im Khān's Rājpūt policy, opened negotiations with Jai Singh and Ajit Singh.[47]

Meanwhile, the rainy season of 1708 was over. The Rājpūt armies invaded Sāmbar. In a battle, the noted warrior, Saiyid Ḥusain Khān, was accidentally killed, and this gave the Rājpūts a notable victory. But they made little progress elsewhere, and contented themselves mostly with plundering.[48]

Even this limited success of the Rājpūts was a blow to Imperial prestige. Mirzā Muḥammad exclaims bitterly: 'If one of the old grandees with a tried and tested following had been nominated the *ṣūbahdār* of Ajmer, and two brave and well-known officers fully equipped with all necessary materials put in charge of Jodhpur, what courage had the Rājpūts to win back their countries...Saiyid Husain Khān Bārahā was a brave and courageous man, but he was a newly risen noble and did not possess the confidence of people, or have sufficient means at his disposal (to cope with the situation).'[49]

On 6 October 1708, the Rājpūt rajas were restored to their *manṣab* at the instance of Asad Khān and Prince 'Aẓīm-ush-Shān

47 *V.V.* ii, 768. See also Irvine i, 67–70. The Mughals were prepared to restore Amber to Jai Singh, and Jodhpur to Ajit Singh, but were not prepared to relinquish their hold on their capitals. The Rajputs demanded restoration of all of their *watans, manṣabs* of 5,000/5,000, and appointment to important posts. (Abdul Rassal, *Narang-i-Zamāna,* ed. A. Baqir, Lahore, 1960, 17–18.)

48 *B.N.*, 421–58, *Akhbārāt,* 10 April 1709, *V.V.*, 772–82.

49 M.M., 57a.

who was then the favourite of his father.[50] But the question of returning their capitals (*watan jāgīr*) was not decided. Asad Khān, who had been put in supreme charge of the provinces of Lahore, Delhi and Ajmer, offered to grant *sanad*s of their homelands to the rajas 'provided they raise their *thana*s from Sāmbhar and Didwana, and accepted appointment to the provinces of Kabul and Gujarāt'. But the Rajas were not willing to be separated, or to accept appointment far away from their homes, and asked for the posts of the *ṣūbahdār*s of Malwa and Gujarāt.[51]

Soon after, differences arose among the Rājpūt rajas. Ajit Singh having reoccupied Jodhpur with the help of the combined forces of the Rana and Jai Singh, showed no eagerness to march against Amber according to his agreement. His absence rankled Jai Singh who therefore delayed in joining the campaign against Sāmbhar. On his finally doing so, and the Rājpūt force having over-run Sāmbhar and Dīdwānā (October–November 1708), Jai Singh proposed that they should be returned to the Mughals in order to facilitate an agreement with them. The Rana supported Jai Singh.

In February 1709, Ajit Singh besieged Ajmer with 20,000 *sawār*. Although Jai Singh had promised to march against Ajmer from Amber by forced marches as soon as news was received that Ajit Singh had left Merta, he did not move out of Amber. Ajit Singh, on extracting Rs 80,000 from the *ṣūbāhdar*, Shujā'āt Khān, left for Devaliy'a for his marriage, and returned to Jodhpur on 30 March (N.S.).[52]

It is, thus, apparent that the united front of the three rajas had started showing cracks as soon as their main objectives had been realized, viz. the recovery of their *watans* by Ajit Singh and Jai Singh, and of the parganas of Pur, Māndal and Bidnur by the Rana. The proposal to post Jai Singh and Ajit Singh to widely separated provinces, such as Malwa and Kabul, coupled with Bahādur Shāh's threat to deal with them sternly on his return to north India led to their uniting once again.

50 In December, Asad Khān reported that the Rājpūt affair had ended. The Emperor was pleased, and remarked—'Well done! In reality, it is Asad Khān who is governing Hindustan' (*Akhbārāt*, 3 December 1708).

51 *Jaipur Records: Wakīl's* reports d. 28, 30 June and 12 July 1709 (O.S.).

52 R. S. A., Shyamal Das Collection; *Akhbārāt*, 6, *Ẕilḥijja*, 1120, 16 February 1709. For Shujā'at Khān's lying report claiming victory, see Kāmwar f. 312b.

In February 1709, after defeating Kām Bakhsh, Bahādur Shāh once more turned his attention towards Rājpūtānā. An uneasy truce had prevailed there since October 1708, following the restoration of the rajas to their *manṣabs*.[53] It appears that a powerful section at the court was in favour of a stern policy towards the Rājpūts. Hence, Ghāzī-ud-Dīn Khān Fīrūz Jang was appointed to Ajmer and directed to march to his charge immediately from Aḥmadabad.[54] It was also reported that the emperor was returning 'resolved to lead an army to punish and chastise the Rājpūts'. In alarm, the Rājpūts sought the meditation of their old friends, Asad Khān and Prince 'Aẓīm-ush-Shān.[55]

The intervention of these powerful figures, combined with the news of a Sikh uprising in the Punjab, tipped the scales in favour of a compromise. The report of the Sikh uprising was received by the emperor near the Narmada, in December, 1709.[56] This was followed, soon afterwards, by the report of the death of Wazīr Khān, the *faujdār* of Sarhind, at the hands of Banda's followers. The possible consequences of a popular uprising such as that of the Sikhs, in close proximity to the Imperial capital and the strategic northwestern area, were considered to be more dangerous than the pending quarrel with the Rājpūts. The latter were old allies of the Mughals and, as one author observes, 'had been used to obeying (the Mughal Emperor) for generations'. It was not considered likely that they would commit further aggression if left in possession of their hereditary lands.[57]

Hence, a settlement was hurriedly patched up with the Rājpūt rajas. Their homelands were returned to them, and their demand for an audience with the Emperor on the march (*sar-i-sawārī*, i.e. not in the court), to which they were to be escorted by Prince

53 On 10 April 1709, Shujā'at Khān, the Governor of Ajmer, reported that Ajit Singh had launched an attack (*Akhbārāt*).

54 On 17 October 1708. Shujā'at Khān Bārahā was replaced by S. 'Abdullāh K. The latter made a number of demands which were accepted. But Shujā'at Khān was restored soon afterwards.

On 12 April 1708, Fīruz Jang was made the absentee Governor of Ajmer. He was dismissed shortly afterwards, and re-appointed on 25 *Rabī*' 1, 15 June (*Akhbārāt*, Kāmwar, Lko. Ms., 93b).

55 *V.V.*, 781–4.

56 *Akhbārāt*, entry d. 4 Rabī' I yr. 4, 4 May 1710.

57 Īrādat, 67.

'Aẕīm-ush-Shān was accepted. It was further agreed that they would be given six months, leave immediately after their audience with the emperor, after which they would serve wherever appointed. On 21 June 1710, while the emperor was on the march, the two rajas were presented before him by Mahabāt Khān, the son of Mun'im Khān. After the customary greetings and presents, they were immediately given six months' leave to return home.[58]

These terms, which one contemporary writer declares as 'far above their status',[59] and another as 'inconsistent with good policy as well as the dignity of the sovereign',[60] could really be only a first step in a sound policy aimed at the reconciliation of the Rājpūts. Bahādur Shāh was keen that the Rājpūts should serve against the Sikhs and, presumably, against the Marāthās as well. In other words, he wanted them to act as the sword arm of the Mughal empire as before. But for such a policy to succeed, an attitude of magnanimity, and not crude suspicion was required. The Rājpūt rajas wanted not only the restoration of their homelands but that they should be granted high *manṣab*s as before, and appointed as *ṣūbahdār*s of important provinces like Malwa and Gujarāt.[61] These two provinces adjoined their homelands as well as each other, and in their prevailing mood of distrust, the two rajas seem to have considered appointment to the charge of these provinces as a guarantee of good faith on the part of the emperor.

The Rājpūt affairs remained in this condition during the remaining years of Bāhādur Shāh's reign. Mun'im Khan was not inclined to accept the demands of the Rājpūt rajas for appointment as the Governors of Malwa and Gujarāt. He urged them to accept, instead, appointment to Kabul and Gujarāt. 'Aẕīm-ush-Shān who posed as the friend of the Rājpūts, promised them appointment 'to the east—or leave to return home if that was not acceptable,' after the rajas had come to the court.[62] But the Rājpūt rajas were not enthusiastic about either of these proposals, and hence they delayed in making their appearance at the court. It was only in October 1711, after repeated summons, and the lapse of more

58 *M.M.*, 58b, K.K., 661. Elliot's translation (Vol. vii, 420) is really only a summary of the original passage.

59 Īrādat, 68.

60 *M.M.*, 58 b.

61 *V.V.*, 949 (*Wakīl*'s report).

62 *V.V.*, 948.

than 15 months after they had secured six months' leave that the two rajas arrived at the court to render service.[63] Mun'im Khān was dead by this time, and prince 'Aẕīm-ush-Shān had become the centre of all affairs. The rajas were appointed to Sādhaurā and served there with 'a large army', guarding the foothills from the raids of Banda's followers.[64]

After two-and-a-half months, Jai Singh was made the *faujdār* of Aḥmadabad Khorā alias Chitrakūt, and Ajit Singh of Sorath in Gujarāt.[65] These fell short of Rājpūt expectations,[66] and they petitioned for permission to return home. In keeping with his promise, the emperor agreed to this, but with the proviso that they should leave a *chauki* behind, and in January 1712, the rajas started back for their homes.[67]

Thus, the Rājpūt policy of Bahādur Shāh underwent a definite evolution. He attempted, at first, to maintain Mughal control over Jodhpur by force of arms, and even to extend the Mughal hold on Rājpūtānā by displacing Jai Singh from the *gaddī* of Amber in favour of his younger brother, and stationing an Imperial *faujdār*

63 The two Rajas reached Sādhaurā on 5 *Ramaẓān* Yr. 5, 17 October 1711 (*J.R.* Misc. papers Vol. i, 217, *Akhbārāt* entries d. 11 and 15 *Ramaẓān*, 23, 27 October, M.M., 39a).

They reached Mertha in December 1710, but nine months later, they were still at Karnāl. They had come with a considerable army and inspite of their assurances, the local people began to flee in panic. Near Delhi, the rajas hunted in the Imperial preserves, which caused much annoyance to the emperor, but he discreetly kept silent (*V.V.*, 948, 786, 924, 943; *Akhbārāt*, 15 *Muḥ.*, 26, *Rabī* II, 22, *Jam.* I, 8, *Jam.* II, 8, *Sha'bān*, Yr. 5, 5 March, 14 June, 9 and 24 July, 21 September 1711).

64 *Akhbārāt*, 1, *Ẕiqa'dah*, 11 December 1711. The Guru threatened reprisals against the rajas, who retaliated by proclaiming in their camps that any Sikh found there would be executed.

65 *Akhbārāt*, 10, 12, 21, *Shawwāl*, 22, 24 November, 3 December 1711. In a letter of instruction bearing Asad Khān's seal and dated 7 *Shawwāl*, 17 November 1711, Jai Singh is asked to punish thieves and to destroy their forts, forbid blacksmiths of the place to make match-locks, realize *mālguẕārī* prevent the *thanadars* from exacting illegal cesses, forbid intoxicants, keep the royal highways safe for travellers, etc.

66 *Cf.* the remark of Aurangzīb in one of his letters that the *faujdārī* of Sorath was not an inferior thing, and that formerly persons of the rank of 5,000 were appointed to it. (*Raqā'im* ff. 9a-b).

67 *Akhbārāt*, 13, *Ẕilḥijjah* Yr. 5, 15 January 1712; Reu's *Marwar*, 303.

at Amber. This led to a serious uprising in Rājpūtānā when Bahādur Shāh went to the Deccan to fight Kām Bakhsh. Pressed by circumstances and by a strong party at the court which favoured conciliation with the Rājpūts, Bahādur Shāh restored their capitals and homelands to Jai Singh and Ajit Singh, but still refused to accord the rajas such *manṣab*s and offices as they coveted.

Thus, the gulf with the Rājpūts was narrowed but not bridged.

THE DECCAN PROBLEM

The Deccan problem, as has been emphasized earlier, was amongst the major problems that the Mughals had to face since the beginning of the seventeenth century, and Bahādur Shāh could not long remain indifferent to it. The problem may be regarded as being a twofold one—the problem of the predominantly Marāthi-speaking areas on the western coast in which Shivāji had demanded independence (*swarajya*), and, secondly, the problem of the plateau extending upto Mysore—a rich and fertile area which had been frequently plundered by the armies from the north, but which had rarely been ruled effectively from northern India. The Mughals had cast covetous eyes on the riches of this area for a long time, but a sustained effort to bring it under direct Mughal rule started only from about 1676. Since the time of Shivaji, the Marāthās had been claiming and levying *chauth* and *sardeshmukhī* from this area, which amounted to 35 per cent of the total revenue.

At the time of Bahādur Shāh's accession, the problem was complicated by the presence of a royal competitor in the Deccan, Kām Bakhsh who had struck coins and had the *khuṭbah* read in his name, thus proclaiming his independence. Aurangzīb had over-run the Deccan plateau, and extinguished the independent states existing there. In order to meet the two-fold problem of establishing a sound administrative system in those parts, and of overcoming the Marāthā opposition, Aurangzīb had spent the last 26 years of his life in the Deccan. But due to difficulties which have been discussed earlier, he could achieve only limited success. With his death, the problem became all the more complicated and finding a solution was difficult. The nobles were already restive at their prolonged stay in the Deccan away from northern India which the large majority of them regarded as their home. A new monarch was not likely to have sufficient authority to compel them to prolong their stay in the Deccan much longer. Besides, continued concentration on the Deccan was liable to have serious repercussions on northern India, the resources of which formed the mainstay of the Mughal empire.

The scheme for the partition of empire ascribed to Aurangzīb was apparently aimed at providing a solution to the twin problems of securing the extension of the Mughal empire to the entire country and, at the same time, setting up in the Deccan a local administration strong enough to counter the Marāthā depredations. Under the scheme, the country was divided into three parts: the first, consisting of Bījāpur and Golkonda was assigned to Kām Bakhsh; the second, consisting of the remaining four *ṣūbahs* of the Deccan and of Malwa, Gujarāt and Agra was assigned to A'ẓam Shāh, and the third, consisting of the rest of the empire was assigned to Bahādur Shāh.[68]

On the eve of the battle of Jājū, Bahādur Shāh had offered to abide by the provisions of this will. He now made a similar offer to Kām Bakhsh. 'Our father entrusted to you the *ṣūbah* of Bījāpur', he wrote to Kām Bakhsh in a letter sent through Ḥāfiẓ Aḥmad Muftī alias Ma'tbar Khān. 'We now relinquish to you the two *ṣūbah* of Bījāpur and Ḥaiderābād with all subjects and belongings, upon the condition according to the old rules of the Dakin, that the coins shall be struck and the *khuṭbah* read in our name. The tribute which has hitherto been paid by the governors of the two provinces we remit. You should do justice to the people, punish the disobedient, and expel the robbers and oppressors from that area'.[69]

68 British Museum (B.M.), Add. 18,881, f 76 b, and I.O.L., *M.S.* 1334, f. 49b. Ḥamīd-ud-dīn Khān gives a different will (Translated by Sarkar in *Ancedotes of Aurangzeb,* 46–9).

English Factory Records also mention the alleged will making the division (see *I.H.R.C. Proceedings,* Vol. XVIII, 1942, 338).

69 K.K., 608, Īrādat, 54, *Ḥadīqat,* 11, *B.N.*, 386–90, Kāmwar, 88b. *Siyar,* 376–7 says that A'ẓam had made a similar agreement with Kām Bakhsh, giving him Ḥaiderābād in addition to Bījapur in return for *khuṭbah* and *sikkah* in his name. But this may be doubted, in view of the extremely strained relations between the two brothers. According to some accounts, Kām Bakhsh had wished to join A'ẓam, but his offer was refused (K.K., 567–70).

Mr Wigmore wrote from Madras on 8 January 1708—'Cawn Bux remains yet possessed of Vijapore, and Shaw Allum they say, is willing he should continue so, but his sons will not consent to it.' (*Factory letters* in *I.H.R.C. Proceedings,* Vol. XVIII, 330).

It is not easy to decide if Bahādur Shāh was sincere in his offer. He may have hoped that the old kingdoms of Bījāpur and Golkonda, united under a Timurid prince, would be able to maintain internal law and order and, at the same time, provide an effective check to the Marāthās.[70] Such a kingdom would also not conflict with the principle of an all-India Timurid monarchy. But the scheme could not be given a trial at all, for Kām Bakhsh scornfully rejected Bahādur Shāh's offer. This enabled the latter to cast on the head of Kām Bakhsh the onus of shedding the blood of innocent Muslims.[71]

If Kām Bakhsh had taken effective possession of all the important forts and fortresses in the provinces of Bījāpur and Golkonda, secured the support and confidence of his nobles, and reached some kind of an understanding with the Marāthās he would have posed a serious threat to Bahādur Shāh. Kām Bakhsh did make approaches towards the Marāthās, but with little success. He failed to bring the Karnātak under his control due to the opposition of Dā'ūd Khān, the deputy of Z̲u'lfiqār Khān. In the north, the commandant of Golkonda, Naẓr Beg Khān, who was in touch with Bahādur Shāh, refused to submit to him.[72] Most of the other nobles also sought to reinsure themselves by entering into secret correspondence with Bahādur Shāh. Matters were made

70 *Cf.* the view of J. D. B. Gribble (*History of the Deccan*, 1898, ii, 337) 'The Deccan under one Prince, who was also a member of the Imperial family, and acknowledged by and allied to the Emperor himself, would before long have developed into a strong and homogenous kingdom extending from sea to sea, and from the Vindhyas to Cape Kamorin. Such a kingdom was the only possible means of subduing the Marathas, and by it the disjointed Hindoo Kingdom of the South would have been conquered without difficulty. It is probable that the course [would have] been far different if, when some 40 years later the English began to take active interest in the political affair of South India, they had come in contact with a strongly established Muslim Kingdom of the Deccan'.

71 The charge brought against Kām Bakhsh by the official historian, Dānishmand Khān, is that 'he collected an army of infidels and plundered the Imperial territories which had no connection with him' (*B.N.*, 385).

72 Bahādur Shāh had made various attempts to retain Ḥaiderābād by granting concessions to the Governor, Rustam Dil Khān (*B.N.*, 130). On 7 April, the *ṣūbahdārī* of the Deccan was offered to 'Aẓ̈īm-ush-Shān (*B.N.*, 257). As no reply had been received from Kām Bakhsh till then, this suggests that Bahādur Shāh was either not sincere about his offer, or felt confident that Kām Bakhsh would reject it.

worse by Kām Bakhsh's suspicious bent of mind which led him to unjustly entertain doubts about the loyalty of Taqarrub Khān, the *Mīr Bakhshī,* and one of his most energetic officers. Hence, he imprisoned Taqarrub Khān and executed him along with a number of his adherents.[73]

The result of all these was that the officers and men of Kām Bakhsh deserted him in large numbers as Bahādur Shāh approached near, till Kām Bakhsh was left with only a small, dispirited following. Deeming flight to be dishonourable, he put up a desperate but futile resistance, and died fighting on the battlefield (13 January 1709).

In this way, the civil war which had kept parts of the country in an unsettled state for almost two years, finally ended with the victory of Bahādur Shāh who now ruled over one of the most extensive empires ever ruled by an Indian king. The victory of Bahādur Shāh strengthened the idea of an all-India monarchy, and implied the defeat, for the time being, of the forces of regional separatism. The idea of the political unity of the country remained one of the cardinal political beliefs in the country, and effected, in some degree or the other, all political movements which developed in the country during the eighteenth century. For instance, it found expression in the continued acceptance of the Mughal king as the Emperor of India even when all power and glory had departed from him.

Bahādur Shāh had next to make suitable arrangements for the administration of the Deccan. At first, the post of the Viceroy of the six *ṣūbahs* of the Deccan was offered to Prince 'Aẓīm-ush-Shān, who had been gradually gaining favour with him. However, 'Aẓīm-ush-Shān preferred the charge of the eastern provinces—Bengal, Bihar, Orissa and Allahabad, some of which he had governed during Aurangzīb's lifetime. The post was therefore conferred upon Ẕu'lfiqār Khān.[74] He was granted full authority in all the revenue and administrative matters pertaining to the Deccan, and allowed to remain at the court and to combine his new appointment

73 For these and other doings of Kām Bakhsh, see K.K., 605–21.

74 *Akhbārāt,* 24 October 1708. Ẕu'lfiqār was appointed on 4 Ẕīqa'dah, 15 January 1709, though a formal *farmān* was not issued till 10 *Muḥ*. Yr. 3, 15 March 1709.

(Copy in '*Sarkar's Collection*', Vol. XIV, 319–20).

with his previous post of *mīr bakhshī*. His old associate and protégé, Dā'ūd Khān Pannī, was made his deputy in the Deccan, and granted the *manṣab* of 7,000/5,000 (5,000 *dū-aspah*), and the governorship of Bījāpur, Berar and Aurangabad, the latter being fixed as his headquarters. All the officers posted in the Deccan were informed of the royal orders that the binding and loosening of the affairs of the Deccan would depend upon the advice of the bakhshī-ul-mamālik, and that he would be responsible for all its affairs (lit. be the *tābi'f* of command and negation).[75]

By virtue of holding two such important posts as those of the *Mīr Bakhshī* and the (absentee) Viceroy of the Deccan, Ẕu'lfiqār Khān became one of the most powerful nobles in the empire. Prior to this, the Mughal emperors had never permitted one person to hold two such posts, whatever may have been the exigencies of the situation. The new departure was a dangerous portent for the future. Moreover, Ẕu'lfiqār Khān was not prepared to tolerate any interference in the revenue or any other matter pertaining to the Deccan. It appears that Mun'im Khān was opposed to the grant of such wide powers to Ẕu'lfiqār Khān. He put forward the argument that the province of Burhānpur (Khandesh) and half of Berar generally known as Pā'īn-Ghat, did not form a part of the Deccan, because Khandesh had been a part of the independent kingdom of the Fārūkīs, and Pā'īn-Ghat had been annexed by Akbar. He wanted to include these *ṣūbahs* in the provinces dependent on Delhi, and to vest the authority over the political and revenue affairs, and the appointment, dismissal and transfer of officers in those areas in the hands of his eldest son, Mahābat Khān, who held the post of the third *bakhshī*. This caused further bitterness between Mun'im Khān and Ẕu'lfiqār Khān, and the dispute reached such heights that it became the common talk of the camp. As Bahādur Shāh disliked taking decisions in matters involving disputes between nobles, the prevailing situation apparently continued.[76]

75 Kāmwarf, 319a (copied by *Siyar*, 360).

76 K.K. ii, 626–7. Ẕu'lfiqār Khān's *dīwān* in the Deccan was Diyānat Khān Khwāfī, the son of the ex-*dīwān* of the Deccan, Amānat Khān. At the instance of Mun'im Khān, Diyānat K. was, at first, superseded and Murṣhid Qulī Khān, the *dīwān* of Bengal, was appointed to succeed him. It seems that Mun'im Khān wanted to use Murṣhid Qulī as a check upon Ẕu'lfiqār Khān, Murṣhid Qulī was not keen to accept the appointment and soon, by the exertions of

Thus, Ẕu'lfiqār Khān remained the Viceroy of the Deccan with sole authority over its affairs. Only one instance will suffice to illustrate the power and authority enjoyed by Ẕu'lfiqār Khān. Upon his advocacy and support, Nīmājī Sindhia, who was 'one of the most considerable *nā-sardār*s of those parts' was raised to the *manṣab* of 7,000/5,000, and the *manṣab*s granted to his sons and grandsons at the same time came altogether to 40,000 *ẕāt*, 25,000 *sawār*. Many *pargana*s in the settled parts of Aurangabad were transferred to him, displacing more than 1,000 *manṣabdār*s, big and small. In spite of considerable clamour and opposition, these measures of Ẕu'lfiqār Khān could not be reversed.[77]

There can be little doubt that the delegation of large powers to the Viceroy of the Deccan, or to his deputy was an administrative necessity. But in the background of the growing feebleness of the central government, and the persistence of strong separatist tendencies in the Deccan, this served to stoke the fires of am-ambition in the breasts of powerful nobles who were already casting covetous eyes on the Deccan. Along with the posts of *wazīr* and *mīr bakhshī*, the post of the Viceroy of the Deccan became one of the chief prizes in the struggle between parties and factions at the court.

The big test of the new viceroy's authority and influence was his ability to secure a settlement of the Marāthā question along lines favoured by him. But here he found it much more difficult to have his own way. After the defeat of Kām Bakhsh, in May 1709 Ẕu'lfiqār Khān introduced Shāhū's *wakīl* Gangādhar Prahlād to the Emperor.

He presented an application for the grant of the *chauth* and *sardeshmukhī* for the six *ṣūbah*s of the Deccan on condition of restoring prosperity to the ruined land. At the same time, Mun'im Khān presented Yādukesh the *wakīl* of Tārā-Bāi, praying for a *farmān* in the name of her son, Shivaji II. She asked only for *sardeshmukhī* without any reference to *chauth*, and also offered to suppress other insurgents and to restore order in the country. A great contention upon the matter arose between the two ministers.

Ẕu'lfiqār Khān, Amānat Khān was made the *dīwān* of the Deccan once again, and Dīyānat Khān, was made his deputy. Thus, Ẕu'lfiqār Khān remained supreme in the affairs of the Deccan.

(*B.N.*, entries d. 18 October 1707, 25 January 1708; *M.U.* ii, 70–3).

77   *B.N.*, 456, 460, 462; K.K., 625–6. This happened in September 1709.

In the end, Bahādur Shāh, who was unwilling to displease either side, ordered that *sanads* for *sardeshmukhi* be given in compliance with the requests of both Mun'im Khān and Z̲u'lfiqār Khān.[78] In other words, he refused to recognize Shāhū as the rightful Marāthā king, as had been done all along by Aurangzīb. He also rejected the claim for *chauth.* Only *sardeshmukhī* was granted, and even for that, the rival claimants were left to fight it out. This was a negation of the policy of giving first priority to the task of restoring peace and order in the Deccan, for fighting each other. Both sides were only too likely to plunder the Mughal territories. In fact, that is what did happen. Bahādur Shāh had no sooner left the Deccan than Shāhū came out of Raigarh and issued an order to his *sardars*: 'The Emperor has granted me the (*sar*) *deshmukhi* of these parts, but not yet the *chauth.* You should therefore raid the Imperial territories and create disorder there (till he agrees to do so)'.[79]

It is difficult to avoid the conclusion that Bahādur Shāh's Marāthā policy was short-sighted and ill-conceived. He was really called upon to choose between the advice of the *wazīr* who was the chief counsellor in matters political, and that of the Viceroy of the Deccan whose special responsibility was the Deccan, including Marāthā affairs. By rejecting the advice of Z̲u'lfiqār Khān he threw away a golden chance of settlement with the Marāthās. The Marāthā power was then at its lowest ebb. Shāhū's position was insecure at home, and if Bahādur Shāh had extended recognition to him, he could have gained Shāhū's gratitude and friendship. Besides, Shāhū's succession had always been favoured by Aurangzīb, and on coming to the throne, Bahādur Shāh himself had tacitly recognized this claim by restoring Shāhū to his former *manṣab,* sending him a *farmān* and other presents in acknowledgement of his congratulations on his succession,[80]

78 K.K., 627, 783, Duff i, 421, *Tārikh-i-Ibrāhīmī,* Elliot viii, 259, *Khazānah,* 42. *M.U.* ii, 351 says that Bahādur Shāh granted 10 per cent as *sardeshmukhī* out of the total collections of (only the five) *ṣūbahs* of Aurangābād, Khāndesh, Berār, Bījāpur and Bīdar.

79 *Akhbārāt,* 21, *Rajab* yr. 3, 21 September 1709.

80 *Akhbārāt,* 15 October 1707, *B.N.*, 114, Kāmwar, 86 a, *M.U.* ii, 342.

Riyasat, 23 and Sinha (*Rise of the Peshwas*), xv wrongly think that Shāhū was given the rank of 10,000/10,000. All ranks of 8,000 and above were reserved for the princes.

Further presents to Shāhū were sent on 24 December (*Akhbārāt*).

and calling upon him to render military help against Kām Bakhsh.[81]

As for the terms to be offered to the Marāthās, Ẕu'lfiqār Khān who was a man of wide experience and well-acquainted with Marāthā character and politics, seems to have been of the opinion that a policy of half-hearted concessions was of no use. He apparently felt that the times were ripe for a bold and far-reaching re-orientation of policy in the Deccan with the object of making the Marāthās partners in the empire from opponents, and of utilizing their military and administrative talents for the maintenance of peace and order in the Deccan by giving them a stake in its prosperity and good governance.

Soon after Bahādur Shāh's departure, news was received of Marāthā depredations in the *ṣūbahs* of Burhānpur, Bījāpur, and Aurangābād. A large band of Marāthās entered the *ṣūbah* of Bījāpur in 1710, and moved in the direction of Ahmadnagar. Rustam Khān Bījāpurī, the Governor, who held the rank of 8,000/8,000, moved against them, but they eluded battle. When this news reached Bahādur Shāh, he reduced the rank of Rustam Khān by 1,000 as a mark of displeasure, but soon relented, and appointed the Khān to Berar in addition to his former charge. Meanwhile, another band of Marāthās invaded Burhānpur, and plundered upto the outskirts of the capital. The Governor, Mīr Aḥmad Khān, came out to fight, but was completely surrounded by the Marāthās. The Khan put up a desperate fight but perished in the course of the battle, while two of his sons were wounded. Another band of Marāthās appeared near Aurangābād and plundered the inhabitants of the surrounding areas. The deputy Viceroy, Dā'ūd Khān Pannī, took the field against them, but the Marāthās refused to fight and moved away at his approach. By this time, the rainy season was approaching and campaigning came to an end.[82]

After the rains, the Marāthās appeared in force once again. Chandrasen Jādhav beseiged the fort of Vijaydurg, and then

81 Shāhū had expressed his inability attend in person, but sent one of his best known sardars, *Nimājī*, with a large force, which did good service. (K.K., 625, Rajwade viii, No. 56, Duff. i, 420.)

Earlier, on his way back after escaping from captivity, Shāhū had demonstrated his loyalty by ostentatiously visiting the tomb of Aurangzīb near Daulatābād (K.K., 583).

82 *Akhbārāt*, 8 February, 19 April, 24 June; K.K., 666.

moved on to Kulbargā; Haibat Rao Nimbālkar, along with Sōmā, Jagannāth etc. invaded Bījāpur but was chased out of the *ṣūbah* by Hīrāman, the deputy of Dā'ūd Khān. Gangā, one of the dismissed *sardars* of Fīrūz Jang, created widespread disturbances in Malwa and Burhānpur. A body of 40,000 Marāthās raided the Junnair area under the instructions of Shāhū, and looted the *jāgīrs* of Zu'lfiqār Khān.[83] The Mughals were apparently powerless to check these inroads, though Dā'ūd Khān Pannī moved about with a large army, chasing the Marāthās. He took over charge from Rustam Khān who had repeatedly failed against them, chased out Santā Ghōrpādē from Khāndesh, made sound arrangements for its defence and sent his nephew, Alāwal Khān to look after Berar. He also tried to sow dissension among the Marāthās by his diplomacy. Towards the end of 1710, Rao Rambhā Nimbālkar joined the Mughals. He was welcomed into Aurangābād by Dā'ūd Khān who secured for him the *manṣab* of 7,000/6,000, and the rank of 5,000 each for two of his lieutenants. The next to desert was Paiṁā Rāj Sindhiā. The most important defection, however, was that of Chandrasen Jādhav who joined the Mughals in March 1711, after a clash with Bālāji Vishwanāth over a hunting incident, though he had been in contact with the Mughals even earlier.[84]

It was probably about this time that Dā'ūd Khān entered into a private pact with Shāhū. According to this pact, the *chauth* and *sardeshmukhī* of the Deccan was promised to Shāhū. However, it was not to be collected by the Marāthā agents, but by Dā'ūd Khān's deputy, Hīrāman, who would pay it to the Marāthās in a lump sum. The *jāgīrs* of the princes and the high grandees were to be exempt from any charge. No written confirmation of this agreement was given to the Marāthās,[85] but it could hardly have been made without the knowledge and active support of Zu'lifqār Khān, and the tacit consent of the emperor.

83 *Akhbārāt*, August 1710 to March 1711.

84 *Akhbārāt*, August 1710 to March 1711. Chandrasen's *wakīl* was presented to Dā'ūd Khān as early as January 1711.

85 K.K., 788, Rajwade viii, 56. Duff, i, 423 dates the agreement in 1709, but *Riyasat*, 68 places it in March 1711. Most authorities are silent on the date, I prefer the latter date on internal grounds—the perceptible decline in the scale of Marāthā operations in the Deccan after March 1711, and the fact that the death of Mun'im Khān in February 1711 had left the field clear for Zu'lfiqār Khān's policies.

The pact was a god-send to Shāhū for it bolstered his prestige in Mahārāshtra at a time when he had reached the nadir of his career. But it failed to bring peace to the unfortunate Deccan. The agreement 'gave birth to an infinity of bickerings and troubles, which always ended in some blood...the hands of the Marāthās stretched everywhere, their agents appeared in all places according to usage, and levied *chauth*'.[86] In December 1711, Mīr Aḥmad Khān, the Governor of Burhānpur, was killed in a fight against a band led by a woman, Tulsi Bāi.[87] The Marāthās beseiged Karnūl, Sholapur, Berinagar and many other places in the Karnātak. Aku Ghorpādē camped in the province with 70,000 men till he was chased across the river by Diler Khān and 'Abd-un-Nabī-Khān. The depredations of the Marāthās gave an opportunity to the *zamindars* who rose up everywhere, and the authority of the Mughals remained only in name in the Karnātak.[88]

Dā'ūd Khān's pact constituted a fundamental departure from the policy of Aurangzīb. The Marāthā claim for the *chauth* and *sardeshmukhi* of the Deccan was conceded in substance, though not in form. But this did not bring to the Mughal empire the benefits that might have been expected, viz., peace in the Deccan, and the establishment of friendly relations with the Marāthās. A major reason for this was that the Marāthā king had ceased to have any real control over the Marāthā chiefs, most of whom owed him only a tenuous allegiance and plundered largely on their own account. In other words, the forces of anarchy let loose in the Deccan as a result of the virtual destruction of the Marāthā state by Aurangzīb could not be controlled easily, or in a short time. Only the joint cooperation of the Mughal authority and the Marāthā King could bring the free-booting Marāthā chiefs under control once again. But past suspicions and Mughal arrogance stood in the path of such cooperation. The refusal of the Mughals to put the agreement for *chauth* and *sardeshmukhi* in writing served to keep suspicions alive, and emphasized the essentially temporary nature of the agreement. The intrigues of the Mughal officials in the Deccan with the domestic enemies of Shāhū also had an unsettling effect, and served to keep the Marāthā civil war going.

86 K.K., 738, 742.
87 *M.U.* iii, 764–5.
88 *Akhbārāt*, December 1711–July 1712.

THE SIKH UPRISING

On 4 May 1710, when the emperor was near the Narmada, news was received from the *dīwān* of Lahore of disturbances created by the Sikhs in the neighbourhood of Lahore and Sirhind under a man who gave himself out as Guru Govind. The emperor ordered the various *faujdārs* to take suitable action, but the uprising spread rapidly, and on 22 May 1710, Wazīr Khān, the *faujdār* of Sirhind, was defeated and killed, and the town ravaged and plundered.[89]

With the help of the local hill rajas and other (upper class) Hindu allies, and by relentless pressure Aurangzīb had been successful in crushing the rebellion of Guru Govind. But the underlying causes of the trouble had remained.[90] When Bahādur Shāh marched from Lahore to contest the throne with A'ẓam, Guru Govind joined him at the head of a small following, and received a *manṣab.* The Guru was present at the battle of Jājū, and, afterwards, accompanied Bahādur Shāh to Rājputānā and the Deccan. In November 1708, it was reported that the Guru had died and left much property behind. There are many stories of the Guru's death, all of which ascribe it, however, to an assault following personal enmity. Bahādur Shāh forebore from applying the law of escheat to his property as he was 'not in need of the property of a *darvēsh*'.[91]

There was apparent peace in the Punjab till the beginning of the Sikh revolt a year and a half later under Band who gave himself out as Guru Govind Singh. It was an age of superstition and the masses could easily be imposed upon. All contemporary authorities agree that the Guru drew his main support from the lower classes—the Jats and Khatris and 'people of such ignoble professions as the scavengers and leather-dressers'. Banda, the 'false guru,' amassed a following of 7,000–8,000 men with 4,000–5,000 ponies at first, but soon increased his strength to 17,000 and then

89 *Akhbārāt,* 5, *Rabī'* i, 23 *Rabī'* I; Irvine i, 96. The date 2 *Rabī'* ii, 30 May given by Irvine (p. 104) when news of the out-break first reached Bahādur Shāh is not correct.

90 See *Introduction* above.

91 *Akhbārāt*: entry d. 7 *Ramaẓān* Yr. 2, 19 November 1708. The traditional date of the Guru's death is 18th October 1708. For the controversy regarding the Guru's death, see I. B. Banerji, *Evolution of the Khalsa,* ii, 147–52; Irvine i, 90–1.

to 40,000 well-armed men. The *faujdārs* of Sonpat and Sirhind and many others were defeated in open battle, and the Sikhs besieged the towns of Sultanpur and Saharanpur, obtaining command of the whole area 'from a few days' march from Delhi to the outskirts of Lahore'.[92] In this area, the Sikhs set up their own administration. They appointed their own *thānedārs* and *taḥṣildārs* to collect revenue, and appointed commandants in the towns they over-ran. Usually, these officers were chosen from the lower classes. 'A low scavenger or leather-dresser had only to leave his home and join the Guru, when in a short space of time he would return to his birthplace with his order of appointment in his hand'.[93]

Even after making an allowance for exaggeration in such statements, the character of the Sikh uprising as a specific form of a lower class movement seems undeniable. The Sikhs persecuted the upper class Hindus no less than the Muslims, and, in most places, the local Hindu *zamindars* and wealthy people sided with the Mughal government. But the Sikhs lacked any clear social and political objectives. The necessary economic basis for the creation of a new and higher social order was lacking. The most that the Sikhs could aim at was a rough kind of egalitarian society with a peasant-clan basis. Such an attempt was bound to evoke the hostility of the privileged classes, and hence, could only hope to succeed if it could rapidly mobilize a large and growing number of peasants. But the religious basis of the Sikh movement restricted its appeal, and made a more rapid growth of the movement difficult.

Consequently, the Imperialists were able to recover from their initial surprise, and to assume the counter-offensive against the Sikhs. Asad Khān was ordered to march against the Guru. Chīn Qulīch Khān, Muḥammad Amīn Khān, Khān-i-Jahān the Governor of Allahabad, Saiyid 'Abdullāh Khān Bārahā and many others were deputed to help him, and suitable advances were made to them for completing their preparations.[94] At the end of June, the emperor left Ajmer and himself marched against the Sikhs. After opening the road between Delhi and Lahore which had been closed for many months, Bahādur Shāh fixed his headquarters at Sādhaurā near the foothills of the Himalayas where the Sikhs had built

92 K.K., 660, 672.
93 Wārid, 392, Irvine i, 98.
94 *Akhbārāt*, 28 June, 6 and 9 July 1710.

several forts for refuge. Lohgarh,[95] which had been built by Guru Govind, and where he and afterwards Banda lived in some sort of regal splendour, was stormed in December 1710. But the chief prize, Banda, got away. Bahādur Shāh blamed Mun'im Khān for his lack of care in allowing Banda to escape, and, according to some authorities, the fierce reproaches of the emperor hastened the death of the *wazīr.*

After the escape of Banda from Lohgarh, Bahādur Shāh seems to have lost interest in the affairs of the Sikhs. He returned to Lahore, leaving the Imperial armies to continue operations against Banda. Thereafter, desultory fighting continued, with the Imperial troops not advancing beyond the foothills and the Guru making occasional descents into the plains for purposes of plunder. The Imperial commanders, Rustam Dil and M. Amīn Khān, chased in vain after the Guru who adopted guerilla tactics and refused to face the Imperialists in a pitched battle. Evidently, the Guru had considerable local support in the plains. Thus, when he invaded the Baith Jālandhar, the Mughal commanders withdrew in panic, and the local Sikhs and their supporters seized the opportunity to slaughter the Mughal stragglers, and put their own armed posts in the towns of Batālā and Kālānaur and in the surrounding villages. When the Imperial armies re-established their sway, they took drastic action against the Sikhs and their sympathizers, many of the innocent suffering with the guilty.[96]

There was a spy scare in the royal camp itself, where many people were suspected of secretly being Sikhs and of passing on information to the Guru. Hence, an order was issued that all Hindus should shave their beards.[97] Hindu *faqīrs, jogis* and *sanyāsīs* who were suspected of spying for the Guru were also expelled from the royal camp.[98]

Inspite of these precautions and efforts and the presence of the emperor, the operations against the Guru were not very fruitful. One cause of this was the mutual jealousy and quarrel of the two

95 Situated half-way between Nāhan and Sādhaurā. Islām Shāh, son of Sher Shāh, had began to build a fort here under the name of Pāwāgarh. It was left unfinished at his death: the ruins remained till Banda restored and extended them. (*Imp. Gazetteer*).

96 Kāmwar, Irvine i, 119.

97 Kāmwar, *Akhbārāt,* 23, *Jam.* II, 19 August 1710.

98 *Akhbārāt,* 27, *Ramaẓān* Yr. 5, 9 November 1711.

Mughal commanders, which led to the disgrace and imprisonment of Rustam Dil in September 1711. In January 1712, when the emperor died, M. Amīn abandoned his post to take part in the civil war at Lahore, and the Guru, seizing his opportunity, recovered Sādhaurā and Lohgarh.[99]

Thus, in spite of concentrating large armies and the best generals in the Punjab for a year-and-a-half, Bahādur Shāh failed to crush the Sikh uprising. The basic cause of this must be considered not so much the weakness of the Imperialists as the nature of the Sikh uprising and the tactics of the Guru. The Sikhs once again proved the truth demonstrated earlier by the Marāthās and the Rājpūts that an army enjoying the support of the local population, making skilful use of the terrain, and led by commanders who followed the methods of guerilla warfare could hold out against a much superior enemy for a long time, if not indefinitely.

The Sikh movement assumed the character of a struggle for an independent Sikh state. If the attempt had succeeded, it would have given impetus to similar movements elsewhere, and largely altered the political picture of the eighteenth century.

DEATH OF MUN'IM KHĀN—BEGINNING OF THE STRUGGLE FOR WIZĀRAT

As has been stated earlier, Z̲u'lfiqār Khān looked upon Mun'im Khān as an interloper and was keen to regain the office of *wazīr* for his family. On 28 February 1711, Mun'im Khān died after a short illness. His death once more brought the question of *wizārat* to the fore. Asad Khān and Z̲u'lfiqār Khān had yielded the *wizārat* to Mun'im Khān very reluctantly. Z̲u'lfiqār Khān now considered that he had the best claim to the vacant office. At first, Prince 'Aẓīm-ush-Shān who occupied a position of great influence at his father's court was of the same view. He and Sa'dullāh Khān,[100] the *dīwan-i-tan* and *khāliṣah*, proposed that Z̲u'lfiqār Khān should be made the *wazīr*, while the sons of Mun'im Khān, Mahābat Khān and

99 *M.M.*, 42 b–44 b, Irvine i, 121.

100 He was the son of 'Ināyatullāh Khān, the *Mīr Munshī* of Aurganzīb. We are told that in ability and hard work he had no parallel in his time, and was considered a second 'Ināyatullāh, nay, even superior to him (M.M., 68 b, *M.U.* ii, 827).

Khān-i-Zamān[101]—should be appointed *mīr bakhshī* and Viceroy of the Deccan respectively. 'Aẕīm-ush-Shān thereby wanted to keep on the right side of Z̲u'lfiqār Khān and, at the same time, to reward the sons of Mun'im Khān who, of late, had become his great friends. But the proposal was opposed by Z̲u'lfiqār Khān and the emperor. The former was not prepared to give up the post of the either chief *bakhshī* or that of the Viceroy of the Deccan. He, therefore, claimed the post of *wazīr* for his father while himself remaining *mīr bakhshī* and the Viceroy of the Deccan. Bahādur Shāh's objection was that the sons of Mun'im Khān were unfit for the posts proposed for them.[102] As for Z̲u'lfiqār Khān's claims, there was no precedent that three powerful posts such as those of the *wazīr*, the chief *bakhshī* and the Viceroy of the Deccan should be held by members of one family, and Bahādur Shāh rightly held that it would be dangerous for the dynasty, 'Aẕīm-ush-Shān was inclined to agree with this view. Hence, Z̲u'lfiqār Khān's demands were turned down. It was then proposed that the Ṣafwid prince, Muḥammad Hāshim, should be formally appointed the *wazīr*, and one of the *bakhshī*s should be asked to carry on his duties. But the prince caused so much offence by his haughty ways that this proposal also fell through. In the end, no *wazīr* was appointed and, as a temporary measure, Sa'dullāh Khān was made the chief *dīwān* and asked to carry on work under the 'supervision and control of Prince 'Aẕīm-ush-Shān'.[103]

It would not be correct to see in this dispute only the overwhelming pride and ambitiousness of Z̲u'lfiqār Khān. Z̲u'lfiqār Khān seems to have come to the conclusion that circumstances demanded the concentration of power in the hands of one man. This belief may be traced back, perhaps, to the latter years of Aurangzīb's reign when the Imperial arms suffered a number of reverses, and was apparently strengthened during the reign of Bahādur Shāh, when Imperial policy seemed to lack a sense of

101 Mahābat K. occupied the rank of 5,000/5,000 at the time, and held the office of third *bakhshī*. Khān-i-Zamān held the rank of 4,000/3,000 (*M.U.* ii, 677).

102 K.K., 677–8, *M.U.* ii, 98.

103 '*Bah niyābat wa iṭṭalā' -i-pādshāhzādah*'—K.K., 678, *M.U.* ii, 98, 831, 504, iii, 677–82. The English factor at Cossimbazar reported that the Emperor had promoted 'Aẕīm-ush-Shān to the 'sole management of all affairs under him' (Wilson ii, p. 16).

direction. Z̲u'lfiqār Khān seems to have felt that the Mughal empire could be saved from imminent disruption only by a person with a close personal knowledge of Imperial affairs, who was able to win the confidence of the Rājpūts, Marāthās, and the Hindus. At the same time it was important to be able to secure the support of the old nobles.[104] Such a person, Z̲u'lfiqār Khān flattered himself, could only be he. From these conclusions followed certain others. Firstly, that the *wazīr* must be made the hub of all affairs, and should control not only the executive and financial affairs which were his special province, but also the army which was the special charge of the chief *bakhshī*. He must also be vested with authority over some *ṣūbahs*, with large resources, otherwise he would not be able to maintain his position in face of the jealousy and hostility which he would inevitably meet from a section of the nobles.

Thus, Z̲u'lfiqār Khān's ambition was not necessarily a guilty or traitorous ambition. But Z̲u'lfiqār Khān's concept of the *wizārat* implied a radical departure from the traditions which had been established under the Mughal sovereigns in India, and re-created the possibility of a serious struggle between the *wazīr* and the monarchy, and between the *wazīr* and the nobles.

Thus, with the death of Mun'im Khān, party struggle at the court moved into fresh grooves and led to new developments which shall be studied hereafter.

General Policy and Administration

From the foregoing account, it should be clear that under Bahādur Shāh, a gradual departure was made from the policies of Aurangzīb. This departure was fairly marked in the sphere of the relations with the Marāthās and, to a smaller extent, with the Rājpūts. But in the case of the Sikhs, for special reasons, the old policy of repression was pursued with renewed vigour.

104 Belief in the imminent disintegration of the Mughal empire was so widespread towards the end of Aurangzīb's reign that Aurangzīb himself echoed them in a number of his letters. Thus, he wrote to Bahādur Shāh '...it is written that after me will come an Emperor, ignorant, narrow-minded, overpowered by injuries—whose words will be all imperfect and whose plans will be all immature. He will act towards some men with so much prodigality as almost to drown them, and towards others with so much vigour as to raise the fear of destruction,...' (*Aḥkām*, 12).

A cautious and hesitating departure from Aurangzīb's policies is visible in the sphere of religious policy and in the dealings of the emperor with his Hindu subjects. Thus, the ban on drinking, and on singing and dancing in the royal court continued[105]—though Bahādur Shāh was far from sharing his father's orthodox outlook. He was a *ṣūfi*—like his *wazīr*, Mun'im Khān—and incurred the displeasure of the orthodox circles by assuming the title of 'Saiyid'. His attempt to have the word '*waṣī*' or heir inserted in the Friday *khuṭbah* after the name of 'Alī led to widespread rioting, and had to be abandoned.[106] However, it led to a definite breach between the Emperor and the orthodox section.

As far as Bahādur Shāh's dealings with the Hindus are concerned, we do not hear of the destruction of any temples or forced conversions in his reign. But the ban on the use of *pālkī*s and 'Arabī and 'Irāqī horses, *rath*s and elephants by Hindus was re-affirmed,[107] and they were also directed not to wear pearls in their ears, and to trim their beards.[108] He is also said to have issued an order that Hindus were not to be employed as news-reporters in the provinces. *Jizyah*, while not formally abolished, seems to have fallen gradually into disuse.[109] Thus, distrust of the Hindus, engendered by political conflict and other factors had not yet been given up, but the orthodox approach was being gradually modified.

105 *Akhbārāt*, 31 August 1709, *B.N.*, 182, 443. According to Manucci (iii, p. 254) Bahādur Shāh indulged in wine drinking himself.

106 K.K., 603, 661, 681; *Akhbārāt*.

107 *B.N.*, 1 *Jamāda* II Yr. 1, 30 August 1707; *Akhbārāt*, 23 *Ramaẓān* yr. 1, 24 *Jam.* II yr. 3, 18 November 1707, 18 December 1708 (re-affirmation of the order).

The exact meaning and scope of this order is not clear. Grant of *Pālkīs* and of 'Arabī and 'Irāqī horses to Hindu Rajas is recorded more than once (*Akhbārāt*; entry d. 17 *Shawwāl* yr. 3, 20 December 1709—to Shāhū; 19 *Jam.* II yr. 4, 6 August 1710 to Raṇa Amar Singh, etc.). From an entry d. 28 January 1708, it appears that soldiers were excluded from the scope of this order. Hence, it would appear that the order applied only to junior Hindu nobles, administrative officials and others who tried to ape the great nobles.

108 *Akhbārāt*, 24 *Ramaẓān* yr. 1, 18 November 1707. Thus, the order was passed much before the Sikh uprising.

109 It was levied at the time of the first Rājpūt War (K.K., 606), but according to Wārid (p. 6), 'in the reign of Bahādur Sḥāh, *jizyah* had fallen into disuse'. According to *V.V.* (p. 395), towards the close of his reign, Bahādur Shāh had contemplated abolishing the *jizyah*, but died before he could do so.

Bahadur Shāh tried unsuccessfully to wrest back from Maharana Amar Singh II the *parganas* of Pur, Māndal and Bidnur which had been ceded to the Mughals in lieu of *jizyah* in 1681, and which had been recovered by the Rana after the death of Aurangzīb. We are also told that when Bahādur Shāh entered Rājpūtānā in 1707–8, since the salaries of the army was in arrears for 40 months, 'mischievous and inconsiderate infantrymen started pressing the indigent Hindus for the payment of *jizyah*'.[110]

In 1710, when Bahādur Shāh was returning from the Deccan, the residents of *Qaṣba* Atodā in Kotah petitioned their ruler, Bhim Singh, for relief from *jizyah*. Bhim Singh replied that if the residents of the neighbouring areas paid *jizyah*, they should also pay.

In an extant paper dated 14 *Rabī*'II R.Y. 5, 2 May 1711, Jai Singh pleaded with Muḥammad Taqī, the *dīwān* of *ṣūbah* Agra, that the residents in his *watan* were unable to pay *jizyah* due to their miserable plight. However, the raja deputed his officials to co-operate with the *amīn-i-jizyah*.[111]

It appears from the above that *jizyah* continued to be levied irregularly in different parts of the empire till the end of Bahādur Shāh's reign. Wārid merely says that in the reign of Bahādur Shāh the orders about *jizyah* had become 'old' i.e. feeble (*taqvīm-i-pārīn*) signifying that they were not enforced strictly.[112]

However, the advantages that might have been secured by the adoption of a more liberal and conciliatory policy were off-set by a deterioration in the sphere of administration, and especially of finances. Bahādur Shāh possessed neither the inclination nor the aptitude for administrative affairs. According to Khāfī Khān '...such negligence was shown in the protection of the state and in the government and management of the country, that witty, sarcastic people found the date of his accession in the words *Shāh-i-bī-khabr*'.[113] However, Bahādur Shāh's neglect of administration was partly made good by Mun'im Khān, the *wazīr*, who was 'a very good man of business', and by Hidāyatullāh Khān (Sa'dullāh Khān), the *dīwān-i-tan* and *khāliṣāh* who 'in ability and capacity for hard work had no equal in his time'.[114]

110 Kāmraj, '*Ibratnāmah*, f. 41a.
111 R. S. A. No. 2478.
112 Wārid, 6.
113 K.K., 628.
114 *M.U.* iii, 675, ii, 827.

Bahādur Shāh was most liberal to all, including the *ulama,* in the grant of lands. He allotted half of Chakla Bareilly, which was in *khāliṣah,* as *madad-i-maash.* When the *mutṣaddīs* objected, he observed, like Aurangzib earlier, that the world was wide, i.e. large enough. The process of alienation of *khāliṣah* lands continued apace under his successors.[115]

The deterioration in the financial situation was a serious matter. From a very early period in the history of the Mughal empire, the kings had been faced with the problem of finding sufficient land for being assigned as *jāgīr* to all their officers. The problem had become progressively more acute, till it had reached the proportions of a crisis in the time of Aurangzīb, as has been noticed earlier. Bahādur Shāh on his accession made it worse by a reckless grant of *jāgīr* and promotions and rewards to all and sundry—so much so that according to Bhīmsen even clerks secured high *manṣabs.*[116] This state of affairs alarmed Ikhlāṣ Khān, the *'arẓ-i-mukarrar,* who was noted for his ability and integrity, and for his strictness in revenue matters and in the taking of accounts. He represented to the *wazīr* that the reckless prodigality of the king was against prudence and the interests of the state, and that leave alone India, the whole world would not suffice to provide *jāgīrs* to all those whom he favoured. He suggested that the *wazīr* should institute an enquiry into the suitability of the appointees, and whether the proposed rank or promotion or reward was not more than they deserved. But neither Mun'im Khān nor Ikhlāṣ Khān were prepared to face the unpopularity of conducting such an enquiry themselves. Ultimately, Muḥammad Sādī Musta'id Khān, the historian, was entrusted with the job. Before an application was forwarded by the '*arẓ-i-mukarrar* and the *wazīr* to the emperor, it had to be checked and certified by Musta'id Khān. But this entailed inordinate delay. The two leading queens, Mihr Parwar and Amatul Ḥabīb, and some other persons close to the emperor started the practice of securing his signature on their applications without referring them to Musta'id Khān for enquiry and approval. But little heed was often paid to such (irregular) grants (by the revenue department). The king instructed the *mutṣaddīs* to do

115 T. *Hindi,* 425.
116 *Dil.,* 167a, *Harcharandas,* 17.

what they thought was proper, with-out heeding his signature which, in consequence, lost its value.[117]

We do not know to what extent Mun'im Khān, Ikhlāṣ Khān and Musta'id Khān could place a check upon the reckless grants of Bahādur Shāh. But the growing crisis of the *jāgīrdārī* system could scarcely be checked by these half-hearted measures. The real nature of the crisis is amply illustrated by the following. It had been the practice of previous emperors that the *manṣabdārs* were required to pay for the upkeep of the royal animals, (or more correctly, the royal transport corps). These expenses continued to be demanded by the *ākhtā bēgīs* and the other *mutṣaddīs* from the *wakīls* of the *manṣabdārs* inspite of the fact that during the reign of Aurangzīb, the income of the *jāgīrs* was very uncertain, and many of them remained deserted and uncultivated. The *jāgīrs* were also in very short supply and after considerable delay and difficulty, the *manṣabdārs* could get only a small *jāgīr*. Notwithstanding this, the *mutṣaddīs* continued to demand the expenses for the upkeep of the animals in full, although the entire income of the *jāgīr* was less than ('was not half or a third of') these sums. Under these circumstances, the distress of the families of the *manṣabdārs* can be imagined. The representations of the *wakīls* of the *manṣabdārs* were of no avail, and they were subjected to torture, imprisonment and harrasment of every kind to make them pay the dues in full. Things reached such a pass that the *wakīls* of the *manṣabdārs* began to resign their jobs in protest.[118]

At length, Mun'im Khān instituted a reform. He passed orders that after a *manṣabdār* had been allotted a *jāgīr*, (but not till then), the charges for feeding the animals should be deducted from his total emoluments, and the balance paid to him as *tankhwāh*.[119] In other words, the upkeep of the animals no longer remained a charge upon the salary of the nobles, but became a central responsibility, and the emoluments of the nobles were scaled

117 K.K., 628–30. The passage is rather obscure at places. *Cf.* Irvine i, 139 for a slightly different version.

118 K.K., 602–3. This passage also is very obscure. *Cf.* Irvine, *Army of the Mughals*, 22.

119 Literally, 'salary', but this salary could be paid in cash (*naqadī*), or by means of a *jāgīr* (*tankhwāh jāgīr*).

down accordingly. 'In this way, the burden of the expenses of the animals was taken away completely from the shoulders of the *manṣabdārs* and their *wakīls*. Actually, the real significance of this order was that the expenses of animals were remitted altogether'.[120]

The reform undoubtedly constituted a substantial relief to the *manṣabdārs*, but it increased proportionately the responsibility of the central government. Keeping in mind the liberality of Bahādur Shāh in the matter of granting *jāgīrs*, it may be doubted whether he was able to keep in *khāliṣah* the lands thus deducted from the *jāgīrs* of the nobles, and to realize from them the funds for the unkeep of the royal animals. Thus, the burden on the state exchequer probably grew.

In any case, there can be little doubt about the serious financial situation in the time of Bahādur Shāh. We are told that when Bahādur Shāh ascended the throne, he found 13 crores coined and uncoined gold and silver in the Agra fort. By the end of the reign, all this had been spent! Khāfī Khān remarks: 'The income of the empire during his (Bahādur Shāh's) reign was insufficient to meet the expenses, and consequently there was great parsimony shown in the government establishments, but specially in the royal household, so much so that money was received every day from the treasury of Prince 'Aẓīm-ush-Shān to keep things going'.[121] The artillery-men in the royal retinue (*wālā-shāhīs*) complained that their salary was six years in arrears.[122]

Thus, the reign of Bahādur Shāh witnessed a sharp deterioration in the financial situation and a further accentuation of the crisis of the *jāgīrdārī* system, although Mun'im Khān and a few others sought to check the worst abuses and to prevent a reckless growth in the ranks and numbers of the *manṣabdārs* and other grantees. In the realm of policy, the association of the state with religious orthodoxy was considerably weakened, a more tolerant attitude was adopted towards the Hindus, and the rigid approach of Aurangzīb to the Rājpūt and Marāthā problems was gradually modified. But these new approaches were still too tentative and half-hearted to yield any definite results. It appears that by a

120 K.K., 602–3.
121 K.K., 683,
122 *Akhbārāt*, 26 October 1711.

process of trial and error, Bahādur Shāh was feeling his way towards a more liberal and acceptable policy, and that he might have succeeded in evolving lasting solutions to some of the problems if he had lived longer. As it was, he failed to reap any definite political advantages from his policy of cautious compromise, and bequeathed to his successors a more difficult situation than the one he had inherited.

CHAPTER III

Z̲u'lfiqār Kh̲ān Struggles for Wizārat

The Problem of Wizārat

The death of Mun'im Kh̲ān brought to the fore the problem which was to dominate politics at the court practically for the next two decades, and which became the focal point, as it were, of all the other problems of the Mughal empire. This was the problem of choosing a satisfactory *wazīr*. The *wazīr* may be called the king-pin of medieval administration, in the Middle East as well as in India. The relationship of the *wazīr* with the king had always posed a problem, for a too powerful *wazīr* threatened to out-top and, ultimately, to displace the king himself, while a *wazīr* who was not powerful enough often proved ineffective.[1] Akbar had attempted to solve the problem by dividing the work of the central government among a number of officials, more or less of the same standing. He entrusted the charge of the revenue department to *dīwans* who were appointed primarily for their expert knowledge of financial and administrative affairs, and who did not necessarily occupy a pre-eminent position in the official hierarchy.[2] Thus, Akbar's *wazīrs* derived their importance from the trust reposed in them by the emperor, and by their position as heads of the finance department.

1 For a fuller discussion, see Tripathi, *Some Aspects of Muslim Administration*, 161–4.

2 *Cf.* Tripathi, *loc. cit.*, 197–209.

But gradually the position of the *wazīr* as the premier noble at the court was re-asserted. During the latter years of Jahāngīr's reign, and more specially during the reign of Shāh Jahān, some of the most eminent nobles of the time were appointed *wazīrs*.[3] In the time of Aurangzīb, at first Mīr Jumlah was appointed the *wazīr* as a reward for his services in securing the throne for Aurangzīb. He was succeeded by Jumdat-ul-Mulk Asad Khān. Both these incumbents held the highest rank obtainable by a noble—that of 7,000/7,000. Apart from transacting the business of their office, they were also entrusted, at one time or another, with important military commands. Thus, by the time Aurangzīb died, the old pre-Mughal tradition of the *wazīr* being the premier noble at the court and the leading counsellor of the king, apart from being the head of the finance department, had been largely re-established. Apart from this, the *wazīr*'s post carried with it substantial patronage and opportunities for private gain. Little wonder, therefore, that the *wazīr*'s office came to be considered a prize post and became the object of much back-stair intrigue among the nobles.

In spite of this subtle change in the character of the *wizārat*, the *wazīrs* posed no threat to the established monarchy in the time of Shāh Jahān and Aurangīb. The personal capacity of these monarchs, and the immense prestige of the Mughal monarchy sufficed to keep the *wazīrs* in their proper place. But whether the institution of *wizārat* would function equally well when a weak, lazy or incompetent king came to the throne was a question which could not be visualized at the time. It seems that the question did agitate the mind of Aurangzīb at times, but he contented himself with the hope that Asad Khān whom he had trained, would somehow tide over the problem.[4] He also toyed with the idea of partition of empire, as has been already noted.

The triumph of Bahādur Shāh in the war of succession led to the elevation of Mun'im Khān to the *wizārat*. He was, till then, only a petty *manṣabdār*, and he owed his appointment entirely to the services rendered by him to Bahādur Shāh in securing the throne. Apart from being appointed the *wazīr*, Mun'im Khān was

3 Thus, the name of Āṣaf Khān in the time of Jahāngīr and of Sa'dullāh K. in the time of Shāh Jahān might be mentioned. Both held the rank of 7,000/7,000.

4 *Aḥkām*, 11.

also rewarded with the rank of 7,000/7,000 (*dū-aspah, sih-aspah*), the (absentee) governorship of Lahore, and numerous gifts in cash and in kind.[5] In a way, the grant of the rank of 7,000/7,000 to Mun'im Khān is even more significant than his appointment as the *wazīr*, for it shows that the idea of the *wazīr* being the pre-eminent noble at the court, and not merely a financial expert was so generally accepted by this time that his sudden elevation from the rank of 1,500 to that of 7,000 occasioned no surprise to anyone—though hardly a single instance of such rapid promotion is met with till that time.[6] The other privileges granted to Mun'im Khān merely serve to emphasize the same point.

The possibility of a clash between a *wazīr* who enjoyed a pre-eminent position in the nobility, and the monarch was avoided in the time of Bahādur Shāh by a number of factors. In the first place, Mun'im Khān never forgot that he owed his position entirely to Bahādur Shāh, and never allowed himself to presume upon his position or past services. He used to say, 'Sovereignty is the particular gift of God, and that no obligation could be laid on sovereigns, so that if anyone thought himself conductive to their success, it was in them vanity and folly'.[7] Secondly, Mun'im Khān was not the leader of any powerful faction in the nobility, so that Bahādur Shāh had no occasion to be jealous or afraid of his power. He was glad to let Mun'im Khān assume the burden of administration, and was sensible enough not to interfere in the conduct of day-to-day affairs, or allow others to do so. In the third place, Mun'im Khān, while not an outstanding administrator, was at least a moderately competent one. He won the respect of everyone by his dignified bearing, his learning, and his consideration for the old, 'Ālamgīrī nobles.[8] But such a happy combination of favourable factors was unlikely to recur, and the

5 *B.N.*, 104, K.K., 626, Kāmwar, 14.

6 The rank of Mun'im Khān was 1,500/1,000 when Aurangzīb died, but he had been raised to the rank of 5,000/5,000 before the battle of Jājū (K.K., 575).

7 Īrādat, 51.

8 'The *wazīr* (Mun'im Khān) had taken pains to convince his master that the ancient nobility were the pillars of the state, and that the welfare of the empire depended on their persons. Their ancestors had held offices, and acquired respect and influence with the people so that it was proper and politic to employ them' (Īrādat, 53–4).

difficulty which Bahādur Shāh encountered in finding a suitable successor to Mun'im Khān posed the problem of *wizārat* sharply. The ultimate solution adopted by Bahādur Shāh—that of dividing up the work of the *wazīr* between several persons—suggested that one solution was to tread the way back to Akbar's practice. But before the traditions of Akbar in this matter could be fully revived. Bahādur Shāh died. This threw the whole question of *wizārat* into the melting pot again.

Z̲u'lfiqār Khān and The League of the Three Princes

After the rebuff suffered by him in securing the post of *wazīr* for his family, Z̲u'lfiqār Khān adopted new tactics for the fulfilment of his ambition. The primary object of his schemes was to checkmate Prince 'Aẕīm-ush-Shān whom he regarded as the principal obstacle in his way to the *wizārat.* 'Aẕīm-ush-Shān was the most energetic and capable of the sons of Bahādur Shāh. He had attracted the attention of Aurangzīb at an early age, and was one of his favourites. As the Governor of Bengal from 1697 to 1706, he had accumulated a vast fortune by monopolizing the internal trade of the province.[9] His role in securing the throne for Bahādur Shāh, and his influence at the court of the latter has been already noted. Soon, he had so far out-stripped his other three brothers—Jahāndār Shāh, Rafi-ush-Shān and Jahān Shāh in wealth, power and influence that it was considered they had no chance against him in a war of succession. In order to realize his ambition, Z̲u'lfiqār Khān now strove to unite the three brothers in a coalition against 'Aẕīm-ush-Shān, on the basis of an agreement to partition the empire.[10]

Thus, the most powerful prince and the most powerful noble at the court were openly ranged against each other. It was in this sense that the civil war at Lahore which followed the death of Bahādur Shāh was different from all the previous civil wars fought by the Mughal princes in India.

Till the last moment, Z̲u'lfiqār Khān was uncertain of his success, and made approaches to 'Aẕīm-ush-Shān for a settlement.

9 *Riyāẓ*, 246, K.K. ii, 686. This practice had brought him a stinging reproof from Aurangzīb.

10 M.M., 9a, K.K., 685.

The precise terms desired by Z̲u'lfiqār Khān are not known. At any rate, the approach which he made through the historian, Irādat Khān, immediately after Bahādur Shāh's death, was curtly turned down by Shaikh Qudratullāh[11] on behalf of 'Aẕīm-ush-Shān, and Z̲u'lfiqār was asked to submit without delay for 'there was no question of any other place'.[12] Approaches through the sons of Mun'im Khān, likewise, bore no fruit.[13]

The nature of Z̲u'lfiqār Khān's ambition may be guaged by the scheme for the partition of the empire which he is said to have drawn up at this time, or a little earlier. According to the scheme, the entire Deccan south of the Narmada was to go to Jahān Shāh; Multan, Thatta and Kashmir to Rafi-ush-Shān, and the rest to Jahāndār Shāh. A novel feature of the scheme was that Z̲u'lfiqār Khān was to be the common *wazīr* for all the three brothers. He was to reside at the court of Jahāndār Shāh in whose name the coins were to be issued and *khuṭbah* read throughout the country, and to exercise his functions through deputies at the court of the other brothers.[14]

It is difficult to decide if the revival of the idea of partitioning of the empire by Z̲u'lfiqār Khān was a confession of bankruptcy in solving the vexed problem of succession, or was in the nature of an experiment to apply the old solution in a new way. The idea of division had failed in the time of Humāyūn, its futility had been further demonstrated in the time of Shāh Jahān and after the death of Aurangzīb. Perhaps, like Aurangzīb, Z̲u'lfiqār felt that the empire had become too unwieldy to be governed effectively from one centre, and that a scheme for decentralization was called for. In Z̲u'lfiqār's scheme, an attempt was made to bring about

11 He is frequently mentioned in the *wakīl's* reports of the period, and is said to have been so influential that even the sons of Mun'im Khān had to make their representations through him. He is also said to have been responsible for Z̲u'lfiqār's exclusion from the *wizārat* in 1711 (M.M., 29b, *V.V.*, 943–6, 952).

12 Īrādat, 76.

13 Nūr-ud-Dīn, 9a.

14 Qāsim, 42–3, *M.U.* ii, 99, *Wārid*, 195, 217. According to Wārid, it was also agreed that Jahāndār would keep 100,000 horses, Rafi-ush-Shān 80,000 and Jahān Shāh 60,000.

Nūr-ud-Dīn (p. 14a) says, however, that the various parts were to be ruled independently by each prince who would be called *Pādshāh.*

decentralization while preserving the basic unity of the empire. Thus, the eldest brother was to be the symbol of unity, and its pivot the *wazīr:* The emperor would reign, and the *wazīr* rule. If the scheme had been implemented, real power would have shifted into the hands of the *wazīr*. According to some authorities, the scheme for partition had originally included 'Aẕīm-ush-Shān, and been formulated with his consent. But in his pride of wealth and soldiers 'Aẕīm-ush-Shān, it is alleged, turned false to his promise after the death of Bahādur Shāh, so that the other princes had no option but to resort to war against him, and allotted the share of 'Aẕīm-ush-Shān to Jahāndār Shāh.[15] It is scarcely likely, however, that 'Aẕīm-ush-Shān could have consented to a scheme which would place real power in the hands of a *wazīr*. The scheme for partition must therefore be regarded as essentially a plan by Zu'lfiqār Khān to realize his ambition of exercising supreme power.

We need not follow in detail the subsequent fighting among the princes. All observers agree that it was largely due to the vigour and intrepidity of Zu'lfiqār Khān that the three princes gained a complete victory over 'Aẕīm-ush-Shān who made the error of standing on the defensive, in the mistaken belief that since his treasure exceeded those of his brothers, their armies would soon melt away and he would gain victory without striking a blow. Zu'lfiqār Khān thus got a chance to seize the initiative. He cut off 'Aẕīm-ush-Shān from Lahore, and secured possession of the treasures as well as the heavy artillery stored in the fort. He then closely invested 'Aẕīm-ush-Shān in his camp.[16]

Probably, the real reason for 'Aẕīm-ush-Shān's conduct was the numerical inferiority of his army compared to those of his brothers.[17] 'Aẕīm-ush-Shān seems also to have hoped for discord

15 *Inshā-i-Mādho Rām,* 73, K.K. ii, 685. But Cf. Kh. Khalīl, a contemporary observer, who says that *Zu'lfiqār Khān* instigated the fight so that the *wizārat* might come to him (*T. Shāhanshāhī*).

16 M.M., 9a, Qāsim, 44.

17 Valentyn iv, 294 estimated the contending forces as follows:

	Horse	Foot
Jahāndār Shāh	20,000	30,000
Rafī-ush-Shān	8,000	8,000
Jahān Shāh	25,000	30,000
	53,000	68,000
'Aẕim-ush-Shān	30,000	30,000

among his brothers whose capacities he despised, and for reinforcements from Chīn Qulīch Khān and others.[18] But he was overwhelmed by the combined armies of his brothers before help could reach from any quarter, and after his army had been thinned by hunger and desertions.

After the defeat and death of 'Aẕīm-ush-Shān, a contention arose between the three brothers about the division of the spoils. Zu'lfiqār Khān had favoured Jahāndār Shāh from the first. Perhaps, as Īrādat suggests, the reason was that Jahāndār was 'a weak prince, fond of his pleasure, averse from business and consequently best suited to the purpose of a minister ambitious of uncontrolled power'.[19] According to another observer, Bahādur Shāh had also made a declaration from his death bed recommending Jahāndār Shāh.[20]

The support of Zu'lfiqār Khān proved the decisive factor in securing victory for Jahāndār Shāh over his other two brothers. On 29 March 1712, a month after the death of Bahādur Shāh, Jahāndār Shāh formally ascended the throne, and was proclaimed the Emperor.

Zu'lfiqār Khān as Wazīr—His Power and Position

After Jahāndār Shāh's accession, Zu'lfiqār Khān became the *wazīr* almost as a matter of right. He also retained the viceroyalty of the Deccan which he continued to govern through his deputy, Dā'ūd Khān. Further, he was accorded the unprecedented rank of 10,000/10,000 *dū-aspah*[21] by the new emperor, and he enjoyed the status and privileges of a prince.[22] His father, Asad Khān,

18 See p. 116 below.
19 Īrādat, 72, Qāsim, 16, 17, Kāmwar, 116–17, and M.M., 10b all substantially agree with Īrādat.
20 Valentyn (*J.U.P.H.S.*, 211), but doubtful since the Dutch had an interest in the victory of Jahāndār.
21 *Akhbārāt*, 1 April 1712. But Harcharan, 24, Wārid, 218, and B.M., 1690 (quoted by Irvine in *J.A.S.B.*, 1896, 161) place his rank at 12,000; Kāmwar, 393, Nūr-ud-Dīn 34b and Yahyā place it at 8,000; *Jauhar* (A.S.B.Ms) f. 35b places it at 10,000.
22 *Akhbārāt*, 3, 7 April 1712. He was also given 4 crore *dām* as *in'ām*, 10 lakh *huns as sih-bandī* and the title of *Yār-i-Wafādār*.

remained the *wakīl-i-muṭtlaq* as before, and received the (absentee) governorship of Gujārāt, and the rank of 12,000/12,000. Jahāndār treated him with great respect, and used to call him uncle (*amwī*).[23] But Asad Khān refrained from taking any interest in public affairs and seldom went to the court. All power remained in the hands of Z̲u'lfiqār Khān, and in all matters relating to war and peace, Jahāndār was guided by his advice.[24] One of Z̲u'lfiqār's protégés, 'Abdus-Ṣamad Khān,[25] was made the *ṣadr* with the rank of 7,000. Sabhā Chand, the *dīwān* of Z̲u'lfiqār Khān, was given the title of Raja, and appointed the *dīwān-i-khāliṣah-sharīfah* (*dīwān* of the crownlands).[26]

Z̲u'lifqār Khān seemed, thus, to have realized his ambitions fully. But he soon discovered that he did not wield as much power as he felt he had a right to expect. This was on account of the underhand opposition of a group of royal favourites who poisoned the ears of the emperor regarding the *wazīr* and interfered in the affairs of the administration. Chief among these favourites was Kokaltāsh Khān, the foster-brother (*koka*) of the emperor. For a long time, Kokaltāsh had been the friend, confidant and guide of

23 *Akhbārāt*, 1 April 1712, Harcharan, 24, Wārid, 218, and Yahyā, 118b. But B.M., 1690 (as quoted in *J.A.S.B.*, 1896) says that his rank was 16,000. No mention by K.K. or Kāmwar.

Whenever Asad Khān went to the court, Jahāndār treated him with great respect and made him sit near the throne (*Jauhar*, 35b).

24 *Siyar*, 392.

25 A Tūrānī adventurer, he had served in the Deccan for a long time. In Bahādur Shāh's reign, he came into prominence, and entered into a marriage alliance with the powerful Chīn family. But some time after this; he fell out with 'Aẕīm-ush-Shān who was then all powerful. At the instance of the latter, he was disgraced, all his property was confiscated, and he was ordered to proceed to Mecca. Just then Bahādur Shāh died. Deeming him a fit instrument for use against 'Aẕim-ush-Shān, Z̲u'lfiqār summoned 'Abduṣ-Ṣamad, and the latter did good service as *mīr ātish* against 'Aẕim-ush-Shān (Wārid, Irvine i, 180–90).

Jauhar (36a) places his rank at 4,000/4,000 only.

26 *Akhbārāt*, 6 April 1712, Valentyn iv, 295, Kāmwar. He was a kayasth and had long been in the service of Zu'lfiqār Khān. On Z̲u'lfiqār's elevation to the *wizārat*, he was also raised from the rank of 900/300 to that of 2,000/1,000. *T Mhdi.* says that he died in *Jamāda I* 1137/January–February 1725, aged nearly 70. Hence, at this time, he must have been 58 years old.

Jahāndār Shāh, and held the charge of all the affairs of that prince.[27] Jahāndār Shāh had promised the *wizārat* to Kokaltāsh if he should become the emperor. Kokaltāsh now deeply resented his exclusion from the *wizārat*, which was inevitable under the circumstances. Not only Kokaltāsh but his entire family—mother, wife and daughter who had close relations with the royal family, bitterly resented his supersession, and constantly intrigued to displace Zu'lfiqār Khān. They played upon Jahāndār's fears, and tried to convince him that 'the *amīr-ul-umarā* entertained designs too ambitious for a subject, to attain which he would dare to shed the blood of princes; that he had already determined upon a revolution, either to seize the throne for himself, or otherwise, if he found that too dangerous, to bestow it on 'Alī Tabār (only surviving son of 'Aẕīm-ush-Shān) or another of the confined princes, more favourable to him than His Majesty'.[28]

Jahāndār allowed himself to be influenced by these suggestions because he disliked the extreme sternness of the masterful *wazīr*, and believed that Kokaltāsh Khān would be more amenable to his wishes. Hence, Kokaltāsh Khān was raised to the rank of 9,000/9,000,[29] and accorded the office of the *mīr bakhshī*; his brother, A'ẓam Khān was promoted to the rank of 8,000 and appointed the Governor of Agra; while his brother-in-law, Khwājah Ḥasan Khān-i-Daurān, was promoted to the rank of 8,000/8,000, and appointed the second *bakhshī*.[30] Kokaltāsh Khān was joined by Sa'dullāh Khān who held the post of the *khān-i-sāman* with the rank of 5,000,

27 Wārid, 223–5, Khush-ḥāl, 68, *M.U.* ii, 100. He had been Jahāndār's deputy in Multan, and in the time of Bahādur Shāh, received the *manṣab* of 2,500/2,250, and the title of Kokaltāsh Khān (*Akhbārāt*, 5 January 1709).

28 Irādat, 97.

29 *Akhbārāt*, 25 April 1712, *Jauhar*, 35 b, *M.U.* i, 817, B.M., 1690 (in *J.A.S.B.*, 1896, *loc. cit.*). However, Wārid, 218 and Harcharan, 24 place his rank at 12,000. Yahyā places it at 7,000 only.

Kokaltāsh was also made the Governor of Multan and Thatta and the *faujdār* of Bakkhar (*Akhbārāt, 26, Ṣafar*, 4 April).

30 *Akhbārāt*, 25 April, 7 and 25 August 1712, Kāmwar, 303, *Jauhar*, 35b, *M.U.* i, 817, K.K., 716.

Kh. Khalīl (p. 4) says that Kh. Ḥasan was made the Governor of Bengal, and his son Nuṣrat Jang, the Governor of Bihar. Another brother, Ẓafar Khān, was made the *dāroghah-i-fil khānah*, with the rank of 3,000/3,000. (*Akhbārāt*, 4 April).

and enjoyed great influence and prestige at the court.[31] After the death of Mun'im Khān, Sa'dullāh Khān had been made use of in order to exclude Z̲u'lfiqār Khan from the *wizārat* and was now afraid of the latter's venom.

Fortified by the clandestine support of the emperor, this powerful clique began to interfere openly in the affairs of the administration, and to set the *wazīr's* authority at naught. Thus, on Kokaltāsh's advice, Sarbuland Khān was appointed the Deputy Governor of Gujārāt without the *wazīr* having been even consulted.[32] By his advice, and in direct opposition to the wishes of the *wazīr*, Khwājah Ḥasan Khān-i-Daurān, whom Khāfi Khān describes as 'one of the lowest men of the time', was appointed the guardian (*aṭālīq*) of Prince A'zz-ud-Dīn for the latter's campaign to check the advance of Farrukh Siyar from Bihar. The *wazīr* had been of the opinion that an old and experienced noble should be nominated to the command, whereas Khwājah Ḥasan Khān-i-Daurān, in the words of a contemporary historian, 'had never even killed a cat'.[33]

Besides the Kokaltāshī faction, there was a second group consisting of the emperor's favourite queen, La'l Kunwar, and her relations, friends and associates, who were also opposed to Z̲u'lfiqār Khān. La'l Kunwar, who is described as a dancing-girl,[34] had been a favourite of Jahāndār since a long time. After his accession to the throne, she was raised to the status of a queen, and even allowed to display the Imperial standard and march with

31 *M.U.* ii, 506, *Akhbārāt*, 31 March, M.M., 66a.

32 *T Muẓ.*, 188–9 Nūr-ud-Dīn, 38b. Valentyn dates the appointment 15 July, which tallies with an entry d. 12 July in the *Akhbārāt*. Another entry d., 29 May, states however that Sarbuland K. was presented to the Emperor by Z̲u'lfiqār Khān, and that he received the *manṣab* of 5,000/5,000 and other gifts.

At Kokaltāsh Khān's instance, Amānat K., the Governor of Gujārāt, was also transferred to Malwa. Out of pique, Z̲u'lfiqār secretly instigated the Raja of Rāmpurā to resist him (*Ḥadiqat*, 23, K.K., 695–7).

33 *Gāhe dar ghurbah tir nah zadah*—M.M., 13b, Īrādat 86, Kāmwar 386, K.K., 696, 716.

34 Or La'l Kumārī. She is described as a singing-girl (*mughīnah)* by Irādat (95) and by Qāsim (55). Irvine calls her Jahāndār's 'concubine'. She was the daughter of Khaṣūṣiyat Khān, a *kalāwant* (musician) descended from the famous musician, Tansen (*Ḥadiqat*, 131). Her father was apparently alive at the time, for he was presented at the court on 16 April, along with three of his sons, and received a *khila't*, flag, *nimah-āstīn*, embroidered turban, *bālāband*, jewelled sword and dagger, waist-band, etc. *(Akhbārāt)*.

drums beating as if she was the emperor in person. Five hundred gentlemen-troopers (*aḥadīs*) followed in her train.[35] She was the constant companion of the emperor and, as such, enjoyed considerable influence over him.

The hostility of La'l Kunwar to Z̲u'lfiqār Khān may be attributed to a feeling on her part that the *wazīr* did not pay due deference to the newly-acquired dignity of her relations, and refused to countenance their claims for the offices usually reserved for the nobly-born. Thus, a proposal to appoint one of the brothers of La'l Kunwar as the governor of a province was turned down at the instance of Z̲u'lfiqār Khān who pointed out that it would cause dissatisfaction among the nobility.[36] On another occasion, Khush-ḥāl Khān, a brother of La'l Kunwar, was arrested by the order of the *wazīr* on the charge of molesting a married lady. His property was confiscated and he was sent to the fortress of Sāmugarh. La'l Kunwar was powerless to intervene.[37]

Contemporary writers relate a number of stories to illustrate how in his infatuation for La'l Kunwar, Jahāndār Shāh neglected even the ordinary proprieties and decencies of behaviour, and lowered imperial dignity and prestige.[38] La'l Kunwar also became a channel for the transmission of imperial favour and patronage. Thus, we are told that the doors of her friend Zuhrah, a vegetable-seller by profession, were crowded from morning to evening by

35 *Akhbārāt, Siyar*, 386, Khalīl, 23, Kāmwar, 385, Nūr-ud-Dīn, 37a, K.K., 689, Wārid, 219.

36 K.K., 689. Khush-hāl (p. 72) mentions the name of Nāmdār Khān, and *Siyar* (385) of Nī'amat Khān, who is called the uncle of La'l Kunwar. Wārid (p. 222) says Khush-ḥāl K. entitled Ni'amat K.

The province in question is variously mentioned as Lahore (Wārid), Agra (*Siyar*), and Multan (Nūr-ud-Dīn).

Valentyn (p. 299) gives a slightly different account, and dates the event 25 April.

According to Nūr-ud-Dīn, both Z̲u'lfiqār and Kokaltāsh opposed this appointment.

37 *Siyar*, 386, *Akhbārāt*, 18 November, 5 December 1713 (slightly different account).

38 Thus almost all contemporary writers relate the story how Jahāndār and La'l Kunwar went out on a *rath* and got drunk (Khush-ḥāl, 15, Irādat, 95–6, K.K., 690, Nūr-ud-Dīn, Valentyn (slightly different)). Other stories are also related by Khush-ḥāl and Nūr-ud-Dīn (See Irvine i, pp. 192–6).

people in search of advancement.[39] Many of La'l Kunwar's relations and friends, too, benefited from the rise in her fortunes. Thus, three of her brothers were appointed to the *manṣabs* of 7,000 and 5,000, and given profitable sinecures and *jāgīrs*.[40]

It was quite natural for the nobles and officials to feel humiliated at the marriage of the monarch to a commoner, who moreover, belonged to a despised profession, and to resent the elevation of her relations to a status of equality with them. On the other hand, the friends and relations of the favourite queen could ill-conceal their new-found sense of importance, and by their swagger and high-handedness made themselves obnoxious to high and low alike.[41]

But the influence of La'l Kunwar over matters political should not be exaggerated. There is little evidence to warrant the belief that the elevation of La'l Kunwar became the occasion for the rise of a large number of men from the lower classes to the rank of the nobility. Even the relations of La'l Kunwar were not appointed to any important offices at the court, or to any posts carrying important administrative duties. La'l Kunwar's influence was mainly non-political, and any attempts to draw an analogy between her and Nūr Jahān are misleading.[42] Nevertheless, the mere fact of her having become an avenue of Imperial patronage and favour

39 Īrādat, 95, Kāmwar, 385, Wārid, p. 219. She was an old friend and the sworn-sister (*dū-gānū*) of La'l Kunwar. It does not seem that she was ever the mistress of Jahāndār. She appears to have gained his regard by advancing him a sum of a lakh of rupees during the civil war at Lahore when he was hard-pressed for money (*Akhbārāt*, 4 April 1712).

40 *Jauhar*, 35b gives the ranks of her brothers as follows:

Khaṣus Khān	7,000/7,000
Nāmdār Khān	5,000/5,000
Khush-ḥāl K.	5,000/5,000
Ni'amat Khān	5,000/5,000

Wārid (p. 219) says *manṣabs* from 7,000–9,000 were conferred upon them. *Jauhar* also stated that through La'l Kunwar, many *kalāwants* received the ranks of 5,000–7,000.

41 Thus, Kāmwar (p. 385) states... 'the fiddlers and drummers who were the brothers and relations of La'l Kunwar, swaggered through the streets of Delhi, committing every sort of outrage'.

Khāfī Khān (p. 689), says, 'It was a fine time for minstrels and singers, and all the fine tribe of dancers and actors.'

Āshūb (p. 127) speaks in the same strain.

42 According to Kāmwar (p. 385), the days of Nūr Jahān were revived for

could not fail to react adversely on the prestige as well as the income of the *wazīr*, the perquisites from the appointees and others seeking imperial favour being a substantial and well-recognized source of income. Here was the main cause of the increasing hostility between La'l Kunwar and Z̲u'lfiqār Khān.

The emergence of these inner rivalries threw the affairs of the empire into confusion. Z̲u'lfiqar was extremely powerful, and Jahāndār dared not dismiss him or even oppose him openly on any issue.[43] Hence, he resorted to secret intrigues to get rid of the *wazīr*, thus creating a pernicious atmosphere which affected every branch of the administration.[44]

General Policy and Administration of Z̲u'lfiqār Khān

It was against this background, and out of conviction as well as a general desire to strengthen his position at the court that Z̲u'lfiqār Khān took a number of steps designed to appease Hindu opinion, and to bridge the gulf which had opened up between the empire and the Rājpūts and Marāthās.

We have already seen that during the brief reign of A'ẓam, Shāhū had been released from captivity at the instance of Z̲u'lfiqār Khān, and the ranks of 7,000/7,000 and the titles of Mirza Raja and Maharaja were conferred on Jai Singh and Ajit Singh respectively. But the policy of conciliation indicated by these steps had made only very gradual headway in the time of Bahādur Shāh.

After becoming Jahāndār's *wazīr*, Z̲u'lfiqār Khān resumed his old policy. First of all, *jizyah* was abolished.[45] This tax, which had

her, and coins were issued in her name. Such coins, even if issued, have not come down to us.

43 Thus, on one occasion, Kokaltāsh and Z̲u'lfiqār Khān quarrelled when the latter set aside an appointment made by Kokaltāsh, and hot words were exchanged. When Kokaltāsh complained to the emperor, he replied that it was no use complaining to him as Z̲u'lfiqār Khān had full authority to do what he liked, and he, the emperor, could not interfere in anything, or utter even a word in protest (*Akhbārāt*, 29, *Ṣafar*, 7 April).

44 Irādat, 103–4.

45 *Akhbārāt*, 7 April 1712. It is significant that this step was taken only nine days after the victory of Jahāndār Shah, and at the instance of Aurangzīb's *wazīr* and life-long friend, Asad Khān.

become a symbol of narrowness of outlook and discrimination towards the Hindus, was removed largely with a view to creating confidence among them, and to clear the way for the establishment of friendly relations with the Rājpūts and Marāthās.

Next, Jai Singh and Ajit Singh were raised to the rank of 7,000/7,000, and granted the titles of Mirza Raja Sawai and Maharaja respectively.[46] Soon after this, Jai Singh was appointed the *ṣūbahdār* of Malwa, and Ajit Singh of Gujārāt. Mandsaur was added to the hereditary kingdom of Jai Singh. Likewise, Ajit Singh was given Sorath, Paltan and Īdar, but was compelled to restore Nāgor to Indra Singh, and Kishangarh and Rūpnagar to Raj Singh. In general, the rajas were satisfied, for as the Rājpūt *wakīl* put it, the emperor 'acceded to all our requests'.[47]

In the case of the Marāthās, the earlier arrangements for the Deccan were continued, and Dā'ūd Khān's pact was left undisturbed. A new development, however, was the grant of an Imperial *manṣab* of 3,000/2,000 and title of Anūp Singh to Shivājī II, the son of Rājāram (the Kolhāpur branch). A *khil'at* and royal *farmān* granting the *Deshmukhi* of Ḥaiderābad were also sent to him.[48] This implied the recognition of the Kolhāpur branch as an Imperial feudatory, inferior in status to the Satārā branch (as evidenced by the lower *manṣab* accorded to the former) but in no way subordinate to the latter. Z̲u'fiqār Khān thus moved towards a solution which seemed also to find favour among a section of the Marāthās, and was, at the same time, most in keeping with Imperial interests. Division of territory had been proposed by Shāhū to Tārā Bāi as early as 1708, but had been rejected by her.[49] Hence, civil war had continued, with resultant unrest

---

See also the present writer's article 'Jizyah in the post-Aurangzīb Period' in the *I.H.C. Proceedings*, 1940, 320–7.

46 *J.R.* Misc. papers Vol. ii, 21. *Farmān* of grant d. 3 *Rabī'* I, 10 April 1712, *Wakīl's* letter and report d. 5 *Sudi Chait*, 1769, 10 April.

47 *Akhbārāt*, 25 November, *Wakīl's* report d. 30 November [The entry in the *Akhbārāt* bears the following marginal comment in pencil by Sir Jadunath Sarkar: 'Mere paper appointments if by Jahāndār'. M.M. (p. 59a) tells us, however, that Ajit had just started for Gujārāt when news reached him that Farrukh Siyar's rebellion had reached serious proportions, and he put off his departure].

48 *Akhbārāt*, 4 September 1712.

49 *Riyāsat*, 13. Shāhū had offered the territory south of the river Warnā.

in the Deccan, and the depredation of Imperial territory by both claimants.[50] The division of Mahārāshtra had an obvious advantage for the Imperialists: it set an internal check on the ambitions of the Marāthās. Nor could Shāhū have any legitimate cause of complaint against such a step for he had failed to crush Tārā Bāi and was, at the moment, actually hard-pressed by her.[51] In 1711, Tārā Bāi had sent her *wakīl* Āyā Mal, to negotiate with the Mughal court. The envoy was instructed to stay at Udaipur and to conduct the negotiations from there.[52] This shows the direction in which the wind was blowing. The division of *swarāj* territory and of the *chauth* and *sardeshmukhi* of the Deccan between the two branches was the logical corollary to the recognition of both the branches as separate feudatories. The grant of the *Deshmukhi* of Ḥaiderābad to the Kolhāpur branch appears to have been a step in this direction. In this regard, the action of Zu'lfiqār Khān foreshadowed that of another shrewd politician, Niẓām-ul-Mulk, who later tried to check the Satārā branch by setting the Kolhāpur branch against it.

There is no clear indication of the Sikh policy which Zu'lfiqār Khān intended to follow. He appointed Muḥammad Amīn Khān to continue the campaign against Banda, and thus apparently continued the coercive policy of Bahādur Shāh and Mun'im Khān. Ajit Singh, the adopted son and the legally recognized spiritual successor of Guru Govind, was at the Mughal court with his mother, and held a royal *manṣab*.[53] Perhaps, it was considered necessary to crush the rising of (the false guru) Banda before any steps were taken to help or appease Ajit Singh.

With regard to the Jats and Bundelas, no change was made in the position obtaining under Bahādur Shāh. Chhatrasāl remained a loyal feudatory, and was summoned to join Prince A'zz-ud-Dīn in his campaign against Farrukh Siyar.[54] Chūrāman Jat had sided

50 See pp. 85–90 above.

51 In 1711–12, the fortunes of Shāhū reached their lowest point, defeats being followed by desertions to the Mughals. Thus in 1710, Rao Rambhā joined Dā'ūd Khān (*Akhbārāt*, 12 October) and in 1711, Chandrasen tentatively approached him (*Akhbārāt*, 28 June 1711).

52 *V.V.*, 944.

53 Harcharan f. 145a. Ajit was presented to Jahāndār Shāh on 23 May 1712 (*Akhbārāt*).

54 *Akhbārāt*, 29 October, 8 December. Churāman promised to help Jahāndār against Farrukh Siyar, but as was his habit, he looted both sides and created much confusion during the battle (Qanungo, *Jats*, 50).

with 'Aẕīm-ush-Shān in the war of succession at Lahore, but he too was pardoned, granted an audience with the emperor, and restored to the *manṣab* which Mun'im Khān had secured for him in 1707.[55]

Ẕu'lfiqār Khān's attempt to grope his way back to more conciliatory policies and thus to give the empire a new lease of life, and at the same time, to concentrate political and administrative authority in his own hands, was bound to create a reaction among the old nobility belonging to the time of Aurangzīb and Bahādur Shāh. The strongest group in the old nobility consisted, at this time, of Chīn Qulīch Khān and Muḥammad Amīn Khān. The rivalry between this family group and Ẕu'lfiqār Khān's family has already been noticed. During Bahādur Shāh's reign, the Chīn family remained in the background. Chīn Qulīch Khān was not satisfied, and resigning his *manṣab*, lived a life of retirement at Delhi. Muḥammad Amīn Khān was made the *faujdār* of Moradabad, and was then commissioned to chase the Sikh Guru. In anticipation of the coming civil war, 'Aẕīm-ush-Shān had approached and won over Chīn Qulīch to his side by promise of high office. When Chīn Qulīch heard the news of Bahādur Shāh's death, he recruited an army and set out for Lahore. But he had marched only a stage from Delhi when he received news of the defeat and death of 'Aẕīm-ush-Shān. Hence, he dismissed his soldiers and returned to Delhi.[56]

When Ẕu'lfiqār Khān became the *wazīr*, he wanted to use his power to crush Chīn Qulīch Khān once for all. But at the instance of 'Abduṣ-Ṣamad Khān, another Tūrānī nobleman who was related to the Chīn family by marriage and was a protégé of Ẕu'lfiqār Khān, Asad Khān intervened and forced Ẕu'lfiqār Khān to give up his intentions. Chīn Qulīch Khān was presented before Jahāndār Shāh when the latter reached Delhi, and the rank of 5,000, and the *ṣūbahdārī* of Malwa was conferred on him.[57] But the Khān was dissatisfied, and soon resigned his office and *manṣab*.[58]

Muḥammad Amīn was confirmed in his commission to pursue the Sikh Guru, and thus remained away from the court.

55 *Akhbārāt*, 26 *Jamāda* II, Yr. 1, 24 November 1707. He had also served in the campaign against the Sikhs.

56 M.M., 99b.

57 *Akhbārāt*, 21, 24 June, M.M., 100a.

58 *Akhbārāt*, 6 August. Shahāmat K. replaced him as the Governor of Malwa.

In this way, this powerful faction remained dissatisfied and dispersed. Z̲u'lfiqār Khān did nothing more to appease Chīn Qulīch, though he did on one occasion support the latter when the soldiers in his retinue clashed with the servants of Zuhrah, the friend of La'l Kunwar, while passing through a narrow street in the town. Zuhrah, it is said, insulted Chīn Qulīch by calling out to him as 'the son of that blind man', and the Khān's followers retaliated by severely belabouring the servants of Zuhrah. Zuhrah complained to La'l Kunwar who spoke to the emperor. But Chīn Qulīch had already approached Z̲u'lfiqār Khān who sided with him, and so Jahāndār Shāh did not dare to take any action against him.[59]

It was only when the rebellion of Farrukh Siyar, the son of 'Aẓīm-ush-Shān, gained serious proportions in the east that Chīn Qulīch was felt to be too important to be neglected any longer. Hence, he was given the *manṣab* of 7,000, and appointed to the army of Prince A'zz-ud-Dīn. But the Khān was not keen to take part in the fight, and prevaricated. He was still at Agra when A'zz-ud-Dīn was defeated by Farrukh Siyar at Khajwah.[60]

Thus, Z̲u'lfiqār Khān failed to win the support of the most important group in the old nobility. The attitude of Chīn Qulīch and M. Amīn Khān was an important factor in the subsequent defeat of Jahāndār and Z̲u'lfiqār Khān at the hands of Farrukh Siyar.

The failure to win over the faction of Chīn Qulīch and Muḥammad Amīn Khān might not have been so serious a matter if Z̲u'lfiqār Khān had been able to rally other sections of the nobility to his side. But he failed to do so due to a number of reasons. According to the contemporary historian, Īrādat Khān, the *wazīr* had become extremely haughty and proud and notoriously false to his word. He says, 'He (Z̲ul'fiqār Khān) studied to ruin the most ancient families, inventing pretences to put them to death, or disgrace them that he might plunder their possessions. Unhappy was the man who was suspected to be rich, as wealth and vexatious accusations always accompanied each other. He established such vexations and abuses as no prior age had beheld, and by which alone he is now remembered. He took enormous emoluments and revenue for himself while he disposed of money to others with a high hand so sparing that even his own creatures felt severe poverty with empty titles for he never allowed jāgīrs to any. The

59 Īrādat, 83, *Siyar,* 386.
60 M.M., 100 a, K.K., 700, 716.

minds of high and low, rich and poor, near and distant, friends or strangers were turned against him and wished his destruction'.[61]

These gross and sweeping generalizations are rather difficult to accept fully. As a matter of fact, Īrādat Khān is not an impartial observer, for he had always been opposed to Zu'lfiqār Khān, being attached first to Mun'im Khān and then to 'Aẓīm-ush-Shān. Further, after Zu'lfiqār's accession to power, when Irādat Khān approached him for employment, Zu'lfiqār treated him kindly but gave him no office. Īrādat Khān comments sourly 'There was no temptation left in employment in a state which had in fact no head, for the ministry was a collection of petty tyrants and abusers of power'.[62]

The general charge of 'oppression' brought against Zu'lfiqār Khān by Īrādat Khān and others[63] seems to be largely based on the many executions and imprisonments, attached with confiscation of property, which took place after the accession of Jahāndār.[64] Īrādat Khān observes 'It had as yet been the usage of this illustrious house, that though a nobleman according to his connections with one of them, appeared against another in the field, that the victor did not put him to death or disgrace him. On the contrary, the fidelity and valour displayed by him in the cause of a defeated rival, were sure recommendations to the conqueror's favour. The princes knew that the stability of power and regulation of empire rested on the support of an experienced nobility and they would frequently observe, 'that the enmity was not to the throne; for whenever a Prince became fixed upon it, they were faithful subjects. If we destroy them, through whom can we administer the government?'[65]

But when the adherents of the defeated princes resorted to Zu'lfiqār Khān for employment, most of them were given a flat

61 Irādat, 96–8.
62 Irādat, 100–1.
63 Thus, Kāmwar, 124a, Wārid, 225–6, K.K., 733, M.M., 66a, Āshūb, 124.
64 The imprisoned nobles included Mahābat K. and Khān-i-Zamān (sons of Mun'im Khān), Ḥakīm-ul-Mulk (chief adviser of Jahān Shāh), 'Aqīdat Khān (son of Amīr Khān) Hidāyat Kesh Khān (*Wāqa' Nigar-Kul* since 1109, 1687–8), M. 'Alī Khān (*bakhshī* of Jahān Shāh), Islām Khān *mīr ātish*, Hamīd-ud-Dīn Khān 'Ālamgīrī, Sarafarāz Khān Bahādur Shāhī, Amīn-ud-Din Sambhalī and more than 20 other nobles (K.K., 688, *Akhbārāt* entry d. 23, *Ṣafar*, 4 March.)
65 Īrādat, 19.

refusal.[66] This was a clear departure from the earlier policy. But Z̲u'lfiqār's personal vindictiveness alone was not responsible for this. It should be remembered that the rebellion of Farrukh Siyar, the son of Prince 'Az̤īm-ush-Shān, had still not been suppressed. Kokaltāsh's responsibility for some of the executions etc. is also not clear.[67] But the main factor was that real power was now in the hands of the *wazīr* who could not afford to take the liberal view that monarchs with an assured position and claim on the loyalty of the nobles had been able to assume.

Irādat also charges Zu'lfiqār Khān with stinginess and reluctance in giving *jāgīrs* to others while he appropriated vast sums for himself. The charge of miserliness in the matter of *manṣabs* and *jāgīrs* was an old one against Z̲u'lfiqār.[68] It should be borne in mind that economy was an urgent necessity as the revenues of the kingdom were insufficient for expenditure, and the treasury was empty.[69] In his munificence, Bahādur Shāh had started squandering *khāliṣah* land and even Mun'im Khān had felt it necessary to take steps against it. But Mun'im Khān had been unwilling to face unpopularity, and had given up when his attempt led to a wave of protests.[70] Z̲u'lfiqār tried to do what Mun'im Khān had shrunk from doing.

Early in Jahāndār's reign, Z̲u'lfiqār Khān issued orders that no *sanads* were to be granted to any *manṣabdār* till his claims had been checked and confirmed. Nor were any increments in rank to be

66 Nūr-ud-Dīn (35b) states that 2,000 to 3,000 old servants were thus rendered unemployed.

67 The execution of Rustam Dil, Mukhlis Khān, and Prince M. Karīm are ascribed to Kokaltāsh Khān (Āshūb, pp. 125–6). It is said that Rustam Dil had raised his hand against La'l Kunwar. Questioned by Farrukh Siyar later, Z̲u'lfiqār Khān disclaimed responsibility for these executions (M.M., 22b, K.K., 732–3).

Irādat (p. 97) suggests that Z̲u'lfiqār, who apprehended opposition from Kokaltāsh, was attempting to get rid of his opponents in this way.

68 See *B.N.*, 416.

69 *Cf.* K.K. (ii, p. 684): 'In the time of Bahādur Shāh, the income of the Empire was not sufficient to meet the expenses, and consequently there was great parsimony shown in the government establishments, but especially in the royal household, so much so that money was received everyday from the treasury of Prince 'Az̤īm-ush-Shān to keep things going.'

70 See pp. 96–7 above.

granted till then. He also attempted to compel the *manṣabdārs* to maintain their stipulated quota of troops and to enforce the regulations regarding the muster of the *manṣabdār's* troops.[71] But economy and strict enforcement of rules were not to the taste of the nobles. In particular, Kokaltāsh Khān and the emperor's favourites complained, and attempted to get round these irksome orders by appointing one of their own nominee as the *'arẓ-i-mukarr* (the official in charge of confirming *jāgīrs*). This led to an acrimonious dispute between Kokaltāsh Khān and the *wazīr* who refused to brook any interference in the revenue department. The dispute was referred to Jahāndār Shāh, but he dared not openly to defy the masterful *wazīr*.[72] But soon, the rules of Z̲u'lfiqār Khān were thrown to the winds, and *manṣabs* were granted to the royal favourities with a liberal hand. Thus, Z̲u'lfiqār's effort to economize only made him unpopular with his own followers.

The charge that Z̲u'lfiqār Khān was deliberately seeking to destroy the old nobility need not be taken seriously for we have already examined his treatment of Chīn Qulīch Khān and Muḥammad Amīn Khān who were his old rivals and formed a most powerful faction in the old nobility. Many nobles of the time of Aurangzīb and Bahādur Shāh continued to hold important posts at the centre as well as in the provinces. The *wazīr* resisted the elevation of new, low-born men, and on more than one occasion defended the old nobles against the pretensions of the friends and relations of La'l Kunwar. Nevertheless, the charge brought by Īrādat Khān reflects the sentiments of a section of the old nobility at their loss of power and influence and possibly, the diminution of their incomes.

In the sphere of revenue administration Z̲u'lfiqār Khān found himself faced with an even more difficult task. During the prolonged absence of Aurangzīb in the Deccan, the administration in northern India had become slack. The financial crisis and the crisis of the *jāgīrdārī* system which was visible in the later years of Aurangzīb's reign, had assumed an acute form in the time of Bahādur Shāh. Apparently, the reforms instituted by Mun'im Khān did not appreciably improve the situation. The result was that in the time of Jahāndār Shāh, the old rules of business were

71 *Akhbārāt*, 22, *Ṣafar*, 16, *Jamada* I, 31 March, 21 June.
72 *Akhbārāt*, 2, *Rabī'* I, 29, *Ṣafar*, 7 April, 9 April.

thrown to the winds, and *ijārah* (revenue-farming) became universal.[73] In other words, the *ẓabtī* system of Todar Mal, which had so far formed the basis of the entire revenue administration, was now finally and completely abandoned, and the government resorted to the practice of making a deal with revenue-farmers, government officials, and middlemen of all types, leaving them to collect what they could from the *raiyat.* It is obvious that this led to the oppression of the people. It also led to a growing divergence between the real and the paper income of the *jāgīrs*, and ultimately resulted in the breakdown of the *manṣabdārī* system itself.

The question is, what responsibility should Zu'lfiqār Khān bear for these consequences of resorting to revenue-farming? It would be unhistorical to fasten on his shoulders the entire blame for the subsequent breakdown of the administration. He was faced with a desperate financial situation and resorted to the easiest and most obvious expedient. With the consolidation of his power and improvement in the political situation, he might have found time to undertake serious administrative reform. For the time being, he was content to leave the financial affairs in the hands of his *ex-dīwān,* Sabhā Chand.[74] Sabhā Chand was not incompetent for the job, but he was thoroughly detested due to his harshness in revenue affairs, his habit of taking bribes, and his foul tongue. In the Deccan, Zu'lfiqār Khān's deputy, Dā'ūd Khān, was all powerful; but he, too 'left all power in the hands of Deccani brahmins, and led a life of ease and pleasure'.[75]

During the reign of Jahāndār Shāh, the price of grain in the capital rose very high. Repeated efforts to curb the high prices by the condign punishment of the grain-merchants and the officials of the royal market proved useless, and this added to the discontent of the people of the capital with the new régime.[76]

73 Wārid, 6. We are told that the *wazīr* and all the other ministers had become accustomed to taking bribes (*M.U.* iii, 720).

74 Kāmwar, K.K., 689.

75 *Mir'āt,* 403, K.K., 964, 748.

76 *Akhbārāt,* 22, *Ṣafar,* 17 *Jamāda* I, 19, *Jamāda* II, 13 *Ramaẓān* (levying of *abwābs* on grain forbidden, and *Chaudhris* of the grain-market tied up and produced before the court), 31 March, 22 June, 24 July, 14 October. Also see Khush-ḥāl, 91, 118.

DEFEAT AND DOWNFALL OF JAHĀNDĀR SHĀH AND Z̲U'LFIQĀR KHĀN

While Z̲u'lfiqār Khān was trying to consolidate his power, and to win the trust and co-operation of the Hindus in general, and the Rājpūts and Marāthās in particular, a serious danger developed in the east. This was the rebellion of Farrukh Siyar, the second son of 'Aẕīm-ush-Shān. As is described later, Farrukh Siyar had proclaimed himself the King at Patna after receiving the news of his father's death. With the adhesion to his side of Saiyid Ḥusain 'Alī Bārahā, the Governor of Bihar, and his brother, Saiyid 'Abdullāh Khān Bārahā, the Governor of Allahabad, he had succeeded in collecting an army, and was marching upon Agra. Many nobles of those parts and some of the adherents of 'Aẕīm-ush-Shān who had fled from Lahore had also joined him.

Even before Jahāndār Shāh had reached Delhi, a royal army under Prince 'Azz-ud-Dīn had been despatched to Agra to deal with Farrukh Siyar. A large sum of money said to be nine crores of rupees was disbursed to him for the purpose. As the prince was considered to be young and inexperienced, he was placed under the tutelage of Khwājah Ḥasan Khān-i-Daurān and Luṭfullāh Khān Ṣādiq, the prince's *dīwān*. Neither of these nobles had any experience of actual warfare, and the appointments were made, as has been noticed above, in opposition to the wishes of the *wazīr*. As more and more nobles rallied to the cause of Farrukh Siyar, the court became alarmed. Prince 'Azz-ud-Dīn was ordered to march from Agra to Allahabad, and Chīn Qulīch Khān was propitiated with the grant of a *manṣab* of 7,000, and asked to join him. The inexperience and pusillanimity of Luṭfullāh Khān and Khān-i-Daurān, and the discord between the latter and Prince 'Azz-ud-Dīn, was a major source of weakness from the outset. The soldiers were dispirited, for the salary of many of them was considerably in arrears. Above all, 'Azz-ud-Dīn himself disliked La'l Kunwar and suspected her of hatching plots against him. The sudden flight of 'Azz-ud-Dīn and Khān-i-Daurān from Khajwah on 28 November 1712, on the eve of battle, can only be ascribed to these internal differences. Their camp, equipage etc. was plundered by the soldiers, and a good part of the material and stores of war fell into the hands of Farrukh Siyar and the Saiyid brothers. This induced many nobles of those parts who had been sitting on the fence till then to throw in their lot with Farrukh Siyar. Some of the nobles attached to 'Azz-ud-Dīn's army also joined Farrukh Siyar. These included Lutfullāh Khān Ṣādiq, the prince's *dīwān*.[77]

News of the flight of 'Azz-ud-Dīn woke Jahāndār to a real sense of danger for the first time. Urgent efforts were made to collect an army and to march from the capital to meet the enemy. The biggest obstacle was the complete lack of money. All the hoarded treasures had been expended by Bahādur Shāh. What remained had been spent during the civil war at Lahore. Jahāndār Shāh had inherited an empty treasury. But he paid no heed to the situation, and made matters worse by his senseless extravagance in illuminations and celebrations of which both he and La'l Kunwar were very fond. The result was that since his accession 11 months ago, the army had not been paid a single pie.

In desperation, Jahāndār broke up all the gold and silver vessels which he could find, sold the jewels and jewelled articles, and even took down the gold ceilings in the royal palaces. The store-houses were thrown open, and goods were distributed to the soldiers in place of cash. Even then, the claims of the army could not be met.[78]

Thus, the last of the reserves accumulated since the time of Babar were exhausted. The financial bankruptcy of the empire was complete. The task of vandalism had been commenced long before the Jats and Marāthās reached the gates of Delhi, by the Timurid princes themselves.

After great exertions and difficulty, an army was at last collected, and on 9 December, Jahāndār set out for Agra. Letters were written to the Rājpūt rajas asking for help, but it was practically certain that the issue would be decided before they could arrive.[79] Even then, the army of Jahāndār was superior to that of Farrukh Siyar in both numbers and artillery. Jahāndār had 70,000–80,000 horse and innumerable foot, whereas Farrukh Siyar had 'not one-third of these numbers'. But Jahāndār's army was demoralized and divided in counsel. Zu'lfiqār and Kokaltāsh Khān

77 K.K., 717, Kāmwar.

78 Wārid, 247–8. Also Irvine, 220–1.

79 *Akhbārāt*, *Farmāns* were actually sent to Jai Singh and Ajit Singh as early as 3 *Rabī'* I, 10 April, summoning them to the court; and on 1 *Rabī'* II, 8 May, they were formally appointed to the army of Prince 'Azz-ud-Dīn, and mace-bearers despatched to escort them to the court. But the rajas delayed in making an appearance.

failed to agree even on a plan of battle. At the instance of Kokaltāsh Khān, it was weakly decided to stand on the defensive on the line of the Jamuna, and to seize all the boats in order to prevent Farrukh Siyar's army from crossing over. But the Saiyids found an undefended ford, and after making a forced night march, crossed the river, and turned the position of Jahāndār Shāh. The battle was fought on 10 January 1713 and was bitterly contested. The lack of co-ordination between Z̲u'lfiqār and Kokaltāsh, the neutrality of Muḥammad Amīn and Chīn Qulīch at a critical moment, and the cowardly flight of Jahāndār from the field of battle before the issue had been finally decided gave Farrukh Siyar and the Saiyid brothers a complete victory.[80]

Thus ended the reign of Jahāndār Shāh and with it, the *wīzārat* of Z̲u'lfiqār Khān. Though of brief duration, the reign of Jahāndār Shāh marks the emergence of several important tendencies to the surface. In the first place, it demonstrated that in the prevailing conditions the only alternative to an all-powerful king was an all-powerful *wazīr*. For when the necessary energy and capacity were wanting in the king, the *wazī*r was the only official with sufficient prestige and authority to lay down policies, run the administration and keep the nobles under control. The difficulties which would arise in such a development were also demonstrated. An all-powerful *wazīr* was likely to arouse the distrust of the king and the envy of the nobility. In such a situation, the *wazīr* could maintain his position only by organizing a bloc powerful enough to meet any rival or a possible combination of rivals, and by enlisting for this purpose the support of independent elements outside the court, viz. Rājpūts, Marāthās etc. This, in turn, created the danger of the establishment of a personal domination by the *wazīr*, which would threaten the dynasty as well as its leading supporters in the old nobility. The logical outcome was a new dynasty and a new nobility directly dependent upon the *wazīr*, or the overthrow of the *wazīr*, in which case the same process might start all over again. During Jahāndār's reign, the situation did not develop to its logical conclusion but all the factors for such a development were present.

In the second place, the reign of Jahāndār Shāh marks the rapid abandonment of the policies of Aurangzīb which had, to some

80 M.M., 15a, Wārid, 255–9, K.K., 700, 718–24, Ījād, 88b–91a. See also Irvine, 219–36.

extent, been maintained by Bahādur Shāh. Thus, the *jizyah* was abolished, large concessions were made to the Rājpūts, and an attempt was made to maintain and extend the accord with the Marāthās. It would appear that Zu'lfiqār Khān was attempting to revive the liberal traditions of Akbar, and to develop a composite ruling class in the country, and, as a logical corollary of it, to establish a national monarchy broadly based upon religious tolerance and the support of the Hindu as well as the Muslim masses. Zu'lfiqār Khān thus underlined the failure of Aurangzīb's attempt to hold the empire together by emphasizing Islam and the Islamic character of the ruling class.

CHAPTER IV

The Saiyid Brothers Struggle for 'New' Wizārat (i)

Antecedents and Early Careers of the Saiyid Brothers

The domination of the affairs of the empire by the brothers Saiyid 'Abdullāh Khān Bārahā and Saiyid Ḥusain 'Alī Khān Bārahā—often referred to as the 'Saiyid brothers', lasted from 1713 to 1721. Outwardly, the history of these years consists of a series of crises caused by a struggle for power between the two brothers who occupied the posts of *wazīr* and chief *bakhshī*, and the Emperor Farrukh Siyar. The culmination of the struggle is reached with the deposition of Farrukh Siyar in 1718, and an attempt by the two brothers at wielding absolute power.

However, the real interest of the period lies not so much in the struggle for power at the court as in the conflict over policies which again brought to the forefront the question of the character and composition of the ruling class, and of the state itself.

Before entering upon a detailed analysis of the important events, it would not be out of place to examine briefly the antecedents and early careers of the two brothers, Saiyid 'Abdullāh Khān and Saiyid Ḥusain 'Alī, who play a conspicuous role in the political developments of the period.

The Saiyids of Bārahā claimed descent from one of the distinguished families of Wasait in Mesopotamia. Much before the advent of the Mughals in India, one of their remote ancestors, Abū'l Farāh came to India with his 12 sons, and settled down in the *sarkār* of Sirhind, between Meerut and Saharanpur. Cut off from the country of their origin, and marrying in the country, they formed numerous settlements and became throughly Indianized in their manners and habits in course of time.[1]

The Saiyids of Bārahā first attracted attention during the reign of Akbar when they won the hereditary right to lead the Mughal van in battle. Their custom was to fight on foot in the Indian fashion.

After the death of Akbar, Saiyid Khān Bārahā played an important part in countering the conspiracy to set Jahāngīr aside in favour of his son Khusrau. Murtaẓā Khān Bārahā was another important figure. Under the successors of Jahāngīr, the Saiyids of Bārahā continued to occupy an important place in the Mughal army, but none of them seem to have attained a high *manṣab*, or been appointed to a high office.

Though reckoned as brave fighters and doughty warriors, the Bārahā Saiyids acquired a reputation for unreliability and ambitiousness. On one occasion, we find Aurangzīb writing: 'To relax the reigns of authority to the Saiyids of Bārahā is to bring a final ruin, i.e. a bad end because these people on getting the least prosperity and promotion boast "There is none like me," stray from the path of right conduct, cherish high handedness and cause impediment'.[2] We do not know how exactly the Saiyids of Bārahā had acquired this reputation.

Ḥasan 'Alī (afterwards 'Abdullāh Khān Quṭb-ul-Mulk) and Ḥusain 'Alī Khān were the two eldest sons of 'Abdullāh Khān Saiyid Miyān. The latter had arisen in the service of Rūḥullāh Khān, the chief *bakhshī* of Aurangzīb, and after receiving a *manṣab* had attached himself to Prince Shāh 'Ālam. Subsequently, he was the *ṣūbahdār* of Bījāpur, and then of Ajmer.[3]

The elder brother, 'Abdullāh Khān, was about 31 years of age and was the *faujdār* of Sulṭan-Nazarpur in Bangalore in 1698. It was in that year that the Marāthās under Nīmājī Sindhia raided the province of Khandesh for the first time. 'Abdullāh Khān put up a disastrous but heroic fight against Nīmājī, and thus won

1 *Tārīkh-i-Sādāt-Bārahā*. See also Irvine i, 201–2.

2 *Aḥkām*, 32, 8.

3 *M.U.* ii, 489–91, *Akhbārāt*, 29 January 1700.

his spurs as a brave warrior.[4] Two years later, in 1700, 'Abdullāh Khān displayed great energy in fighting another Marāthā general, Hanumant. He sacked Hanumant's base camp, made his nephew, Jānoji, a prisoner and converted him to Islam. Z̲u'lfiqār Khān who was passing that way commended 'Abdullāh Khān's bravery, and recommended him for a rise from the rank of 800 to 1,000, and his younger brother, Ḥusain 'Ali for a promotion from the rank of 700 to 900. But Aurangzīb turned down the recommendation, saying 'It is difficult for me to consent to their promotion in one step', and sent them two robes and daggers only as a mark of royal favour.[5]

Soon after this, 'Abdullāh Khān joined the service of Jahāndār Shāh who was the eldest son of Shāh 'Ālam, and was the Governor of Multan. Ḥusain 'Alī was appointed the *faujdār* of Ranthambhor and later of Hindaun-Bayānā.[6]

In 1702, in a battle against a Billoch *zamindar,* Jahāndār Shāh assigned the honours of battle to his favourite, 'Īsā Khān Main. This annoyed 'Abdullāh Khān who claimed the honours for himself. In high dudgeon, he quitted Jahāndār's service, and repaired to Lahore. There he remained unemployed till 1707 when Mun'im Khān, who was on his way to Agra for the war against A'ẓam, secured for him the *manṣab* of 3,000.[7] Ḥusain 'Alī also joined Bahādur Shāh near Delhi, and was granted the *manṣab* of 2,000.[8]

The Saiyids fought well at Jājū, losing one brother, Nūr-ud-Dīn 'Alī Khān, and Ḥusain 'Alī being wounded. They received a rise of 1,000 each, but were not satisfied, and pressed their claims with some vigour, which annoyed Prince Jahān Shāh who was his father's favourite at the time.[9] Hence, they received no employment, but were compelled to follow in the wake of the court, thereby incurring heavy expenses.

In 1708, 'Aẓīm-ush-Shān appointed Ḥusain 'Alī his deputy in the governorship of Bihar.[10] 'Abdullāh Khān remained unemployed. At one time during the Rājpūt War, he was offered the governorship

4 K.K., 457.
5 *Aḥkām,* 32.
6 *M.U.* i, 322, iii, 132, Irvine (i, p. 203) is not correct in thinking that both 'Abdullāh and Ḥusain 'Alī joined Jahāndār Shāh.
7 *M.U.* i, 825–6, iii, 130, Qāsim, 56.
8 *M.U.* i, 322, iii, 132, K.K., 456.
9 *Akhbārāt, B.N.,* 309, Wārid, 237, Irvine i, 204–5.
10 *Akhbārāt,* 1 April 1708.

of Ajmer. But he made a number of far-reaching demands; viz. the forts of Jodhpur and Mertha and the *faujdārī* of Ranthambhor must be made over to him, he should be exempted for 10 years from repayment of the advances made to him for his expenditure and from having the horses of his army branded, his personal followers must be admitted to *manṣabs*; his *jāgīrs* in the Deccan should be confirmed, Rājpūts who applied for service should be given *manṣabs* in accordance with his recommendations etc. His demands were accepted formally, but they were not to the liking of the emperor and his advisers. Hence, the old *ṣūbahdār* Shujā'at Khān was soon reinstated, and 'Abdullāh Khān remained unemployed.[11]

'Abdullāh Khān was again called upon to serve during the Sikh campaign. At the battle of Anantpur in 1710, he fought on foot as was the custom of the Bārahā Saiyids, and after great slaughter, won a signal victory.[12]

In 1711, when 'Aẕīm-ush-Shān was looking around for adherents, he appointed 'Abdullāh Khān his deputy in the governorship of Allahabad.[13]

Thus, the two Saiyid brothers were indebted to 'Aẕīm-ush-Shān for their appointments. They enjoyed a reputation for bravery, but were considered haughty and ambitious. Their career had in no sense been remarkable, and it is probable that they would have died as obscure nobles had it not been for the circumstances created by the civil war and the rebellion of Farrukh Siyar.

EARLY RELATIONS OF FARRUKH SIYAR AND THE SAIYID BROTHERS

Although 'Abdullāh Khān and Husain 'Alī were clearly under an obligation to 'Aẕīm-ush-Shān for their employment, they did not proclaim 'Aẕīm-ush-Shān when news was received of the death of Bahādur Shāh. Farrukh Siyar, the second son of 'Aẕīm-ush-Shān, had been camping at Patna for some months before this occurance. The prince had been his father's deputy in the governorship of Bengal since 1707, and had recently been recalled to the court.

11 *Akhbārāt*, 17 October 1708, M.M., 58a.

12 *Akhbārāt*, 28 May, 4 June 1710, Irvine i, 105–6.

13 *Akhbārāt*, 10 January 1711.

Leaving Rājmahal about June 1711,[14] he had reached Patna at the commencement of the rainy season,[15] and had not resumed his journey at the time of this occurence. In reality, he was reluctant to proceed to the court for he enjoyed little favour with his father as compared to his brothers.[16] According to some others, it had been predicted that he would be king on the death of Bahādur Shāh, and so he delayed purposely.[17]

Farrukh Siyar's prolonged stay at Patna was apparently not to the liking of the Governor Ḥusain 'Alī Khān, and relations between the two became strained. While in Bihar, Farrukh Siyar led an expedition against one Ri'āyat Khān who had secured control of the fort of Rohtas by producing before the commandant a forged *farmān* of appointment. As Rohtas was a very powerful fort, Farrukh Siyar had to recourse to duplicity. He inveigled Ri'āyat Khān out of the fort on a false assurance of safe conduct and then massacred him along with his entire family.[18] Farrukh Siyar's action lowered him in the public esteem, and created an unfavourable impression on Ḥusain 'Alī.[19]

When on 15 March 1712, news reached Patna of the death of Bahādur Shāh, Farrukh Siyar at once proclaimed his father, 'Aẕīm-ush-Shān, as king, and struck coins and had *khuṭbah* read in his name. Ḥusain 'Alī who had gone out against some malcontents in the direction of Rājgīr, did not like this.[20] Apparently, he wanted to sit on the fence till the results of the contest at Lahore were

14 'Izz-ud-Daulah Khān-i-Jahān, the Governor designate, reached Rājmahal on 1 June 1711, and so Farrukh Siyar must have left soon after (*Riyāẓ*, 240).

15 From Patna, he sent an *'arẓdāsht* pleading the approach of the rainy season and the advanced pregnancy of his wife for his inability to march further (Kāmwar).

16 *M.U.* i, 322–3.

17 According to Nūr-ud-Dīn (p. 40a) and M.M., sovereignty on the soil of Bihar had been predicted for him by an astrologer.

But according to *Riyāẓ*, he had been hailed as King by the famous *ṣūfi* saint of Burdwan, Ṣūfi Bāyizīd, as early as 1697 when, as Prince, he had visited him to seek blessings for his father (*Riyāẓ*, 242–3).

18 K.K., 708–10. The capture of Rohtas was reported to Bahādur Shāh on 1 February 1712, and on the 10th, a robe an elephant, and an *arwish* were sent to the prince as rewards (*Akhbārāt*). Irvine (i, 205) wrongly states that it was Ḥusain 'Alī who had proceeded against Rohtas.

19 K.K., 710.

20 Nūr-ud-Dīn, 40, K.K., 711, M.M., 14b, *Jauhar,* 26b.

known. He came back to Patna and, according to one writer, wanted to arrest Farrukh Siyar who had only a small following with him. But he was prevented from doing so by Aḥmad Beg who was Farrukh Siyar's chief lieutenant and who exerted himself to collect an army on his behalf.[21] Farrukh Siyar wrote flattering letters to the governor who was at last persuaded to give his support to the prince. This seems to have happened *before* the result of the contest at Lahore was known.[22]

When news arrived of the defeat and death of 'Aẕīm-ush-Shān, Ḥusain 'Alī wanted to draw back. The prince himself wanted to commit suicide in despair. But Farrukh Siyar's mother threw herself on the support of Ḥusain 'Alī, appealed to his sense of generosity and his old relations with 'Aẕīm-ush-Shān, and fired his imagination by promises of high office. 'Whatever the result, you will be the gainer', she is reported to have told him. 'If defeated, your name will stand recorded as a hero till the day of judgement; if successful, the whole Hindustan will be at your feet, and above you none but the Emperor.'[23]

Ultimately Ḥusain 'Alī agreed to join Farrukh Siyar, partly because he was afraid he was already too deeply committed, and

21 M.M., 14a.

22 K.K., 710–11 Qāsim (80), Īrādat, and Kh. Khalīl (25) state that the Saiyids joined Farrukh Siyar immediately after he reached Patna.

On the other hand, M.M. (p. 14b) and Wārid (pp. 232–5) state that the Saiyids joined after the news of Jahāndār's victory. But Wārid's chronology is unreliable—he made Farrukh Siyar leave Rajmahal after the news of his father's defeat. Nūr-ud-Dīn (ff. 39b–41a) upon whom Wārid bases himself is not clear, stating that Ḥusain 'Alī 'objected about joining Farrukh Siyar till the termination of the affair of his father'.

The reports of the English factor at Patna tend to support K.K. (Wilson ii, XXIX).

For a further discussion, see the present author's article 'Early Relations of Farrukh Siyar and the Saiyid Brothers' in *Medieval India Quart.*, Vol. ii, 1955, pp 135–46.

Mr S. H. Askari ('Bihar in the First Quarter of the 18th Century', *I.H.C.*, Vol. V, pp. 394–405) thinks that Ḥusain 'Alī held a second coronation after he joined Farrukh Siyar, the first coronation being held immediately following the news of 'Aẕīm-ush-Shān's death, on 6 April 1712.

I have failed to trace in any contemporary authority reference to a second coronation at Patna.

23 Nūr-ud-Dīn, 41a, Wārid, 323.

partly due to his dislike of Jahāndār Shāh and his disgust at the absolute authority enjoyed by Ẕu'lfiqār Khān at his court.[24]

But the mutual suspicion and ill-will between Farrukh Siyar and Ḥusain 'Alī did not end with the latter's adherence to his cause. Ḥusain 'Alī, we are told, was afraid of 'the notorious low-down cunning and deceitful nature of Farrukh Siyar'.[25] The reports of the English factor at Patna give a graphic account of the heights to which the mutual suspicion and ill-will reached. Farrukh Siyar was hard pressed for money and formed a plan of levying contributions on all the rich merchants, including the English and the Dutch, and of plundering the town. But Ḥusain 'Alī deemed it dishonourable and also against good policy. In particular, he took the English and the Dutch under his protection. Hence, 'Hosain Aly exerted to preserve the town and had put his forces at the gates (of the town) with orders to oppose any that shall molest or offer to plunder'. Najm-ud-Dīn 'Alī Khān, the younger brother of Ḥusain 'Alī, foiled several attempts by Farrukh Siyar to plunder the city. Farrukh Siyar went so far as to offer Ḥusain 'Alī a fourth share of the booty if he would withdraw his opposition but to no avail. The result was that two parties came into existence, 'one composed of the Nabob and several others, and the other composed of a rascally crew'. It was rumoured that Farrukh Siyar was trying to get Ḥusain 'Alī out of the way by sending him to Bengal, 'to fetch Moorshid Aly Cawn or treasure or his head', and that 'the Nabob freely accepts his new employment that he may get free of the king and it's supposed will never return but will join with Cawn Bahadoor Cawn ('Izz-ud-Daulah Khān-i-Jahān, the Governor of Orissa'). Ultimately Ḥusain 'Alī's appointment was cancelled due to these suspicions, and instead, Muḥammad Raẓā and Mirzā J'afar were sent against Murshid Qulī who inflicted a crushing defeat on them.[26]

The ill will between Farrukh Siyar and Ḥusain 'Alī kept growing till there were differences of opinion between them on practically every point. In addition to this, there were altercations and misunderstanding among their followers. This delayed preparations for marching on the capital.

24 Wārid, 236, *Tārīkh-i-Fatḥiyah, M.U.* i, 323.
25 M.M., 14a.
26 Wilson ii, 50–6, 81, 86, Ijād, 51a.

At this time, Khwājah 'Āṣim (later entitled Khān-i-Daurān) who had been present in the battle at Lahore and had escaped with great difficulty after 'Aẕīm-ush-Shān's defeat, reached Patna. He rapidly established his influence over Farrukh Siyar, and strove to bridge the differences between him and Ḥusain 'Alī. At length, through his efforts, mutual suspicions abated sufficiently—at least to outward appearances, for the march towards the capital being commenced on 18 September 1712.[27]

In reality, however, Ḥusain 'Alī was far from happy, and relations between him and Farrukh Siyar continued to be strained. Thus, the two did not see eye to eye on the treatment of Sīddhishta Nārāyan, the *zamindar* of Bhojpur in Shāhbād, and one of the most powerful men in those parts. Ḥusain 'Alī had a long-standing quarrel with Sīddhishta Nārāyan, but Farrukh Siyar intervened through Ghāzī-ud-Dīn Aḥmad Beg, and persuaded the Raja to join him. A number of Rājpūts who had been imprisoned by Husain 'Alī were ordered to be released. Ḥusain 'Alī did not approve of these proceedings, but gave way at the instance of Ghāzī-ud-Dīn Aḥmad Beg.[28]

It is difficult to say whether the differences between Farrukh Siyar and Ḥusain 'Alī were essentially personal, or extended to the sphere of policy. While in Bihar, Farrukh Siyar, at the instance of Saiyid Ḥusain 'Ali, issued a proclamation abolishing the *jizyah.*[29] This was an important political move on Ḥusain 'Alī's part with far-reaching implications. But there is no evidence that Farrukh Siyar was, at that stage, opposed to the move.

However, Ḥusain 'Alī continued to sulk and took little part in public affairs till the royal camp reached Allahabad early in November, when 'Abdullāh Khān, the elder brother of Ḥusain 'Alī, came and resolved the ill-will between him and Farrukh Siyar.[30] Thus, 'Abdullāh Khān played an important role in cementing the alliance with Farrukh Siyar. Indeed, since the time of his arrival in the camp, he seems to have become the dominant figure in the alliance, outstripping his younger brother in the management and control of all affairs.

27 Ījād, ff. 53b–55b.
28 Ījād, ff. 62b–63b.
29 *Akhbārāt*, entry d. 17 *Rabī'* ii yr. 2, 12 April 1713. See also the present writer's article 'Jizyah in the post-Aurangzeb Period' *I.H.C.*, 1946, 320–7.
30 Ījād, 74a.

We have already noticed that in 1711, 'Aẕīm-ush-Shān had nominated Saiyid 'Abdullāh Khān his deputy in the governorship of Allahabad. Apparently, 'Abdullāh Khān did not fare well in his new charge for he accumulated large arrears of salary to his soldiers. At the time of Bahādur Shāh's death, a convoy of treasure from Bengal, consisting of the tribute of that province and income from the *jāgīrs* of 'Aẕīm-ush-Shān, had reached the boundary of the province of Allahabad. 'Abdullāh Khān deemed it a golden opportunity to meet his hard-pressing obligations. He seized the convoy which was said to contain 28 lakhs of rupees, and distributed the money among his followers.[31]

'Abdullāh Khān could scarcely have expected that such a serious offence would be forgiven by Jahāndār Shāh, particularly as his relations with Jahāndār Shāh had been strained since the time he had quitted his (Jahāndār's) service and joined that of his rival, 'Aẕīm-ush-Shān.[32] Hence, 'Abdullāh Khān opened correspondence with Farrukh Siyar, and the latter hastened to send him a *farmān* confirming him in his post, and sanctioning belatedly the money which he had already seized for his expenses.[33] Meanwhile, 'Abdullāh Khān also petitioned Jahāndār Shāh, mainly, it seems, with a view to gaining time till Farrukh Siyar should approach.

Thus, 'Abdullāh Khān's adherence to Farrukh Siyar's cause was entirely due to personal reasons, and his supersession by Jahāndār Shāh was not so much its cause as its logical result.[34]

On 5 November 1712, Farrukh Siyar reached Jhūsī and received 'Abdullāh Khān in audience. The previous assurances given to the two brothers were reaffirmed—though it is not clear whether they were formally invested with the office of *wazīr* and *mīr bakshī* at this time or not.[35]

31 K.K., 711, 715.

32 See p. 128 above.

33 Ījād ff. 64; K.K., 711, 715; Qāsim (Sarkar Ms.) 450.

34 Jahāndār Shāh attempted too late to reconcile the Saiyids by the restoration of Allahabad, and the grant of the *manṣab* of 7,000/7,000 *dū-aspah*, 2 crore *dam* as *in'ām* to 'Abdullāh Khān, and the rank of 7,000/7,000 to Ḥusain 'Alī (*Akhbārāt*, 13, *Rajab*, 10, *Ramaẓān*, 16 August, 10 October).

This suggests that the real importance of the Saiyids was far greater than what appears from their rank and office, and that this was recognized by Jahāndār Shāh only belatedly.

35 Irvine (i, p. 213) asserts, apparently on the authority of Ījād, that formal

From the foregoing review of the early relations of Farrukh Siyar and the Saiyid brothers, it should be apparent that the favourites of the emperor, Khān-i-Daurān and Mīr Jumlah, were not responsible for the ill-will between the two parties at the outset. In fact, the influence of Khān-i-Daurān was cast on the side of reconciliation at this stage. But later, fresh grounds of discord and hostility arose in which the 'favourites' played a definite role.

According to Yahyā, the *mīr munshī* of Farrukh Siyar, after the battle of Agra, Farrukh Siyar offered the post of *wakīl-i-muṭlaq* to 'Abdullāh Khān on the plea that he had promised the *wizārat* to Aḥmad Beg. This would have made 'Abdullāh Khān largely a figurehead, leaving real power in the hands of the Emperor's favourites. But 'Abdullāh Khān was fully alive to the implications of Farrukh Siyar's proposal, and rejected it on the ground that he had won the crown for the Emperor by his own sword and right arm, and that his title to be the *wazīr* was indisputable. As Farrukh Siyar had just succeeded to the throne, and his position was not yet secure, he thought it wise to give way.[36] But this revealed his lack of confidence in and continued suspicion of the Saiyids.[37]

Position and General Policy of the Saiyids After the Accession of Farrukh Siyar

After the flight of Jahāndār Shāh from the field of battle and the formal proclamation of Farrukh Siyar, 'Abdullāh Khān was made the *wazīr* and Ḥusain 'Alī the *mīr bakhshī* with the ranks of 7,000/7,000. They were also granted the governorships of Multān and Bihar respectively, and allowed to govern them through deputies. Saiyid Najm-ud-Dīn 'Alī Khān and a number of their younger brothers and other kinsmen were also admitted to *manṣabs*. The

---

engagements were entered into with the Saiyid brothers at this juncture, making over the post of *wazīr* to 'Abdullāh Khān and that of *mīr bakhshī* to Ḥusain 'Alī.

I have failed to find any support for this statement in Ījād.

36 Yahyā, 122a. See also K.K., 727–8, and M.M., 23a.

37 *Cf.* the action of Shāh Jahān who, after his elevation to the throne, did not appoint his leading supporter, Āṣaf Khān, to the post of *wazīr*, but relegated him to the post of *wakīl*. Farrukh Siyar may have attempted to ape Shāh Jahān's action.

maternal uncle of 'Abdullāh Khān, Saiyid Muẕaffar Khān Bārahā, was made the Governor of Ajmer.

But apart from these posts, the Saiyids claimed no special position for themselves or their kinsmen. Indeed, far from seeking to establish a monopoly of power for themselves, they were keen to conciliate and to win over the nobles of the time of Aurangzīb and Bahādur Shāh. At the outset, the general policy laid down was that all the 'Ālamgīrī nobles were to be confirmed in their (former) ranks, while promotions in *ẕāt* rank of 300 and above granted by Bahādur Shāh were held over till they had been subjected to a scrutiny. After some time, exemption from this rule was granted to nobles serving in the Deccan and in the *ṣūbah* of Kabul, and the ranks enjoyed by them at the time of Bahādur Shāh's death were confirmed.[38] Most of the old nobles were continued in service.

If the Saiyids had their way, even Asad Khān and Ẕu'lfiqār Khān who were held responsible for the death of 'Aẕīm-ush-Shān and his son, Prince Muḥammad Karīm, would have been pardoned, and granted high offices. But Farrukh Siyar, acting in defiance of their wishes, desired to make an example of these two nobles. He treacherously imprisoned and executed Ẕulfiqār Khān, and disgraced Asad Khān. There can be little doubt that Farrukh Siyar acted against the best interests of the empire and the monarchy, for he destroyed two of the most experienced nobles who would also have acted as a counter to the power and authority of the Saiyids.

Farrukh Siyar regretted his action later on.[39] The conclusion Ḥusain 'Alī drew from the execution of Ẕu'lfiqār Khān was that Farrukh Siyar was 'a man who paid no regard to claims of gratitude and was devoid of faith, a breaker of his word and altogether without shame. In these circumstances, it was incumbent upon them to act according to their own design without regard to the objects of the sovereign',[40]

38 *Akhbārāt*, 30, *Muḥ.*, 4, 10, *Ṣafar*, 14, *Rabī'* I yr. 2, 26 February, 2 and 6 March, 10 April 1713.

39 K.K., 732–3, M.M., ff. 22a–b, Irvine, 248–53. Ẕu'lfiqār K. had declined 'Abdullāh Khān's offer of securing him a pardon, and was led into a trap by Taqarrub Khān, a personal follower of the emperor, who took the most binding oaths for his safety.

40 Wārid, 276.

The only powerful faction that now remained in the nobility was the one consisting of Chīn Qulīch Khān, M. Amīn Khān and 'Abduṣ-Samad Khān. 'Abdullāh Khān realized the importance of this powerful group and wanted to win it over to his side through Chīn Qulīch Khān. At 'Abdullāh Khān's request, Chīn Qulīch was accorded the rank of 7,000/7,000 and the title of Niẓām-ul-Mulk, and appointed the viceroy of the Deccan, with powers to select the lands to be held in *jāgīr* for furnishing his pay and that of his followers, and to suggest the *manṣab* to be granted to the chief *zamindars* there. Dā'ūd Khān Pannī, the former deputy-Viceroy, was transferred to Gujārāt as the deputy-governor.[41] 'Abdullāh Khān used to say that he regarded Niẓam-ul-Mulk as his 'elder brother'. He called at Niẓām-ul-Mulk's residence before the latter left for the Deccan and costly gifts were exchanged between them as a token of friendship.[42]

M. Amīn Khān, the cousin of Niẓām-ul-Mulk, whose neutrality at a critical moment had helped the Saiyids to win the battle of Agra, was appointed the second *bakhshī* with the title of I'timād-ud-Daulah. His son, Qamar-ud-Dīn Khān, was made the *dāroghah* of the *aḥadīs*.

'Abduṣ-Ṣamad Khān had been the chief lieutenant of Z̲u'lfiqār Khān. But since he was related to Niẓām-ul-Mulk by marriage, he was pardoned, granted the rank of 7,000/7,000, and appointed the governor of Lahore. The choice was a wise one, for 'Abduṣ-Ṣamad Khān was to prove a very successful governor. He put down the Sikh and Afghan depredations with a firm hand, and restored prosperity to that much harrassed, strategic province.

In most of the other provinces, the old nobles were reinstated in their former offices, while a number of posts which gave constant access to the emperor went to his personal favourites. The emperor and the Saiyids did not see eye-to-eye on all these appointments. We shall examine the nature of their differences a little later.

41 K.K., 740, M.M., 23a.

42 Niẓām-ul-Mulk was appointed on 4 *Ṣafar*/2 March 1713; on 15 *Ṣafar* further honours were conferred upon him and he was given leave of departure. On 23 *Ṣafar*, 'Abdullāh Khān and Ḥusain 'Alī visited him and presents were exchanged. On 12 *Jamāda* I, 6 June, he crossed the Narmada which was then in floods, on an elephant (Letter to Jai Singh). He entered Burhānpur on 29 June which fact was reported to the emperor on 2 *Rajab*, 22 September. (*Akhbārāt*)

After making the various appointments, the problem which Farrukh Siyar and the Saiyid brothers faced next was of devising a suitable policy towards the Rājpūts, Marāthās, Sikhs and a number of other allied problems. While in Bihar, Farrukh Siyar, at the instance of Ḥusain 'Alī, had issued a proclamation abolishing the *jizyah.*[43] This order was confirmed after the victory of Farrukh Siyar at Agra.[44] But it appears that formal effect was not given to it till Ḥusain 'Alī submitted a petition in April 1713 praying that a *parwānah* be sent to the *daftar-i-diwāni* (confirming the order of abolition).[45] Similarly, the pilgrim-tax was also abolished from a number of places,[46] though the ban on the Hindus using *pālkīs* and 'Irāqī horses continued for some time.[47]

As for the Rājpūts, immediately on Farrukh Siyar's accession Jai Singh, Ajit Singh, the Mahārānā and others had sent letters of felicitation and submission which were placed before the Emperor by Ḥusain 'Alī.[48] Messengers were sent to Jai Singh and

43 See p. 133 above.

44 This was done on 16 January 1713, six days after the victory over Jahāndār (B.M., 1690, f. 163, Kāmwar, 390, Khush-ḥāl, 99, Irvine i, 246).

45 *Akhbārāt,* 2, 12 April 1713. *V.V.* (p. 935) gives a story that Bihari Das, the *wakīl* of Udaipur, gave friendly advice to 'Abdullāh Khān that 'the Hindus were alienated on account of (the imposition of) *Jizyah*... if he abolished *Jizyah,* the foundations (*bunyād*) of his power would be strengthened.' Abdullāh Khān agreed to this and got the emperor to excuse *jizyah.*

Tod (ii, 935) states that *jizyah* was abolished at the instance of Khemsi Bhandāri after Ḥusain 'Alī's Mārwār campaign.

Khush-ḥāl states that *jizyah* was abolished at the instance of Chhabelā Rām, and this is supported by Shiv Dās, who has reproduced a copy of an '*arẓī* submitted by Chhabelā Rām's nephew, Girdhar Bahādur, in 1720 to Muḥammad Shāh, stating that when Chhabelā Rām had joined Farrukh Siyar, he had secured a promise from him to abolish *jizyah* if victory was granted to his arms. According to this agreement (*qarār-dād*) the *jizyah* was abolished. (Shiv Dās *Iqbālnāmah,* 329).

46 *Bālmukundanāmah* No. 27, *Akhbārāt,* 14 August 1714—complaint that the *faujdār* of Allahabad was charging four annas per pilgrim attended to; 12 January 1716 *ditto* for Agra.

47 The order was confirmed on 11 December 1713 and reaffirmed on 10 June 1714. But on 20 October 1715, the *wakīls* and *mutaṣaddīs* who had used *pālkīs* in the time of Aurangzīb were allowed to do so, and on 19 November 1716, the order was cancelled altogether at the instance of Mukham Singh, the *wāqi'-nigār Kul* (*Akhbārāt*).

48 *Akhbārāt,* 29 and 31 January, 6, 12, 18 and 20 February 1713, Kāmwar, 394.

Ajit Singh summoning them to the court.[49] But they feigned fear and apprehension in coming to the court because of the perfidious conduct of the emperor in the case of Ẕu'lfiqār Khān. However, they expressed their readiness to accept any service in the provinces to which they might be appointed, and promised to come to the court after two or three years when their fear had abated. At the same time, privately, they petitioned for the *ṣūbahdārīs* of Malwa and Gujarāt, or Malwa and Burhānpur.[50]

The attitude of the Rājpūt rajas provoked the ire of Farrukh Siyar. At a meeting which was attended by Ḥusain 'Alī, Mīr Jumlah and Khān-i-Daurān, he remarked 'I have no doubt about the loyalty of Jai Singh, but it is now certain that he is in league with Ajit Singh. We must use statecraft and stratagem (to deal with them). It is not possible that we send both (the Rajas) to the same quarter, as that would be against the interests of the empire'. In other words, like Bahādur Shāh before him, Farrukh Siyar felt that the union of Jai Singh and Ajit Singh was a threat to the empire. Hence, in the same meeting, it was decided that after *Ramazān* (c. 20 October), Ḥusain 'Alī would leave for Mārwār with an army to chastise Ajit Singh.[51] At the same time, both Jai Singh and Ajit Singh were raised to the rank of 7,000/7,000, and Jai Singh was appointed the *ṣūbahdār* of Malwa, and Ajit Singh the *ṣūbahdār* of Thatta. This move was designed to disrupt the alliance of the two rajas. It succeeded in doing so. Jai Singh accepted the offer of Malwa and left for his charge, but Ajit Singh who 'had his eyes on Gujarāt, felt it beneath his dignity to accept Thatta, and refused to obey'.[52]

This provided a justification for the war against Ajit Singh.[53] At

49 *Akhbārāt*, 14, 16 July 1713.

50 M.M., ff. 59b–60a.

51 *J.R.*—Pancholi Jagjiwan Ram's Report to Jai Singh d. 7 *Ramaẓān* Yr. 2, 27 September 1713.

52 M.M., f. 60a, Khalīl, 40. The rajas were appointed on 6 *Shawwāl* Yr. 2, 26 October 1713 (*Akhbārāt*, and Jai Singh's letter d. 11 *Shawwāl*, Kamwar, 12 *Shawwāl*). The rajas were asked to proceed to their charge immediately without waiting for regular and formal *farmāns*. (Ḥusain 'Alī's letter to Jai Singh d. 1125, *Misc. Papers*, Vol. II, p. 159. In reply, Jai Singh informed the Emperor that he had sent his *peshkhānah* towards Ujjain. (Letter d. 11 *Shawwāl*, *Misc. Papers* ii, 153).

53 According to Irvine (i, 236), the cause of the war with Ajit Singh was

first, Farrukh Siyar decided to lead the campaign himself, in order to vindicate the Imperial prestige which, it was felt, had been sorely offended by Ajit Singh's disobedience of the Imperial orders. Another reason for Farrukh Siyar's annoyance was that Ajit Singh had assassinated Muhkam Singh and Mohan Singh, sons of Indra Singh of Nāgor, both of whom were Mughal *manṣabdārs*.[54] However, in the middle of December, the campaign against Ajit Singh was entrusted to the chief *bakhshī*, Ḥusain 'Alī Khān, who set out at the head of a large army on 6 January 1714.

With the commencement of the Mārwār campaign, the struggle between the Saiyid brothers and Farrukh Siyar enters a new phase. Hitherto, it had not gone beyond personal ill-will and mutual recriminations. Now, at the instigation of his favourites, the emperor went so far as to intrigue against the life and honour of the two brothers. Apparently, the Saiyids did not see eye-to-eye with the Rājpūt policy of Farrukh Siyar. Ḥusain 'Alī had been in secret touch with the Rājpūt rajas all along, and had been discussing schemes of a compromise with the Jaipur *wakīl* at the court, Pancholi Jagjiwan Rām.[55] On his part, Farrukh Siyar was apparently keen to separate the two brothers so that he could deal with them one by one. Shortly after the departure of Ḥusain 'Alī for Mārwār, he sent secret letters to Ajit Singh, promising him favours if he would defeat and kill the *mīr bakhshī*.[56]

The result of this back-hand intrigue was somewhat unexpected for Farrukh Siyar. Ḥusain 'Alī came to know of the emperor's plot

---

that 'after forbidding cow-slaughter, forbidding call for prayers from the Alamgiri mosque, besides ejecting Imperial Officers from Jodhpur... he had occupied Ajmer.' But Jodhpur had been evacuated by Bahādur Shāh in 1709, and there is no mention of its subsequent re-occupation by the Mughals. It seems that Irvine confused the events of 1707 or of 1720 with those of 1713.

54 This incident took place on 25 August 1713. The emperor was enraged and wanted to destroy Jaswantpurā, but was dissuaded by Ḥusain 'Alī who pointed out the futility of the step and told Farrukh Siyar that Ajit's treachery would be seen to. (J.R.—'*Sarkar Collection*', Vol. XIV, No. 73).

Also *V.V.*, 841, Tod ii, 175, Ojha, *Jodhpur* ii, 554–5.

55 *J.R.*, report of Jagjiwan Rām, d. 27 September 1713. One compromise offered by Ḥusain 'Alī was that Jai Singh should be appointed the *ṣūbahdār* of Malwa or Burhānpur, and Ajit Singh of Lahore, Awadh, Allahabad or Banāras (Agra may have been meant).

56 Kāmwar, 13 *Ẕīqa'dah*, 12 December, K.K., 738, Shiv Dās, 10.

against him, either because the emperor's letters fell into his hands, or, as some contemporary observers have suggested, because Ajit Singh communicated their contents to Ḥusain 'Alī in order to induce him to make peace. Letters from 'Abdullāh Khān also reached the *mīr bakhshī* urgently recalling him to court as he ('Abdullāh) was finding it difficult to maintain his position in the face of opposition from the emperor's favourites.[57]

In March 1714, a treaty was concluded between Ḥusain 'Alī and Ajit Singh. By its terms, Ajit Singh agreed to give his daughter in marriage to Farrukh Siyar (*dolā*), to send his son, Abhai Singh, to the court with the *mīr bakhshī,* and to attend in person when ever he was summoned. He also agreed to give *peshkash* and to accept the appointment to Thatta.[58]

According to one writer, the treaty was made at the instance of Jai Singh who persuaded Ajit Singh that this was the best course for him in the circumstances.[59] But the most important part of the treaty was a private pact between Ḥusain 'Alī and Ajit Singh which was kept secret for the time being. According to it, Ḥusain 'Alī promised that as soon as Ajit Singh had marched a couple of stages towards Thatta, and thus publicly demonstrated his obedience of the Imperial orders, he would be appointed to Gujarāt. In compliance with this understanding, Ajit Singh left for Thatta, and as soon as he had marched a few stages, he was appointed the *ṣūbahdār* of Gujarāt.[60]

Thus, Ḥusain 'Alī followed a policy exactly the reverse of the one he had been sent out to implement. Instead of separating the two Rajas, he gave them Malwa and Gujarāt, thus conceding the last of the demands which Jai Singh and Ajit Singh had been making since the time of Bahādur Shāh. This may be said to mark the beginning of an alliance between the Saiyid brothers and the Rājpūts.

Meanwhile, relations between the two brothers and Farrukh Siyar were rapidly reaching the point of a crisis.

57 *Ibid.*

58 M.M., 60a, K.K., 738, *M.U.* i, 321, Qāsim, 80. According to *Iqbāl* (Rampur) 6, Ajit gave to Ḥusain 'Alī 50 lakhs in cash, 50 horses, 10 elephants, and 50 lakhs in jewellery as *peshkash.* These figures seem somewhat difficult to credit.

59 Khush-ḥāl (Sarkar Ms.) 378.

60 M.M., 60a (the only authority to mention it). The formal *farmān* was not issued till 14 December 1714 (*Akhbārāt*).

The First Trial of Strength—Its Causes and Consequences

We have already seen that the relations between the Saiyid brothers and Farrukh Siyar were far from cordial from the very beginning. After the accession of Farrukh Siyar, these relations steadily deteriorated till an open breach was precipitated towards the end of the year 1714.

From the outset, the struggle was essentially for power. The Saiyids wanted not merely the appearance but the substance of power, while Farrukh Siyar, though lacking in any real ability, had the ambition of exercising personal authority. Concretely, the Saiyids desired that 'no business should be transacted or *manṣab*s given or promotions and appointments made without their advice and consultation'.[61] Farrukh Siyar felt that this claim went much beyond the traditional powers and functions of the *wazīr* and that if acquiesced in, it would inevitably reduce the emperor to the position of a figure-head.

Thus, the real issue was two divergent concepts of the *wizārat.* Like Z̲u'lifiqār Khān earlier, the Saiyid brothers felt that the interests of the empire were bound up with the concentration of effective power in their own hands, and hence, they wanted to make the *wazīr* the real hub of affairs, while the king merely reigned. They clearly felt that they had secured the crown for Farrukh Siyar by the strength of their arms, and hence considered their claims for supreme power to be indisputable. Farrukh Siyar, on the other hand, stuck to the concept of the *wazīr* being merely the chief adviser of the king and the head of the revenue department, but not having any power of independent initiative.

This divergence in outlook manifested itself from the very beginning. After his appointment as the *wazīr*, 'Abdullāh Khān promised the post of *ṣadr* to Saiyid Amjad Khān who had held the same post in Bahādur Shāh's time, and that of the *diwān-i-khāliṣah* to Luṭfullāh Khān Ṣādiq.[62] But on his way from Agra, Farrukh Siyar

61 K.K., 379, M.M., 60 (Ṣarkar Ms.). *M.U.* (i, p. 328) says that 'Abdullāh Khān wanted that no appointments should be made *in his department* without consulting him.

62 He was the *wakīl* of Prince Jahān Shāh in the time of Bahādur Shāh, and had deserted him during the war of succession at Lahore, making his way into Jahāndār's favour by a big bribe (30 lakhs according to Wārid). He was

assigned these offices to his own followers—his tutor, Afzal Khān, being made the *ṣadr* and Raja Chhabelā Ram Nāgar[63] being made the *diwān-i-khāliṣah* and *tan*.

When Farrukh Siyar arrived at Delhi, 'Abdullāh Khān objected to these appointments. On behalf of the Emperor, it was argued that when a sovereign deputed power to a minister, it was for the minister to recognize the limits of that power and not make appointments to high offices without previous sanction. Upon this 'Abdullāh Khān flew into a rage and declared that if his very first exercise of power was contested, there was no point in his being the *wazīr*.[64]

After some time, a compromise was arrived at. The *wazīrs*' nominee, Luṭfullāh Khān, was allowed to retain the post of the *dīwān-i-tan*, but the post of the *dīwān-i-khāliṣah* was entrusted to Mu'tamad Khān—an old Bahādur Shāhī noble and the ex-*khān-i-sāmān* and *dīwān* of Jahān Shāh. Chhabelā Ram Nāgar was appointed the Governor of Agra. Afẓal Khān remained in charge of the *ṣadr's* office.[65]

But the substance of the dispute remained unsettled.

The ill-will and mutual discord between the king and his ministers was further accentuated by the activities of some of the personal favourites of the king, who thought that their opportunity lay in fomenting the discord between the two sides.

---

appointed the *dīwan* of Prince 'Azz-ud-Dīn when the latter was sent to check Farrukh Siyar, and after the flight of that prince, joined Farrukh Siyar. Later, he is said to have assisted Mīr Jumlah in seducing the officers of Jahāndār Shāh (K.K., Irvine i, 227).

Luṭfullāh K. traced his descent from one of the Imāms. His family had come to India in the time of Balban and settled down at Panipat, and its members occupied honourable positions under the later sovereigns of Delhi (*Gulshan-i-Ṣādiq*, Punjab Public Lib. Ms., p. 42).

63 A Nāgar brahman from Gujarāt, according to Harcharan (p. 33), his real name was Hirday Rām. He had long been employed in the revenue service of 'Aẓīm-ush-Shān along with his brother, Dayā Rām, who was killed fighting on 'Aẓīm-ush-Shān's side at Lahore.

Chhabelā Rām was the *faujdār* of Korā-Jahānabād at the time, and deserted to Fārrukh Siyar when Prince 'Azz-ud-Dīn reached that side. (*Ajā'ib-ul-Āfāq*, f. 19b, 29b, K.K., 728. See Irvine, pp. 214–18 for details.)

64 K.K., 729–30.

65 M.M., 23a, K.K., 721, *Akhbārāt*, 17, 27 February and 8 March 1713.

Two of the leading favourites of the king were Khān-i-Daurān and Mīr Jumlah.

Mīr Jumlah was a native of Tūrān, and had been the Qāẓī of Dacca and later of Patna in the time of Aurangzīb. He had gradually won the confidence of 'Aẕīm-ush-Shān who was then the governor of Bihar and Bengal, and, allegedly, also acquired great influence over his second son, Farrukh Siyar. Mīr Jumlah was at Lahore with Aẕīm-ush-Shān when Bahādur Shāh died. After the defeat and death of 'Aẕīm-ush-Shān, he made his way to Agra where he joined Farrukh Siyar.[66] He earned the gratitude of the latter by inducing two of the important nobles, Chīn Qulīch and M. Amīn Khīn, to remain neutral in the battle of Agra.[67] After the victory, he was raised to the rank of 6,000 *z̲āt*, and also rewarded with the posts of the *dāroghah-i-khāwaṣṣān* and the *dāroghah-i-ghusalkhānah* (superintendent of the private-retinue and the privy audience-chamber), and a few other minor posts.[68]

Khān-i-Daurān (Khwājah Āṣim)[69] had also been in the employ of 'Aẕīm-ush-Shān. His elder brother, Khwājah Anwar, was a boon companion of 'Aẕīm-ush-Shān, and his virtual prime minister till his death while fighting against a rebel, Raḥīm Khān, in 1697. His accumulated treasures, which were very considerable, were inherited by Khwājah 'Aṣim who, though much older than Farrukh Siyar, joined that prince in wrestling, archery, polo etc.[70] Khwājah 'Āṣim

66 *M.U.* iii, 7, 11 *Tārīkh-i-Hinḍī,* 522–3.

67 K.K., 700. According to the *Jangnāmah* of Shri Dhar Murli (*J.A.S.B.*, 1900), the Saiyids had their own agents at the court of Jahāndār Shāh for seducing his officers.

68 M.M., 24a, Kāmwar, 17 January 1713, *Akhbārāt,* 9 March, 28 May 1713, *M.U.* iii, 711.

69 Khwājah 'Aṣim's grand-father, Khwājah Abū'l Muḥsin came to India from Badakhshān (Tūrān) and settled down in the Punjab. His son, Kh. Muḥammad Qāsim, enrolled as a *wālā-shāhī* of 'Aẕīm-ush-Shān. Subsequently, the family shifted to Agra.

Khwājah Qāsim had five sons: Kh. 'Āṣim and Kh. Muẓaffar were real brothers, and the other three were Kh. Anwar, Kh. Ja'far and Kh. Bāqar. Kh. Ja'far was a *faqīr.* He called himself the *mujtahid* of the age and was suspected of *shī'ah* tendencies. He acquired a great name in the time of Farrukh Siyar, and even had some hand in the political events of the period. Except Kh. Muẓaffar, none of other brothers rose to a high position (Āshūb, 253, *M.U.* i, 819, '*Imād,* 23).

70 *Riyāẓ,* 235–7.

soon acquired so much influence over the young prince that complaints reached 'Aẓīm-ush-Shān, who recalled Khwājah 'Āṣim to Lahore. After the defeat and death of 'Aẓīm-ush-Shān, Khwājah 'Aṣim fled to Bihar and joined Farrukh Siyar. He was made the *dāroghah-i-dīwān-i-khāṣ* and, for same time, also held the post of *Mīr Ātish* though he did not play any prominent part in the battle of Agra. After the victory, he was promoted to the rank of 6,000/6,000 with the title of Khān-i-Daurān, confirmed in the post of the *dāroghah-i-dīwān-i-khāṣ* and also appointed the *bakhshī* of the *wālā-shāhīs* (the Emperor's personal troops).[71]

Thus, neither Mīr Jumlah nor Khān-i-Daurān had much experience of administrative or military affairs. But both of them—especially Mīr Jumlah, were extremely ambitious. Mīr Jumlah is described as a man of learning and a friend of the learned, a friendly, generous and upright man from whom many received kindness. But '(he) was unwilling that the reins of the government of Hindustan should pass into the hands of the Bārahā Saiyids. When he saw that the sovereign power was entirely under the control of the two brothers, he could not suppress his envy and rivalry'.[72] Mīr Jumlah and Khān-i-Daurān resented their supersession by the Saiyid brothers whom they regarded as comparative new-comers and upstarts. Hence, they tried to induce the Emperor by all means in their power to oust their rivals. Farrukh Siyar, who was already suspicious of the Saiyids and dreaded their power and influence, lent a ready ear to these persuasions. He also hoped to find in Mīr Jumlah a more willing tool for his ambition of exercising personal power.

Thus, Farrukh Siyar, Khān-i-Daurān and Mīr Jumlah ranged themselves in opposition to the Saiyid brothers, and upheld the principle of the personal rule of the monarch. As opposed to this, the Saiyids were firmly of the opinion that the task of running the administration should be left in the hands of the *wazīr* and the *mīr bakhshī*. This became the central issue in party politics during Farrukh Siyar's reign, all other issues being linked with it.

Mīr Jumlah and Khān-i-Daurān gradually gained a complete

71 *Khazānah-i-Āmrah* 246, *Sawāniḥ-i-Khushgū* (O.P.L. Ms.) ff. 140a–b, '*Imād* 35, *M.U.* i, 819, *Akhbārāt*, 16 February 1713 (for further increments see entries d. 9 March, 28 May, 6 June, 8 July, 19 November 1719), Kāmwar, 396, 398, K.K., 729–30.

72 K.K., 732, *T. Hindī*, ff. 523.

ascendency over the mind of Farrukh Siyar who had always been led by others, and had no independent opinion or judgement of his own.[73] The accession of Farrukh Siyar was followed by a spate of executions and confiscations, chief among the victims being Z̲u'lfiqār Khān and Asad Khān, Sādullāh Khān the *diwān-i-tan*, Hidāyat Khān the *wāqī' nigār-i-kul*, Sīdī Qāsim the *kotwāl*, and many others. All these were popularly ascribed to the influence of Mīr Jumlah who, it was said, wanted to destroy the old nobility in order to clear his own way to power.[74] It may be doubted if the Saiyids had any hand in them for they preferred, as we have seen, a very different policy. The most heinous crime committed by Farrukh Siyar, allegedly at the instance of Mīr Jumlah, was the blinding of all his younger brothers so as a deprive the Saiyids of a possible tool in case they should wish to displace him.[75]

These events led to a widening of the breach between the King and his ministers. Other disputes also arose. Thus, on reaching Delhi, the Saiyids had occupied the residences lately belonging to Z̲u'lfiqār Khān and Kokaltāh Khān. It was suggested to the emperor that the wealth of generations which was hoarded there had been appropriated by the Saiyids, whereas he, the emperor, had inherited only an empty treasury.

A foolish superstition that after Bahādur Shāh his youngest descendant would reign, who in turn would be followed by a Saiyid also influenced the impressionable mind of the emperor.[76]

In spite of these differences and the growing ill-will, there was no open breach between Farrukh Siyar and the Saiyids till, emboldened by the secret support of the Emperor, the favourites started interfering in the administration.[77] Farrukh Siyar authorized Mīr Jumlah to sign all papers on his behalf, and repeatedly

73 K.K., 730.

74 Mīr Jumlah's part in the assassination of Z̲u'lfiqār Khān has been already discussed. (See p. 136 above). The execution of Sa'dullāh Khān is also ascribed to Mīr Jumlah 'who was envious of his reputation as a second 'Ināyatullāh Khān' (M.M., p. 68b). The execution of Shaikh Qudratullāh, the favourite of Prince 'Aẓīm-ush-Shān, is inscribed by M.M. (pp. 27b–29b) to Mīr Jumlah's fear that the Shaikh would regain his old influence. See also K.K., 740, Wārid, 150b, Kāmwar, 144, M.M., 30 ff. Irvine, 275–81.

75 Wārid, 277, K.K., 740, Kāmwar, 219a.

76 Wārid, 277.

77 Thus, at Mīr Jumlah's instance, Ḥaidar Qulī was made the *dīwān* of the Deccan with very wide powers. He was made the *dīwān* of all the *ṣūbahs* of

declared: 'The word and signature of Mīr Jumlah are my word and signature'.[78] Mīr Jumlah resorted to the practise of entertaining proposals directly from the aspirants to *manṣab*s and promotions, and set the emperor's signature upon letters of appointment without having them passed through the *dīwān-i-wizārat*. This was contrary to all the established rules of procedure, and also effected the prestige and authority of the *wazīr* and deprived him of the perquisites of appointment which were a well-known and substantial source of income. Hence, Mīr Jumlah's practice caused great umbrage to the Saiyids.[79]

Mīr Jumlah was encouraged in his conduct by 'Abdullāh Khān's disinclination to attend to the details of administration. He was primarily a soldier, and preferred to leave all the affairs of state and ministerial duties in the hands of his *dīwān*, Ratan Chand.[80] Ratan Chand was haughty and overbearing and, according to one writer, 'had a mouth as insatiable as the nethermost hell for swallowing gold and silver'.[81] He would do nothing without a suitable bribe for himself and for 'Abdullāh Khān, which was in addition to customary (but illegal) fees for appointments. Mīr Jumlah refrained from these extortionate practices, and also showed despatch in business. Hence, he was preferred by candidates for office and *manṣab*. Out of pique, Ratan Chand influenced 'Abdullāh Khān, who made it a practice to set aside any appointment in

the Deccan in addition to being the *dīwān* for the whole of the Deccan. The *amānat* of all the *khāliṣah* lands, and the superintendentship of all the diamond mines was also granted to him. 'In fact, except the *wāqī'-navīs* and the department of Justice, he was entrusted with authority over all other departments' (K.K., 740, *M.U.* iii, 476). Niẓām-ul-Mulk did not get on with Ḥaidar Qulī, and after some time, on his own responsibility he ordered him to go back to Delhi. Niẓām-ul-Mulk thus gained supreme control of the executive and revenue affairs of the Deccan.

78 K.K., 739.

79 K.K., 739, Khush-ḥāl, 102.

80 K.K., 739, Khush-ḥāl, 102, *Siyar*, 396, Khālīl, 55, Qāsim, 78.

Elliot (vii, 447) calls Ratan Chand a grain-merchant. There is no evidence to warrant the belief that Ratan Chand ever kept a shop, though he was a *bania* by caste, and a resident of Jānsath. He had long been an associate of the Saiyids: in 1712 he had fought bravely against 'Abdu'l Ghafūr on 'Abdullāh Khān's side, and as a reward had received the title of Raja and the rank of 2,000 (K.K., 692, 712).

81 Qāsim, 87.

which he suspected the hand of Mīr Jumlah. Thus, the efficiency of the administration suffered, and much annoyance was felt by the emperor and the parties concerned.[82]

On another score, too, Farrukh Siyar had justifiable cause for complaint against the Saiyid brothers. Under Ratan Chand, the practice of revenue-farming (*ijārah*) became universal. Even *khāliṣah* lands were farmed out. Whenever an '*āmil* was appointed, Ratan Chand would take from him a contract or lease in writing and realize the money from his banker.[83] Farrukh Siyar rightly considered this practice to be a ruinous one, and had issued standing orders forbidding *ijārah.*[84]

Mīr Jumlah took advantage of all these factors, and impressed upon Farrukh Siyar that the Saiyids were unfit for high office and that there would be no peace and prosperity in the empire as long as they had a hand in the administration. He charged them, further, with being haughty and ease-loving, and of looking upon the emperor as their creation, and of lowering his prestige by disregarding his authority.[85]

Hoping to overawe the Saiyids and make them retire from their offices voluntarily, Farrukh Siyar began to augment the military power of his favourites. Mīr Jumlah was permitted to keep 5,000 Mughal *sawār*s who were to be paid directly from the state treasury and were allotted *jāgīr*s in the *sūbah* of Lahore. Earlier, Mīr Jumlah had been made the *ṣūbahdār* of Bengal and raised to the rank of 7,000/7,000.[86] Khān-i-Daurān, too, was placed at the head of 5,000 *wālā-shāhī*s and allotted *jāgīr*s in the *ṣūbah*s of Delhi and Agra. He had earlier been appointed the *ṣūbahdār* of Agra and raised to the rank of 7,000. A number of relatives of these two favourites were also pushed forward till each of them had over 10,000 men at his command.[87]

82 K.K., 739.

83 K.K., 773, 919, *Mir'āt* ii, 141, Khush-ḥāl, 399b, Yahyā, 123b, *Siyar,* 407. *Jāgīr* lands were sometimes farmed out even in the reign of Aurangzīb (*Cf.* S. A. Rashid, *A Calendar of Oriental Records,* Allhd. 1956, ii, 13). The practice seems to have become universal in the time of Jahāndār Shāh (Wārid, 6), and was apparently continued by Ratan Chand.

84 *Akhbārāt,* d. 23 *Rajab,* Yr. 4, 25 July 1715.

85 M.M., 31a, K.K., 739, Qāsim, 78–9.

86 M.M., 31a, Kāmwar, 399, *Akhbārāt,* 28 May 1713, *Iqbāl,* 2.

87 M.M., 31a, *Iqbāl, 2,* Kāmwar, *Akhbārāt,* 24, 25 *Ramaẓān,* 14, 15 October 1714.

This was the situation which Ḥusain 'Alī confronted on his return from Mārwār.

After due deliberations, Ḥusain 'Alī came to the conclusion that it would not be possible for them to maintain their position at the court unless they gained control of one of the more important *ṣūbahs*, and could utilize its resources. Accordingly, he demanded and secured for himself the viceroyalty of the Deccan in place of Niẓām-ul-Mulk.[88] His intention was to revive Ẕu'lfiqār Khān's practice of discharging his duties in the Deccan through a deputy, and to remain at the court himself. Hence, he nominated Dā'ūd Khān Pannī as his deputy, stipulating with him for an annual sum of money in return for full freedom to carry on the local administration.[89] This was a vicious practice, but Farrukh Siyar could not logically object to it because shortly before this, his favourite, Mīr Jumlah had been permitted to make a similar pact with Murshid Qulī Khān, the Deputy Governor of Bengal.[90] However, on the advice of Mīr Jumlah, Farrukh Siyar turned down Ḥusain 'Alī's request, and ordered that he should proceed to the Deccan personally.[91]

A crisis now developed. Like Bahādur Shāh before, Farrukh Siyar regarded the combination of three such powerful posts as those of *wazīr*, chief *bakhshī* and the Viceroy of the Deccan in one family as a threat to the dynasty. On the other hand, the Saiyids were not prepared to relinquish any of the offices they held. Rather, they regarded Farrukh Siyar's order a clever move on the part of their enemies to separate them in order to deal with them one by one. Hence, the Amīrul-Umarā Ḥusain 'Alī, after considering the course pursued by the king and Mīr Jumlah, refused to go to the Deccan and leave his brother alone at the court'.[92]

Apparently, the emperor also objected to Ḥusain 'Alī's private agreement with Ajit Singh, and delayed issuing a *farmān* confirming the appointment of the latter as the Governor of Gujarāt.[93]

88 *Akhbārāt*, 11, *Ramaẓān* Yr. 3, 20 September 1714, Kāmwar, 20, *Ramaẓān*, 29 September.

89 K.K., 739.

90 *Akhbārāt*, 3, *Jamāda* I, Yr. 2, 28 May 1713.

91 K.K., 739, *M.U.* i, 326, iii, 712, Khalīl, 56.

92 K.K., 739.

93 The agreement had been made in April, and in June Ajit Singh had left for Thatta. But he was not appointed to Gujarāt till 23 *Ẕilḥijjah* Yr. 3, 30 December 1714, i.e. till the dispute with the Saiyids was over. Even then,

It was at this juncture that Ḥusain 'Alī discovered a plot to murder him.[94] The brothers thereupon retired to their houses, and fearing an attack by the emperor's supporters, 'meditated the levying of soldiers and throwing up lines of defence round their residence'.[95] Thus, the Saiyids clearly showed that they were determined not to yield to threats of force.

Pressed to contemplate an open trial of strength, the emperor and his advisers hesitated and faltered. Mīr Jumlah and Khān-i-Daurān shrank from measuring their strength with that of the Saiyids of Bārahā, for they 'were only carpet knights, not true fighters'.[96] Realising their weakness, they advised Farrukh Siyar to open negotiations with M. Amīn Khān, the second *bakhshī*, who was an experienced warrior, having won his spurs under Aurangzīb.

We are told that M. Amīn Khāṇ was willing to undertake the task, but in reward he wanted the *wizārat* for himself. For the emperor and his favourites, this was a remedy worse than the disease: for if the Saiyids were got rid of with the help of M. Amīn Khān, it would be still more difficult to get rid of him afterwards.[97]

Thus, the dilemma confronting Farrukh Siyar and his advisers was that lacking any real strength and confidence in themselves, they could only juggle with powerful pieces in an attempt to keep real authority in their hands. A ruler more competent than Farrukh Siyar might have succeeded in this game for some time, but it could not but lead to disaster and ruin for the empire in the long run since it meant the negation of strong and effective rule by the centre.

Ajit was not trusted, and Ḥaidar Qulī Khān, the *dīwān* was granted special powers so that he could act as a check upon him (*Mir'āt* ii, 5–6, *Akhbārāt: J.R.*—copy of *farmān* of appointment).

94 According to M.M. (31b), the plot was to make Ḥusain 'Alī a prisoner when he came to present to the emperor a son who had been born to him recently (*Akhbārāt* mentions the birth of a son on 15 May 1714, and also on 17 November). But the plot was revealed to the Saiyids by some palace servants (according to M.M.), or by Luṭfullāh Khān Ṣādiq (according to *Aḥwāl*), or by the Queen-mother herself (according to K.K., 740).

95 K.K., 740. Kh. Khalīl (p. 57) a supporter of the Saiyids, states that for some days artillery was placed round the Imperial fort, and by 'Abdullāh Khān round his house, and there were preparations for war.

96 M.M., 33b, Qāsim, 79.

97 M.M., 32b.

Failing to coerce the Saiyids, Farrukh Siyar fell back on compromise. Emissaries were sent to the brothers, the queen-mother herself visiting them and taking the most solemn oaths on her son's behalf. At last, it was agreed that both Mīr Jumlah and Ḥusain 'Alī should assume personal charge of their provinces.[98] It was further stipulated that Ḥusain 'Alī would come to pay his respects to the emperor only after the departure of Mīr Jumlah whom the Saiyids considered the evil genius of the Emperor. At the time of his visit, all the arrangements in the fort were to be in the hands of the employees of the Saiyids.[99]

According to this agreement, Mīr Jumlah left the court on 16 December. On the 20th, Ḥusain 'Alī entered the palace, with his men posted at all strategic points. The most solemn vows were exchanged and, outwardly, cordial relations between Farrukh Siyar and the Saiyids were restored. On 20 May 1715,[100] Ḥusain 'Alī left for the Deccan, carrying with him the authority to appoint and dismiss all *jāgīrdārs* and office holders in the Deccan, and to transfer the commandants of the forts. It was even rumoured that Farrukh Siyar had been compelled to hand over the royal seal to Ḥusain 'Alī so that the latter may not have to depend on his formal assent for appointments etc.

Further, it is said that before leaving Delhi, Ḥusain 'Alī warned Farrukh Siyar that if his brother was molested or Mīr Jumlah recalled, he could count on his return from the Deccan in 20 days.[101]

98 Khāfi Khān (p. 741) says that Jumlah was appointed to Bihar only. M.M. (p. 35a) says, however, that Mīr Jumlah was appointed to both Bengal and Bihar. The *Akhbārāt refer* to him as the *ṣūbahdār* Bengal (15 and 25 December 1715 and 18 January 1716). The English factors reported that Jumlah was coming as the Governor of Bengal, and sent their agents to contact him (Wilson ii, 212, 220, 242). However, Mīr Jumlah did not proceed beyond Patna.

99 K.K., 741, Wārid, 284, Khalīl, 60. Qāsim (p. 87) ascribes the sending away of both these nobles to the advice of 'elderly people' who stressed the dangers of disunity, and the need of appointing a brave noble like Ḥusain 'Alī to the Deccan. M.M. who totally fails to understand the whole point of the dispute, ascribes Ḥusain 'Alī's departure to his disgust with recent affairs.

100 *Akhbārāt*, Mīr Jumlah's actual departure was not reported till April 1715. Ḥusain 'Alī stayed on near Delhi for a month after this. On 28 May, he reached Rewari which is 50 miles from Delhi.

101 K.K., 742.

Thus ended the first trial of strength between the Saiyid brothers and Farrukh Siyar. The outcome was, to all outward appearances, a great triumph for the Saiyids. The emperor not only failed to dislodge them from their offices, but had to accept the humiliating condition of handing over the charge of the fort to their men before they would come to pay their respects to him. Thus, the ministers dictated and imposed their own conditions on the monarch who tacitly accepted the special position of the Saiyids.

In fact, however, the struggle revealed the weakness of their position to the Saiyids, and forced them to accept a compromise. They found pitted against themselves not only the monarchy but also a strong section of the nobility, including the powerful group led by M. Amīn Khān. The Bārahā clan, by itself, was too small to maintain them in power, and in the hour of trial, when it was rumoured that the emperor had decided to dismiss them, many even among the Bārahās had begun to waver.[102] Hence, they felt the necessity of creating a strong territorial base for themselves. But it was impossible to create such a base unless one of the brothers took charge of it personally. It was, perhaps, for this reason that Ḥusain 'Alī dropped his original demand for permission to govern the Deccan through a deputy, and agreed to proceed to it himself.[103]

Thus, on the main point at issue, the Saiyids had to yield. They also agreed to hand over the charge of the *mīr bakhshī*'s office to one of the emperor's favourites, Khān-i-Daurān.[104] This was partially offset by the departure of Mīr Jumlah for Bihar at the same time. However, Mīr Jumlah was not sent away in disgrace, for he

102 M.M., ff. 33b, 34a.

103 Some of the relations of the Saiyids were of the opinion that the control of two strong territorial units would be preferable to the precarious *wizārat* and *mīr bakhshīgiri.* Saiyid Khān-i-Jahān and Asadullāh Khān, the uncles of the Saiyids, are said to have advised them to ask for Bengal and the Deccan. The Saiyids thought the idea to be a good one but felt that they would be accused of mediating independence (*Aḥwāl,* p. 93b in Irvine i, p. 300).

It would be seen that an additional reason was that the Saiyids had not yet lost hope of gaining full control over the central government.

104 Khān-i-Daurān was appointed on 8 June 1715 (Kāmwar). At the time of the dispute, Khān-i-Daurān had secretly promised through his brother, Kh. *Ja'far* the holy man, not to join any conspiracy against the Saiyids in future (M.M., p. 34b, *M.U.* i, pp. 819–30). He may have been acceptable to the Saiyids for this reason.

was accompanied by 7,000 Mughal troops, these being over and above his quota as a governor. The Saiyids, doubtless, hoped for some respite from intrigues after Mīr Jumlah's departure, but he remained a constant source of danger to them. Nor did the agreement produce even a temporary abatement in the emperor's hostility towards them. As a matter of fact, as soon as Ḥusain 'Alī's back was turned. Farrukh Siyar sent secret instructions to Dā'ūd Khān Pannī[105] transferring him from Gujarāt to Burhānpur, and ordering him to resist Ḥusain 'Alī. Dā'ūd Khān proceeded from Gujarāt by forced marches, and reached Burhānpur on 13 August. A battle was fought on 6 September, in which Dā'ūd Khān was defeated and killed. The secret letters sent to him by Farrukh Siyar fell into the hands of Ḥusain 'Alī, thus giving the Saiyids fresh proof of the duplicity of their royal master.

In addition to the continued hostility of the emperor and his friends, the Saiyids had to reckon with the powerful group of M. Amīn Khān, Niẕām-ul-Mulk and 'Abduṣ-Ṣamad Khān. M. Amīn's part in the conspiracy against the Saiyids has been already noted. Niẕām-ul-Mulk showed his resentment at his supersession in the Deccan by neglecting to call on Ḥusain 'Alī though he passed within a few miles of the latter on his way back to Delhi. Ḥusain 'Alī was surprised and aggrieved, for he had looked upon Niẕām-ul-Mulk as a sworn friend. But the latter's resentment at his supersession was not unexpected.[106] If Niẕām-ul-Mulk and M. Amīn

105 Dā'ūd Khān Pannī had been appointed the Governor of Burhānpur on 27 *Rabī'* II Yr. 3, 12 May 1715, at the instance of Ḥusain 'Alī (*M.U.* i, 326–7, Kāmwar, *Akhbārāt.* Irvine i, 390 is not correct in giving 29 *Jamāda* I as the date of his appointment).

According to Shiv Dās (Rampur Ms. p. 16), Dā'ūd Khān had reached Burhānpur to greet Ḥusain 'Alī when he received a *farmān* appointing him to the Deccan, and a special *shuqqa* from the Emperor urging him as a faithful servant to resist Ḥusain Alī. Dā'ūd Khān had only a small following but he decided to comply with the order, and died fighting.

K.K., 751 tells us that Ḥusain 'Alī learnt of Dā'ūd Khān's hostile intentions only when he reached Akbarpur ferry on the Narmada.

106 Niẕām-ul-Mulk reached Delhi on 11 *Rajab*, 1127, 13 July 1715 (*Akhbārāt*, Kāmwar, 402). The date 11 *Jamāda* II, 13 June 1715 given by Irvine (i, 327) and Y. Khan (*Āṣaf Jāh*, 77–8) is not correct. Y. Khan also states that Niẕām left Aurangabad in May which is not correct. K.K. (ii, 750) gives early *Safar* (early February) as the date of his departure from Aurangabad, and we learn

now joined hands with the emperor, the position of 'Abdullāh Khān would become untenable.[107]

Thus, the trial of strength settled no basic issues and left 'Abdullāh Khān alone to face a treacherous master and a hostile court, till such time as the Saiyids could gather sufficient strength to finally settle the issues in the manner they desired.

---

from the *Akhbārāt* that in February, the Niẓām defeated Gangā near Burhānpur (*Akhbārāt,* entries d. 10, 11 *Rabī'* II, 15–16 April).

Thus, Niẓām-ul-Mulk reached Delhi two months after the appointment of Dā'ūd Khān to the Deccan, and he could not have had any hand in it (*Cf.* Irvine i, 328).

107 Qāsim (pp. 79, 86) makes out that the Tūrānīs had all along been eager to remove the Saiyids from the court but wanted to employ strategem (*ḥikmat-i-'amli*) rather than courage and bravery.

CHAPTER V

The Saiyid Brothers Struggle for 'New' Wizārat (ii)

Position of 'Abdullāh Khān

For the next few years following the departure of Ḥusain 'Alī from the court, both Farrukh Siyar and the Saiyid brothers busied themselves in recruiting allies wherever they could be found. Farrukh Siyar turned to the old nobles, specially to the group consisting of M. Amīn Khān, Niẓam-ul-Mulk, and their associates. He also tried to enlist Jai Singh and Ajit Singh on his side. 'Abdullāh Khān and Ḥusain 'Alī sought to counteract these moves. They attempted to retain the support of the old nobles and the Rājpūt rajas, while extending their connexions with other elements, including the Jats and the Marāthās.

As a result of this factional struggle, administration was neglected and the condition of the state went from bad to worse. 'Abdullāh Khān placed more reliance than ever on his *dīwān* and chief lieutenant, Ratan Chand. The influence of Ratan Chand was felt in all departments—even in the appointment of *qāẓīs*. In the revenue department, specially, he acquired so much authority that no one dared to oppose him, and the *dīwān-i-tan* and the *dīwān-i-Khāliṣah* became 'mere cyphers'. Ratan Chand leased the revenues to the highest bidders. Even *khāliṣah* lands were leased out. In this way, while he made a handsome profit for his master, the revenue of the state from both *khāliṣah* (crown-lands) and the *jāgīr* (assigned) lands declined.[1] Whenever 'Abdullāh Khān appointed an *'āmil*, he took from him a contract or lease in writing, and realized the money from his bankers in advance. This practise was frowned upon by Farrukh Siyar who wanted that the entire income and expenditure must be accounted for. But 'Abdullāh Khān paid no heed to his objections.[2]

The condition of the *jāgīrdārs* also deteriorated further. Due to the growing divergence between the real and the paper income of the *jāgīr*, they found it more difficult than ever to make the two ends meet. The smaller *manṣabdārs* were apparently hit the harder. To mitigate their hardship to some extent, Luṭfullāh Khān, the *dīwān-i-tan*, started the practice of granting cash stipends in place of *jāgīr* to officers whose ranks were between 50 and 1,000. However, it seems that the stipends fixed were too low, and were, perhaps, paid very irregularly.[3] In consequence, many nobles—even the bigger ones—did not maintain any *sawārs*, and sent false reports in collusion with the *mutṣaddīs*. Thus, there was a general deterioration in the administration.[4]

An indirect result of these developments was to encourage the growth of a numerous class of bankers, contractors and revenue-agents. Many nobles belonging to ancient families felt overshadowed by this new class. Their sentiments find an echo in Khāfi Khān's complaint that 'Under Ratan Chand, excepting Bārahās and *banias* no one found any favour', and that 'the nobility of every province carried on their existence in disgrace and distrust'.[5] Another contemporary observer, Khush-ḥāl Khān remarks that 'Ratan Chand replaced the principles of kingship by the principles of shop-keeping, i.e. he put everything to sale'.[6]

While the administration was thus rapidly heading towards a break-down, political rivalries dominated the court. Whenever the emperor planned a hunt or went on an outing, rumour went round that an attack on 'Abdullāh Khān was intended. The effective force at the disposal of 'Abdullāh Khān at this time is estimated

1 K.K., 773, Kāmwar, 405.

2 K.K., 773, Yahyā, 123b, Irvine i, 335–6.

3 Khush-ḥāl, 339b (B.M.).

4 *Akhbārāt*, 17 April 1713. Early in the reign, *sawār* rank had been abolished for those holding *manṣabs* below 500 (*Akhbārāt*, 25, *Ṣafar* Yr. 1, 23 March 1713.

5 K.K., 902, 775.

6 Khush-ḥāl, 102. However, the author praises the financial skill and business acumen of Ratan Chand.

at between 15,000 and 20,000 men.[7] This was not enough to safeguard his position in a hostile court. Hence, he enrolled more men every time the emperor went on a hunt or there was rumour of a plot against him.[8]

The Saiyids were conscious of the weakness of their position, and endeavoured to gather in their hands the necessary resources to finally settle the question of power. Events so shaped themselves as to give them the opportunity they desired.

In January 1716, Mīr Jumlah entered Delhi surreptitiously in a state of great financial distress. At the time of his departure for Bihar, he had been accompanied by 7,000 Mughal troops which were in addition to the contingent permitted to the governor of that province. For the upkeep of these additional troops, he had been granted nine lakhs of rupees in cash and in the shape of assignments on the Bengal treasury.[9] But Mīr Jumlah had failed to deal satisfactorily with the *zamindars* of Bihar who were notoriously turbulent. At the same time, he had woefully mismanaged his finances so that he was unable to pay his Mughal soldiers. The latter, in turn, committed every sort of excess and oppression upon the people in order to extort money from them.[10]

Reports reached the emperor about these oppressions, and also that Mīr Jumlah was committing breach of the royal privileges by witnessing fights of lions etc. He had also misappropriated 30 lakhs of rupees from the tribute which was annually remitted from Bengal to Delhi.[11]

In consequence Mīr Jumlah was removed from the governorship of Bihar in November 1715, and was replaced by Sarbuland Khān.

7 Wilson ii, 95–6, K.K., 795 says he had 20,000 men but they were continuously increasing. M.M., 69b places the figures at only 7,000–8,000. M.M., 96b places the figures at only 7,000–8,000.

8 K.K., p. 770, Qāsim, 90. *Cf.* the remarks of Owen (*Fall of the Moghul Empire*, p. 141) that the Saiyids had 'real reason to fear, rather than to initiate resort to violence'.

9 M.M., 31a.

10 M.M., 48a–51a (graphic details), Qāsim, 89, K.K., 769. But according to Shiv Dās (pp. 8–10), Mīr Jumlah had dismissed all his Mughal troops on reaching Patna and employed Hindustani troops. The oppressions were committed by the disbanded Mughal soldiers.

11 M.M., 46a. Shiv Dās (p. 9) gives the figure of Rs 18,000,000 and 200 elephants which seems preposterous.

Soon afterwards, he was also deprived of the absentee governorship of Bengal.[12]

Ruin stared Mīr Jumlah in the face. His last hope was to appeal to his old patron, the emperor. Hence, he fled secretly to Delhi. But he was followed there by 7,000–8,000 of his disbanded soldiers clamouring for their salaries which had not been paid for the last 12 to 13 months. They beseiged the house of Mīr Jumlah and created great disorder in the streets of the capital. 'Abdullāh Khān was afraid that these disorders might be used as a pretext for an attack on his house. He engaged more men and 'the officers of Saiyid Quṭb-ul-Mulk ('Abdullāh Khān) with suitable forces, ready accoutred, mounted on elephants and horses held themselves ready for a conflict'. Bārahās flocked into the city hearing that the *wazīr* whom they considered not only their countryman but their kinsman, was in danger from his enemies.[13]

The emperor was greatly annoyed by this unwanted trouble and tension which put him in a difficult situation. In anger, he forbade Mīr Jumlah the audience, and deprived him of all his titles and of his *manṣab* and *jāgīr*.[14]

Thus, the affair took a turn quite different from what Mīr Jumlah had expected. In despair, he applied to his old enemy, 'Abdullāh Khān. At the latter's instance he was appointed the *Qāẓī* of Lahore, and ordered to leave without an audience. Seven or eight months later, his *manṣab* and titles were also restored at the instance of 'Abdullāh Khān.[15]

The result of these developments was that a dangerous rival was removed from the path of 'Abdullāh Khān who now felt more secure, while the position of Farrukh Siyar was correspondingly weakened.

12 *Akhbārāt*, 5 November, 1715, M.M., 46b.
K.K., 770 is not correct in stating that Mīr Jumlah was dismissed from Bihar *after* he came to the court.

13 K.K., 771, *Siyar*, 405–6.

14 M.M., 46b. But K.K. (p. 769) says 'When Mīr Jumlah waited upon the Emperor, he was coldly received and he was severely censured for the wretched state of the people of Patna and for having come to the court without permission.'

15 On 3 March, he was escorted to Narela by Niẓām-ul-Mulk, and from there went to Sarhind where he stayed for seven to eight months at a wayside inn, hoping to rouse the emperor's commiseration. At length, on 11 June 1716, his titles were restored at the instance of 'Abdullāh Khān (Kāmwar, Irvine i, 332).

Another event which was destined to have far-reaching consequences was the arrival at the court in July 1715 of an English embassy under John Surman. The English had well-established factories at Surat, Patna, Murshidabad etc. and were steadily increasing their share in the export trade of Surat as well as the Eastern provinces. They applied for permission to carry on their trade in Bengal, Bihar and Orissa free of duty. The English were convinced that 'at Delhi everything was for sale', and that the emperor's favourite, Khān-i-Daurān, the acting chief *bakhshī*, was all powerful. 'The Vizier's Chief Muttsuddys viz. Duan Colsa and Duan Tanki (the *dīwān-i-khāliṣah* and the *dīwān-i-tan*) are entirely under his (Khān-i-Daurān's) command so that the poor vizier has but the title with very little authority' they wrote back.[16] Hence, they neglected the *wazīr* and sent their petition to the emperor through Khān-i-Daurān.

It was only after the expenditure of much time and money and the failure of two petitions presented through Khān-i-Daurān that the English realized that they had followed a totally wrong procedure, and that Khān-i-Daurān had little power to interfere in the revenue administration. Once the English applied through the correct channels, i.e. through the *wazīr*, things moved with a rapidity which surprised them. What was even more surprising to them, the *wazīr* put his seal on the grant 'without accepting a farthing'.[17]

This grant, which forms a landmark in the growth of the East India Company's importance in India's trade, has been popularly ascribed to the successful treatment of Farrukh Siyar by one Dr Hamilton. But it would be wrong to exaggerate the role of Dr Hamilton, for it was the *wazīr*, 'Abdullāh Khān, rather than Farrukh Siyar who was responsible for the grant of the English petition. The revenue department had expressed the view that a grant of this nature had no precedent, and was against the best interests of the empire. But these objections were over-ruled by the *wazīr*.[18] His motives in doing so can only be guessed at. Perhaps, he was impressed by the English threat that unless their petition was granted they would withdraw from Surat and ruin the trade of that

16 Wilson, *English Factory Records*, ii, XXIV–XXVII, 48–173.

17 *Ibid.*

18 *Ibid.*

port.[19] Or, he might have hoped that the grant would further encourage the export trade, and thus yield indirect benefits to the empire.

At any rate, the events demonstrated the personal dominance of the *wazīr* in revenue matters.

THE RECALL OF JAI SINGH, AND THE OUTBREAK OF THE JAT WAR

Ever since the departure of Ḥusain 'Alī from the court, Farrukh Siyar had been casting about for a suitable tool to get rid of the Saiyids. His attention was drawn towards Raja Jai Singh who, as the Governor of Malwa, had recently won a big victory against the Marāṭhā invaders, driving them across the river Narmada with heavy losses. The news reporters hailed it as the biggest victory gained by the Imperial arms since the days of Aurangzīb.[20] Although Jai Singh owed his initial appointment as the Governor of Malwa to Ḥusain 'Alī, as has been noticed above, Farrukh Siyar set about trying to detach him from the Saiyids. His attempts to do so were facilitated by a number of factors. Jai Singh had felt greatly annoyed at the intervention of Ḥusain 'Alī in the Kotah-Bundi dispute against his protégé and brother-in-law, Budh Singh. Budh Singh had sided with Bahādur Shāh in the battle of Jājū, and as a reward, he had been granted 54 forts which included the fort of Kotah. Bhim Singh, the son of Rām Singh Hāṛa, had been displaced from Kotah since he had sided with A'ẓam Shah. But Bhim Singh had refused to evacuate Kotah, and when Farrukh Siyar ascended the throne, he arrived at Delhi and ingratiated himself with Ḥusain 'Alī. Budh Singh not only avoided coming to the court despite repeated summons, but adopted a hostile attitude during Ḥusain 'Alī's campaign against Ajit Singh, and attacked Kotah. Bhim Singh hurried back to Kotah, and after repulsing Budh Singh's attack, also ousted him from Bundi. At Ḥusain 'Alī's instance, he secured Bundi also in formal grant from the emperor. In high dudgeon, Budh Singh repaired to Jai Singh at Ujjain, and made the

19 Wilson xlviii. Similarly, while negotiating with Prince Buland Akhtar in 1709 for the right to trade free of duty in Bengal, Bihar and Orissa, the English had threatened to retaliate at Hugli if their petition was not accepted (Wilson i, 297).

20 *Akhbārāt*, 6 and 17 June; *Wāqi'ah Papers*, 28 and 29 May; *Letters*, 25 May. Also see *Sardesai Comm.*, 68–9.

latter promise to intercede with the emperor on his behalf.[21] Relations between Jai Singh and the Saiyid brothers became cool from this time. Jai Singh showed his hostility by refusing to wait on Ḥusain 'Alī when the latter passed through Malwa on his way to the Deccan, after the quarrel with Farrukh Siyar. Instead, he left Ujjain on the pretext of dealing with a rebel *zamindar.*[22] According to the etiquette of the times, this was a gross breach of manners on his part, and Ḥusain 'Alī wrote an angry letter to Farrukh Siyar, accusing him of having instigated Jai Singh's action.[23]

Another reason for Jai Singh's dissatisfaction with the Saiyids was their tacit support to the Jats. Jai Singh resented the rise of a Jat power under Chūrāman Jat on the borders of his hereditary dominions. Apart from the irritation caused to him by the constant plundering activities of the Jats, relations between the house of Amber and the Jats had been strained since the time of Aurangzīb when Jai Singh's father, Ram Singh, had fought a series of exhausting wars with Rājārām Jat. After the death of Rājārām, the headship of the Jats had passed to Chūrāman Jat, the son of Bhajjā. For sometime, Chūrāman carried on the usual plundering activities. But after the battle of Jājū in 1707, he presented himself before Bahādur Shāh through Mun'im Khān and obtained the rank of 1,500/500, and was placed in charge of the road between Delhi and Agra.[24] Subsequently, he took part in the Sikh campaign of Bahādur Shāh, and was present at the siege of Sādhaura and Lohgarh. At the battle of Lahore, he was a partisan of 'Aẕīm-ush-Shān, but his only part in the battle was to plunder. However, he was pardoned by Jahāndār Shāh and presented with a robe and asked to accompany the army against Farrukh Siyar. But when the tide of battle turned against Jahāndār Shāh, Chūrāman was the first to plunder—his Jats invading the women's quarters and causing great confusion and alarm.

21 *Akhbārāt*, September, October, December 1713. Bhim Singh reached the court on 8 September 1713 and, at Ḥusain 'Alī's instance, was raised from 2,500 *z̲āt* to 3,500 *z̲āt*, and granted the title of Maharao. After the capture of Bundi (*Akhbārāt*, February–March 1714), he was raised to 5,000/4,000 (2,000 *dū-aspah*). Budh Singh reached Ujjain on 22 November 1714.

22 *Akhbārāt*, 21 and 30 July; *Wāqi'ah Papers*, 21, 22 and 24 July 1715. The rebel *zamindar*'s headquarter was Garh Banera near Bhilsa, 80 *kos* from Ujjain.

23 *M.U.* iii, 326.

24 M.M., 65a, *B.N.*, 164.

Early in his reign, Farrukh Siyar had appointed Chhabelā Rām Nāgar as the Governor of Agra with orders to chastise the unruly Jat leader. Chhabelā Rām employed extra troops and further stiffened his forces with guns brought from the Agra fort. But he failed to bring the Jat leader to book, for the local *zamindars* rendered him no help. It was also suspected that Chūrāman received secret encouragement from the Saiyids.[25]

After a short time, Khān-i-Daurān replaced Chhabelā Rām as the Governor of Agra. Khān-i-Daurān preferred the methods of peace to those of war. At his instance, Chūrāman was presented at the court and placed in charge of the royal highway from Delhi to the banks of the river Chambal. But gradually, Chūrāman fell out of favour. He had used his position to lay hold of many *parganas*, and he interfered with the *jāgīrdārs*. Complaints were also received that he was (illegally) levying road-dues (*rāhdārī*), and secretly manufacturing arms and ammunition. He had also usurped royal territories and erected a mud fort at Thūn which he had made his headquarters.[26]

In September 1715, Farrukh Siyar sent a *farmān* to Jai Singh directing him to appear at the court with Rao Raja Budh Singh, Raja Chhatrasāl Bundela, Rao Durga Das etc. Farrukh Siyar promised to restore Bundi to Budh Singh, and also to appoint Jai Singh at the head of a large army to chastise the Jats. Hopes of other high favours were also held out to him.[27]

Thus, Farrukh Siyar hoped to kill two birds with one stone, viz. to crush the Jats who had made a nuisance of themselves, and also to win Jai Singh over to his side. However, despite his keenness to proceed against the Jats, Jai Singh was reluctant to embroil himself in the factional politics at the court. He, therefore, ignored the summons of the emperor, and in October 1715, left Ujjain for Amber. It was not till June 1716, that in response to repeated and the most pressing summons from Farrukh Siyar, that Jai Singh finally appeared at the court.[28] On his arrival, orders were passed that Bhim Singh should be expelled from Bundi which should be

25 M.M., 65b.

26 M.M., 65b, *Akhbārāt*, 25, 27 April, 1, 9 and 30 July 1715; 20 March, 31 August 1716 *et passim; Letters* d. 25 April 1715.

27 *Akhbārāt, farmān* d. 19 *Ramaẓān Yr.* 4 and 18 September 1715; M.M., 65b.

28 *Akhbārāt,* An urgent summon was sent to Jai Singh on 31 March 1716 after the affair of Mīr Jumlah.

placed under *khāliṣah* (for safe-keeping), and then handed over to Budh Singh.[29] Soon after this, Jai Singh was nominated to the command of an expedition against the Jats. 'Abdullāh Khān was not even consulted on the subject.[30]

In November 1716, Jai Singh invested the Jat strong-hold of Thūn with 50,000 men. But due to the thick jungles, the broken terrain, the hostile attitude of the local populace, shortage of provisions, and difficulties of transport the siege proceeded slowly. The rains of 1717 were very late in coming. The price of grain rose abnormally high, and Jai Singh had to bring the grain from his own country at an enormous cost. The Jats were joined not only by the Mewatis but by many Afghans who came from Shahjahanpur and Bareilly and were employed by Chūrāman at three rupees per day. Even the local *zamindars* would not help the Imperialists. The Jats became so bold that they plundered right up to Agra and Delhi, waylaid convoys of grain and merchandize, and conducted a kind of guerilla war against the Imperialists.[31]

Farrukh Siyar was impatient at the delay, and repeatedly wrote to Jai Singh to that effect. Thus, on 13 March 1717, he wrote: 'Seven months have passed since that high Raja was given charge of the destruction of the Jats villains, with a large army, a big park of artillery and copious treasure. Uptil now, the fort has not been invested (even) from one side, not to speak of its conquest. The jungle remains for half a *kos* around the fort, and the Jats come out under its shelter and attack the royal army. Now the rainy season is approaching fast and, it seems, will pass in the same way. If under the supervision of Raja Gaj Singh you set the army to clear the forest, and yourself devote full attention to it, the task could be accomplished in a week. If, God forbid, the campaign is not finished now, once the rains begin, the mud fort will become still more difficult (to conquer).'[32]

However, the delay can hardly be attributed to negligence or incompetence on the part of Jai Singh. Jai Singh proceeded methodically, cutting down all trees around the fort and setting up block-houses on the road eastward to Agra. Progress was

29 M.M., 60a–b, *Akhbārāt*, 6 August 1716. Earlier, on 1 January, Budh Singh had been given the *zamindari* of Momīdānah (*Akhbārāt*).

30 M.M., 60b.

31 *Wāqi'ah Papers*, Kāmwar, 418–20, *Iqbāl*, 33–7.

32 *J.R.* (*Add. Pers.* ii, 143).

necessarily slow. It must be remembered that he was fighting against the same race and the same terrain which baffled Lord Lake in the nineteenth century.

At the capital, 'Abdullāh Khān harped on the waste of men, money and material. He pointed out that two crores of rupees had already been spent and that much more was likely to be needed before the siege terminated. When the siege had lasted a year and a half, and victory was still not within sight, Farrukh Siyar felt compelled to agree to a peace with the Jats. The terms were negotiated over the head of Jai Singh, through 'Abdullāh Khān's uncle, Khān-i-Jahān, who had been sent to Thūn in November 1716, with the ostensible purpose of helping Jai Singh, but really to thwart him. According to the terms of the treaty, the Jat leader agreed to pay 50 lakhs of rupees to the state in cash and goods, besides a private gift of 20 lakhs to the *wazīr*. He also surrendered Thūn, Dīg etc., and agreed to serve wherever he was appointed.[33]

Farrukh Siyar yielded to 'Abdullāh Khān's demands very ungraciously, while Jai Singh felt robbed of victory which he had deemed within his grasp, and was sore and bitter on this score.

The Jat War further strained the relations between Farrukh Siyar and the Saiyids. At the same time, the alliance of the Saiyids with the Jats who were considered rebels and disturbers of the realm marked a new stage in the struggle between the parties at the court.

Deepening of the Political Crisis at the Court

Meanwhile, the struggle for power between Farrukh Siyar and the Saiyid brothers was assuming a deeper significance.

Early in 1717, 'Ināyatullāh Khān Kashmīrī, who had gone to Mecca towards the beginning of the reign after the execution of his son, Sa'dullāh Khān, returned to the court. Farrukh Siyar was now of the opinion that it was a mistake to have rooted out the old 'Ālamgīrī nobles who were experienced administrators and who could have acted as a counterpoise to the Saiyids. 'Ināyatullāh Khān 'had been trained under Aurangzīb, knew the rules of business, and was spoken of as being economy-minded'. Hence, at the behest of some of his advisers, Farrukh Siyar proposed to appoint him as the *dīwān-i-tan wa khāliṣah*. He was also made the

33 *Letters* No. 192, *Iqbāl*, 37–8, M.M., 84b–86a.

(absentee) Governor of Kashmīr, and granted the rank of 4,000 in April 1717.[34]

In view of 'Abdullāh Khān's authority in revenue matters, 'Ināyatullāh Khān refused to accept the post of the *dīwān-i-tan* without an understanding with the *wazīr.* After sometime, an agreement was arrived at with the help of Ikhlāṣ Khān,[35] by which 'Ināyatullāh undertook not to make any proposals or recommendations to the emperor in revenue matters without the advice and consultation of 'Abdullāh Khān. In return, it was stipulated that 'Abdullāh Khān would come to his office in the fort at least once or twice in the week, and attend to his business personally, *i.e.* not leave it in the hands of Ratan Chand. Previous to this, he had not attended his office for four–five months on end. We are told that this was due to Farrukh Siyar's 'intrigues, his irascible temper and voluptuous habits, and the consequent neglect of the administration'.[36]

For some time, things went smoothly. But soon disagreement arose. First of all, 'Ināyatullāh, who was an admirer of Aurangzīb, produced a letter from the *Sharīf* of Mecca stating that the levying of *jizyah* was obligatory (*wājib*) according to the *shara'*.[37] Next, 'Ināyatullāh examined the titles to *manṣabs*, the calculation of salaries and the yield of *jāgīrs*,[38] and proposed to reduce or set aside the *manṣabs* of 'Hindus and eunuchs and Kashmīrīs (who) by force and cunning had acquired *manṣabs* beyond their deserts and

34 K.K., 774, M.M., 70a. The English factor, Surman, describes him as being 'an uttar enemy to Bribery' (*Early Annals* ii, 268). I'tiṣām Khān and Rai Rāyān, who held the posts of the *dīwan-i-khāliṣah* and the *dīwani-i-lan* respectively, had resigned their offices shortly before the arrival of 'Ināyatullāh Khān. The reason for this was that I'tiṣām Khān sided with the Emperor, and Rai Rāyān with the Saiyids, so that there were objections against them from both the sides, and they felt powerless.

35 Originally a Khatri, he had been converted to Islām, and held various posts under Aurangzīb and Bahādur Shāh. Ẕu'lfiqār Khān raised him to the rank of 5,000/4,000 and appointed him the *dāroghah-i-'arẓ-i-mukarrar* and the *dīwān-i-tan.* After the execution of Sa'dullāh Khān, he had retired to the home of the Bārahās, and devoted himself to writing (*M.U.* i, 350–2, *Akhbārāt*).

36 K.K., 774.

37 *Letters.* Explaining the measure to Jai Singh, Farrukh Siyar wrote, 'It is a matter of faith, I am helpless (to intervene)'. *V.V.*, 954, K.K., 772, M.M., 70a.

38 'Ināyatullāh examined the *āwārjah* and *taujīh.* Probably, the former was a descriptive roll of the *manṣabdārs* along with a record of their *manṣabs*, while the latter contained an assessment of the yield of *jāgīrs.*

accumulated in their hands the most profitable (*sair ḥāsil*) jāgīrs, with the result that there was a scarcity of *jāgīrs* for the others. Men of low rank whether of the *dīwānī* or the *bakhshī* or the *khān sāmānī* office had become *manṣabdārs* and obtained *jāgīrs*. People belonging to old families had been reduced to the dust'.[39]

It is probably that both the measures were motivated largely by financial considerations, and aimed at improving the pecuniary position of the state, which had deteriorated as a result of revenue-farming, growing lawlessness and administrative laxity.[40] But the *jizyah* was odious to the Hindus who felt it to be a penalization of faith. Besides, it affected most the petty officials and other middle class elements, since the poor were exempt from paying it, and the incidence was too light to be felt as a burden by the rich. The second measure was aimed at the very numerous class of subordinate officials which consisted mainly of Hindus and Hindustanis (i.e., Indian Muslims). These elements clamoured against the new proposals. Ratan Chand took up the cudgels on their behalf and opposed the new reforms. 'Abdullāh Khān therefore refused to implement these measures. He also showed displeasure at the re-imposition of the *jizyah.* Thus, the pact with 'Ināyatullāh Khān broke down. After this, we are told, 'the Hindus became hostile to 'Ināyatullāh Khān, and determined to oppose him in every way'.[41]

By his resistance to 'Ināyatullāh's measures, 'Abdullāh Khān rallied to his side the subordinate officials, and appealed to the Hindu sentiment generally. From this time onwards, the Saiyids came to be regarded as the champions of the Hindus and the Hindustanis. However, it would not be correct to interpret the struggle at the court as primarily one between the Hindustanis and the Mughals, as contemporary and later writers often represent it to be. As has been noticed already, the Saiyid had made no attempt to monopolize the higher offices for themselves or for any group or section. Rather, they had gone out of their way to conciliate and appease the old 'Ālamgīrī nobles, and had given

39 K.K., 775, M.M., 70a.

40 Khush-ḥāl, 102. The finances of the empire were not in order, and the pay of the soldiers was sometimes several years in arrears, so that they made incessant clamour and often insulted the men in-charge (*Akhbārāt*, 11 August 1713, K.K., 774).

41 K.K., 775.

high posts to such individuals as M. Amīn Khān and Niẓām-ul-Mulk. The struggle at the court was in reality partly a personal and partly a political struggle which cut across racial and religious groups. The main issue in the political struggle seems to have been whether an attempt was to be made to associate elements like the Marāthās and Jats in addition to the Rājpūts, in the higher ranks of the nobility. Fundamentally, the question was whether a political equilibrium could be created in the prevailing conditions, without sharing state power with these elements. The question was by no means a new one; it had been faced also by Aurangzīb. In Aurangzīb's lifetime and after his death, the prestige of the Imperial arms had suffered, while the activities of the Marāthās, and to some extent of the Jats and the Sikhs, had assumed a ubiquitous guerilla character which rendered a quick victory impossible. The internal cohesion and stability of the Mughal government had also declined. In these circumstances and under the pressure of a hostile faction at the court, the Saiyids moved in the direction of forming an alliance with the Marāthās and the Jats as well as with many individual Rājpūt princes. Thus, they took a definite step towards forming a more broad-based state. They realized the urgent necessity of a broad policy of religious toleration, in order to secure the good will of the Hindus generally. But the policies of the Saiyids were opposed by a group which raised the old slogan of 'religion in danger', accusing the Saiyids of being pro-Hindu and of not observing the letter of the law. They also invoked the policies of Aurangzīb, and tried to represent the Saiyid policies as dangerous innovations.

Thus, the struggle for power at the court gradually involved the question of the character of the state itself. The policy followed by the Saiyids was more in consonance with the liberal, tolerant spirit of Akbar, and was conducive to the growth of a national state and monarchy. Their opponents sought to preserve the privileges of a comparatively narrow group, and took their stand upon the apparently orthodox and uncompromising principles of Aurangzīb. There were other points of conflict too.

In interpreting the struggle which followed it should be borne in mind that the real nature of the issues was only dimly realized by the two sides. For both of them the question of power remained the most immediate and pressing issue. In order to gain power both sides were prepared to modify the principles for which they apparently stood. Personal and group loyalties also played a part. This renders necessary the exercise of the utmost caution in judging the position of individuals and groups, and complicates the study of the more significant conflict of principles and policies.

The Saiyid–Marāthā Pact

When Niẓām-ul-Mulk arrived in the Deccan as the viceroy in 1714, he refused to accept Dā'ūd Khān's agreement for the payment of the *chauth* and *sardeshmukhī* of the Deccan to Shāhū, and ousted the *kamā'ishdārs* of Shāhū from Aurangabad and several other districts.[42] This led to the resumption of general hostilities with the Marāthās. Niẓām-ul-Mulk inflicted a couple of defeats on them, but was unable to destroy the small mud forts (*garhī-chah*) which they had built in every district and which served as a base of attack or a place of refuge to the Marāthā bands, and was the real basis of their system of organized plunder in the Deccan.[43]

When Ḥusain 'Alī replaced Niẓām-ul-Mulk as the Viceroy of the Deccan, he followed the same policy for some time. He refused to countenance the Marāthā claims for *chauth* and *sardeshmukhī*, and resisted them wherever he could. The result was that the Marāthās appeared everywhere and plundered and desolated every place. The Imperial commanders failed to cope with the situation. In 1715, Khāndū Dābhādē inflicted a crushing defeat on Ḥusain 'Alī's *mīr bakhshī*, Ẕu'lfiqār 'Alī Khān.[44] In retaliation, Raja Mukham Singh the *dīwān* of Ḥusain 'Alī, and Chandra Sen, Nīmājī etc. ravaged the Marāthā country upto the outskirts of Satārā.[45]

42 K.K., 743, 783. It does not seem that Niẓām-ul-Mulk ousted the Marāthā *chauth* collectors from the whole of the Deccan.

43 For a detailed description of this system, see K.K., 738, 742–3, *Ḥadīqat* ii, 68–75. We are told that Farrukh Siyar was 'not enthusiastic' about the policy of Niẓām-ul-Mulk 'lest it plunge him in a sea of trouble with the Marathas' (*Āṣaf Jāh*, 79).

44 K.K. ii, 777–8, Kāmwar entry d. 2 *Rabī'* I yr. 5, 25 February 1716, *Riyasat*, 80–1.

45 *Akhbārāt: Harkāra's* report d. 19 February 1717. This took place in early January. The Imperial *harkāra* wrote that this was the first time after the Emperor Aurangzīb's death that a royal army had penetrated upto the Marāthā capital, and that it was a warning to the villains.

S.P.D. xxx, 236–40 confirm this report. Also K.K., 779, *M.U.* ii, 331.

But this victory did not prove of much avail to Ḥusain 'Alī for he failed to defeat and to crush the Marāthā bands which roamed the Deccan, retiring when the Imperialists appeared in overwhelming strength, and reoccupying their former positions as soon as they withdrew. Matters were rendered more difficult for Ḥusain 'Alī by the underhand opposition of Farrukh Siyar who wrote letters to Shāhū and to all the *zamindars* and *dīwāns* in Karnātak to oppose the Viceroy.[46] The result was that Husain 'Alī's authority in Bijāpur, Ḥaiderābād and the two Karnātaks was reduced almost to a cypher.[47]

Also, contrary to the terms of the agreement of 1714, Farrukh Siyar began to interefere in matters of appointment etc. in the Deccan.[48]

Consequently, on the advice of Saiyid Anwar Khān, and through the instrumentality of Shankarāji Malhār,[49] Ḥusain 'Alī opened negotiations with the Marāthās. This was done sometime in the middle of 1717.[50] Reports of these negotiations reached the Emperor, but he was powerless to circumvent them. Ultimately, in February 1718, Ḥusain 'Alī reached an agreement with Shāhū granting him the *swarajya* of Shivaji with certain reservations,[51] and the right of collecting the *chauth* and *sardeshmukhī* of the six *ṣūbahs* of the Deccan through his own collectors. The recent Marāthā

46 K.K., 780, *Tārīkh-i-Ibrāhimī* (Rampur Ms. and Elliot viii, 260), *M.U.* i, 328.

47 K.K., 780, 787–8.

48 K.K., 773, *Akhbārāt* entries d. 19, 27 October, 22 November 1715. In the sixth year, Ḥusain 'Alī had asked for and obtained confirmation of his right to appoint and dismiss all *ṣūbahdārs*, *bakhshīs*, *faujdārs*, *qil'adārs*, *wāqi'-nigārs*, etc. in the Deccan (*Akhbārāt*, 3 May 1717). For examples of Farrukh Siyar's interference, see K.K., 773, 787.

49 K.K., 784, *S.P.D.* vii, 28. Shankarājī was originally a *kārkun* under Shivaji, and was, subsequently, *sachiv* under Rājāram. He retired in 1698 and settled down at Banaras. He came to Delhi and joined Ḥusain 'Alī when the latter went to the Deccan (Duff, 105, 164, 171, 197–8, K.K., 784).

50 B.M., 26,606 quoted by Dr A. G. Powar in his paper 'Some Original Documents of Mughal-Marāthā Relations' in *I.H.R.C. Proceedings*, 1940, 204–12. Several papers dated September 1717, exchanged between Shāhū and Ḥusain 'Alī are quoted too.

Also *Akhbārāt*, 8, 11 December 1717.

51 In lieu of Khandesh, he was to get the adjoining districts of Pandhārpur and Trimbak (Duff i, 363).

conquests in Berar, Gondwānā and Karnātak were also confirmed.[52]

In return for these concessions, Shāhū agreed to pay a *peshkash* of 10 lakhs, to maintain a body of 15,000 horse to be placed at the disposal of the viceroy, and 'to make the country populous, to punish all malefactors... and if any one's property should be stolen or destroyed, to get it restored and to punish the thieves and if he does not do that, to give it himself'. No taxes were to be charged besides the established ones,[53] and it was specifically stipulated that *rāhdārī* was not to be charged.[54] For the *sardeshmukhī* only, Shāhū undertook to pay the *peshkash* customary upon a hereditary grant, viz. 651 per cent of one year's income.[55]

As soon as the agreement had been concluded, Ḥusain 'Alī wrote to the emperor for its formal ratification. But Farrukh Siyar could hardly be expected to confirm a pact clearly aimed against him. Besides, 'several well-wishers of the state urged that it was not proper to admit the 'vile enemy' to be over-bearing partners in matters of revenue and government'.[56] Hence, the proposal was rejected. Meanwhile, Shāhū gave out that the emperor had consented to make the grants, and without waiting for the formal confirmation, started collecting his dues.[57] He also sent 10,000

52 Copies of these *sanads* are given in '*Sanads and Treaties*' Nos 2, 3, 4 and Dr A. G. Powar *loc. cit.*, 205–8. See also Duff i, 363, 368–9, K.K., 784, *Ḥadiqat* 86, *T. Ibrāhīmī* (Rampur Ms., Elliot viii, 260).

Riyasat (p. 82) quotes not the terms agreed upon, but the terms set forth by Shāhū. Dr Powar quotes a series of papers setting forth such demands. They need to be treated with caution in determining the final terms because it was the Marāthā practice to demand much more than what they hoped to get.

53 Dr Powar *loc. cit.*, 207. K.K. (p. 784) says that Shāhū and his men were to share in so many other sources of Government collections that they got nearly half of the rent-roll.

54 K.K., 785. However, the Marāthās continued to collect *rāhdārī* as before.

55 Dr Powar *loc. cit.*, 207–8. This came to Rs 117,516,762, but Shāhū agreed to pay only Rs 11,719,390/12/- as many districts were desolate (Duff i, 363, 368–9). It was stipulated that one-fourth of the sum of ten lakhs promised in lieu of the grant of *swarajya* was to be paid on receipt of the *sanad*, and the remainder on the taxes being fixed.

It does not seem that these sums were ever paid. In a paper dated 1724, it was stated that Shāhū had not paid even 10 lakhs till then (Dr Powar, *loc. cit.*, 212).

56 K.K., 786, *M.U.* i, 329–30.

57 Rajwade iii, 99–100. Ḥusain 'Alī promised to secure the royal *farmān* in nine months.

Marāthā horsemen under Santoji and Parsoji Bhosle and Bālājī Peshwa to join the viceroy, according to the terms of the agreement.[58]

There can be little doubt that the terms of the agreement with the Marāthās were against the best interests of the empire. Ḥusain 'Alī not only conceded the claim for *chauth* and *sardeshmukhī* which was, perhaps, inevitable, but also agreed that the Marāthās should collect their dues through their own agents, thus creating an *imperium in imperio.* But Farrukh Siyar had clearly brought this trouble on his own head, and could hardly blame the Saiyid brothers.

EVENTS LEADING TO THE DEPOSITION OF FARRUKH SIYAR

The conclusion of the pact between Ḥusain 'Alī and the Marāthās brought the affairs of Farrukh Siyar to a crisis. The Saiyids had now secured that superiority for which they had been manoeuvring since the first breach with Farrukh Siyar three years ago. Anticipating their next move, Farrukh Siyar had posted M. Amīn Khān to Malwa as early as November 1717. The ostensible purpose of this appointment was to drive out the Marāthās who had been harrying that province for the past several years. The emperor had written to Jai Singh 'This year the Marāthās are pouring into Malwa like ants and locusts. They have reduced to dust the towns and villages by their plunder and devastation. In the royal dues, much loss has been incurred and the entire province is under siege.

'One royal servant with a mighty force will be appointed as your deputy so that the above mentioned *ṣūbah* may not become desolate (lit lampless) and remain in our possession. After the victory he will be recalled'.[59]

58 Duff i, 363.
59 *Letters,* d. 12, *Ramaẓān yr.* 5, 16 August 1717; Nos 160, 187 (*Misc. Papers.,* vol. iii), *M.U.* i, 330.

As late as 5 May 1717, Farrukh Siyar had assured Jai Singh, 'Whatever may be, I shall never take Malwa from you' (*Letters*). Explaining the appointment of M. Amīn Khān he wrote to Jai Singh 'M. Amīn Khān Bakshī-ul-Mamālik 'Itimād-ud-Dāulah has been sent with a mighty force to drive out and destroy the Marāthās who have been camping in Malwa. He will give *taqāvi* to the subjects, and collect revenue from them without their being afraid of the looting and destruction of their villages. He has also been instructed to chastise the

M. Amīn Khān wrote to Jai Singh asking for his co-operation in the chastisement of the 'oppressers'. But his real motive was to check Ḥusain 'Alī, should he march north. Farrukh Siyar also made a number of other appointments to Ḥusain 'Alī's northern province (Burhānpur), with the intention of weakening the Saiyid hold on that province. Thus in 1718, he appointed Jān Niṣār Khān—an old noble who had exchanged turbans with 'Abdullāh Khān's father and was on friendly terms with the Saiyids, as the Governor of Burhānpur. Three other men were appointed a little later: Ẓiyā-ud-Dīn Khān an Īrānī, as the *dīwān-i-deccan* in place of Diyānat Khān deceased, Jalāl-ud-Dīn Khān as the *dīwān* of Burhānpur, and Faẓlullāh Khān as the *bakhshī* of Burhānpur.

In the Deccan, it was widely rumoured that Farrukh Siyar had decided upon war against Ḥusain 'Alī.[60] Hence, Ḥusain 'Alī set aside the nominations made by the emperor. This gave great umbrage to Farrukh Siyar, and he projected a wild plan to arrest 'Abdullāh Khān when he came to offer prayers on the occasion of 'Īd. But the secret of the plot leaked out to 'Abdullāh Khān who engaged a large number of men from all sections of the population. 'Hitherto he had engaged few who were not Saiyids or inhabitants of Bārahā.'[61] Thus, 'Abdullāh Khān was forced to extend further his connections among non-Bārahās.

Afghāns (who have been helping the Marāthās). He will proceed by way of Agra and will drive the Marāthās to the other side of the Narbada. *A farmān has been sent to the Amīr-ul-Umarā to send a suitable force either under the nāi'b ṣūbahdār of Khandesh (Burhānpur), or of Berar (to be cooperative with him).*' According to K.K. (p. 787), the *ṣūbahdārī* of Malwa was promised to M. Amīn Khān as soon as he reached the border of Malwa. Rumour had it that the *farmān* of appointment had actually been made out and handed over to him secretly.

60 It was rumoured that Jān Niṣār was coming as the advance guard of M. Amīn Khān to invade the Deccan, and that they had 150,000 *sawārṣ* between them. For a while, there was wild panic at Burhānpur. Hearing of this, Jān Niṣār Khān went to Burhānpur with only a small party. Husain 'Alī heaved a sigh of relief. Jān Niṣār Khān was courteously received, but as Burhānpur was on the northern frontier, Ḥusain 'Alī did not give him charge of that province immediately. Ẓiyā-ud-Dīn Khān, who carried a letter from 'Abdullāh Khān was made the *dīwān-i-deccan*. Jalāl-ud-Dīn Khān was made the *dīwān* of Berar, while Faẓlullāh Khān was completely ignored. Even Ẓiya-ud-Dīn Khān was given no real powers except that his seal was put on *sanads* and pay-bills (K.K., 773, 787, 790; *Siyar*, 409–10; *M.U.* iii, 36).

61 M.M., 96a, K.K., 792, 770, *Siyar*, 411.

In desperation, Farrukh Siyar now decided to call together some of the old grandees of the state who looked upon the Saiyids as being upstarts, resented their dominance, and disliked their policy which they regarded as being against the best interests of the Empire. Accordingly, in August–September 1718, he summoned to the court his father-in-law, Ajit Singh from Jodhpur, Niẓām-ul-Mulk from the *faujdārī* of Moràdabad, and Sarbuland Khān, his maternal grand-uncle, who was the Governor of Bihar.[62] Each of these nobles was instructed to come 'with a large following.'[63] We are told that 'the combined strength of the various rajas and nobles, and the personal forces (*khāṣah*) of Farrukh Siyar was about 70,000–80,000 *sawārs*'.[64]

62 Sarbuland Khān had the reputation of being a courageous soldier. As the *ṣūbahdār* of Awadh (April 1713–June 1714), he had sternly repressed its turbulent *zamindars*. As a result when he was appointed to Allahabad in June 1714, the Imperial news reporter wrote that 'at the mere news of his appointment, the *zamindars* are returning to duty and sending their *wakīls* to the Khān (for the settlement of their affairs)' (*Akhbārāt*, 24 September 1714). He is said to have employed 15,000 extra *sawārs* and destroyed 500 fortresses while he was the governor or Allahabad (June 1714–November 1715). As the Governor of Bihar (November 1715–February 1718), he defeated and killed Shiv Singh, the son of Dhīr, a notorious *zamindar* of those parts, whom no *ṣūbahdār* had been able to suppress since the days of Aurangzīb (*Akhbārāt* 24 September, 14 October 1715, 11 February 1715, 16 December 1716; Kāmwar, pp. 240–1).

The English factor at Patna reported that as the Governor of Bihar he managed everything himself and the *diwān* had not the least authority (Wilson ii, p. 236).

63 Shiv Dās 44 (text of the secret *shuqqa* of recall) Sarbuland Khān reached the court on 8 July 1718, Niẓām-ul-Mulk on 24 September 1718, and Ajit Singh on 30 August 1718 (*Akhbārāt* Kāmwar). K.K. (p. 792) states that Ajit Singh was summoned from Ahmadabad. This is not correct. Ajit Singh had been superseded in Ahmadabad in July 1717, and was at Jodhpur at the time (*Mīr'āt* ii, 12).

Sarbuland Khān was told that his presence was required for advice, and also because the Emperor wanted to consult him about the maladministration of Bengal and Orissa (Shiv Dās p. 45).

64 *Siyar*, 412. *Iqbāl* (102) says that Sarbuland Khān came with 50,000 *sawārs*, a greater number of foot and a large park of artillery. M.M. (94b) places the figure at 7,000 *sawārs* more foot and a large park of artillery. Qāsim supports M.M. K.K. gives no figures.

'Abdullāh Khān's strength is variously estimated at 15,000, 20,000, and 30,000 *sawārs*.[65] Thus, a combination of these three powerful figures in opposition would have placed 'Abdullāh Khān in great difficulty. But such a coalition was prevented from coming into existence by various factors, not least the pusillanimity and short-sightedness of Farrukh Siyar and his advisors who were afraid that if they ousted the Saiyids with the help of these powerful nobles, it would be even more difficult to get rid of them afterwards. Hence, Farrukh Siyar picked on a newly-risen favourite, M. Murād Kashmīrī for the post of the *wazīr*. Contrary to popular belief and assertions, M. Murād was not of low-birth,[66] but he was the usual type of courtier, i.e. a sycophant and a braggart. His rise alienated Khān-i-Daurān and the old nobles who were no more prepared to take orders from M. Murād than from Mīr Jumlah earlier.[67]

While the enthusiasm of Nizam-ul-Mulk and Sarbuland Khān had been thus cooled, Farrukh Siyar, in his usual heedless way, completely alienated them. He deprived Sarbuland Khān of the

65 According to the English, he had 15,000 or 20,000 troops who constantly attended him (Wilson ii, pp. 95–6). K.K. (p. 795) says that he had 20,000 troops but that they were continually increasing. M.M. (p. 96b) says that after the *nawāb* learnt of the plot to arrest him on the occasion of 'Īd (p. 1718), he ordered 20,000 *sawārs* to be raised. Till then he had employed only 7,000–8,000 personal (*khāngī*) troops. This is confirmed by K.K. (p. 792), though *Siyar* (p. 412) says, 'earlier he had kept not more than 4,000–5,000 *sawārs*'. Shiv Dās mentions 30,000 *sawārs kalam-bandī* (i.e. actual, not on paper only) as his strength (Rampur Ms., 30,B.M. Ms., 96).

66 M. Murād was related to the mother of Farrukh Siyar, and had long been in Imperial service, having entered the service in the time of 'Ālamgīr. He was an old friend of Mun'im Khān, and in Jahāndār's time, through the influence of Kokaltāsh Khān, he acquired the rank of 5,000. After the fall of Jahāndār Shah, he joined the Saiyids, and had been in favour with Ḥusain 'Alī before the latter left for the Deccan (Kāmwar, 428, Shiv Dās pp. 40–1, M.M., 77b, 81a, 84b. See also Irvine i, pp 340–5).

67 M.M., 103a Wārid (p. 297) says that after this, Khān-i-Daurān used to carry every secret of the emperor to the Saiyids. Kāmwar (p. 432) remarks 'from the coming to the front of I'tiqād Khān (M. Murād) many nobles who had been favourably inclined towards Farrukh Siyar were alienated and joined Quṭb-ul-Mulk and exerted themselves in his favour… They were extremely jealous of the promotion of I'tiqād Khān which seemed to them without any cause.'

governorship of Bihar without confering any new post upon him,[68] and took away the *faujdārī* of Moradabad from Nīẓām-ul-Mulk, converted it into a province, and conferred it upon his new favourite, M. Murād.[69] Thus, both these nobles became ripe for defection. 'Abdullāh Khān played his hand cleverly and won them over by promising the governorship of Kabul to Sarbuland Khān, and of Bihar to Niẓām-ul-Mulk.[70] Meanwhile, M. Amīn Khān, finding his means unequal to the task of checking Ḥusain 'Alī in Malwa, had left his charge and returned to the court. In exasperation, Farrukh Siyar dismissed him from his *manṣab* and office. But 'Abdullāh Khān intervened on his behalf also, and won him over by securing his restoration to his *manṣab* and office.[71] He also secured the support of 'other fortune seekers by rendering them assistance and enquiring after their affairs'. Ajit Singh had always been a partisan of the Saiyids. He had been further alienated when Farrukh Siyar dismissed him from Gujarāt on the ground of 'oppression,' and conferred the province on his favourite, Khān-i-Daurān.[72] Hence, on his arrival at the court, Ajit Singh adhered to the side of the *wazīr.*

68 K.K., 792, M.M., 110a. Sarbuland K. left the court on 26 September. He resigned his *manṣab* and returned to Delhi on 25 November (*Akhbārāt*).
69 K.K., 792, 802, M.M., 110a, Kāmwar and *Akhbārāt* entry d. 7 January 1719, *Iqbāl*, 47.
70 *Akhbārāt*, Niẓām-ul-Mulk was appointed to Bihar in February 1719, and Sarbuland Khān to Kabul on 7 January 1719.
71 K.K., 902. M.M. (p. 111a) gives a somewhat different account. M. Amīn had been recalled from Malwa by Farrukh Siyar. When M. Amīn reached near Delhi, 'Abdullāh Khān expressed suspicion at his recall, and at his instance, M. Amīn was forbidden from entering Delhi and dismissed from his *manṣab* and office. Having thus alienated M. Amīn from Farrukh Siyar, 'Abdullāh Khān cleverly won him over to his side by having him restored (Kāmwar, Shiv Dās, p. 44).
72 *Mir'āt* ii, 12. This was sometime in April 1717, when Ajit Singh had gone on a pilgrimage to Dwārkā. On 10 August, Ajit's son, Abai Singh had been superseded as the *faujdār* of Sorath (*Akhbārāt*).

The Rājpūt sources (*Jodhpur Khyāt*, quoted in Ojha's *Marwar* ii, p. 567) ascribe this to Ajit's friendship with the Saiyid brothers, and the machinations of Jai Singh (Reu, *Jodhpur*, p. 311).

In a letter to Jai Singh d. 4 *Jamāda* II yr. 6, 16 May 1717, Farrukh Siyar gave misgovernment as the reason for Ajit Singh's supersession. 'Maharaja Ajit Singh has made Gujarāt which is the pride of Hindustan (lit. its lamp

Thus, by the end of 1718, Farrukh Siyar had been almost completely isolated. The only noble of consequence on his side remained Jai Singh. A decisive section of the old nobility, including such powerful figures as M. Amīn Khān, Niẓām-ul-Mulk and Sarbuland Khān had no hopes left from Farrukh Siyar, and either decided to side actively with the Saiyids, or adopted a position of neutrality in their conflict with Farrukh Siyar. Thus, the Saiyids were in a position to dictate their will to the Emperor.

The Saiyids now had three possible courses before them: first, to depose Farrukh Siyar and set themselves up as the monarchs, as had been done by successful rebels in the time of the *sulṭanat*; second, to depose Farrukh Siyar and choose a new Timurid prince who could be relied upon to rule according to their wishes; and, third, to keep Farrukh Siyar on the throne but shear him of all power and capacity for mischief by securing control of all the offices which gave access to him. The first course was never seriously considered and was, perhaps, considered unworkable.[73]

---

and light) dead and deserted (lit. lampless) by his oppressions and excesses. *Jāgīrdārs* big and small, people high and low and the citizens of Ahmadabad have appealed (against him). Because the care of the world and the happiness of the people are incumbent on the sovereign, we have no alternative but to dismiss him and to appoint Ṣamṣām-ud-Daulah (Khān-i-Daurān) in his place' (*J.R.: Add. Pers.*, Vol ii, p. 3).

The charge of oppression against Ajit Singh seems to have been of old standing. On 22 August, 5 and 27 September 1715, there were complaints that the Rājpūts of Ajit Singh were laying their hands on the royal *maḥāls* and the *Jāgīrs* of the royal *manṣabadārs*, and that the *mutṣaddīs* and the *jāgīrdārs* dared not say anything as the news-writers were in collusion with the Raja. Gulā'b Chand, *Karorī Sā'ir*, was also said to be charging 5 per cent toll on the goods of all Muslims (*Akhbārāt*).

73 According to a Bārahā tradition (*Tārīkh-i-Sādāt-i-Bārahā*, Jansath Ms., pp. 300, 314) one Jalāl Khān of Muzaffarnagar or his son Diyānat Khān proposed that one of the two brothers should ascend the throne. Irvine (i, p. 388), however, considers this story to be of doubtful veracity.

Qāsim (p. 101) tells us that M. Amīn had declared that if the Saiyids chose to ascend the throne, he would be the first to salute them. But, says the author, 'this was all a figment of his imagination: the Saiyids never laid any claims to the throne.'

Subsequent rumours that the Saiyids had formed the project of murdering all the scions of the Timurid dynasty one by one and then dividing the empire

The choice lay between the second and the third course. 'Abdullāh Khān, who was a shrewd politician, as is evident from his deft handling of the situation during his brother's absence, favoured the last course. He wanted, as a contemporary writer puts it, 'to treat Farrukh Siyar as Mahābat Khān had treated Jahāngīr',[74] i.e. to keep him a virtual prisoner in his hands. In this way, he hoped to secure the reality of power without incurring the odium of raising their hands against the lawful sovereign.

Early in 1718, 'Abdullāh Khān had written to Ḥusain 'Alī to come to the north at once, as his relations with the emperor were worsening daily and he was in fear of his life.[75] In September 1718, Farrukh Siyar recalled Mīr Jumlah from Lahore. As this was a breach of the agreement made with Ḥusain 'Alī, the latter now had a valid excuse for marching to Delhi. In October 1718, Ḥusain 'Alī left Aurangabad. At Burhānpur he was joined by a Marāthā army of 10,000 horse under Peshwa Bālājī Vishwanāth, the combined forces of Ḥusain 'Alī and the Marāthās numbering about 25,000 horse and 10,000 foot. The ostensible pretext for coming to the court without permission was that a (fictitious) son of Prince Akbar had been handed over by Shāhū and it was necessary to escort him to Delhi.[76]

Ḥusain 'Alī, who was of a haughty and impatient temperament, had already made up his mind about the deposition of Farrukh Siyar. This decision was known in his innermost circle by the time he reached near Delhi.[77] He entered Delhi with drums beating like an independent sovereign, defying Imperial etiquette, and repeatedly said that he no longer reckoned himself among the servants of the monarch, adding 'I will maintain the honour of

---

among themselves (*Aḥwāl,* Irvine i, p. 432) seem to have been so much bazar gossip.

74 Khush-ḥāl, 416 (Sarkar Ms.).

75 See copy of the letter in Shiv Dās (Rampur Ms., pp. 41–5). 'Abdullāh Khān wrote that Farrukh Siyar had demanded the surrender of Ratan Chand and Chūrāman, and made an attempt on his life.

76 *Iqbāl,* 49–50, K.K., 793, 795. In April 1714 and 1717, the *Akhbārāt* had brought news of disturbance in the Deccan created by a suppositious son of Prince Akbar.

77 K.K., 825. It is alleged that Ratan Chand was among those who instigated Ḥusain 'Alī against Farrukh Siyar (K.K. p. 805), but it is not known if he advised deposition.

my race and care neither for the loss of my *manṣab* nor for royal censure'.[78]

A tussle now began between 'Abdullāh Khān and Ḥusain Alī. On 19 February, a conference was held by Ḥusain 'Alī, 'Abdullāh Khān, Ajit Singh and Bhim Singh Hāṛā, and it was decided that the Saiyids should demand the posts of the *dāroghah-i-dīwān-i-khāṣ* and *mīr ātish* before Ḥusain 'Alī would go to the fort for an audience with the emperor, and hand over the captive prince to him. The Saiyids also demanded that Jai Singh should be ordered to leave for Amber, that the other posts which gave access to the emperor—such as the post of the *dāroghah-i-khawāṣṣān*—should also be filled by their nominees, and that the fort should be placed under their control at the time of the interview.[79] On 20 February, on the advice of his favourite, I'tiqād Khān (M. Murād Kashmīrī), Farrukh Siyar decided to yield to the demands of the Saiyids, Jai Singh was asked to leave for Amber, and the posts of the *dāroghah-i-dīwān-i-khāṣ, mīr ātish, dāroghah-i-khawāṣṣān, dāroghah-i-jilau* (Supt. of the Royal attendants and the Special Retinue) and the *nāẓir-i-ḥaram* were conferred upon the nominees of the Saiyids. However, Farrukh Siyar made the proviso, that the old incumbents should continue to hold office as deputies, till *Nauroz*, which was about a month off.[80]

The departure of Jai Singh was followed by the defeat of his protégé, Budh Singh, at the hands of Bhim Singh who had allied himself with the Saiyids. On 22 February, Ḥusain 'Alī had an interview with the emperor after posting his men at all strategic points in the fort. But the differences between the two sides could not be bridged. The Saiyids were impatient at the delay in the handing over of actual charge of the various offices to their

78 Shiv Dās, 58, K.K., 804, *M.U.* i, 330. Ḥusain 'Alī's troops destroyed the crops and looted the bazars like a hostile army. In particular, the country of Jai Singh was thoroughly ravaged. These facts were brought to the notice of Farrukh Siyar but he could do nothing about them.

79 M.M. (Sarkar Ms.), 238, K.K., 805, Qasim 97, *M.U.* iii, 135. Amīn-ud-Dīn Sambhalī got a message from a friend who had direct access to the Saiyids that the conference had decided to depose Farrukh Siyar and to raise a captive prince to the throne. Accordingly, Amīn-ud-Dīn wrote a strong letter to Farrukh Siyar advising military resistance to the Saiyids.

80 M.M., 238, K.K., 806, Irvine i, 375. The *ṣūbahdārīs* of Lahore and Agra were conferred on the Saiyid nominees at the same time.

nominees, and suspected that Farrukh Siyar was only playing for time in order that he might resort to some new trick.

Hence, they refused the proffered compromise. On 26 February, 'Abdullāh Khān had a stormy interview with Farrukh Siyar during which the latter refused to make any further concessions, openly abused the *wazīr*, and retired into the *ḥaram*. 'Abdullāh Khān thereupon turned out the royal favourite, I'tiqad Khān, and all the royal guards from the fort, and took possession of it.[81]

Inspite of this break, 'Abdullāh Khān was in favour of keeping Farrukh Siyar on the throne and maintaining the *khuṭbah* and *sikkah* in his name, since all the important offices were in their hands or, he felt confident, would soon be. He sent messages to the effect to his brother,[82] and repeatedly asked Farrukh Siyar to come out of the *ḥaram* and dismiss their remaining opponents. Farrukh Siyar refused. Meanwhile, wild rumours of the death of 'Abdullāh Khān and Ḥusain 'Alī at the hands of Ajit Singh, M. Amīn and others spread in the town, and several nobles took courage to come out in defence of the monarch. The Marāthā troops of Ḥusain 'Alī clashed with the Mughal troops of M. Amīn Khān, and were assailed by the riff-raff in the city and the unemployed Mughal soldiers. After about 2,000 of them had been slain, they were compelled to leave the town.[83] Though militarily ineffective, this demonstration of popular attachment to the house of Timur confronted the Saiyids with the danger of a sudden landslide against them, and impressed upon them the urgent necessity of making a decision quickly, specially as Jai Singh was hovering 40 miles from Delhi with 20,000 horsemen.

Hāshim 'Alī Khān, Ikhlāṣ Khān, and M. Amīn Khān, who held frequent consultations with Ḥusain 'Alī, advised the deposition of Farrukh Siyar.[84] M. Amīn Khān had already given this advice to Ḥusain 'Alī a few days earlier. Opinion now veered round in favour of deposition. Even Khān-i-Daurān and Ajit Singh gave the same advice.[85] Ḥusain 'Alī sent a peremptory note to 'Abdullāh Khān asking him to finish the job in hand or come out of the fort, and

81 K.K., 807, M.M., 239, Shiv Dās, 59, Qāsim, 145–6, Irvine i, 377–8.
82 Khush-ḥāl, 416, Qāsim, 150, *Ḥadīqat*, 89, M.M., 263 (Sarkar Ms.).
83 K.K., 812–13, M.M. (Sarkar Ms.), 262–3, Qāsim, 102—figures probable much exaggerated.
84 M.M., 263, Khush-ḥāl, 416, Qāsim, 99, *Ḥadīqat*, 89, *M.U.* iii, 135.
85 M.M., 263, Qāsim, 99, Khush-ḥāl, 416, Wārid, 309, K.K., 814–16.

let him (Ḥusain 'Alī) take over. As Farrukh Siyar refused to come out of the *ḥaram* and comply with 'Abdullāh Khān's demands, 'Abdullāh Khān had no option but to bow down to the recommendation of all his associates in favour of deposition. A party of Afghāns was sent into the *ḥaram*. They dragged Farrukh Siyar out, blinded him and threw him into jail. A youth of 20 years, Rafi'ud-Darjāt, was proclaimed the Emperor. Shortly afterwards, on 29 April 1719, Farrukh Siyar was murdered and buried in the crypt of Humāyūn's tomb.

'Abdullāh Khān afterwards regretted the deposition of Farrukh Siyar, and blamed his brother for his haste. Farrukh Siyar's preference for sycophants and upstarts had prevented the old nobles from forming a coalition to oust the Saiyids. In destroying Farrukh Siyar, the Saiyids had thus destroyed their most effective shield against the old nobles. The political, economic and administrative problems facing the empire had become more acute during the preceding period of factionalism and misgovernment, and the Saiyids were now called upon to solve them. The ability of the Saiyids to hold on to power would depend largely upon their success in devising satisfactory solutions to the problems posed by the old nobles, and the various problems inherited from the preceeding rulers. They were thus faced with a situation of stupendous difficulty.

CHAPTER VI

The Saiyid 'New' Wizārat

POWERS AND POSITION OF THE SAIYIDS

After deposing Farrukh Siyar and setting up a new monarch, the Saiyid brothers distributed among their nominees all the posts which gave direct access to the Emperor. The *dāroghah-i-dīwān-i-khāṣ*, the *dāroghah-i-ghusal-khānah*, the *Nāẓir-i-Ḥaram*, and even the eunuchs and personal attendants of the emperor were hand-picked by the Saiyids. Saiyid Himmat Khān Bārahā was nominated the guardian (*aṭālīq*) of the emperor, and it is said, without his orders even the food of the emperor could not be served. The emperor could not talk to any noble unless his 'guardian' or one of the Saiyid brothers was present. Whenever the emperor went out for public prayers or for hunting, a select body of Bārahās surrounded him. Thus, the emperor lost all personal liberty, and all access to him was controlled by the Saiyid brothers.[1] This was considered necessary because, in a great measure, the power of the Saiyids rested on the control of the Emperor's person.

This state of affairs continued under Rafi'-ud-Daulah who succeeded Rafi-ud-Darjāt after the latter's death from consumption on 11 June 1719. But Rafi'-ud-Daulah also succumbed to the same disease, and on 28 September 1719, the Saiyids raised Muḥammad Shāh, the son of Jahān Shāh who was the youngest son of Bahādur Shāh, to the throne. On Muḥammad Shāh's accession, a slight

1 K.K., 816, 818, 831, 842; Kāmwar, 410, 413; *T. Muẓ.*, 218, 224; *Siyar*, 420, Āshūb, 151, Wārid, 312.

relaxation of control was made, and the hereditary doorkeepers and attendants were allowed to return to their former posts. But in all matters of state, the emperor continued to be powerless.[2]

But apart from those posts which gave access to the emperor, the Saiyids followed a policy of effecting as few changes as possible. In the provinces, most of the governors and other officers were confirmed in their previous posts.[3] This was done in order to restore law and order rapidly, to screen the violent transfer of power at the centre, and to reconcile the old nobles to the new set up.

At the court, the property and *manṣabs* of a number of the personal favourites of Farrukh Siyar—such as Muḥammad Murād Kashmīrī, Amīn-ud-Dīn Sambhalī, Ghāzī-ud-Dīn Aḥmad Beg, and the emperor's relations like Sa'ādat Khān, Shā'istah Khān etc. were confiscated. But the property of many more was spared.[4] There were no bloody executions, and even some of the close favourites of the late emperor such as Khān-i-Daurān and Mīr Jumlah, were left in possession of their *manṣabs* and *jāgīrs* and given employment. In general, the Saiyids made no attempt to monopolize the high offices of state. M. Amīn Khān continued to be the second *bakhshī*, another Tūrānī, Roshan-ud-Daulah Ẓafar Khān was made the third *bakhshī*, and even 'Ināyatullāh Khān, whose policies had been strongly opposed by the Saiyids, was allowed to continue as the *khān-i-sāmān* and the (absentee) governor of Kashmir. The post of *ṣadr* was given to Amīr Khān, an old 'Ālamgīrī noble, and then to Mīr Jumlah.[5] Apart from the two highest offices of state and the viceroyalty of the Deccan which the Saiyids held since 1715, and the offices which controlled access to the emperor, the only new posts given to Bārahās or the personal employees and

2 Kāmwar, 413, Irvine i, 416.

3 Kāmwar, 422, *T. Muẓ.*, 218, Irvine i, 404.

4 Thus, M.M. (p. 120a) states that except for some people like M. Murād Kashmīrī, 'all *manṣabdārs*, imperial servants and *jāgīrdārs* were given *sanands* of confirmation and even the *wālāshāhīs* of the late emperor were retained'.

Kāmwar (p. 441), however, says that 'the *manṣabs* of more than 200 *manṣabdārs* of the time of 'Ālamgīr, Bahādur Shāh and Farrukh Siyar were confiscated, and distributed by the two brothers among their followers'. K.K. is silent, but *Siyar* (p. 420) as also *Iqbāl* (p. 138) follow M.M.

5 Kāmwar, 444. Mīr Jumlah was made the *Ṣadr* on 21 October 1719 and continued to occupy the post till his death on 3 January 1732 (*Tārikh-i-Muḥammadī*).

dependents of the Saiyids were the *ṣūbahdārīs* of Agra and Allahabad, and the *faujdārī* of Moradabad.[6]

But the Saiyids had yet to stabilize their power. Two things were necessary for this: first, to gain effective control of all parts of the empire so as to deny a rallying centre to their opponents; and, second, to organize a strong bloc of supporters to maintain their position in the face of possible opposition from rival sections inside the nobility.

Early Revolts against the Saiyids

Inspite of the conciliatory policy adopted by the Saiyids, two centres of resistance and overt challenge to their authority were rapidly formed: the first at Agra, and the second at Allahabad.

The revolt at Agra was organized by an adventurer named Mitr Sen[7] and a couple of his associates whose primary objective was to take advantage of the disturbed condition of the empire to gain wealth and position for themselves. To achieve this, they proclaimed as emperor a scion of the Timurid dynasty, Nekū Siyar, who was a prisoner in the Agra fort. By themselves, the rebels had little power or importance, but the Saiyids were afraid that Nekū Siyar might become the rallying centre of all elements hostile to them. Rumour was rife that Niẓām-ul-Mulk, Jai Singh, and Chhabelā Ram Nāgar, the Governor of Allahabad, were coming to the aid of Nekū Siyar. Nekū Siyar's partisans appealed for help not only to these nobles but also to the Afghāns and the local *zamindars*.[8] Jai Singh had actually moved out several stages from

6 Agra was given to S. Ghairat K., the cousin of the two brothers. Shāh 'Alī K. was appointed to Allahabad after Girdhar Bahādur had been ejected from it. Ajmer, however, was taken from S. Khān-i-Jahān Bārahā the uncle of the Saiyids, and given to Ajit Singh. Ṣaif-ud-Dīn 'Alī K. the younger brother of 'Abdullāh K. and Ḥusain 'Alī, was made the *faujdār* of Moradabad. S. Najm-ud-Dīn 'Alī K. was the *mīr¯atish* for sometime, but the post was soon given to S. Ṣalābat K. a proteģé of Khān-i-Daurān, and after his death, to Ḥaider Qulī Khān (Kāmwar).

7 An employee of Nekū Siyar, he was reputed to have had some knowledge of medicine, and to have made his fortune by money-lending. It was this obscure figure who now proclaimed Nekū Siyar the Emperor, and became his *wazīr*, with the title of Raja Birbal and the rank of 7,000 (K.K., p. 825, Kāmwar).

8 Shiv Dās, 71.

Amber and was camping at Toda Tank, 80 *kos* from Agra. After the deposition of Farrukh Siyar, many nobles such as Taqarrub Khān, Shā'istah Khān etc. had taken shelter with Jai Singh to await the turn of the times. Amber had thus become a centre of opposition to the Saiyids. It was feared that many other nobles who had joined the Saiyids at the last moment would also go over to Jai Singh.[9]

In his opposition to the Saiyids, Jai Singh was supported by Rana Sangram Singh. Sangram Singh had ascended the *gaddi* in 1710, and had been awarded the *manṣab* of 5,000 by Bahadur Shah which was higher than the ranks of Ajit Singh and Jai Singh at the time. Farrukh Siyar had raised his rank to 7,000/7,000.[10] With the intervention of Jai Singh, the Rana had been able to recover Rampura. Dungarpur and Banswara were also placed under his over-lordship.[11]

When Jai Singh moved from Amber to help Neku Siyar's rebellion, the Rana gave him financial help. He also wrote to Chhabelā Rām Nāgar, denouncing the Saiyids as 'traitors to the salt', and pressed him to march to the aid of Neku Siyar, informing him that Pancholi Jag Jiwan Ram was marching via Malwa with a large army to aid Jai Singh. The Rana also expressed the hope that Nīẓām-ul-Mulk who had a large artillery, and the Marāthās would cooperate so that 'with the help of the three sides the cherished objective would be attained'.[12]

However, the rebellion failed to spread beyond Agra and did not receive any support from the high grandees. Even Niẓām-ul-Mulk, who passed Agra enroute to Malwa, gave no help.[13] Mitr Sen appealed to the Saiyid brothers and other prominent nobles to accept Nekū Siyar as the Emperor, and 'Abdullāh Khān was said to be in favour of accepting the suggestion. But Ḥusain 'Alī, considering it a personal affront, declined, and resorted to stern measures.

9 K.K., 832, Kāmwar, 430. To check Jai Singh, 'Abdullāh K. appointed Nuṣrat Yār Khān Bārahā to go and sit at Kālādham (*Bālmukundnāmah*, letter No. 23). Ḥusain 'Alī had appointed S. Dilāwar 'Alī K. for the purpose.

10 Bahādur Shāh *Akhbārāt*, 17, 28, Rabī' II, R.Y. 5, 5, 16 June 1711; Farrukh Siyar: *Akhbārāt*, 26, *Sha'bān* R.Y. 2. 17 September 1713.

11 *Mir'at*, 225.

12 Maharana's letter to Chhabelā Rām, *Ajaī'b-ul-Āfāk* ff. 57b–58a.

13 K.K., 827–8, 832, Shiv Dās, 79–80.

The Allahabad rebellion was due to the personal apprehensions of Chhabelā Ram, an old servant of Farrukh Siyar and the Governor of Allahabad. He suspected the intentions of the Saiyids towards him, and his suspicions were strengthened when the Saiyids attempted to displace him from Allahabad, and sent a force under Shāh 'Alī Khān with instructions to seize the fort. In reality, the Saiyids had no desire to destroy Chhabelā Ram, but they considered his possession of such a strong fort as Allahabad dangerous, especially as it lay athwart the route from which the vital Bengal treasures came to Delhi.[14] They were even prepared to grant Awadh to Chhabelā Ram,[15] in exchange for the *ṣūbahdārī* of Allahabad, but the latter refused to place any trust in their word, and rose in open revolt (August 1719). Soon afterwards, Chhabelā Ram died. But the rebellion was continued by his nephew, Girdhar Bahādur.

These two rebellions occupied all the energies of the two brothers during the first fourteen months of their domination. It took three months of siege before hunger and treachery brought about the surrender of Agra (12 August 1719). Another nine months were spent in negotiations and warfare with Girdhar Bahādur before he agreed to evacuate Allahabad (11 May 1720). The terms granted to the latter were generous and practically the same as had been proffered to him even before the commencement of the hostilities. He was granted the governorship of Awadh with all the *jāgīrs* dependent on it, and two or three other important *faujdārīs* which he desired to possess, with an additional gift of rupees 30 lakhs as *in'ām*.[16] It is significant that even then Girdhar Bahādur refused to place any reliance in the words of the Saiyid brothers, and stipulated that Ratan Chand should be the guarantor and intermediary.[17]

14 The Bengal treasure had been the mainstay of the Delhi government even towards the end of Aurangzīb's reign. At the time of Chhabelā Ram's rebellion, a convoy of 90 lakhs was waiting at Patna. The financial affairs of the brothers were not too good, as is evident from letters written at this time by 'Abdullāh K. to Chhabelā Ram asking him to escort the treasure beyond his borders as the soldiers had not received their salaries for years (*Bāl.*, 7, 27).

15 *Bāl.*, Nos 3, 8; Shiv Dās, 76.

16 Shiv Dās, 68; K.K., 846; *Bāl.*, Nos 8, 19, 4; *T. Muẓ.*, 230.

17 K.K., 838.

Political Problems of the Saiyids

These developments could not fail to reflect unfavourably on the military power of the Saiyids. The Saiyids could not afford protracted military operations, and needed to proceed cautiously, so that the coalition which had brought about the deposition of Farrukh Siyar might be maintained and consolidated. This implied two things: first, the consolidation and extension of the alliance with the Marāthās and Rājpūts; and second, the solution of what might be called 'the problem of the 'Ālamgīrī nobles'.

Active attempts were made by the Saiyids to consolidate their alliance with the Rājpūts and the Marāthās, and to appease 'Hindu opinion' generally. Immediately after the deposition of Farrukh Siyar, the *jizyah* was abolished once again at the request of Raja Ajit Singh.[18] As a further gesture of goodwill, Ajit Singh's daughter who had been married to Farrukh Siyar after being duly converted to Islam, was allowed to renounce her new faith and return to her home with her father, taking all her wealth and property with her. This step, which Khāfī Khān calls 'unprecedented', caused great indignation among a section of the Muslims in the capital, and specially among the *Qāẓīs* who ruled that it was illegal to renounce Islam. But the Saiyids, paid no heed to them.[19]

Jai Singh Sawai had always been hostile to the Saiyids. He had actually come out of Amber with the intention of supporting the rebellion at Agra. He had also given shelter to certain nobles who had fled from Delhi with rebellious intentions.[20] Yet, through Ajit Singh, the Saiyids opened negotiations with him. At last, after the fall of Agra and under threat of an invasion from Ḥusain 'Alī, Jai Singh withdrew from Toda Tank. The Saiyids decided to be generous, and Jai Singh was granted a large sum of money and the *faujdārī* of Sorath in Aḥmadabād. Ajmer, which was considered to be a most important charge and entrusted to the highest grandees and generally to Muslim nobles only on account of its religious associations, was granted to Ajit Singh along with the

18 Kāmwar, 442, K.K., 816, Reu, *Hist. of Marwar,* 314 (Letter from the Maharana), *Mir'āt* ii, 23, Tod i, 424.

19 K.K., 833, *T. Muẓ.*

20 These were Rūhullāh K. II who had been appointed the *faujdār* of Aḥmadabād, Tahawwur Khān Tūrāni, and S. Ṣalābat Khān, the brother-in-law of Farrukh Siyar, who had been the *mīr ātish* (K.K., 832, Kāmwar).

ṣūbah of Gujarāt.[21] Other honours were also conferred on the Raja who thus became one of the most powerful and influential noble in the empire. The two Rājpūt rajas together constituted a very powerful faction in the empire. The returning confidence felt by the Hindus is reflected in Khāfi Khān's 'complaint' that 'from the environs of the capital to the banks of the Narbada, the infidels were engaged in repairing temples and attempting to forbid cow-slaughter'.[22]

The Saiyids continued to make attempts through Ajit Singh to win over Jai Singh actively to their side. At their instances, Ajit Singh met Jai Singh at Manoharpur, and took him to Jodhpur where he was fêted and feasted.[23] Shortly afterwards, Ajit Singh solemnized the marriage of his daughter to Jai Singh.[24] Some tangible accord might have resulted from all this had the Saiyids remained in power longer. For the moment, Jai Singh refused a request by Niẓām-ul-Mulk for joint action against the Saiyids,[25] but did not join the Saiyids either. The Saiyid pact with the Rājpūts, therefore, touched only Ajit Singh.

The pact with the Marāthās was strengthened by the formal grant, under Imperial signature, of the *sanads* for *sardeshmukhī* and *chauth.*[26] Within a month of Farrukh Siyar's deposition, the Marāthā

21 K.K., 838. Elliot (vii, p. 485) has confused Sorath with Surat. The *farmān* of Jai Singh's appointment is dated 19 *Ẕilḥijjah,* 1132, 2 November 1719 (Reu, *Marwar,* p. 318).

22 K.K., 860. No formal order prohibiting cow slaughter was passed by the Saiyids but on his own responsibility Ajit Singh prohibited it in the two *ṣūbahs* under his charge, an action which Khāfi Khān says 'exceeded his authority' (K.K., 936, *T. Hindī,* 43b [B.M. Ms.]).

23 *Bāl.,* 11–12, Reu, *Marwar,* 318–20. Ajit met Jai Singh at Kālā Pahār in November 1719 and is mentioned as having signed a treaty with him on 22 *Jamada* II, 1 May (*Bāl,* 5, 31).

24 Jai Singh was married, under tight personal security to Princess Suraj Kunwari to whom he had been bethrothed when she was a child, and had just come of age. (*Byava Bahi* No. 1 of Jodhpur gives the date of marriage as *Baisakh Badi* 9, 1776 V.S. *shravanādi,* 1 May 1720.) See also Ojha, *Marwar,* 588; *Bāl.* Nos, 5, 11, 31.

25 *Āṣaf Jāh,* 113.

26 Copies in B.M. Ms., 26, 216 quoted by Dr A. G. Powar in the *I.H.R.C.* XVII, session, *loc. cit.* The *sanads* in question are dated the first year of Muḥammad Shāh's reign. As M. Shāh's reign had not commenced by then, and it could not be foreseen that his reign would be pre-dated to commence

troops which Ḥusain ʻAlī had brought with him from the Deccan left Delhi, taking with them the *sanads* and the family of Shāhū. Though comparatively cheaper,[27] these troops were unpopular with the Delhi populace and the north Indians generally. Hence, the Saiyids were not keen to detain them at Delhi more than was absolutely necessary. Although no Marāthā soldiers now remained in north India, Marāthā support continued to be the mainstay of the Saiyid power in the Deccan. ʻĀlam ʻAlī', Ḥusain ʻAlī's deputy in the Deccan, was virtually under the guardianship of Shankarājī Malhār, who had been the minister of Rājārām at one time. It is said that Ḥusain ʻAlī had instructed ʻĀlam ʻAlī to follow Shankarājī's advice in all matters, and as the latter had many connections with the Satārā court, good relations with Shāhū were thus assured.[28]

It was not only among the Rājpūts and the Marāthās that the Saiyids sought to extend their connections. They sought to bind Chūrāman Jat still closer to themselves by further concessions. He was given charge of the royal highway from Delhi to Gwāliar and took part in the siege of Agra, receiving favours for his services.[29]

That the Saiyids had no intention of seeking any narrow monopoly of political powers, or of following a policy of racial or religious exclusion is amply born out not only by the foregoing instances, but also by their attitude towards the nobles belonging to the time of ʻĀlamgīr and Bahādur Shāh. As in the earlier period, the Saiyids attempted to win this section over to their side and to secure their cooperation in the task of administration by granting them increments in rank and honour, and by appointing them to high offices. Thus, most of the old incumbents were confirmed in their previous offices. In a letter to Niẕām-ul-Mulk, ʻAbdullāh Khān explained his general policy in the following words: 'The high and mighty task of administering Hindustan is not one that can be

---

from Farrukh Siyar's deposition, these *sanads* must have been confirmatory *sanads* granted by the Saiyids *after* Muḥammad Shāh ascended the throne. See also Duff i, 368–9.

27 Marāthā soldiers were paid at the rate of 8 annas daily, whereas the average pay of a trooper under the Saiyids was Rs 50 per month (*Riyasat*, 92–3, *Iqbāl*, 128).

28 *Burhān-ul-Futūḥ*, 167a, Khush-ḥāl.

29 Shiv Dās, 69, Kāmwar, 423.

accomplished single-handed, without the help of prominent nobles and officers of state. Under the circumstances, is it better that I should bring forward new (untried) men and become dependent on them, or that I should continue to take the help of one like you who has ever been a friend?'[30]

However, in seeking to translate this policy into practice, the Saiyids faced a number of serious difficulties, such as the fears and suspicions aroused by the deposition of Farrukh Siyar, the jealousy and resentment of some of the old nobles at the domination exercised by two such comparatively newcomers as the Saiyid brothers, the ambition of individuals like M. Amīn Khān and Niẓām-ul-Mulk who desired to exercise supreme power, or to carve out separate spheres of influence for themselves, the vaulting ambition of the Marāthās, and, finally, growing differences between the two brothers over matters, both personal and political.

The differences between the brothers related to the sharing of the spoils of victory, and of political power. They also differed over the attitude to be adopted towards the old nobles in general, and Niẓām-ul-Mulk in particular. Ḥusain 'Alī charged that 'Abdullāh Khān had taken advantage of his position inside the fort to take possession of all the buried treasures of Farrukh Siyar, and the goods in his jewel-house, imperial establishments etc. He also objected to the fact that 'Abdullāh Khān had resumed the *jāgīrs* of more than 200 Farrukh Shāhī and other nobles and distributed them among his followers. For sometime, there was great tension and even talk of fighting between the brothers till Ratan Chand brought about an agreement by pointing to the 'Tūrānī' danger.[31]

After the capture of Agra, the lion's share of the booty was appropriated by Ḥusain 'Alī. 'Abdullāh Khān moved from Delhi on the pretext of barring Jai Singh's advance from Amber, but really in order to claim a share in the booty. Once again, Ratan Chand brought about a settlement, but 'Abdullāh Khān was not satisfied

30 *Bāl*, 2. The letter was written sometime in 1720 when Niẓām-ul-Mulk was the Governor of Malwa.

'Abdullāh Khān used to say, 'We are three brothers of whom Niẓām-ul-Mulk is the eldest and Ḥusain 'Alī the youngest' (*Ḥadīqat*).

31 Kāmwar, pp. 441–2.

with his share of the booty.[32] Hence, each of the brothers wanted to lead the campaign against Allahabad personally. Ultimately, as a compromise, the command had to be entrusted to Ratan Chand.

Underneath differences lay a subtle struggle for power between the two brothers. Husain 'Alī was much more energetic than 'Abdullāh Khān, and he rapidly out-classed the latter in the exercise of real power. But he was of a hot and hasty temperament, and failed to weigh the situation carefully before coming to a decision, and did not penetrate to the heart of a problem. As Khāfi says, 'He (Ḥusain 'Alī) deemed himself superior in military and governmental matters to his brother, though he was forgetful of the real matter and unacquainted with stratagem.

'In his judgement it seemed that there were sufficient administrators with him and his brother, and as his adopted son, 'Ālam 'Alī, was acting as the *ṣūbahdār* of the Deccan with a sufficient army, it would be well to send Niẕām-ul-Mulk to be the *ṣābahdār* of Malwa, (which was) half-way between Delhi and the Deccan'.[33]

Thus, Ḥusain 'Alī greatly over-estimated the strength and stability of their position, and failed to appreciate sufficiently the wisdom and moderation of 'Abdullāh Khān's policy. The subsequent misfortunes of the Saiyids were due, in good part, to the unseemly haste of Ḥusain 'Alī in attempting to put down all potential rivals and the resentment caused by his arrogant and untactful behaviour.[34] 'Abdullāh Khān had suggested that Niẕām-ul-Mulk should be appointed the Governor of Bihar, which was a province with notoriously turbulent *zamindars* and which yielded little money. In this way,'Abdullāh Khān wanted to remove Niẕām-ul-Mulk from the court, and appoint him to a place where he would be worried by lack of money and of suitable means and material. He could then be dealt with later, as the situation required. But

32 The booty is placed at one crore (ten million) by *T. Muẕ.* (p. 229). Rs 18,000,000 by Shiv Dās (p. 73), and two to three crores by K.K. (p. 837).

At the intervention of Ratan Chand, 'Abdullāh Khān received 21 or 28 lakhs, supposed to represent his share of the booty after deducting the expenses. 'Abdullāh Khān felt cheated (Qāsim, pp. 117–18, *M.U.* i, 331).

33 K.K., 847.

34 Thus, it is said that on one occasion he boasted that anyone at whom he cast the shadow of his shoe would become the equivalent of emperor 'Ālamgīr. On another occasion, he ignored court etiquette and sat down in the presence of the Emperor without his permission (Yahyā, 125a, K.K., 821).

at Ḥusain 'Alī's instance, the appointment was cancelled and Niẓām-ul-Mulk was appointed to Malwa instead. Niẓām-ul-Mulk accepted the appointment on a promise by the Saiyids that the province would never be taken away from him—at any rate, not for a long time. He left Delhi in March, 1719, accompanied by his son, Mughal Khān, and more than a thousand *manṣabdārs* who also took their families with them at his instance. He refused to leave his son behind at the court as his *wakīl*, despite repeated requests from the Saiyids.[35]

It is apparent that Niẓām-ul-Mulk trusted the Saiyids as little as the Saiyids trusted him, and that a showdown between the two was inevitable sooner or later. For the Saiyids, however, the problem represented by Niẓām-ul-Mulk was not one of dealing with an individual only. The problem of Niẓām-ul-Mulk was, to some extent, the problem of the bulk of the old nobility belonging to the time of 'Ālamgīr and Bahādur Shāh. Many of these nobles prided themselves on their Īrānī and Tūrānī ancestry. Even though most of them had been settled in India for several generations, they assumed a superior air towards the Indians, or the Hindustan-zā, i.e., Muslims born in India. These nobles, and specially the Tūrānīs, attempted to identify themselves with the Mughal monarchy and tacitly claimed a monopoly of political power—a claim which was hardly supported by the practise of the Great Mughals. These proud nobles felt a sense of humiliation at their domination by a section of the despised Hindustani nobles.[36] Many of them resented the growing alliance of the Saiyids with the

35 K.K., 847–58.

36 Thus, Khāfī Khān observes: 'The two Saiyids, the real rulers, thought themselves masters of the pen and sword, and as opposed to their judgement and the sword of the Bārahās, the Mughals of Īrān and Tūrān were as nobodies. They did not remember that these Mughals had come a thousand or two thousand miles from their native countries and that by courage and sound judgement, the wide realms of Hindustan had been won for the Emperor Babar by hard fighting. For two hundred years they had lived in favour of the House of Taimur and they now felt the ignominy of their emperor being without any power in the state' (K.K., 905, 860).

Cf. also the remarks of Āshūb, 153–4, 139.

On the other hand, Rustam 'Alī says, 'Many Hindi and Tūrānī nobles were opposed to Ḥusain 'Alī Khān due to personal grudge and jealousy' (*T. Hindī*, p. 469).

Rājpūts and Marāthās and their attempt to mollify Hindu opinion by abolishing the *jizyah* and other discriminatory cesses. Still others may have felt the Saiyid rule a barrier to the fulfilment to their own individual ambitions. These sections had not really reconciled themselves to the Saiyid domination but were watching the developments, and awaiting a favourable opportunity to strike a blow against them. Under these circumstances, an attempt on the part of the Saiyids to take a strong attitude towards Niẕām-ul-Mulk stood in danger of being interpreted by these nobles as part and parcel of a policy designed to root out all the old nobles. This was a risk the Saiyids could ill afford to take, because the alternative course was to bring forward new, untried men which created the danger of a breakdown of the administration, and an opportunity to the Rājpūts, Marāthās, Jats etc. to augment their power.

Unfortunately for the Saiyids, events so shaped themselves that they were drawn to take the very step they wished to avoid most, viz., the driving of Niẕām-ul-Mulk into open rebellion.

The Revolt of Niẕām-ul-Mulk and the Downfall of the Saiyids

Ever since Niẕām-ul-Mulk had taken charge of Malwa, reports had been pouring in that he was collecting men and materials of war in excess of his requirements as the governor, and that he had an eye on the Deccan. When questioned by the Saiyids, Niẕām-ul-Mulk explained his action by pointing to the necessity of checking the Marāthās who were harrying the province with 50,000 horse.[37] The Saiyids, however, suspected that Niẕām-ul-Mulk had other intentions. Nor were these suspicions unreasonable on their part, because from Malwa Niẕām-ul-Mulk had sent his son, Mughal Khān, to Jai Singh Sawai to concert measures against the Saiyids. The Saiyids also had some other complaints against Niẕām-ul-Mulk—notably about the employment of one Marḥamat Khān whom Ḥusain ʿAlī had dismissed from the post of the *qilaʿdār* of Māndū for his negligence in not attending upon him when he passed that fort on his way to Delhi in 1719. Niẕām-ul-Mulk's employment of Marḥamat Khān was considered by the Saiyids to

37 Shiv Dās, 79–80 (Niẕām's letter to ʿAbdullāh), K.K., 851.

be a defiance of their authority.[38] The Saiyids had also complained to Niẓām-ul-Mulk about his ravaging certain villages, transferring the *zamindar* of *pargana* Nilam against their wishes etc.[39] They also suspected Niẓām-ul-Mulk of having instigated the uprising of Nekū Siyar.[40]

But these complaints might not have led to an open breach with Niẓām-ul-Mulk had other more urgent considerations not intervened. It seems that Ḥusain 'Alī was desirous of governing the Deccan along with Malwa, Gujārāt, Ajmer and Agra personally and that for this purpose he wanted to make Malwa his headquarters.[41] The reasons for this were two-fold. In the first place, the Saiyids apprehended danger from the Marāthās, and, it seems, wanted to maintain a stricter control on the affairs of the Deccan than was possible from Delhi. We are told that at the time of his visit to Delhi in 1719, Bālāji Vishwanath had been instructed by Shāhū to secure the cession of the forts of Daulatabād and Chanda, recognition of certain conquests of Parsoji Bhonsle in Berar, and an authority for levying *chauth* which had for some time been imposed by the Marāthās in Malwa and Gujārāt. Shāhū's plea was that only if he was given such an authority could he control the chiefs who had already levied contributions there.[42] Secret emissaries from Tārā Bāi had reached Niẓām-ul-Mulk who, we are told, 'had formed the secret design of conquering the Deccan, and of setting free that land of treasures and soldiers'.[43]

The Saiyids were afraid lest the entire Deccan problem should be opened afresh because of the vaulting ambition of the Satara house, and the intrigues of Niẓām-ul-Mulk. Hence, it appears that they wanted to divide the empire into zones of authority among

38 K.K., 849, 858, *Siyar,* 425, *Iqbāl,* 55–66. K.K. suggests that the Saiyids were afraid of the military capacity and reputation which Marḥamat had earned in Malwa, and wanted a pretext to remove him from Niẓām-ul-Mulk's employment. But *T. Muẓ.* (p. 232) says that Ḥusain 'Alī considered Marḥamat's employment a definance of their authority.

39 *Bāl.*, 31, K.K., 851.

40 Wārid, 315.

41 K.K., 851, 857, 859; *Siyar,* 425, Aḥwāl, 172a.

42 Duff i, 365–6.

43 K.K., 858. After his rebellion Niẓām-ul-Mulk was joined by a contingent from Tārā Bāi at Burhānpur (*Āṣaf Jāh,* p. 118).

themselves so that both the north and the south might receive due attention. A partition of the empire on these lines had also been suggested as a solution to the growing differences between the two brothers. As a first step towards such a division, the Saiyids wanted to remove Niẓām-ul-Mulk from Malwa. Ḥusain 'Alī offered Niẓām-ul-Mulk the choice of the governorship of Agra, Allahabad, Burhānpur and Multan,[44] assuring him that he would be sent the *sanad* of whichever *ṣūbah* he chose.[45] But Niẓām-ul-Mulk objected to giving up Malwa so soon after his appointment, particularly in the midst of the harvest season before the advances (*taqāvī*) and the money spent by him had been recovered. He protested that he had accepted Malwa on the solemn promise of not being removed (soon), and that he looked upon the order of transfer as a breach of promise.[46] As early as November 1719, Ḥusain 'Alī had deputed a strong force under his *Bakhshī* Dilāwar 'Alī Khān, to settle a dispute in Bundi, with instructions to keep a watch on the Malwa border after finishing the job. Dilāwar 'Alī had finished

44 K.K., 851, 857, 859; *Siyar*, 425. According to Kāmwar, a *farmān* was sent to Niẓām-ul-Mulk promising him that he would be appointed to Agra as soon as he reached the court. Qāsim (pp. 195–6) mentions the *ṣūbah* of Allahabad. Shiv Dās (p. 56) simply says that Ḥusain 'Alī transferred Niẓām-ul-Mulk from Malwa.

45 K.K., 850. This seems to imply that Niẓām-ul-Mulk was given the option of proceeding to his charge without coming to the court first, as was customary in such cases.

46 K.K., (pp. 851, 859) treats the transfer as a virtual declaration of war, and says that Ḥusain 'Alī had decided to destroy Niẓām-ul-Mulk. This decision he ascribes to Ḥusain 'Alī's overwhelming conceit and underestimation of his enemies.

On the other hand, *Siyar* (pp. 424–5) holds Niẓām-ul-Mulk's ambition responsible for the breach.

T. Muẓ. (pp. 231–50) and *Ḥadīqat* (pp. 94–100) follow K.K. *Aḥwāl* (p. 155b) steers a middle course. According to the author, on hearing the news of Niẓām-ul-Mulk's preparations in Malwa, the Saiyids, after many consultations, decided to send a *farmān* of recall by the hands of mace-bearers, while a force was moved across the Chambal. If the governor submitted, all would be well; if not they could still fight or negotiate. If he fled to the south, their generals could pursue. 'Ālam 'Alī at Aurangabad was warned to be on the alert. Thus, 'Niẓām-ul-Mulk would inevitably be caught between two fires (if he rebelled).'

This would appear to be most plausible explanation in the circumstances.

his assignment in Bundi, and at this time, was hovering on the Malwa border. He was now warned to be alert and letters were sent to 'Ālam 'Alī to be vigilant in guarding the Deccan.[47]

Having taken these precautions, the Saiyids despatched a mace-bearer to escort Niẓām-ul-Mulk back to the court. This move of the Saiyids did not come as a surprise to Niẓām-ul-Mulk, for he had been repeatedly warned by M. Amīn and Dia'nat Khān that the Saiyids intended to move against him after the conclusion of the affair of Girdhar Bahādur (in Allahabad). He had also received special messages from the emperor and his mother asking him to liberate them from the grip of the Saiyids.[48] Hence, he decided to disregard the order to return to the court, and unfurled the banner of revolt. He left Ujjain, ostensibly for the court, but turned south, and crossed the Narmada into the Deccan.[49]

In the Deccan, Niẓām-ul-Mulk was immediately joined by the governors of Berar and Khandesh. The strong fort of Asīrgarh yielded to him without a shot being fired. Some of the nobles who joined him—Ṭāhir Khān the Governor of Asīrgarh, Nūrullāh Khān and Anwārullāh Khān of Burhānpur, had been the protégés and the trusted men of the Saiyids.[50]

These desertions reveal the political weakness of the Saiyids, and their profound unpopularity at the time. The Saiyids had confirmed the old nobles and officials in their positions, but many of them considered the new régime disgraceful and the Saiyids as being traitors to the salt. Niẓām-ul-Mulk exploited these sentiments. He sedulously preached:

47 *Aḥwāl*, 157a; K.K., 844, 851, 859; Shiv Das, 152. Niẓām-ul-Mulk complained of the presence of the *bakhshī* on his borders, and pointed out that it was causing a great deal of loss in life and property to the people of the province, and that these, 'unseemly blandishments were totally against the promise given by the Saiyids'.

48 K.K., 851.

49 This was towards the middle of *Jamāda* II, *c.* 24 April. Irvine (ii, 22) is not right in thinking that the news of Niẓām-ul-Mulk's rebellion reached the Saiyids about 9 *Rajab*, 17 May *after* he had crossed the Narmada. K.K. (p. 856) definitely states that the news of the Niẓām-ul-Mulk's rebellion reached Agra by the end of *Jamāda* II. In a letter to Ajit Singh written about 4 *Rajab*, 12 May. 'Abdullāh K. says, 'Niẓām-ul-Mulk by this time must have crossed the Narbada' (*Bāl.*, 31).

50 K.K., 871–3, 867, 852–3; *Ḥadīqat*, 99; *M.U.* iii, 877. Others like 'Iwaẓ Khān and Rao Rambhā Nimbālkar also joined Niẓām-ul-Mulk.

(i) That whatever he was doing, he was doing for the honour and the prestige of the royal house, the Saiyids having decided to subvert the Timurid dynasty;[51]

(ii) That the Saiyids had determined to ruin and disgrace all Īrānī and Tūrānī families and that his own destruction was the first step in the direction; and, finally,

(iii) That the Saiyids were allied with Hindus and were pursuing anti-Islamic policies detrimental to the empire.[52]

These slogans, and particularly the slogan of monarchy in danger became the rallying cry of the anti-Saiyid movement led by Niẕām-ul-Mulk.

These developments threw the Saiyids into great fear and perplexity and divided their counsels. The emphasis of Niẕām-ul-Mulk on racial and religious issues sharpened the differences between the two brothers on the policy to be pursued towards the old nobility. Ḥusain 'Alī Khān—whom Niẕām-ul-Mulk once described as being in character a mere soldier who, on seeing any thing unfavourable, burns with anger and at once becomes an enemy—felt that the 'Mughal' nobles, and especially the Tūrānīs could no longer be trusted. As a first step, he favoured the assassination of M. Amīn Khān who was the second *bakhshī* and the cousin of Niẕām-ul-Mulk. 'Abdullah Khān regarded such a course as 'ungenerous and, any rate, dishonest and inexpedient'. It seems that he wanted to treat Niẕām-ul-Mulk's rebellion as the aberration merely of one individual, and not the symbol and proof

51 Thus, after the conquest of Burhānpur, Niẕām-ul-Mulk is said to have assembled all the prominent men of the town and told them, 'The only object of my exertions is to free the emperor from the tyranny of the selfish people who have placed such strict restraints on his liberty that he cannot even come to the Friday prayers' (Note the emphasis on religion). (*Ḥadīqat* ii, 98, K.K., 855). Similarly, in a letter to M. Khān Bangash, Niẕām-ul-Mulk declared

Bah ḥam-dīgarī hamchūn kār-i-man pardāzand ki Ḥaẕrat Ẕill-i-subḥānī az dast-i-ẕālimān bar-āwurand, wa bah istiqlāl-i-tamām ba-akhtiyār-i-khud shawand (*Khujastah,* 322).

52 This aspect is emphasized by almost all the contemporary writers. The alliance of the two brothers with Ajit Singh and Chūrāman Jat, the dominance of Ratan Chand 'the vile infidel' in their affairs, the abolition of *jizyah* is emphasized by all writers as causes of the alienation of the old nobles. In particular, see K.K., 905, Āshūb, 150–4.

of the disaffection of the entire body of the 'Mughal' nobility. He even favoured the conciliation of Niẓām-ul-Mulk by granting the Deccan to him. He sarcastically remarked that Niẓām-ul-Mulk's rebellion was only the first fruit of the deposition of Farrukh Siyar, and accused Ḥusain 'Alī of having precipitated a premature clash with Niẓām-ul-Mulk. Khān-i-Daurān and Ratan Chand supported 'Abdullāh Khān's proposal for a compromise, remarking that 'war would end in the death of the Saiyids'.[53]

At 'Abdullāh Khān's insistence, Ḥusain 'Alī gave up the idea of removing M. Amīn and, as a further gesture to the 'Mughals', a Tūrānī nobleman, Ḥaider Qulī Khān, was given the important post of *Mīr Ātish.* But Ḥusain 'Alī rejected the proposal for compromise as being the counsel of defeat and one which was bound to be rejected by Niẓām-ul-Mulk, and would, therefore, weaken their position.[54] He blamed his brother for lack of initiative and courage. Finally, at his instance, Dilāwar 'Alī was ordered to march against Niẓām-ul-Mulk from the North, while 'Ālam 'Alī, the deputy of Ḥusain 'Alī in the Deccan, marched from the south so as to crush Niẓām-ul-Mulk between their combined forces. Letters were also despatched to Shāhū and to Bālājī Vishwanāth requesting them to assist 'Ālam 'Alī.[55]

However, Niẓām-ul-Mulk proved too quick for the Saiyid commanders. He fell upon Dilāwar 'Alī before the latter could be joined by 'Ālam 'Alī, and completely routed him on 19 June 1720. He then turned round to face 'Ālam 'Alī who had meanwhile been joined by a strong body of Marāthā horsemen under Peshwa Baji Rao.[56]

53 K.K., 867. Ḥusain 'Alī had also desired to exile 'Abdus-Ṣamad Khān.

54 *Ibid.* (*Cf.* Elliot's translation, vii, p. 492, where the passage has been given quite a different meaning).

55 *Aḥwāl, Bāl.*, 31. In reply, Shāhū assured 'Abdullāh Khān of his sympathy and support for 'Ālam 'Alī Khān and his lasting friendship for Ḥusain 'Alī. He also promised the help of an army. Already a Marāthā army was approaching Haiderabad after campaigning in the Karnātak. 'Abdullāh Khān showed his gratitude by the despatch of the *sanads* of *deshmukhi* requested by Bālāji Vishwanāth. This must have been in confirmation of the previous grant, since the original grants were taken by Bālāji with him when returning from Delhi (*Bāl.*, 14, 15).

56 In fulfilment of Shāhū's promise, Baji Rao joined 'Ālam 'Alī with 15,000–16,000 horsemen (*S.P.D.* x, 5, xxx, 265, K.K., 874, *Ḥadīqat* ii, 101).

This unexpected blow threw the Saiyids into the utmost consternation. 'Abdullāh Khān once again urged a compromise with Niẕām-ul-Mulk in order to gain a breathing spell. Some of the well-wishers of the Saiyids, like Dia'nat Khān Khwāfī, the *dīwān-i-tan wa khālīṣah,* pointed out that Ḥusain 'Alī's family was still in the Deccan, and that in order to prevent its falling into the hands of Niẕām-ul-Mulk a cautious policy was necessary. M. Amīn Khān, the cousin of Niẕām-ul-Mulk, was secretly delighted with the turn of affairs, but offered to help in bringing about an accomodation with Niẕām-ul-Mulk.[57]

In the end, a double-faced policy was decided upon. *Farmāns* and letters couched in hypocritical language were sent to Nīẕām-ul-Mulk, granting him the viceroyalty of the Deccan and condemning and repudiating Dilāwar 'Alī Khān's action. Niẕām-ul-Mulk was asked to permit 'Ālām 'Alī and the *mīr bakhshī*'s family to leave the Deccan.[58] At the same time, preparations were pushed ahead for leading a grand army to the Deccan, and 'Ālam 'Alī was instructed to await its arrival.[59]

But Niẕām-ul-Mulk was too shrewd to be taken in by such an apparent manoeuvre. He turned the tables upon his rivals by making use of their *farmān* in a way they had not foreseen. He gave it the widest possible publicity, thus making himself the legally constituted viceroy of the Deccan in the eyes of all and sundry, and making 'Ālam 'Alī a rebel who was defying Imperial authority by refusing to hand over charge to him. 'Ālam 'Alī not only lost moral authority, but many waverers now threw in their lot with Niẕām-ul-Mulk.[60]

It is not necessary for our purposes to treat in detail the subsequent story of the defeat and downfall of the Saiyids. Suffice it to say that 'Ālam 'Alī and his Marāthā confederates were completely routed by Niẕām-ul-Mulk in a battle at Shakar Khera on 10 August

57 *M.U.* i, 333, Irvine ii, 34–5.

58 Shiv Dās, 83–5-copies of letter and *farmān* (full text in Irvine ii, 35–6).

59 *Bāl.*, 25, 12, 11; *Iqbāl,* 88, K.K. 886. The letter to 'Ālam 'Alī is d. 27 *Rajab,* 4 June 1720.

60 Shiv Dās 93, Qāsim *cf.* English factors who again reproduce bazar rumours: 'as expected he (Niẕām-ul-Mulk) refused the Phirmaund and seerpao sent him by the king—returning reply that it came from the Syed who kept the king prisoner from whom he hoped to deliver him' (*Bengal Consultations,* Range i, Vol. iv, 139).

1720.[61] Soon after this, Ḥusain 'Alī was assassinated while on his way to the Deccan with the Emperor. This was the outcome of a plot hatched by M. Amīn Khān, the second *bakhshī*, Ḥaider Qulī Khān, the *Mīr Ātish*, and some others like Sa'ādat Khān (later Burhān-ul-Mulk) and Mīr Jumlah.[62] 'Abdullāh Khān was then on his way to Delhi. When he heard the news, he pushed on to the capital, and raised a new puppet to the throne under the name of Ibrāhim Khān, and attempted to rally his supporters. The Bārahās[63] stood by him to the end, as also Chūrāman Jat. Many Afghāns, too, joined, perhaps out of a mercenary motive, though M. Khān Bangash, the only prominent Afghān noble at the time, went over to the side of M. Amīn Khān and the Emperor Muḥammad Shāh. Some old nobles of Farrukh Siyar living in retirement at Delhi, such as Ghāzī-ud-Dīn Aḥmad Beg, M. Murād Kashmīrī etc. also agreed to join 'Abdullāh Khān. Khāfī Khān says that 'any butcher, cook or cotton-carder who presented himself, mounted on some wretched pony was employed, and given Rs 80 per month.'[64] But the hastily

61 According to K.K. (886, 899), 'Ālam 'Alī had been advised by the Marāthās to wait behind the walls of Aurangābād for the arrival of Ḥusain 'Alī, and in the meantime, to let them carry on guerilla warfare. But in his pride, 'Ālam 'Alī rejected the advice. Niẓām-ul-Mulk, it is said, had offered him safe conduct to the north, which too he refused (*Iqbāl*, 92).

62 K.K., 902–5, Wārid, 317–18, Qāsim, 135–6, Shākir, 20–1, Harcharan 30–1, Shiv Dās, 101–2, *T. Muẓ*, 271–3, Irvine ii, 56–61. Two despatches from the court to Jai Singh give the details of the assassination (*J.R.*, Add. Pers. Vol. ii, Nos 193, 198).

63 On the eve of the battle of Ḥasanpur, 'Abdullāh Khān was joined by 10,000–12,000 *sawārs* (Bārahās and Afghāns), and by 150 carts full of Bārahās 'who rallied to the cause of their clansman at the behest of Ṣaif-ud-Dīn 'Alī Khān who had been sent by Ḥusain 'Alī to recruit troops in Bārahā' (K.K., 918).

Many of the soldiers of Ḥusain 'Alī who under compulsion had joined Muḥammad Shāh after Ḥusain 'Alī's assassination, deserted to 'Abdullāh Khān in groups of 200–300 on the eve of the battle (K.K., 918). Likewise, Raja Mukham Singh and many other private employees of the Saiyids who had been forced to join Muḥammad Shāh also deserted to 'Abdullāh Khān (K.K., 920, 925).

The only prominent Bārahā who went against the Saiyids was Saiyid Nuṣrat Khān Bārāhā who had a personal grudge against 'Abdullāh Khān and was a particular friend of Khān-i-Daurān (*Siyar*, 436–7, *T. Muẓ.*, 273).

64 K.K., 915–16, 897–8, 918.

collected army of 'Abdullāh Khān could not stand against the armies of M. Amīn Khān, Muḥammad Khān Bangash, and the Emperor Muḥammad Shāh. On 13 November 1720, 'Abdullāh Khān was defeated at Ḥasanpur near Delhi and taken prisoner.

Thus ended the 'new' *wizārat* of the Saiyid brothers.

☆ ☆ ☆

The inability of the Saiyids to consolidate their power may be ascribed largely to the opposition offered by an important section of the old nobles belonging to the time of Aurangzīb and Bahādur Shāh. This section looked upon the Saiyids as upstarts, and was not prepared to be over-shadowed by them in conducting the affairs of the empire. The general policy and approach of the Saiyid brothers to the various political problems facing the empire was also not to its liking.

The leading role in the opposition to the Saiyids was played by a small but powerful group centring round Niẓām-ul-Mulk and M. Amīn Khān. These capable and ambitious nobles aspired to exercise supreme power in the state. They also disliked the Saiyid policy of making large concessions to the Rājpūts, Marāthās etc., and to the Hindu opinion generally, regarding it as being a departure from the policies of Aurangzīb, contrary to the Islamic character of the state and against the best interests of the empire and the monarchy.

Apart from posing as the defenders of Islam and the monarchy, the opponents of the Saiyids appealed to the narrow interests of a section of the nobility by depicting the Saiyids as anti-Mughal, and by accusing them of seeking to monopolize power from themselves and their creatures. However, neither the policy and the practice of the Saiyids, nor an analysis of the actual party groupings support such an interpretation. The Saiyids attempted, as we have seen above, to associate in the higher ranks of the nobility all sections including the various ethnic groups at the court, the nobles belonging to the time of Aurangzīb and Bahādur Shāh, and the Rājpūts, Marāthās etc.[65] But it suited their

65 *Cf.* Owen, '*Fall of the Moghul Empire*', 149, 163. The author considers that an important cause of the downfall of the Saiyids was the numerical weakness of the Bārahā community. Since the Saiyids never attempted to base their power on any one community, this explanation is hardly sufficient.

opponents to misrepresent the policy of the Saiyids, and to give to the anti-Saiyid struggle the outer character of a struggle between the Mughals and the Hindustanis.

Politically, the biggest error of the Saiyids was the deposition of Farrukh Siyar. The question has been argued on a moral plane, whether 'the Saiyids were disloyal to their king', or whether they 'treated him as the case required'.[66] Irvine has opined that the deposition of Farrukh Siyar was, perhaps, unavoidable 'but the way of doing what had become almost a necessity was unduly harsh and the taking of the captive's life was an extremity entirely uncalled for'.[67]

This really is to beg the question. The execution of Farrukh Siyar, though performed with unnecessary cruelty, was a logically unavoidable corollary of his deposition. As long as he was alive, the Saiyids could not feel secure. What the Saiyids had to decide was whether they could realize their objectives without deposing Farrukh Siyar. 'Abdullāh Khān was apparently of the opinion that they could. He felt that there was no harm in leaving the *sikkah* and the *khuṭbah* in Farrukh Siyar's name as long as all the important offices remained in their control, and were filled by their nominees. The deposition, for which Ḥusain 'Alī seems to bear the primary responsibility, created apprehensions in the minds of many nobles about the ultimate intentions of the Saiyids, and alienated their own supporters who were not prepared for such extreme measures.[68] From being looked upon as brave individuals who were fighting an ungrateful master for the preservation of their life and honour, after the deposition the Saiyids began to be considered tyrants and traitors to the salt who had brought infamy to their family. All contemporary writers, including those favourable to the Saiyids are agreed in condemning the deposition as an act of infamy and disgrace.[69] Considering the weakness of their

66 *M.U.* i, 344.

67 Irvine i, 395.

68 *Cf. Jauhar,* 50. We are told that even men who owed their fortunes to the Saiyids used to pray secretly for their downfall (Qāsim, 151).

When Niẓām-ul-Mulk reached the Deccan, many nobles who owed their positions to the Saiyids, including the commandants of some important forts, had deserted the Saiyids, and joined him (*ibid.,* 157).

69 Thus, K.K. (901) calls the downfall of the Saiyids a heavenly retribution for their faithlessness to their master. Qāsim (Sarkar Ms., 158) who is

actual position, it was a political blunder, for it enabled their rivals, the 'Chīn' group, to appear as the champions of the Timurid monarchy and to utilize the public revulsion against the Saiyids for their own ends.[70]

Secondly, the Saiyids over-estimated their strength and resources, disagreed among themselves about the policy to be pursued towards the powerful 'Chīn' group, and ultimately precipitated a premature showdown with it. It would appear that 'Abdullāh Khān understood better than Ḥusain 'Alī the real weakness of their position. By patient and careful diplomacy, he had succeeded in detaching M. Amīn Khān, Niẓām-ul-Mulk and Sarbuland Khān from Farrukh Siyar. He was keen that the understanding with these nobles should be maintained and, if possible, strengthened. Hence, he favoured a cautious and conciliatory policy towards them. On the other hand, Ḥusain 'Alī who was inclined to be haughty and overbearing, apparently held the view that such a policy was unworkable. He desired that Niẓām-ul-Mulk, M. Amīn Khān and others should be destroyed at the earliest possible moment, or at any rate, rendered incapable of any mischief. This divergence of outlook and approach accentuated the differences which had already appeared between the two brothers over the division of power and the spoils of victory.

The Saiyids did not enjoy supreme power long enough for a proper estimate to be made of their administrative capabilities. The spirit of party strife which grew right from the accession of Farrukh Siyar paralyzed the administration, and 'everywhere *zamindars* and malcontents raised their head.' Established rules of business were ignored.[71] The dependence of the Saiyids on subordinates like Ratan Chand made them unpopular, and reflected unfavourably on their administrative competence. The responsibility for bribe-taking and harshness in revenue-farming

---

generally favourable to the Saiyids, refers to the deposition as an act of disloyalty (*namakḥarāmī*). So, too, *Siyar,* Kāmwar strongly denounces it, as also *Ḥadīqat* (89), *Jauhar* (48a), *Khush-ḥāl* (416) and Wārid (309).

70 Thus, Ajit Singh was pelted with stones in the streets of Delhi for his part in the deposition and subsequent execution of Farrukh Siyar. Even the beggars refused the charity of the Saiyids for some time (K.K., 900, Qāsim, 151).

71 *M.U.* i, 309, Āshūb, 152, 136.

is ascribed to these subordinates.[72] On the other hand, it is not denied even by those writers who are strongly opposed to the Saiyids that they strove hard to maintain law and order, and that their military reputation and capabilities prevented a final breakdown of the administration.[73]

By concentrating power in their hands, the Saiyids sought to save the Mughal empire from the process of disintegration which had inevitably followed the accession of a weak or incompetent king. Simultaneously, they pursued policies which, if persisted in for some time, might have led to the development of a composite ruling class consisting of all sections in the Mughal nobility as well as the Rājpūts and the Marāthās. In the ultimate analysis, the political structure which had been evolved by the Mughals could be consolidated and developed only by the further growth of such a ruling class in the country. The major obstacle in this process was that apart from the Saiyids there were no powerful groups or sections at the court or outside it which were actively interested in such a development. The 'Ālamgīrī nobles, or the section often described as the 'Mughals' were generally averse to sharing power with anyone, deeming only themselves fit for the task of governing the empire. Most of the Marāthā *sardar*s were mainly concerned with establishing domination over the Deccan, and were not interested in the maintenance of the Mughal empire. Although Shāhū's interests coincided with those of the Saiyids for the time being, he had little desire to see the Mughal empire revived and

72 K.K., 941–3. The author relates how 'Abdullāh Khān returned the escheated property of 'Abdul Ghafūr Bohra without accepting anything for himself. In the case of the Surman Embassy also, he did not accept 'a farthing'.

73 Rustam 'Alī says 'As is well known, this Emperor (Muḥammad Shāh) so long as *Amīru-l-Umarā* Husain 'Alī Khān lived, strictly observed, by virtue of the efficient management of that great Saiyid, all the ancient laws and established rules of his ancestors. The achievement of all undertakings, the arrangement of all political affairs, and the execution of all wars were carried on in an excellent manner by the wisdom of that high nobleman' (*T. Hindī*, Elliot viii, 42, 43).

The Saiyids were worried by self-seekers (Shiv Dās 136). Even K.K. (942) admits that 'the inhabitants of those countries which were innocent of contumacy or selfishness made no complaint of the rule of the Saiyids'.

Iqbāl (128) says that unemployment was rare in the time of the Saiyids and any soldier or person who reached their audience, generally secured a job worth Rs 50 per month at the lowest.

strengthened, and felt little sympathy with the Saiyid desire to evolve a composite ruling class. However, the Saiyids failed to utilize the Marāthās even to the limited possible extent. 'Ālam 'Alī, Ḥusain 'Alī, deputy in the Deccan, rejected the advice of Baji Rao to let the Marāthās carry on a harassing warfare against Niẕām-ul-Mulk, and to avoid a pitched battle till reinforcement should arrive from northern India.

The Rājpūts had a larger interest than the Marāthās in the maintenance of the Mughal empire, having secured many opportunities of advancement and gain in the service of the empire. They might have been expected to give full support to the Saiyids whose policies were in consonance with their own desires. Ajit Singh and Jai Singh were also beholden to the Saiyids for many favours. However, neither of these rajas made any effort to render military aid to the Saiyids in their hour of need, preferring to engross themselves in their local ambitions.

Thus, the Saiyids were brought face to face with the old dilemma that the forces of integration were woefully weak in Medieval society, and only a strong central government could keep the forces of disintegration in check. In the absence of a competent monarch, a strong central government could have been established by a *wazīr* if he enjoyed either the support of a powerful section of the nobility, or the backing of a well-established monarchy. The former the Saiyids could not secure, for reasons already indicated. The Saiyids were keen to preserve the Timurid monarchy as a symbol of unity. But the traditional suspicion between the monarch and an all-powerful *wazīr* vitiated the atmosphere, and made co-operation between the two extremely difficult to achieve. Personal factors further aggravated the differences.

Although the Saiyid experiment lacked the elements of permanence for the reasons described above, the 'new' *wizārat* which they sought to establish is not without significance. The Saiyids made a definite break with narrow, exclusionist policies, and moved in the direction of establishing a state essentially secular in approach and national in character. Their downfall did not imply the automatic negation of this process which they had stimulated and strengthened: it continued to work apace and influenced the political and cultural developments of the succeeding period.

CHAPTER VII

Niẓām-ul-Mulk and the End of the Struggle for Wizārat

The Wizārat of M. Amīn Khān

A year and three months elapsed between the defeat and downfall of the Saiyids, and the assumption of the *wizārat* by Niẓām-ul-Mulk. In the first three months of this period, M. Amīn Khān Chīn, the cousin of Niẓām-ul-Mulk, was the *wazīr*. M. Amīn Khān was granted the rank of 8,000/8,000 *dū aspah sih aspah*, along with the absentee governorship of Multan. His son, Qamar-ud-Dīn Khān, was appointed the second *bakhshī* with the rank of 7,000, and also obtained the *faujdāri* of Moradabad, and the posts of the *dāroghah-i-aḥadī* and the *dāroghah-i-ghusalkhānah* both of which were important posts since they implied control over access to the emperor. Other persons who had taken a leading part in the conspiracy against the Saiyids were also rewarded. Sa'ādat Khān was made the Governor of Awadh, and Ḥaider Qulī the Governor of Gujarāt in addition to being appointed the *mīr atish*. Mīr Jumlah remained the *ṣadr*, and Khān-i-Daurān the chief *bakhshī*. Niẓām-ul-Mulk retained charge of the Deccan and of Malwa. 'Abdus-Ṣamad Khān retained Lahore, with the addition of Kashmir in the name of his son, Ẕakariyah Khān. Not many changes were made in the other *ṣūbahs*.[1]

1 K.K., 911, 938, Shiv Dās, 133, Kāmwar, 444.

From the very beginning, the new *wazīr* showed little inclination to fulfill the chief professed aim of the anti-Saiyid movement viz., 'the restoration of the emperor to the full enjoyment of his powers'. He was, if anything, more domineering than the Saiyids, and we are told that the share of Muḥammad Shāh was only to sit on the throne and to wear the crown.[2] The emperor felt afraid of the *wazīr* and had given him all authority, 'paying no heed to the complaints of the people'. The other nobles felt that the emperor was powerless, and they, too, were afraid of the *wazīr*.[3] All that the emperor gained from the overthrow of the Saiyids was a certain measure of personal liberty, but in the affairs of state he had no authority.

Nor could M. Amīn make any sharp break with the general policy of the Saiyids. He made a proposal for the revival of *jizyah* but due to the opposition of Jai Singh and Girdhar Bahādur had to abandon the attempt. However, to save the prestige of the *wazīr*, and to conciliate the orthodox elements, it was declared that the tax had (only) been deferred until 'the recovery of the prosperity of the *raiyat* and the settlement of the country'.[4]

In the case of the Marāthās, the agreement made by the Saiyids for the payment of *chauth* and *sardeshmukhī*, was confirmed by the grant of fresh *sanads*.[5] Niẓām-ul-Mulk, on his part, had already agreed to Shāhū's demand for *chauth* and *sardeshmukhī*, and strengthened the agreement by a secret meeting with Peshwa Baji Rao on 4 January 1721—the first of a series of meetings between these two remarkable men.[6]

2 Wārid (Hyderabad Ms.) 339, K.K., 940.

3 *Iqbāl*, 130.

4 *Iqbāl*, 131, K.K., 936, Kāmwar (entry d. 24 December 1720). Shiv Dās gives copies of the '*arẓī*' submitted by Jai Singh and Girdhar Bahādur (Patna Ms., 339–40). *Iqbāl* further says, 'out of regard for the *shara*', Jai Singh presented most of the *maḥāls* of his *Jāgīrs* and *zamindari* in lieu of *jizyah*'.

For a further discussion, see the present writer's paper 'Jiẓyah in the post-Aurangzeb Period', *I.H. Congress*, 1946, 320–7.

5 Duff i, 473, *T. Muẓ*, 307, *Riyasat*, 160.

6 *S.P.D.* XXX, 266, and apparently the meeting referred to in x 5. No details are available. Niẓām-ul-Mulk had already promised Shāhū that he would abide by the grants of Husain 'Alī, and on 3 December 1720, issued a *sanad* under his own signature confirming the grants in question. He also ordered a number of *thanas* claimed by Shāhū to be handed over to him (see also Dr Powar's article in *I.H.R.C.* XVII, 209–10).

Thus, the victory of M. Amīn Khān and Niẕām-ul-Mulk did not lead to any immediate changes in the policies initiated by the Saiyids, despite their denunciation of the Saiyids for adopting allegedly 'pro-Hindu' policies. Ajit Singh had always been a staunch supporter of the Saiyids. He was removed from Gujarāt for 'mal-administration', but even in his case M. Amīn was half inclined to restore the province to him.[7]

ARRIVAL OF NIẔĀM-UL-MULK AND HIS EARLY DIFFICULTIES

M. Amīn Khān died after a short illness on 27 January 1721. After some discussion, the Emperor sent a summon to Niẕām-ul-Mulk in the Deccan to come and assume the *wizārat.* Niẕām-ul-Mulk had aspired to that office after the downfall of the Saiyids and had actually started for northern India when news arrived of the appointment of M. Amīn Khān as the *wazīr.* Not wishing to enter into a contest with his cousin, he had cancelled his visit, and left for the Karnātak which was being raided by the Marāthās.[8]

When the royal summons reached Niẕām-ul-Mulk, he took some time to settle the affairs in the Karnātak, and so did not reach the court till 20 February 1722. In the interval, Muḥammad Shāh had full opportunity to show his aptitude for government. But he proved himself to be a weak-minded and frivolous person, negligent of the affairs of state and completely under the influence of his favourites. He was never long of the same mind, being, as a Marāthā *wakīl* observed, 'fickle by nature'.[9]

7 *Mir'āt* i, 37. Muhar 'Alī Khān, the *nā'ib* of Ḥaider Qulī, was afraid that Ajit might be restored. He came from Khambāyat with an army and ousted Nāhar Khān, the *nā'ib* of Ajit Singh, and his *dīwān* Anūp Singh. Ajit was not officially dismissed from Gujarāt till *Rajab,* 1133, May 1721, i.e. till after the death of M. Amīn Khān.

8 In a letter to Sa'd-ud-Dīn Khān, the *Khān-i-Sāmān,* Niẕām-ul-Mulk wrote, 'In view of the agreement arrived at between ourselves and 'Itimād-ud-Daulah (M. Amīn Khān), the latter would have done well not to claim the *wizārat.* This being left behind was odious to us, but in view of our relationship with 'Itimād-ud-Daulah, we controlled our feelings and tolerated this' (Quoted in *Āṣaf Jāh,* 139–40).

9 *S.P.D.* XIV, 47. Rustam 'Alī calls him, 'the asylum of negligence' (*T Hindi,* 535).

Chief among the favourites who came to the forefront during this period were Ḥaider Qulī Khān and Kūkī Jiū. Ḥaider Qulī Khān (Muḥammad Raẓā) was a native of Iṣfrain, and had been a follower of 'Aẓīm-ush-Shān. When Farrukh Siyar came to the throne, he received the title of Ḥaider Qulī through Mīr Jumlah and was made the *dīwān* of the Deccan, with the superintendentship of all the crown-lands, numerous other perquisities, and the power to appoint and remove all subordinates. Niẓām-ul-Mulk did not get on with him and sent him back to Delhi on his own authority. He was then made the *dīwān* of Gujārāt and the *mutṣaddī* of Surat, where office he amassed a vast fortune. 'Abdullāh Khān did not like him and removed him from his office in 1718 upon the complaint of 'Abdul Ḥaī', the son of 'Abdul Ghafūr Bohrā whose property, amounting to 85 lakhs of rupees in cash and kind, had been confiscated by Ḥaider Qulī on the false pretext that he had died childless.[10] When he arrived at the court, Ḥaider Qulī somehow won the favour of Ratan Chand, and was appointed to the army sent against Agra and Allahabad. Soon afterwards, he was made the *mīr ātish.* This gave Ḥaider Qulī the opportunity to plot against the Saiyids, and for his part in the assassination of Ḥusain 'Alī he was raised to the rank of 6,000/6,000. He rose in the favour of the emperor every day, and by the time Niẓām-ul-Mulk arrived to assume the *wizārat,* he had risen to the rank of 8,000/7,000.[11]

Kūkī Jiū is described as a woman of great charm and intelligence, and a friend of the emperor's mother. In collusion with Khwājah Khidmatgār, who was said to be one of the emperor's close companions, she realized large sums by way of *peshkash* from applicants for jobs. It is said that the emperor himself took a share in this illegal income. Kūkī had become so influential that it was popularly rumoured that she kept the royal seal in her charge.[12]

The interference of the royal favourites in administration, and the sleepless jealousy of the chief *bakhshī,* Khān-i-Daurān Ṣamṣām-ud-Daulah, created great difficulties for the new *wazīr.* He found

10 *Mir'āt* ii, 4–5, *M.U.* iii, 746. 'Abdul Ghafūr was reputed to be one of the richest merchants of the world at that time. It is a tribute to the character of 'Abdullāh Khān that he returned the property of 'Abdul Gahfūr to his son without accepting even a pice for himself.

11 K.K., 940, Wārid, 43, *M.U.* iii, 746.

12 Shiv Dās, 154, Wārid, 43, K.K., 940.

that the established rules of business had been thrown to the winds, the old nobility was neglected, income was declining, and the empire was fast sinking into its grave.

When Niẓām-ul-Mulk complained of Ḥaider Qulī's interference in the administration, the emperor ordered Ḥaider Qulī to proceed to his governorship of Gujarāt. Arriving in Gujarāt, Ḥaider Qulī adopted a haughty and over-bearing attitude, and began to assume the airs of an independent prince. He usurped the *jāgīrs* assigned to Imperial nobles; employed 'Arabs, Ḥabshīs and Franks (Europeans) to strengthen his artillery department; escheated goods without obtaining permission; and infringed royal privileges by hearing complaints while seated on a raised platform, witnessing animal fights, awarding fringed *pālkīs* to his followers etc. It was alleged that he dared to do all this because he enjoyed the secret support of the emperor.[13]

At length, Niẓām-ul-Mulk, who had been removed from the governorship of Malwa a short time back, persuaded the emperor to grant him the *ṣūbah* of Gujarāt in the name of his son, Ghāzī-ud-Dīn Khān, and set out for Gujarāt in December 1722, on the plea of curbing the pretensions of Ḥaider Qulī.[14] His real motives, however, would seem to be different. He had come to Delhi with mixed motives—partly because he fondly believed that he could set the affairs of the empire right, and partly to see what he had to hope and fear from the new emperor. The first of these hopes seemed likely to prove illusory, or, at any rate, to be a far more difficult task than he had apparently imagined. Meanwhile, his position in the Deccan was being jeopardized. Mubāriz-ul-Mulk, whom he had appointed his deputy in the Deccan in his absence, had repudiated the pact with Shāhū for *chauth* and *sardeshmukhi*, and this had led to a recrudesence of trouble with the Marāthās.[15] In 1723, Peshwa Baji Rao entered Malwa at the head of a large army in order to lead what was to be the first of a series of extending Marāthā operations into that strategic province.

Niẓām-ul-Mulk met Baji Rao on 24 February 1723, at Badākshā (or Bolāshā) near Jhābua in Malwa, and remained with him for a

13 Wārid, 7–8, *Mir'āt* ii, 45–7, K.K., 940, Shiv Dās, 143, Shākir, 16.

14 K.K., 947. Girdhar Bahadur had succeeded Niẓām-ul-Mulk in Malwa in September 1722 (Kāmwar).

15 K.K., 962–3, *Ḥadīqat*, 136, *Riyasat*, 163.

week (till 2 March).[16] We have no information regarding the nature of the discussions and the conclusions arrived at, and can only make guesses and draw inferences. The meeting was followed by a joint campaign against Dost Muḥammad Khān, the *Nawab* of Bhopal.[17] Shortly afterwards, Niẕām-ul-Mulk assumed charge of the *ṣūbah* of Malwa, and Baji Rao returned to the Deccan.

From the above, we may conclude that the trend of the talks was friendly, and resulted in some kind of an accord. On the side of Niẕām-ul-Mulk, there was every reason for him to be friendly to the Peshwa. He had not yet made up his mind whether to make a bid for power at Delhi, or to return to the Deccan. Meanwhile, it was no use creating enemies. On Baji Rao's side, too, the motives for friendship with Niẕām-ul-Mulk were equally strong. Niẕām-ul-Mulk was the Imperial *wazīr.* He was also one of the most powerful nobles in the empire, and the master of the Deccan. He had till then, given no cause for hostility to the Marāthās, having accepted Shāhū's claim for *chauth* and *sardeshmukhī.* The young Peshwa was, therefore, keen to secure the friendship of such a powerful person.

It was typical of the diplomacy of Niẕām-ul-Mulk, however, that while attempting to utilize the Peshwa's friendship, he was careful to seek safe-guards against an over expansion of the latter's power. His assumption of the *ṣūbahdārī* of Malwa—for which permission from the emperor was apparently obtained later,[18] was aimed at containing the Marāthās in the south and preventing their northward expansion.

Thus, already we see Niẕām-ul-Mulk formulating the policy on which he was to act throughout his life, i.e. maintaining his supremacy in the Deccan and keeping a line open to Delhi, and of seeking to circumscribe the power of the Marāthās without affecting an irreparable breach with them.

After the meeting, Niẕām-ul-Mulk resumed his march towards Gujarāt. Ḥaider Qulī, who had failed to find support from any quarter, was seized with panic. Feigning madness, he left for Delhi with a very few followers. On hearing this, Niẕām-ul-Mulk appointed

16 *S.P.D.* xxx, No. 310, xxii, 4, K.K., 946, Rajwade ii, 48.

17 *S.P.D.* xxx, 267, xxii, 4: Vad ii, 144, and *T. Fatḥiyah* (as quoted in *Aṣaf Jāh, loc. cit.*). The author was actually present at the siege. The Niẕām was very boastful, but failed to take Islāmnagar after a long siege.

18 Kāmwar simply says that at Sironj, on 25 May 1723, Niẕām-ul-Mulk appointed 'Aẕīmullāh Khān as the Deputy Governor of Malwa, K.K. is silent.

his cousin, Ḥāmid Khān his deputy in Gujarāt, and from Jhalod turned back towards Delhi.[19]

Thus, Gujarāt also passed under Niẓām-ul-Mulk's control.

NIẒĀM-UL-MULK'S SCHEME OF REFORMS, AND HIS DEPARTURE FOR THE DECCAN

On 3 July 1723, Niẓām-ul-Mulk returned to the court. He found that under the influence of Kūkī, corruption and bribery had increased. The courtiers and Imperial favourites had seized the most profitable and easily manageable *jāgīrs*. Even the *khāliṣah* land had been distributed in assignments. Revenue-farming (*ijārah*) which led to high prices on the one hand, and rank-renting resulting in the impoverishment of the peasantry and steadily declining revenue on the other, had become fully prevalent. Bribe-taking flourished from top to bottom under the guise of presents or *peshkash*. The result was that the old nobles spent their time in poverty and unemployment, and the Imperial treasury had not the money to pay the soldiers and the *manṣabdārs* cash salaries. The small *manṣabdārs* were the hardest hit. They lacked the wherewithal to maintain themselves and their contingents, and many of them took to trade.[20]

In order to restore the efficiency of the administration, and to repair the finances of the empire, Niẓām-ul-Mulk drew up a detailed report and placed it before the emperor. His main demands—which he had apparently been pressing upon the emperor since his arrival at the court, were as follows: that only fit nobles and soldiers should be employed, as in the time of Aurangzīb; that the farming of *khāliṣah* lands should be discontinued; that the *jāgīrs* should be re-distributed and *khāliṣah* lands (given in *jāgīrs*) resumed; that bribe-taking must stop, and lastly, that the *jizyah* should be levied as in the time of Aurangzīb.[21]

19 K.K., 946, *Mir'āt* ii, 48.

20 K.K., 947, Wārid (A.U.L. Ms.), 8–9, *Siyar*, 458.

21 *Ibid.* K.K. says that Niẓām-ul-Mulk also proposed an expedition to restore the Ṣafwid monarch who had been recently expelled from Iṣfaḥān by M. Ḥusain Afghān. Irvine (ii, 132) rightly says that such a proposal accords ill with the cautious character of Niẓām. Probably there was some vague talk of such an expedition. Isfaḥān fell on 21 October 1722. The news reached Delhi on 10 March 1723. Niẓām-ul-Mulk left for Gujarāt in December 1722

These proposals were not at all to the liking of the emperor, while the favourites were afraid that if Niẕām-ul-Mulk was once allowed to establish himself at the court, they would lose all their influence. The favourites also stood to lose the most from the proposed reforms. Hence, they represented to the emperor that the circumstances of the empire were different from those in the time of Aurangzīb, and that an attempt to restore the old rules would merely disturb the revenue and the administrative system. They sought to sow suspicion of Niẕām-ul-Mulk's intentions in the mind of the emperor by dwelling upon his ambitiousness and love of power, and by harping upon the danger that a successful general like him would present to the dynasty.[22] They seized upon the proposal to revive the *jizyah* and represented to the emperor, singly and in groups, that the tax was 'inopportune', and that 'the only purpose of Niẕām-ul-Mulk's proposals was to create confusion in the administration and to sow discord and hate between the state and its servants.' The contemporary writer, Wārid, laments that 'the nobles had become lax in matters of faith and religion', and ascribes their opposition to the revival of *jizyah* to 'the instigation of the Hindus.' However, the favourites were opposed to Niẕām-ul-Mulk for reasons of their own. The latter's insistence on the reimposition of *jizyah* enabled them to secure the sympathy and support of the Hindu nobles and officials also, and to isolate Niẕām-ul-Mulk. Even 'Abdus-Ṣamad Khān, who was related to Niẕām-ul-Mulk by marriage, opposed the re-imposition of *jizyah*.[23]

The result was that the emperor gave his formal assent to the proposals of Niẕām-ul-Mulk but shelved them in reality. The virtual rejection of his scheme of reforms placed Niẕām-ul-Mulk in a difficult situation. He could imitate the Saiyid by resorting to a *coup de main*, disperse his enemies, and reduce Muḥammad Shāh to the position of a puppet, or even set up a new emperor. Niẕām-ul-Mulk probably had the power to do so—indeed, he was in a more favourable position than the Saiyids to consolidate his power after a coup. But Niẕām-ul-Mulk seems to have considered such a course dishonourable as well as futile. The nobility was far too

---

and returned in July 1723. His position at the court was already precarious and it is doubtful if he could have seriously made a proposal of this nature.

22 Wārid, 643; Shiv Dās, 150, 153; K.K., 940.

23 Wārid, 40 (O.P.L. Ms.), K.K:, 949.

heterogeneous and internal jealousies among them too strong to permit any individual, however capable he might be, to exercise supreme power on their behalf. The only alternative was to set up a new dynasty which, in the circumstances, was unthinkable. On the other hand, to remain at the court as a helpless onlooker went against the grain, and would also jeopardize Niẓām-ul-Mulk's position in the Deccan. The royal favourites were not slow to point out that Niẓām-ul-Mulk's retention of the viceroyalty of the Deccan in addition to his being the (absentee) Governor of Gujarāt and Malwa, and the *wazīr* endangered the monarchy. There was no precedent in Mughal history of the concentration of so much power in the hands of one noble. Hence, moves were set afoot to deprive Niẓām-ul-Mulk of the Deccan.

Niẓam-ul-Mulk had always looked upon the Deccan as the land of his dreams. He had spent most of his youth there, and since the dispossession of the Saiyids, he considered it to be his own by right of the sword. He was not at all willing to relinquish it in favour of a precarious *wizārat* at the court. News of renewed activity of the Marāthās in the Deccan, and his own distrust of his deputy, Mubāriz-ul-Mulk whom he had tried to remove from the Deccan by suggesting his name for the vacant governorship of Kabul, convinced Niẓām-ul-Mulk that he must return to the Deccan if he was to retain possession of it.[24] The visit to Delhi had been essentially in the nature of an exploratory visit. Having personally witnessed the utter imbecility of the court and the emperor's complete lack of a will of his own, he determined to go his own way, conscious that there was little harm that the court could do him, and convinced of the futility of wasting his energies in efforts to reform the court, and in setting right the affairs of the Empire.

For sometime after the rejection of his proposed reforms by the emperor, Niẓām-ul-Mulk kept up a show of negotiations. But it was obvious that he had already made up his mind to return to the Deccan. With the death in December 1723 of Raja Gūjar Mal, the *dīwān-i-khāliṣah,* who had been carrying on negotiations with the emperor on behalf of Niẓām-ul-Mulk, the last hope of a compromise disappeared.[25]

In December 1723, Niẓām-ul-Mulk marched to his *jagīr* in Moradabad for 'a change of air'. From Agra he sent a report that

24 *M.U.* iii, 735–6.
25 K.K., 949, Kāmwar, 267.

the Marāthās had invaded Malwa and Gujarāt which were under his son's charge, and that he must march south to expel them. As Niẓām-ul-Mulk approached Malwa, the Marāthās re-crossed the Narmada. Just then, news reached Niẓām that he had been superseded in the viceroyalty of the Deccan by his deputy, Mubāriz Khān, and that attempts were being made through Jai Singh to enlist the support of Kanhoji and other Marāthā *sardars* against him.[26] The emperor had also opened negotiations with Shāhū.[27] Niẓām-ul-Mulk now threw off all pretence, and marched south to assert his claims.

On 11 October 1724, with the aid of Baji Rao, Niẓām-ul-Mulk defeated Mubāriz Khān at Shakar Khēṛā near Aurangābād.[28] From this battle may be dated the independent principality of Ḥaiderābad. The break-up of the Mughal empire had begun.

Jat and Rājpūt Affairs

The gradual rise of a Jat power on the borders of Rājpūtānā and the Agra *ṣūbah*, and a revival of the power and importance of the Rājpūt princes had been two notable features of the preceding years. The alliance of the Saiyids with these sections had served to emphasize this process, and to give greater confidence to the Jats and Rājpūts.

After the downfall of the Saiyids, the question of the relationship of the Mughal state with these elements engaged the attention of the court circles once again. Chūrāman Jat had abandoned the Saiyid brothers when the tide of fortune turned against them, and joined the imperialists. However, on the eve of the battle of Ḥasanpur against 'Abdullāh Khān, he had deserted once again, and plundered the baggage in the rear of the Imperial armies. He continued his contumacious ways even after this, and aided the Bundelas in their opposition to Diler Khān, the deputy of Muḥammad Khān Bangash who was the governor of Allahabad. In 1721, Chūrāman harried the armies of Sa'ādat Khān when the latter marched against Ajit Singh of Jodhpur. Matters came to a head, however, when in February 1722, Chūrāman's son, Mukham Singh, defeated and killed Nīlkanth Nāgar, the deputy of Sa'ādat Khān who was

26 *J.R.* (Misc. Vol. i, 75), Vad i, 12.
27 *S.P.D* x, 1 Dighe, '*Baji Rao*', 13.
28 *S.P.D* xxx, 269–71 and Nos 333–4, K.K., 955.

then the governor of Agra. Sa'ādat Khān failed to make any impression on the Jats. Hence, at the instance of Khān-i-Daurān, Jai Singh was appointed in April 1722 to lead an army against them.[29]

Although Jai Singh was keenly desirous of curbing the Jat pretensions, with his previous failure in mind he refused to move till he was also appointed the Governor of Agra. This was done on 1 September 1722, and, soon afterwards, Jai Singh left Delhi at the head of an army of 14,000–15,000 *sawārs*. By this time, Chūrāman had died and his son, Mukham Singh, had assumed the leadership of the Jats.

Jai Singh laid siege to Thūn, the Jat stronghold, and proceeded by systematically cutting down the jungle, and closely investing the garrison. A couple of weeks passed in this way.[30] It is difficult to say how long the siege would have lasted, but dissensions broke out among the Jats. Badan Singh, the cousin of Mukham Singh, came over to the side of Jai Singh and pointed out the weak points in the Jats' defences. Mukham Singh's position now became precarious. One night, he set fire to the houses, exploded the magazines, seized as much cash and jewellery as he could, and fled to Ajit Singh who gave him shelter. Jai Singh now entered the fortress in triumph and levelled it to the ground, having the ground ploughed up by asses as a sign of comtempt.[31]

For this victory, Jai Singh received the title of *Rājah-i-Rājeshwar*. The terms granted to the Jats are not mentioned by any contemporary author. Badan Singh succeeded to the headship of the Jats, and received the *zamindari* of Chūrāman. It may be inferred that while the important fortresses were destroyed, Chūrāman's family was not deprived of the entire state they had gradually won. Henceforth, Badan Singh humbly styled himself a feudatory of Jai Singh. But apparently, he was a good administrator, and under his watchful stewardship the Jat House of Bharatpur gained in power silently and steadily for the next two decades. Thus, the setback to the growth of the Jats' power was more apparent than real.

The fall of the Saiyids from power also led to a number of changes in the political set-up in Rājpūtānā. During the period of Saiyid domination, Ajit Singh Rathor had risen to the position of

29 Shiv Dās, Irvine ii, 120–1.

30 *Wāqi'ah Papers of the Maharaja's Army*.

31 *Akhbārāt*, Irvine (ii, 123) gives 18 November as the date of the fall of Thūn.

being the most important of the Rājpūt Rajas, holding the *ṣūbahdārī* of both Gujarāt and Ajmer. Ajit Singh had always been an indifferent administrator, and his earlier governorship evoked numerous complaints from the people of high-handedness and oppression on the part of the raja and his subordinates. Moved by these complaints, in 1717, Farrukh Siyar had removed the raja from his charge on the ground of 'mis-government'.[32] But when the Saiyids gained supreme control of affairs, they re-instated the raja in his previous charge, and also appointed him the governor of Ajmer. Ajit Singh once again left the affairs of Gujarāt in the hands of subordinates, refusing to leave Jodhpur and assume personal charge of the *ṣūbah* in spite of repeated and pressing requests from 'Abdullāh Khān.[33]

After the downfall of the Saiyids, the emperor appointed Ḥaider Qulī Khān as the governor of Gujarāt, and Muẓaffar 'Alī Khān, the younger brother of Khān-i-Daurān as the Governor of Ajmer.[34] When Ajit Singh heard of this, he marched from Jodhpur at the head of 30,000 troops, and occupied Ajmer. After assuring the Muslims of the place that their religious practices would in no way be interfered with, he assembled all the chief men of the town and produced a *nishān* from Jahān Shāh, the emperor's father, conferring upon him the perpetual governorship of Ajmer and Gujarāt. He also petitioned the emperor to be allowed to retain charge of either Gujarāt or Ajmer.[35]

At the court, everything was in confusion. Muẓaffar 'Alī Khān, the governor-designate, had not proceeded a few stages beyond Delhi. He was a newly-risen noble and lacked the means to raise a suitable force. The Imperial treasury was empty—the recent civil war having exhausted everything. The army was, in consequence, ill-paid and discontented. The court was full of factions and dissensions. In view of all this, Khān-i-Daurān favoured a settlement with Ajit Singh, arguing that even if he was beaten in the field, he would be-take himself to the mountains and deep valleys of his hereditary dominions, where no one would be able

32 See 175 above.

33 *Bāl*, 29, 5.

34 This was in *Rajab*, 1133, May 1721. According to *Mir'āt*, there was rumour that Ajit Singh might be left in charge of Ajmer.

35 *Siyar*, 453, *T. Muẓ*, 317, K.K., 938 (confused), *Mir'āt* ii, 37–8, *Iqbāl*, 375.

to pursue him.[36] In other words, he was afraid of the repetition of a situation like the one with which Aurangzīb had been faced in 1679. A rival faction, led by Ḥaider Qulī and a number of other nobles, opposed the idea of leaving Ajit Singh in charge of Ajmer on the ground that it was adjacent to Delhi and contained innumerable shrines and places venerated by the Muslims.

While the court was still debating the issue, news was received that Muẓaffar 'Alī Khān's troops, having failed to receive their pay, had mutinied and seized everything on which they could lay their hands, compelling Muẓaffar 'Alī to seek shelter in Amber. Taking advantage of this situation, the Rathors under Abhai Singh raided the Imperial territories. In Nārnol, the *zamindars* and local 'bandits' became so bold as to rise up in arms and plunder the town. Thus, the vaccillation of the court worsened the situation.[37]

The *ṣūbahdārī* of Ajmer now went abegging. Khān-i-Daurān, Ḥaider Qulī, and Qamar-ud-Dīn Khān the son of the late *wazīr* M. Amīn Khān accepted the post by turn, but shrank from the cost and the difficulty of the operation.

At last, Nuṣrat Khān Bārahā was appointed to the vacant *ṣūbahdārī*. By this time, Niẓām-ul-Mulk was approaching Agra from the Deccan. Ajit Singh now deemed discretion to be the better part of valour, and hastened to withdraw from Ajmer and to send letters of apology.[38] He could take this action without loss of prestige because through the intercession of his friend, Khān-i-Daurān, he was pardoned and allowed to retain charge of Ajmer (March 1722). The motives of Khān-i-Daurān can only be guessed at. He may have desired to deprive Niẓām-ul-Mulk of the credit of putting down the rebellion of Ajit Singh, as some historians allege. Or, he may have already started his attempts to bring into being a party consisting mainly of Indian-born Muslims and Rājpūts to resist the narrow and exclusionist policies advocated by a section of the nobles.

36 *Ibid.*

37 *Ibid.*

38 K.K., 938, *Siyar*, 453–4.

Elliot (vii, 517) says that Niẓām gave Ajit Singh 'a sharp warning'. This seems to be a mistranslation of the following passage from Khāfī Khān: '*Dar-īn-ẓamān akhbār āmadan-i-Niẓām-ul-Mulk Bahādur Fatḥ Jang Rājah Ajīt Singh rā az khwāb-i-ghaflat bīdār sākht*'.

Later, Niẓām expressed disapproval of the easy manner in which Ajit Singh's rebellion had been passed over (*T. Hindī*).

As Ajit Singh was acutely distrusted by a powerful section at the court, it was decided to appoint Nāhar Khān, who was the *faujdār* of Sāmbhar and the *dīwān* of Gujarāt, as the *dīwān* at Ajmer. He was granted wide powers in order that he might act as a check on the Raja. Ajit Singh, who had an old aversion to Nāhar Khān, was enraged at this, and had the latter treacherously murdered when he entered Rājpūtānā and camped near the Rājpūts in the mistaken belief that they were friendly (6 January 1723).[39]

When the news reached Muḥammad Shāh, he was enraged beyond words, and appointed an army under Sharf-ud-Daulah to 'track the villainous Ajit to his rat's hole'. Jai Singh, Girdhar Bahādur and others who had just finished the Jat campaign were asked to help him.[40] Just then, Ḥaider Qulī Khān, who had fled from Gujarāt on Niẓām-ul-Mulk's approach, reached near Delhi. At Qamar-ud Dīn's instance, he was pardoned and appointed the Governor of Ajmer.

Ḥaider Qulī proceeded vigorously. He moved on Jodhpur by way of Sāmbhar. Ajmer was reached on 8 June 1723, and the new *ṣūbahdār* then beseiged Garh Patili. After a siege of a month and a half, the fort surrendered.[41]

Ajit Singh now deemed it opportune to sue for peace. He sent his son Abhai Singh, to the Imperial commander with several elephants and presents. At the court, Khān-i-Daurān was as keen as ever to conciliate the Rājpūts. Hence, Ajit Singh was pardoned and restored to his *manṣab.* His request for being exempted from personal appearance at the court was also granted.[42] Abhai Singh, the son of Ajit Singh, appeared at the court in his place. Shortly afterwards, news arrived of the murder of Ajit Singh (7 January 1724) at Jodhpur by one of his sons or by poisoning. Khān-i-Daurān now obtained for Abhai Singh the title of *Rājah-i-Rājeshwar* with the rank of 7,000/7,000, and the permission to leave for Jodhpur to occupy his father's *gaddī.*[43]

Thus, we see that the downfall of the Saiyids led to the loss of the pre-eminent position which the House of Jodhpur had acquired. But it did not result in the decline of the power and importance of the Rājpūts as such. Jai Singh was appointed the Governor of

39 *Mir'āt* ii, 38.
40 *J.R.* Letters.
41 Kāmwar (B. M. Ms., 264–6), *T. Hindī,* 497, Irvine ii, 114.
42 *Ibid.*
43 *T. Muẓ,* 337.

Agra, and then of Malwa. He was the close personal friend of the chief *bakhshī* Khān-i-Daurān, and wielded considerable influence at the Mughal court for more than a decade. Khān-i-Daurān also attempted to win over to his side Abhai Singh who retained an important position in Rājpūtānā. Thus, the Rājpūts continued to play an important part in the politics at the Mughal court.

☆ ☆ ☆

The departure of Niẓām-ul-Mulk from the court marks the end of an epoch in the history of the Mughal empire during which a series of ambitious nobles attempted to save the empire from dissolution by concentrating supreme power in their own hands, and carrying out reforms in the administrative system. The withdrawal of Niẓām-ul-Mulk signified that henceforth ambitious nobles would devote their energies to the carving out of separate principalities for themselves.

Outwardly, the main interest during the foregoing period centres round the attempts of the *wazīrs* to consolidate their position and their clash, in this process, with other powerful individuals and groups in the nobility and with the monarchy. Underlying and inter-penetrating this struggle was, however, another struggle—a struggle between those who wanted to revive and carry forward the liberal and nationalist traditions of Akbar and those who wanted to persist in the policy of exclusionism and religious discrimination which had become identified with the name of Aurangzīb.

The relationship between these two processes is by no means a simple one. Z̲u'lfiqār Khān and the Saiyid brothers attempted to strengthen their position by conciliating the Hindu sentiment in general, and by winning over to their side the Rājpūts and the Marāthās in particular. It would not be correct to assume that these nobles acted from interested motives only and that they deliberately pursued a policy in disregard of the interests of the empire. Self-interest and conviction seem to have pushed them in the same direction.

In their clash with the Saiyid brothers, Niẓām-ul-Mulk and M. Amīn Khān attempted to rally the 'Ālamgīrī nobles to their side by appealing to the sentiments of race and religion. After assuming control of the government, they attempted, therefore, to reverse many of the liberal and conciliatory measures adopted by the

Saiyids. Thus, *jizyah* was sought to be re-imposed and a punitive expedition was sent against Ajit Singh, partly with the idea of putting the Rājpūts in their proper place. But even these limited objectives could not be realized, largely because the position of the sections which favoured a tough policy towards the Rājpūts and desired a strict enforcement of the various injunctions of the *shara*' had become weakened. It is significant that even 'Abduṣ-Ṣamad Khān, who was considered to be a pillar of the 'Tūrānī' faction and the 'orthodox' group, opposed the proposal of Niẓām-ul-Mulk for the re-imposition of *jizyah*.

From the account in the foregoing chapters, it will be apparent that the policy associated with the name of Aurangzīb was abandoned within half a dozen years of his death. Subsequent efforts to revive his policy did not find much support at the Mughal court itself. This suggests that the forces of liberalism in Indian society were really stronger than appears at first sight, and that the large number of orthodox measures introduced by Aurangzīb are not indicative of the final triumph of the forces of orthodoxy over those of liberalism in Indian society even for a limited period.

The defeat of the forces of orthodoxy at the Mughal court early in the eighteenth century was a factor of far-reaching importance. It restored the Mughal court to the position of being the leader of the movement for the promotion of a composite culture borrowing freely from the various cultural elements present in the country, a culture which was enriched by the contribution of the Hindus and the Muslims alike. The cultural importance of the Mughal court increased as its political importance diminished. The twin symbols of the new cultural process might be considered to be the Urdu language and the Emperor Muḥammad Shāh. From the time of Wālī Deccani Urdu came into its own at the Mughal court, and provided a new meeting point between the Hindus and the Muslims. Muḥammad Shāh extended his patronage to the fine arts and specially to music which made significant progress during his reign. The court also continued to occupy the position of being a school of manners for the entire polite society.

These developments were not without political significance. They helped to foster and to preserve cordial relations between the Hindu and Muslim upper classes in northern India and thus to prevent the prolonged political tussle between the Marāthās and the Mughal empire from degenerating into a series of bitter communal feuds.

CHAPTER VIII

The Marāthā Advance Towards North India (1725–31)

General Features

The decade following the departure of Niẕām-ul-Mulk from the court and his establishment as a semi-independent ruler in the Deccan, witnessed a rapid shrinkage in the area under the actual control of the Mughal emperor. It was during this period that hereditary *nawabs* arose in a number of areas. Even since his appointment to the Punjab in 1713, 'Abdus-Ṣamad Khān had ruled it with little interference from outside, putting in an occasional appearance at the court and sending his quota of tribute regularly. He died in 1726, and was succeeded by his son Ẕakariyah Khān who ruled in the same manner.[1] In Bengal, Murshid Qulī Khān, who had dominated the affairs of the province since the last years of Aurangzīb's reign, died in 1727. His death was followed by a civil war between his grandson, Sarfarāz Khān, and his son-in-law, Shuja' Khān, for the control of the province. The latter came out successful, and was duly recognized as the governor by the court.[2] Nothing could better illustrate the crumbling of Imperial authority. The case of Awadh was equally significant. Sa'ādat Khān had been appointed the Governor of Awadh in 1722, after the downfall of the Saiyids. He ruled Awadh with a high hand, and took possession of the *jāgīrs* of the Imperial *manṣabdārs* there, which led to a

1 *M.U.* ii, 517. In 1737, Ẕakariyah Khān was also made the Governor of Multan.
2 *Siyar*, 470, *Riyāz*, 277–8.

dispute with Muẓaffar Khān, the brother of the *Bakhshī-ul-Mamālik* Khān-i-Daurān, in 1726–7. As a result, Sa'ādat Khān was removed from Awadh, and appointed to Malwa. According to Imperial orders, Sa'ādat Khān left for Malwa, but from Agra he suddenly crossed the Jamuna, and proceeding to Awadh took possession of it.[3] Thus, even in areas near Delhi, powerful nobles began to set the Imperial authority at nought.

A further sign of the growing desire of the nobles to carve out independent principalities was that in Gujarāt each successive governor had to eject his predecessor by force of arms.[4]

The Rājpūt rajas were not slow to follow the example of the nobles. The Mughals had maintained a truce in Rājpūtānā, preventing the Rājpūts from encroaching on areas outside Rājputānā, and also placing a check upon the ambitions of the stronger Rājpūt states to expand at the cost of their weaker neighbours. With the decline in Mughal power and prestige, the leading Rājpūt states felt free to resume the old process of conquest and expansion. Jai Singh Sawai cherished the ambition of establishing a hegemony from the Sāmbhar Lake in the west to Agra and Mathura in the east, and extending upto the Narmada in the south. By grants from the emperor, usurpation and conquest he expanded considerably the dominion inherited by him.[5] A significant step in this direction

3 *T. Hindī,* 508–9. Acc. to A. L. Srivastava '*First Two Nawabs*', 78–9, the independent state of Awadh might be dated from this time.

4 Ḥaider Qulī was the first to attempt independence in Gujarāt. After him, Ḥāmid Khān, then Sarbuland Khān, then Abhai Singh attempted to set themselves up as *de facto* rulers of the province (See *Mir'āt* ii, 45–166, Irvine ii, 166–215 for details.) Sarbuland also seized all the *parganas* assigned in *jāgīr* to nobles and courtiers (*Mir'āt,* 99.)

5 The *Jaipur Records* permit us to follow the expansion of Amber under Jai Singh in detail. Thus, 27 May 1714—Grant of Rs 48,350 on *pargana* Bhangarh, probably a renewal (No. 35).

10 September 1716: Grant of *pargana* Malarna in *jāgīr* then worth Rs 333,272 per year (No. 48).

5 April 1717: Grant of Rs 80,000 *jāgīr* in *pargana* Amarsar.

9 October 1717: *Jāgīr* yielding Rs 2½ crores given to his contingent. It included Umara and Barwar (No. 40).

In the following decade were wrested 50 *parganas* from Zain Khān of Jhunjhun, these being granted to him for a quit rent of Rs 25 lakhs.

These were supplemented by conquests from his neighbours. Thus , in 1729, Jai Singh virtually annexed the Rāmpurā district from Udaipur, and

was the crushing of the Jat power. The Maharajas of Jodhpur, likewise, aggrandized themselves at the cost of their neighbours. They seized several areas belonging to the Mughal province of Gujarāt, and dreamt of a hegemony from Lake Sāmbhar to Aḥmadabād and the sea.[6]

Apart from this, the period also witnessed the rapid growth of Afghān power in northern India. Between Delhi and Awadh, the Rohilla power was growing silently.[7] Muḥammad Khān Bangash set up a second Afghān centre at Farrukhābād, and attempted to subdue the war-like Bundelas. He led a campaign into Bundelkhand in 1728, ostensibly aimed at the recovery of his *jāgīrs* which had been usurped by the Bundelas, but with the real object of establishing his influence in those quarters.[8] Khande Rai, the agent of Jai Singh, wrote that 'seventy to eighty thousand Pathans in Gwalior and Dholpur, hearing the name of a Pathan, have flocked to him and are committing all manners of excesses'.[9]

Thus, the sphere of the emperor's effective authority rapidly shrank to an area extending in an arc roughly from Sahāranpur to Nagor in the west, Farrukhābād in the east, and from the line of the Ganges in the north upto the Narmada in the south. Even inside this area, the Jats had usurped many areas, and the *zamindars* were raising their heads on every side, so that 'every *zamindar* became a raja, and every raja a maharaja'.[10]

This was the background to the growing encroachment of the Marāthās on Malwa and Gujarāt. Only the utmost vigilance, resourcefulness and determination could have enabled the Delhi

---

attempted to bring Bundi under his vassalage by setting up his own nominee on its throne.

In 1731, he annexed many districts around Amber belonging to the Emperor (*T. Hindi*, 524).

6 The Rathors were attempting to seize the Shekhāwātī confederation, and in 1725 seized Nagore which was an Imperial feudatory state. In 1733–4, Abhai Singh attempted to conquer Bikaner (Ojha, *Hist. of Jodhpur* ii, 608–10). As the Governor of Gujarāt, Ajit Singh annexed certain places which the Mughals failed to recover.

7 See *Gulistān-i-Rahmat*, and Dr B. Prasad's article 'Ali Muhammad Khan Ruhella' in *J.I.H.*, Vol. v, 380–98.

8 *J.A.S.B.*, 1878, 288–90.

9 *J.R.*, Hindi letter d. 1724, v, 47–8.

10 Āshūb, 263.

court with its depleted resources to successfully meet the Marāthā threat. As it was, the court remained engaged in factional squabbles, and woefully under-estimated the Marāthās, leaving the local governors to cope with the situation as best as they could with their own limited resources. The result was that the Marāthās rapidly established themselves in these provinces, and made a bid for their outright annexation. This posed a serious threat not only to the Delhi court, but also to all the other 'principalities' in north as well as in south India.

It is outside the scope of this work to attempt to trace these events in detail. In the following pages, we shall study the various stages in the Marāthā conquest of Gujarāt, Malwa and Bundelkhand, and the impact of this process on north Indian politics and the parties at the Mughal court. But first it is necessary to analyse briefly the origin and development of the Marāthā policy of expansion, and the relations between the Marāthās and Niẓām-ul-Mulk in the Deccan.

The Marāthās and Their Policy of Expansion

As has been noted already, the Marāthā movement was a complex movement, combining an earlier movement for socio-religious reform with the movement for regional independence led by the Marāthā *sardars*. There were contradictions between the political, socio-religious, and the economic aspects of the movement, these contradictions being rooted ultimately in the interests of different social groups. The Marāthā *sardars* who were the dominant element in Marāthā society, had little interest in socio-religious reform, or in securing the welfare of the peasantry unless their own interests were involved. After the death of Shivaji, the peasantry was neglected, and the links between the political and the socio-religious reform movement were weakened. With the death of Aurangzīb and the withdrawal of the Mughal armies from Marārāshtra, the divergence between the interests of the Marāthā *sardars* and the Marāthā peasantry became even clearer. Intent on personal gain and plunder, the Marāthā *sardars* refused to subordinate their individual interests to the national good, and made the re-establishment of a centralized administrative system impossible. A seal was set on this process by Peshwa Bālāji Vishwanāth who made a complex division of the revenues between Shāhū and his *sardars* in 1719. Broadly speaking, this system implied placing on the Marāthā *sardars* the entire responsibility for the collection of *chauth* and *sardeshmukhī*. Out of these collections, a fixed share was to be paid to the raja—*sardeshmukhī* plus 34 per cent of the *chauth*. The raja thus became largely dependent on his *sardars* for his finances. Care was also taken to divide the responsibility for the collection of *chauth* and *sardeshmukhī* in such a way that no individual Marāthā *sardar* could easily dominate a large compact area. Inside Mahārāshtra, the semblance of a centralized system of administration under the care and supervision of the peshwa was kept up. But here, too, some of the evils of the system of *zamindari* asserted themselves.[11]

The arrangements made by Bālāji have often been criticized, and their defects are obvious enough. While the Marāthā *sardars* were given an added incentive for the plundering and over-running of the Mughal territory, they were made practically independent of the king. In the ultimate resort, there was no substitute for a strong central authority if the Marāthā movement was to hold together. But the arrangements should be regarded as reflecting a particular political reality, rather than an ideal set of regulations. The hope of effective political unity among the Marāthās centred more and more in the institution of the *peshwa* which became a prime factor in Marāthā politics from this time onwards.

The real founder of the institution of the hereditary *peshwa* was Baji Rao. In 1720 Shāhū appointed Baji Rao to the vacant office of his father, in recognition of the signal services of the latter. There is no clear evidence that at this juncture Shāhū regarded the post as hereditary in the family of Bālāji[12] though the incumbents of the leading posts already tended to regard them as their hereditary preserves. Baji Rao placed the issue beyond doubt by his success in the field of battle, and by steadily arrogating authority to his office till it became the focal point in the Marāthā political system.

The rapid decline of the power of the Mughals, and the conflict between various factions at the court gave an opportunity to the Marāthā *sardars* which they were not slow to seize. The struggle now was no longer one for the national survival and freedom of the

11 See Sen, '*Adm. System*', 272–3. Duff, 370–6.

12 See K&P ii, 182, 183 for the *Pratinidhi* Shripatrao's arguments against the appointment of Baji Rao.

Marāthās, but for the domination and control of as much land as possible. This change from the defensive to the offensive by the Marāthās, from struggle for national survival to empire-building was not accomplished overnight. The change in the character of the struggle was becoming apparent during the last years of Aurangzīb's reign when the Marāthās began regular raids into Gujarāt and Malwa. But the new trend was not given the shape of a definite policy till the coming of Baji Rao on the scene. A prolonged controversy at the Marāthā court between Baji Rao and the *Pratinidhi* Shripat Rao preceded the adoption of the new policy. From the near-contemporary account of Chitnis,[13] a rough idea may be formed of the approach and general line of argument adopted by the two men, though it would be dangerous to accept literally the purple passages and the long speeches put by Chitnis in the mouth of the protagonists. Apparently, the main issues posed were: (i) the direction and timing of Marāthā expansionist activities, (ii) the attitude of Niẓām-ul-Mulk and the possibility of maintaining friendly relations with him, and (iii) internal administration, and particularly the problem of controlling the Marāthā *sardars* and of putting the finances and the army etc. in order. Lastly there was the question of power—who was to dominate the councils of the king, the *peshwa* or the *pratinidhi*?

The *pratinidhi* was not opposed to an exapansionist policy as such, but he wanted that attention should first be given to the overrunning of the Konkan where the Sidi of Janjira had recovered many areas, and the completion of the conquest of the Karnātak begun by Shivaji. After consolidating Marāthā positions in the Deccan, they could think of conquest further afield in northern India. The *pratinidhi* emphasized the necessity of caution, and of not provoking the Mughals too far lest it bring another invasion of the Marāthā homeland. Above all, he was keen to befriend the powerful Niẓām-ul-Mulk. Hence, he wanted that large scale expansionist activities should be deferred till the finances had been placed on a sound basis, and a strong army and a stable administrative system created.

On the other hand, Baji Rao dwelt upon the weakness and imbecility of the Mughal court which was torn by factions and internecine feuds so that Marāthā aid was sought, and by its means

13 Chitnis, *Life of Shahu Maharaj*, 60–1 *et passim.*

kings were made and unmade. He dismissed the conquest of the Karnātak as a domestic affair which could be left to the *Huzarat* (household) troops. Pointing to Shivaji's dream of a Hindu domination, he dwelt upon the (alleged) friendship of the Hindu powers to the Marāthās, and discounted the power of the Niẓām, offering to hold him in check as well as to effect a northward drive. Finally, he appealed to the predatory instincts of the Marāthā *sardars* by pointing to the riches of northern India, the Deccan having been reduced to ruin by prolonged warfare. He is supposed to have ended with the famous words, 'Strike, strike at the trunk and the branches will fall off themselves. Listen but to my counsel and I shall plant the Marāthā banner on the walls of Attock'.[14]

It does not seem correct to imagine that Baji Rao's policy of northward expansion implied that he was disinterested in the south. As early as the year 1724, when the emperor had asked for Marāthā help against Niẓām-ul-Mulk, Baji Rao had demanded the cession of the *ṣūbah* of Ḥaiderabad, and the virtual right to nominate the Mughal viceroy of the Deccan.[15]

Thus Baji Rao too, was interested in Marāthā supremacy over the Deccan. But he did not apparently share the *Pratinidhi*'s facile optimism that the Marāthās could overrun the Karnātak without the bitter opposition of the Niẓām, or that they could obtain the mastery of the Deccan in the face of a clever and determined foe like Niẓām-ul-Mulk with the resources of Mahārāshtra alone. Hence his fixed determination of over-running and bringing under Marāthā domination the rich and flourishing provinces of Malwa and Gujarāt. Marāthā *sardars* had raided and regularly exacted contributions from these provinces since the early part of the century. Baji Rao gave to these sporadic raids a systematic form and political content, for he perceived as well the political and strategic value of these provinces. With the Marāthās securely established in Malwa and Gujarāt, a wedge would be interposed between the Niẓām and Delhi. The Marāthās would then surround the Niẓām's territories on three sides, and could, at their convenience, turn against the Niẓām without fear of his getting succor from Delhi, or raid the *dū'āb* and the regions to the east and west of it.

14 *Ibid.*

15 *S.P.D.* x, 1. The Deccan figured prominently in Baji Rao's negotiations with the emperor in 1736, and with Niẓām-ul-Mulk after the battle of Bhopal in 1738.

Thus, the establishment of a Marāthā domination in Malwa and Gujarāt was the first step towards the establishment of a large and powerful Marāthā empire. It seems historically inaccurate to think that Baji Rao set himself any tasks beyond this. His peroration about the planting of the Marāthā flag on Attock was only a politician's hyperbole. The task was clearly beyond Marāthā strength for a long time to come, and Baji Rao was too much of a practical statesman to set before himself any such impossible objectives.

THE MARĀTHĀS AND NIẒĀM-UL-MULK

Marāthā relations with Niẓām-ul-Mulk passed through a number of phases, and had a considerable bearing on Marāthā activities in Malwa and Gujarāt.

As the Viceroy of the Deccan from 1715 to 1717, Niẓām-ul-Mulk resisted the Marāthā claims for the *chauth* and *sardeshmukhī* of the Deccan, and was almost constantly at war with them—though with little lasting success. After his successful rebellion against the Saiyids, Niẓām-ul-Mulk respected the Imperial *farmān* granting the *chauth* and *sardeshmukhī* of the Deccan to the Marāthā, but resisted the stationing of Marāthā agents in the neighbourhood of the capital, Aurangābād. Shortly afterwards, on 4 January 1721, he had his first personal meeting with Baji Rao.[16] Though Niẓām-ul-Mulk established friendly relations with the young *peshwa*, no lasting agreement resulted. The most important point of conflict between the Marāthās and Niẓām-ul-Mulk was the Karnātak. Niẓām-ul-Mulk looked upon the Karnātak as his by right of succession to the kingdoms of Bījāpur and Golkonda. However, scant attention was paid to his claims by the Marāthās who had been interested in the Karnātak at least since the time of Shahji, and had always regarded it as a kind of happy hunting ground which they were determined to plunder and to lay under contribution.[17]

In October, 1721, Niẓām-ul-Mulk left Aurangābād for Delhi, and did not return till 1724. During his absence, his deputy,

16 *S.P.D.* xxx, 266, No. 909, and apparently the meeting referred to in x, 5, 10, 11. See also Dr Powar's paper, *loc. cit., I.H.R.C.* XVII, 204–15, *Riyasat* 160–1.

17 Niẓām-ul-Mulk marched upto the Fardāpur pass in 1721 to check Ghorpāde's invasion of the Karnātak, and near Trichinopoly, the Mughal and Marāthā forces clashed (*Āṣaf Jāh*, 139–40, Vad i, No. 3).

Mubāriẕ-ul-Mulk, repudiated the agreement for *chauth* and so there was a general resumption of hotilities with the Marāthās. However, Niẕām-ul-Mulk attempted to maintain good relations with the Marāthās, and met Baji Rao in Malwa in 1723, with the results already noted.[18]

When Niẕām-ul-Mulk rebelled in 1724, the emperor attempted to enlist the support of the Marāthā *sardar*s against him and wrote to Shāhū. Mubāriz Khān also opened direct negotiations with the Marāthās.[19] Niẕām-ul-Mulk checkmated these moves by arranging another personal meeting with Baji Rao. Baji Rao was present at Shakar Kherā with a contingent of Marāthā horsemen which did good service, and for which Niẕām-ul-Mulk rewarded Baji Rao.[20] It has been suggested that in return for Marāthā support, Niẕām-ul-Mulk agreed not to oppose Marāthā advance into Malwa and Gujarāt.[21]

It was against this background that Baji Rao and the *pratinidhi* disputed about the future of Marāthā relations with Niẕām-ul-Mulk. The *pratinidhi* had some reason to hope for the continued goodwill of Niẕām-ul-Mulk, especially as the victory over Mubāriẕ Khān had been followed by two joint Marāthā-Niẕām expeditions into the Karnātak. But the *pratinidhi* failed to comprehened the deeper purposes of Niẕām-ul-Mulk, and the inner motives of his policy.

18 See pp. 209–10 above.

19 Mubāriẕ Khān was advised by some well-wishers to seek the help of Kanhoji Bhosle, but he did not accept the suggestion (*Riyasat*, 169).

From an extant letter of Kanhoji to Jai Singh, it appears that Kanhoji was prepared to help, but the Khān declined to accept it. Kanhoji wrote, 'According to the *farmān* of H.M. and the letter of that Most High Raja (Jai Singh), Mubāriẕ had been provided with 10,000 horse and other necessaries of war, and asked not to fight till he reached these quarters. The Khan did not do so, and on account of haste gave up his life'. (*J.R.*, Misc., Vol. i, No. 277)

Shāhū had instructed Kanhoji to remain neutral in the conflict between Niẕām and Mubāriẕ (Vad i, 12).

20 K.K., 955, *S.P.D.* xxx, Nos 333–4. According to *T. Fatḥiyah* (quoted in *Aṣaf Jāh*, 162), Niẕām-ul-Mulk conferred upon Baji Rao a *manṣab* of 7,000 in recognition of his services.

21 Dighe, 13, Dr Powar, *I.H.R.C.* XVII, 207. But in two extant letters to Jai Singh, Niẕām-ul-Mulk vigorously denies the charge, pointing to the greatly enhanced power of the Marāthās and his difficulties in attempting to meet their threat. (*J.R., Letters*, Vol. V, No. 485)

Faced with the implacable hostility of the Delhi court, Niẓām-ul-Mulk was not loth to acquiesce in Baji Rao's schemes of expansion towards the north. But he could not afford to let the Marāthās grow so powerful as to bring Malwa and Gujarāt completely under their sway. This would isolate him from Delhi, and jeopardize his position in the Deccan. Hence, the policy of Niẓām-ul-Mulk was to ward off the hostility of both the court and the Marāthās by keeping them embroiled with one another, and at the same time, not to allow one of them to become so powerful as to dominate the other. He wanted to keep the Marāthās at play by professing friendship, while keeping a line open to Delhi in case the Marāthās grew too powerful. He also attempted to interpose internal checks on the growth of Marāthā power by allying with disgruntled groups and individuals among the Marāthās while he conserved and consolidated his own power. It was a complex policy, and required a shrewd and calculating politician like Niẓām-ul-Mulk to work it. While Niẓām-ul-Mulk sometimes over-reached himself, he was successful, on the whole, in maintaining his position, and evoked a grudging admiration from even Baji Rao who strove for good relations with him even while resisting his intrigues and opposing him by force of arms at times.

In 1728, affairs between Niẓām-ul-Mulk and the Marāthās moved towards war. Niẓām-ul-Mulk was uneasy and apprehensive at the growing sweep of Marāthā operations in Malwa and Gujarāt. He also resented Marāthā encroachments in the Karnātak and though he joined in the two expeditions to the Karnātak launched by Shāhū in 1725–6 and 1726–7, he issued secret orders to his commander to oppose the Marāthās.[22] Hostility between the courts of Satārā and Kolhapur, and the differences between Baji Rao and the *pratinidhi* helped him. While the bulk of the Marāthā armies were in the Karnātak, he suspended payment of *chauth* and *sardeshmukhī* on the ground of a dispute upon the matter between Shāhū and Shambhāji (the Kolhapur Raja), and posing as the representative of the Mughal emperor, invited Shāhū to submit the dispute to his arbitration. He also sent him messages suggesting the dismissal of Baji Rao. In the meantime, he effected a junction with the armies of the Kolhapur Raja.[23]

22 Sardesai, *New Hist.* ii, 90–1.
23 *Ḥadīqat*, 138. For details, see Dighe, 14–18, *Āṣaf Jāh*, 185–7. The exact

Shāhū was dumbfounded and was almost persuaded to accept Niẓām-ul-Mulk's claim for arbitration. But he quickly recovered, and sent express messages of recall to the Marāthā forces, alerting the commanders of the Marāthā forts for defence. Hurrying back from the Karnātak, Baji Rao decided on immediate war, rejecting the peace overtures made by Niẓām-ul-Mulk who had no real desire for war.[24] After a brief but brilliant campaign, Baji Rao brought Niẓām-ul-Mulk to bay at Pālkhed. On 6 March 1728, by the treaty of Mungi Shivgaon, Niẓām-ul-Mulk re-affirmed Shāhū's claim for the *chauth* and *sardeshmukhī* of the Deccan, and agreed not to offer any protection to Shambhāji of Kolhapur.[25]

While it is historically wrong to imagine that this treaty established Marāthā supremacy in the south,[26] it did place the claims of Shāhū to the *chauth* and *sardeshmukhī* of the Deccan beyond dispute. It also enabled Baji Rao to finally supplant the *pratinidhi* at Shāhū's court, and to devote his undivided attention to the affairs of Malwa and Gujārāt. But it was not long before Niẓām-ul-Mulk re-commenced his intrigues. The presence of Niẓām-ul-Mulk in the Deccan and his constant intrigues made Baji Rao tread warily, and rendered more difficult his task of establishing a Marāthā hegemony in Malwa and Gujārāt.

THE MARĀTHĀ ADVANCE INTO MALWA AND GUJARĀT

Gujārāt had been raided by the Marāthās intermittently since 1705, and Malwa since 1699; but it was only after 1720 that the Marāthā raids in these provinces became a regular and organized feature in pursuance of a fixed policy on the part of the *Peshwa*. Although claims to the *chauth* of Malwa and Gujarāt had been advanced as early as the reign of Shivaji, they do not seem to have been officially put forward in any negotiations with the Mughals till 1717. In that year, in the course of his negotiations with Ḥusain 'Alī, Shāhū asked for the recognition of the Marāthā claims over

---

nature of Shambhāji's claims is not clear. He apparently claimed the right to realize *sardeshmukhī* from the Karnātak, and regarded Shāhū's expeditions in that area as encroachments.

24 Duff. ii, 407.

25 *S.P.D.* xv, 90–1. See also *New Hist.* ii, 98–100, Dighe, 20.

26 *Cf.* Dighe, 20.

Gujarāt and Malwa. At the time of his visit to Delhi in 1719, Bālāji Vishwanāth was instructed to try and secure the *chauth* of these two provinces also.[27]

These claims were not conceded, and Marāthā raids into the two provinces assumed larger and larger proportions. In 1724, when Niẓām-ul-Mulk rebelled, both he and the emperor bid for Marāthā support. The Marāthās once again demanded the recognition of their claims over the two provinces.[28] But in view of the financial and strategic importance of these provinces, neither of the two was prepared to hold out any such promise to the Marāthās. However, after his defeat by Baji Rao in 1728, Niẓām-ul-Mulk was compelled for some time to disregard the Marāthā advance in Malwa and Gujarāt, and even to connive at the passage of their armies across his territory.[29] Thus, it was not till 1728 that the Mughals felt the full brunt of the Marāthā strength in Malwa and Gujarāt.

It is not necessary for our purposes to trace in detail the progress of Marāthā arms in Gujarāt and Malwa. The Marāthā conquest of these provinces proceeded in three stages. The first stage was the establishment of their claim for *chauth* and *sardeshmukhi*. Next, this claim was substituted by a demand for the cession of territory, and the provinces were divided into spheres of influence among the Marāthā *sardars*. The final step was outright annexation.

In Gujarāt, the Marāthā claim for the *chauth* and *sardeshmukhi* of the *ṣūbah* were accepted by the Imperial governor, Sarbuland Khān, in May 1726.[30] The principle of *chauth* and *sardeshmukhi* having been once conceded in the Deccan, there could be little moral objection to a similar arrangement for Gujarāt, if it was demonstrated that the Marāthās were too strong to be successfully resisted by force of arms. But the grant of *chauth* and *sardeshmukhi* did not result in the ceasing of the plundering activities of the

27 Duff. i, 273, Chitnis 51.

28 *S.P.D.* x, i.

29 *Siyar,* 463–4.

30 Vad i, No. 105. An order d. 1 *Ramaẓān* 1138 H., 3 May 1726 sets out the basis on which the *chauth* of Gujārāt was to be divided among the various Marāthā *sardars*. Irvine (ii, 192–3) dates this settlement in October 1726, apparently on the basis of *Mir'āt* (ii, 92–3). But this was only a confirmation of the earlier agreement signed by Sarbuland Khān with Ambāji Pant Purandare.

Marāthā *sardars*. The chief lieutenants of the Dabhade, Pilāji Gaekwad and Kanthā Kadam, fell out among themselves over the division of the *chauth*, resulting in constant fights between them. Further, Baji Rao contested the claim of the *pratinidhi* who had been assigned the *chauth* of Gujaṛāt by Shāhū. In February, 1727, the governor Sarabuland Khān made a pact with Baji Rao stipulating for the payment of *chauth*, provided Baji Rao helped to establish peace in the province.[31] But Baji Rao was too busy in the Deccan and then in Malwa, so that the pact was not confirmed. Meanwhile, the Marāthā *sardars* gradually seized 28 districts of Gujarāt, i.e. the entire south Gujarāt.[32] In 1730, Baji Rao entered Gujarāt politics again. The earlier agreement for *chauth* was confirmed by Sarbuland Khān in April 1730.[33] This resulted in his being replaced by Abhai Singh. However, Abhai Singh also signed a pact with Baji Rao in February, 1731, by which he agreed to pay a fixed sum of 13 lakhs in lieu of *chauth*, on condition that Baji Rao expelled Gaekwad and Kanthā Kadam from Gujarāt.[34]

Thus, by 1732 the Marāthās had not only secured recognition of their right of *chauth* and *saradeshmukhi* of Gujarāt from the governor, but also obtained control of the districts from which they could effectively realise their claims. The defeat of the Dabhade at the hands of Baji Rao at Tiloi in 1731 did not improve matters for Abhai Singh. Shāhū now patched up an agreement between the two *sardars*, and assigned the greater part of Gujarāt to the Dabhade.

Despairing of ousting the Marāthās by force of arms, in 1733 Abhai Singh invited Pilāji Gaekwad to a conference, and

31 *S.P.D.* xv, 86, 84–5. The English date given by the Editor is wrong. It should be 20 February 1727 (o.s.) or 2 March (n.s.).

The terms were modelled on Ḥusain 'Alī's agreement of 1719. The Marāthās were to maintain peace, and keep 2,500 horsemen for the service of the governor in return for *chauth*, and were not to send more than 2–3 men in each district as collectors. In return for *sardeshmukhi*, they were to give a *peshkash* of Rs 413,080/13.

32 *S.P.D.* xv, 82.

33 *Letters of Abhai Singh* (quoted by V. Reu, *I.H.R.C.*, 1938, 124–6; 1942, 328–32).

34 *Mir'āt* ii, 134–5. This was really a renewal of the pact signed the previous year by Sarbuland Khān. Baji Rao was to get six lakhs immediately, and the remainder after he had expelled Kanthāji and left those parts (*Surat Factory Diary*, 614).

treacherously murdered him. However, this was of little avail to him. The Marāthās rallied under Umā Bai Dābhāde to avenge the death of one of their prominent *sardars*. Abhai Singh soon found the situation beyond his control, and withdrew into Marwar. The stage was now set for the next step, annexation. The rest of the province rapidly passed under Marāthā sway. It only remained to legalise the position by a formal grant from the emperor.[35]

The first concerted move for the enforcement of the claim for *chauth* from Malwa was made under the leadership of Baji Rao in 1723.[36] In 1725, regular Marāthā officials, such as Keso Mahādeo, Keso Vishwanāth, Godāji Deokolā and Udāji Pawār were appointed to collect *chauth* from south Malwa.[37]

In June 1725, Girdhar Bahādur was appointed the *ṣubahdār* of Malwa. He was a man of courage and determination and refused to surrender to the Marāthās. He turned out the Marāthā *kamāvishdārs*, and disregarded the representations of Shāhū not to disturb the collection of *chauth*. Dayā Ram, the cousin of Girdhar Bahādur, moved about the province with a well-equipped army, and showed great activity in chasing out the Marāthā *sardars*.[38] Thus began a conflict which ended only with the death of Girdhar Bahādur and Dayā Ram at the battle of Amjharā in November, 1728.[39] Baji Rao then swept into Bundelkhand, and beseiged M. Khān Bangash at Jaitpur, forcing the latter to relinquish all his conquest in Bundelkhand. In return, the grateful Raja agreed to pay *chauth*.[40] The Marāthā armies camped in Malwa throughout that summer. Three years later, Baji Rao divided the province into spheres of influence among his *sardars*.[41]

35 In 1736, in the course of his negotiations with the Emperor, Baji Rao demanded the cession of both Malwa and Gujarāt (*Siyar*, 468–9).

A last effort was made by the Imperialists to recover Gujarāt in 1740 by appointing Fakr-ud-Daulah, the brother of Roshan-ud-Daulah, as the Governor of Gujarāt (*T. Muẓ*, 240). But the governor-designate did not even leave for his charge. The last traces of Mughal rule in Gujarāt disappeared with the fall of Aḥmedabād in 1753.

36 Baji Rao's *Roznishi*, 223–4, *S.P.D.* xiii, 3, xxx, 310.

37 *S.P.D.* xii, 6–9.

38 *S.P.D.* xiii, 6–9, *Ajā'ib* No. 180. For details see R. Sinh, '*Malwa*', 158–62.

39 *S.P.D.* xiii, 28, 25, 27, 17; *Ajā'ib*, Nos 182, 201; '*Malwa*', 164–5, 199–207.

40 *S.P.D.* xii, 38, 39, xxx, 55, 304–6; *J.A.S.B.*, 1878, 297–302.

41 *S.P.D.* xxii, 54, 82.

The North Indian Reaction

The ever-extending sweep of the Marāthā operations and their growing demands and aspirations caused serious concern to the Delhi court and to the various semi-independent or autonomous princes and *nawab*s of north India, such as the Kachhwāhās of Amber, the Rathors of Jodhpur, the Bundelas, Sa'ādat Khān of Awadh etc.

None of them had any desire to see the Delhi government regain its power and authority. At the same time, they could not ignore the Marāthā threat, or repel it by their individual efforts. The need of the hour was a united front. But their mutual jealousies and suspicions made the forging of such a front a difficult task. Much depended on the attitude of the emperor and his advisors. If they followed a well-defined and firm policy, many of the princes and the *nawabs* could perhaps be induced to help. Lack of firmness at the Delhi court led to wavering in their ranks, and efforts to make individual deals with the Marāthās, thereby accelerating the process of the disintegration of the political and moral authority of the emperor. Thus, the Marāthā advance towards north India accentuated the inner problems of the empire and hastened its internal decay. For all practical purposes, north India became divided into a number of semi-independent states or principalities, each determining its own interests.

In the following pages, we shall attempt to analyse the attitude of the various north Indian powers towards the Marāthās and their relations with each other and the court.

Jai Singh Sawai dominated the affairs of Amber from his succession to the *gaddī* in 1700 to his death in 1743. His attitude towards the Marāthās during this long period underwent several changes as might well be expected. In 1701, at the seigs of Khelna, he did good service against the Marāthās, and was rewarded by a rise (or rather restoration) of his *manṣab*. Subsequently, he performed good service in guarding Khandesh and Malwa from the depredations of the Marāthās, and was nominated the *nā'ib ṣūbahdār* of Malwa by Bīdār Bakht. But Aurangzīb disapproved of his appointment.[42]

As the Governor of Malwa from 1713 to 1715–17, Singh put up a stout resistance to the Marāthās, and inflicted a crushing defeat

42 'Ināyat, 68a, 72b, 75a–b.

upon them in 1715, so that the Marāthās kept away from Malwa for two years.[43] Jai Singh's absence from Malwa after 1715 with half the Kachhwāhā contingent in connection with the Jat campaign, and the negligence of his deputy, encouraged the Marāthās to resume their raids. Jai Singh was keen to return to the province after his unsuccessful Jat campaign. The emperor promised to depute a high noble with a powerful army to clear the province of the 'Deccanis' in co-operation with him.[44] But in November 1717, the province was suddenly taken away from him, and given to M. Amīn Khān.

Jai Singh did not come into direct contact with the Marāthās again till October 1729, when he was appointed the Governor of Malwa for the second time. His governorship did not last more than a couple of months. In 1732, Jai Singh became the governor of Malwa for the third time, and accepted the Marāthā claim for *chauth*. In 1735, he invited Baji Rao to northern India in order to induce the emperor to accept his demands and to make peace with the Marāthās.

It is obvious that between 1719 and 1732 a big change took place in Jai Singh's attitude towards the Marāthās. It is now possible with the help of the mass of the Persian and Marāthi records available to us to determine the time and causes of this striking change.

We are told that contact between Jai Singh and the young *Peshwa*, Baji Rao, was first established in 1719, when Bālājī Vishwanath and Baji Rao accompanied Ḥusain 'Alī to Delhi to receive the *sanads* of the *chauth* and *sardeshmukhī* of the Deccan. Though no occasion can be found when Jai Singh could have met Bālājī Vishwanath and Baji Rao at Delhi as asserted by Duff,[45] it is possible that some kind of an indirect contact was established between these two important personages, either at this time or soon afterwards. This appears likely as it is now clear that a Marāthā envoy lived at Delhi almost without a break after Bālājī's visit of 1719. The names of Malhār Dādājī Barwe, Ānand Rao

43 See p. 160 above.

44 *J.R.* (Add. Pers. ii, 160).

45 Duff. i, 393. *Riyasat* (80) says that Shankarājī Malhār was instrumental in establishing friendship between Jai Singh and the Peshwa.

Jai Singh remained at Amber during the entire period when the Saiyids were the *de facto* rulers at Delhi.

Sumant, Dādājī Pant Nānā and Mahāḍeo Bhatt Hingane might be mentioned in this connection.[46]

Between 1725 and 1730, the Marathas advanced not only into Malwa, Bundelkhand (then a part of *ṣūbah* Allahabad) and Gujarāt, but also into Rājpūtānā. The routes of their advance were from Mukandarā pass and across the Chambal from Malwa via Harauti, and from Gujarāt via Īdar and Jālor. In both cases, the Marāthā entry into Rājpūtānā was facilitated by internal disputes among the Rājpūts. In 1725, the Marāthās started hovering on the outskirts of Kotah-Bundi, but found an entry only after 1732. They were, however, invited into Marwar by Mukund Singh and Rai Singh, the younger brothers of Abhai Singh, after a civil war between these two and Abhai Singh following the murder of Ajit Singh in 1724. Mukund Singh and Rai Singh, it seems, even proposed a matrimonial alliance with the Marāthās. Failing to remove Abhai Singh from Jodhpur they attempted to gain Īdar for themselves. In order to help them, the Marāthās invaded Īdar in the middle of 1725, and ravaged some areas belonging to the Rana. In March 1726, the two brothers, along with their Marāthā allies prepared to make a dash on Jodhpur. Jai Singh and Rana Sangram Singh sent their forces to support

46 Hingane (probably Govind Pant s/o Mahādev Bhatt) returned from Delhi with the Peshwa, and Shankarāji followed with the *sanads* (*Hingane Daftar*, *Nos* 8, 9; *Marāthā Wakīls* i, *Burhān-ul-Futūḥ* 167a). But Mahādev Dādāji Barwe continued to live at Delhi, and in 1720, after the assassination of Ḥusain 'Alī, sent an 'express' to Baji Rao, urging him to come forward boldly and to seize the vacant situation at the court (*S.P.D.* xxx, 24).

In 1721, Ānand Rao Sumant accompanied Niẓām-ul-Mulk to Delhi (*S.P.D.* xxii, 3), but he seems to have left soon afterwards, for he was with Mubāriz Khān in 1722 (*Riyasat*, 163). In his alleged speech before Shāhū urging the Marāthās to strike at the root of the empire, Baji Rao mentions one Dādāji Pant Nānā who had prepared the ground for Marāthā expansion by establishing friendly relations with the Rājpūt Rajas (Chitnis, 61). This would be in 1722 or 1726.

An entry dated 1724 in the *peshwa*'s *Roznishi* (expense register) mentions that Rs 2000 was paid to Māyā Ram *Wakil*, at Delhi, as his salary for the previous year (*S.P.D.* xxx, No. 353). Māyā Ram is again mentioned as the *Wakil* at Delhi in 1728 (*S.P.D.* xxii, 40). From 1732, Yādav Rao Prahlād lived at Delhi as the accredited Marāthā representative. Hingane is again mentioned as being at Delhi in 1734, but does not seem to have been posted to Delhi till Baji Rao's death (*Hingane Daftar*, 8–9).

Abhai Singh.[47] It was to dissuade Shāhū from helping Anand Singh and Rai Singh and also to gauge the Marāthā intentions in Malwa and Gujarāt that Jai Singh sent his agent, Joshi Shambhu, to the Maratha court in 1725. The report and suggestions of Joshi Shambhu and the subsequent negotiations of the Rana and Jai Singh with the Marāthās have already been discussed (see Appendix C).

A new chapter in north Indian politics commenced with the year 1725. The new phase began with the efforts of both the emperor and Niẓām-ul-Mulk to seek support from the Marāthās. As has been seen, the Marāthās preferred to support Niẓām-ul-Mulk, in 1725 and again in 1728. The attitude of Jai Singh and Sangram Singh towards the Marāthās was conditioned partly by this, and partly by the fact that both of them had their own interests in Malwa which they did not wish to lose. They were, no doubt, also aware of the strategic importance of the area for the defence of Rājpūtānā. Jai Singh's desired to maintain his position in Malwa, even in collaboration with the Marāthās, was based on these considerations.

Rana Sangram Singh supported Jai Singh's Marāthā policy. When Jai Singh was made *ṣūbahdār* of Malwa for the third time, not feeling himself strong enough to defend Malwa against the Marāthās single-handed, he made an agreement with the Rana in 1732 whereby the latter would send 24,000–25,000 *sawārs* to Malwa, and share in the proportion of 1:2 the income from land, including *ijāra* from the *jāgīrs* of *manṣabdārs*, and *peshkash* from the *zamindars*.[48]

Thus, by 1725, direct relations had been established between the Rājpūt princes and the Marāthās. According to two extant papers in the *Jaipur Records*, a Marāthā agent named Jadu Rai reached Udaipur in 1725 and opened negotiations with the Rājpūt rajas for a general peace settlement. It appears that Jai Singh and the Mahārānā proposed the following terms:

(i) Shāhū should be taken into Imperial service, and granted *jāgīrs* worth 10 lakhs in each of the two provinces (of Gujarāt and Malwa), and (ii) four of Shāhū's principal men should be called and accorded *manṣabs*.[49]

47 G. R. Parihar, *Marwar and the Mughals*, pp. 27–30.

48 Letter of Aya Mal to Jai Singh, dt. *Ashoj Badi*, 13, 1789, 16 October 1732, *RSA*.

49 *J.R.* (*Hindi Letters* v, 65–8, 85–6). These were apparently the terms proposed by the Marāthā *Wakil* himself.

The rajas forwarded these proposals to the emperor, and while emphasizing their loyalty to him and their readiness to abide by his wishes, expressed the opinion that it would be in the best interests of the empire to accept them. They also suggested to Sarbuland Khān, the Governor of Gujarāt, that he should come to an agreement with the Peshwa, and advised him to write direct to Shāhū before they put him in touch with his plenipotentiary, Jadu Rai.[50]

However, the rajas privately entertained doubts whether the terms would satisfy the Marāthās who, they felt 'really want the *chauth* of Malwa and Gujarāt which comes to 50 lakhs (annually).' They were also suspicious of the Marāthā *bonafides.* Thus, in a letter to Jai Singh the Mahārānā writes. 'The Deccanis are extremely selfish: you yourself know them well'. In another letter, he urges that 'the salvation of the (Rājpūt) Rajas lay in uniting against the Deccanis'.[51]

The hopes of the rajas for a compromise were based on the existence of internal differences among the Marāthās, and the friendship of the Niẕām. 'Previously, when the elder Maharaja (Jai Singh) went against the Deccanis, Shivaji laid the keys of his 84 forts before him,' wrote an anonymous observer from Udaipur. 'But these are not so (strong). There is an internal enemy in their camp: there is not one kingdom but two. This will be a source of happiness and success (for us). Their power is as yet new (literally, only four days old) but they are gaining strength daily.... The Nizam is friendly to us'.[52]

It is difficult to decide whether a lasting agreement with the Marāthās was possible on the term proposed by the two rajas. The Marāthās were in the habit of regarding every concession as a sign of weakness, and raising fresh demands till they became the dominant partners.[53] On the other hand, the *peshwa* did not, as

50 *Ibid.*

51 *J.R.*: memorandum from Rana Sangram Singh to Jai Singh, d. *Ashādh Sudi,* 24 1782, 24 July 1726 (N.S.) [The date will be 1725 if the year used is not *Shrāvanādi.* But the paper contains a reference to Sarbuland Khān in Gujarāt, and Sarbuland did not reach Gujarāt till December 1725. Hence, the date 1725 indicated by Sir Jadunath in the margin does not seem to be correct (*Hindi Letters* v, 65–8)].

52 *J.R.* (*Hindi Letters* v, 85–6).

53 *Cf.* Duff, 432.

yet, know the full measure of his own power, and he had to reckon with the hostility of the Niẓām, and the opposition of the *pratinidhi* at home. Shāhū's influence, too, was cast on the side of moderation. The financial condition of the Marāthā kingdom was unsatisfactory, and it is possible that in return for a fixed annual sum of 20 lakhs the Marāthạs would have been willing to give up their claim for the full *chauth* of Malwa, and save themselves the cost of years of difficult campaigning with no guarantee of success.

The motives of the two rajas in urging such a pact can only be guessed at. They might have felt that the claims of the Marāthās were irresistable in the long run, and that it was in the best interests of the empire to accept them gracefully while there was still time, before they were faced with other exhorbitant Marāthā demands, and the claim for the full amount of the *chauth* of the two provinces.

Jai Singh might also have hoped that in case of an agreement with the Marāthās, he would be able to secure the *ṣūbahdārī* of Malwa for himself, and thus extend his sphere of influence upto the Narmada. But there does not seem anything treasonable in the proposals. The attempts of some modern writers to prove that Jai Singh acted out of religious sympathy for the Marāthā ideal of a *Hindū-pad-pādshāhī* seems to rest on the doubtful veracity of some letters in the Mandloi *daftar.*[54] It is not borne out by the activities of Jai Singh, or by the contemporary Persian chronicles and Marāthā records.[55]

In October 1729, Jai Singh was appointed as the Governor of Malwa for the second time. He once again urged peace with the Marāthās by conceding to them the *chauth* of Malwa and Gujarāt, setting forth his arguments in a remarkable memorandum which he submitted to the emperor. He pointed out that the 'Marāthās had

54 R. Sinh (*Malwa*, 96–8, 196–9 and *Appendix* I) has established conclusively that the alleged letters of Jai Singh expressing sympathy with the political objectives of the Marāthās are crude forgeries.

55 The gravity of the charge brought against Jai Singh by some of the contemporary Persian chronicles is that he calmly sat at home, supervising the building of Jaipur, and was content to let Imperial governors be defeated without doing anything to help them (Wārid, 119–20, Qāsim, 379, Āshūb). But some other writers make similar charges against Niẓām-ul-Mulk (*cf. T. Hindī*, 550).

tasted Malwa for a long time past. If this year, by reason of our heavy concentration of troops, they were unable to enter the *ṣūbah* or are chastised (after they have entered), you know what heavy expenditure would be necessary for this object every year in the future. I, therefore, suggest that as Raja Shāhū has been ranked as an Imperial *manṣabdār* since the days of Aurangzīb, Your Majesty should give him a *jāgīr* worth ten lakhs of rupees in the name of his (adopted) son, Khushāl Singh, on condition that he prevents any future disturbance in Malwa, and that an auxiliary contingent of his troops serves the *ṣūbahdār* of that province. This will give peace to the land and save us from the expense of campaigning (every year)'.[56]

Thus, it is evident that Jai Singh urged the same policy that a shrewd politician like Niẓām-ul-Mulk pursued throughout his life[57] and recommended to his sons from his death-bed—a policy of trying to live amicably with the Marāthās by judicious compromise, and going to war only as a last resort.[58]

The Marāthā *wakīl*, Dadu Bhīmsen, gave a *sanad* on behalf of Shāhū, under-taking to fulfil Jai Singh's terms. 'Even if five to six lakhs are realized from the *jāgīr* this year, it is acceptable' he wrote. 'In three or four years it should give about ten lakhs'.[59] For settling further details, Jai Singh sent Dip Singh as his envoy to Shāhū. Dip Singh concluded a pact promising 11 lakhs for Malwa

56 *J.R.* (Add. Pers. ii, No. 188, see Appendix B).

57 Thus, in 1725, Niẓām-ul-Mulk wrote to Jai Singh, 'Previously the co-ordination and efforts of many *ṣūbahdārs* were required to subdue the Marāthās. In the time of Aurangzīb and other emperors before him, immense treasure was spent for this purpose, and high Rajas, both cash-holders and *jāgīrdārs* were appointed. Today, the Marāthās have penetrated into the very bones and fibre of the body politic, and their power has increased beyond all bounds' (*J.R., Misc. Papers*, Vol. v, No. 485, 59–61).

58 In his dying will, Niẓām-ul-Mulk wrote '....it behoves the ruler of the Deccan, in his dealings with the Marāthās, who are the *zamindars* of this country, to seek peace and agreement with them. But he should maintain pre-eminently the dignity and prestige of Islam, and never allow them to overstep the bounds...' (Quoted in *Aṣaf Jāh,* 285).

The policy of Jai Singh may have been inspired by Niẓām-ul-Mulk himself. *Cf.* R. Sinh, *Malwa,* 194–5.

59 *J.R. Add. Pers.*, Vol. ii, No. 96, d. 19 *Sha'bān,* Yr. 12, 9 March 1730. Repeated as No. 218 d. 12, *Rabī'* I Yr. 14 (Yr. 12), 15 September 1732.

and 15 lakhs for Gujarāt in lieu of *chauth*. Further, it was stipulated that the Marāthā troops would not cross the Narmada.[60]

At the court, the emperor, never long of one mind, wrote 'agreed' on Jai Singh's memorandum. Then he changed his mind, and charging Jai Singh with 'negligence and sloth', removed him from the governorship of Malwa, and appointed M. Khān Bangash in his place. The latter was ordered to march post-haste to the Narmada, and to drive out the Marāthās from Malwa.[61]

Thus, the policy urged by Jai Singh was not given a trial at all.[62]

For some time after the downfall of the Saiyids, the House of Jodhpur was under a cloud. Two campaigns were undertaken against Ajit Singh between 1720 and 1724, as has been noted already.[63] Ajit Singh was pardoned and restored to *manṣab* in 1724. Soon after this, he was murdered by his son Bakht Singh,[64] and was succeeded by his second son, Abhai Singh.

Abhai Singh lived quietly at Jodhpur between 1724 and 1730 when he was appointed as the Governor of Gujarāt in place of Sarbuland Khan.[65] Abhai Singh perceived at once that he could

60 *S.P.D.* x, 66, 67, 31, 71, 74, 73. Dip Singh went to pay a visit to the Nizam, after he had concluded the agreement, and told him that the visit had been undertaken at the emperor's orders. Sardesai (*Life of Baji Rao*, 149) thinks that Jai Singh's object was to establish peace between the Emperor, the Marāthās and Niẓām-ul-Mulk. But the latter was then intent on his scheme of putting down Baji Rao with the help of a coalition consisting of the Dābhāde, the Senapati and others. He told Dip Singh, 'I place absolutely no trust in the promises of the Marāthās.... or of Baji Rao as an individual. I do not trust him for a *cowrie*' (*S.P.D.* x, 66).

61 *Khujastah*, 347–8, *J.AS.B.*, 1878, 309.

62 Dighe (*Baji Rao*, 120) declares 'The policy of appeasement had been tried with disasterous results'. But what had really produced disaster was not a policy of so-called appeasement, but of half-hearted resistance and refusing to follow either the peace policy advocated by Jai Singh, or the policy of united resistance urged by M. Khān Bangash and some others.

63 See 179–82 above.

64 *J.R. T. Muẓ.*, 337, Kāmwar, *T. Hindi*, 497, Irvine ii, 117–18. *T. Muẓ* thinks that Ajit Singh was murdered at the instance of the *wazīr*, Qamar-ud-Dīn Khān, who hinted that the sins of Ajit Singh were too many to be forgotten. According to Kāmwar, the assassination was due to Ajit Singh's incestuous relations with his daughter-in-law, the wife of Bakht Singh.

65 This appointment is ascribed to the influence of Khān-i-Daurān who wanted to detatch Abhai Singh from the 'Tūrānī' party (Āshūb, 371,

not resist the Marāthā claim for *chauth* with his limited resources. Hence, he confirmed the grant of *chauth* to Baji Rao, and tried to befriend him in order to expel with his help the other Marāthā *sardars* like Kanthāji Kadam and Pilāji Gaekwad from Gujarat.[66] This was followed by a meeting with Baji Rao in February 1731. In return for 13 lakhs as *chauth*, the latter promised to oust Kanthājī Kadam and Pilāji from Gujarāt.[67] Abhai Singh protested vehemently to the court against Khān-i-Daurān's policy of reliance on Niẓām-ul-Mulk and fighting Baji Rao with his help. 'Niẓām-ul-Mulk has sent Baji Rao the original of the emperor's orders communicated to him, M. Khān Bangash and ourselves, in order to convince Baji Rao that in fighting Niẓām-ul-Mulk he was fighting his own man and weakening his own side', he complained. Abhai Singh thought it a great stroke of policy on his part to have befriended Baji Rao and pitted him against Niẓām-ul-Mulk. He claimed that he was thus serving the emperor's cause.[68] But Abhai Singh was soon to be disillusioned. The *peshwa* rendered him no help once he had defeated his rival, the Senapati Dābhāde, at Dabhoi in 1731. The Gaekwads continued to encroach on Gujarāt. In 1732, Abhai Singh treacherously murdered Pilāji, and seized Baroda. But he failed to gain any lasting advantage, and after losing Baroda in 1734, retired to Delhi where he joined hands with the party led by the *wazīr* Qamar-ud-Dīn Khān in urging armed resistance to the Marāthās.[69]

Mir'āt ii, 115, *Siyar*, 462). Sarbuland's policy of granting *chauth* was not approved by the court at the time.

66 *S.P.D.* xv, 82.

67 *Mir'āt* ii, 133–5, *Surat Factory Records*, 614.

68 Abhai Singh's letter d. 14 *Sudi Chait*, 1787 (*Shrāwanādi*), 10 April 1731, quoted by V. Reu in *I.H.R.C. Proc.*, 1939, 112–14.

Niẓām-ul-Mulk complained to M. Khān Bangash that Abhai Singh was trying to befriend Baji Rao (*Khujastah*, 331). The Emperor's instruction to the governors of Malwa and Gujarāt evidently was to co-operate with the Niẓām, for the latter wrote thanking the Emperor for his orders (*Gulshan-i-Aj'ib*, quoted in *Aṣaf Jāh*, 198).

V.V., 847 has got the facts all wrong. It asserts that Baji Rao came and besieged Baroda, and that the Niẓām came upto Surat to help Abhai Singh who wrote him a letter of thanks.

69 *Mir'āt* ii, 120–50, Letters of Abhai, cited by Reu in *I.H.R.C.*, 1938, 1939, 1942. But Abhai Singh took no active part in the campaigns. According to

Thus, a sharp divergence came to exist between the attitudes of Jai Singh and Abhai Singh towards the Marāthās. This shows that religious considerations played little role in determining the relations of individual Rājpūt rajas with the Marāthās.

Unlike both the Kachhwāhās and the Rathors, the Bundelas rendered active assistance to the Marāthās from 1728 when Chhatrasāl summoned their help to repel an invasion by M. Khān Bangash, the Governor of Allahabad. The Bundela chief agreed to pay an annual tribute of Rs 65,000 which was converted into a *jāgīr* for the Peshwa after Chhatrasāl's death in 1731.[70] In 1733, the former defensive agreement was supplemented by an agreement for offensive action. It was agreed that the Bundelas would join the *peshwa*'s standard and give him aid when he invaded foreign territory or marched on Delhi. Chhatrasāl's son, Hirdesa, with his eye on Orchha, dreamt of extending his territory in that direction, and the *peshwa* promised to share the state with him half and half.[71]

Thus, the fear of the Imperial Governor of Allahabad and the desire to aggrandize themselves at the cost of their neighbours and the empire threw the Bundelas into a partnership with the Marāthās. Consequently, the Marāthās acquired a very useful base to strike at the vital *Dū'āb* area which formed a part of the dominions of Sa'ādat Khān. From the *Dū'āb*, the Marāthās could strike eastwards into Bihar and Bengal, or march on Delhi.

The establishment of the Marāthās in Bundelkhand brought the Marāthā danger to the door steps of Sa'ādat Khān. Ever since his appointment to Awadh, in 1722, Sa'ādat Khān had been consolidating his position there by subduing the local *zamindars*, and extending his dominions towards the line of the Jamuna in the south, and eastwards towards Bihar.[72] His interests thus clashed

---

Ghulām Ḥusain, 'he retired to his country where he devoted himself to the intoxication of opium. He slept the whole day and spent the whole night in asking what was to be done; yet whenever he was sent for by Khān-i-Daurān, he used to expulpate himself by alleging the necessity of defending his own hereditary dominions and by bringing forward such futile excuses'. (*Siyar* 474).

70 *S.P.D.* xii, 34, xxx, 288.

71 *S.P.D.* xiv, 7–9, *Br. Ch.*, 44. *S.P.D.* xxx, 210–11.

72 Thus, about 1728, he leased the *sarkārs* of Banaras, Jaunpur, Chunargarh and Ghazipur from one Murtaẓa' Khān. In 1735, he was given the *faujdārī* of

with those of Jai Singh and M. Khān Bangash both of whom had their eyes on the rich *Dū'āb* lands. This made cooperation between them, even against the Marāthās, extremely difficult. The jealousy between M. Khān Bangash and Sa'ādat Khān was of old standing. The latter had refused to help when M. Khān was besieged by the Marāthās at Jaitpur in 1728.[73]

Sa'ādat Khān seems to have remained away from the court for most of the time till 1733, when the growing threat of the Marāthās to *Dū'āb* brought him to Delhi. He then urged a policy of determined resistance to their growing encroachments.

M. Khān Bangash was a typical Afghān adventurer. In gratitude for his help against Jahāndār Shah, Farrukh Siyar granted him a tract of land around modern Farrukhabād. Soon, M. Khān converted Farrukhabād into a centre of Afghān power. After the assassination of Ḥusain 'Alī, he rose to the rank of 6,000, and then of 7,000. He was appointed the *ṣūbahdār* of Allahabad[74] in 1722, and remained in charge of that province till 1729. His constant preoccupation during this period was to chastise the Bundelas who had seized many royal lands on the other side of the Jamuna, and had virtually confiscated all the *jāgīrs* of the Imperial *manṣabdārs* in Bundelkhand. In November 1726, he led a campaign against the Bundelas, with the results already noted.[75] It is said that Khān-i-Daurān prevented the emperor from giving him any help by pointing to the danger that a successful Afghān general would present to the monarchy.[76]

M. Khān Bangash warned Jai Singh about the seriousness of the Marāthā danger, and the real nature of their ambitions. He wrote, 'The Marāthās are deceitful and would overthrow him and the Bundelas after they have established themselves in their country.' The only way, he suggested, was that 'the Maharaja Dhiraj (Jai Singh) who had *jāgīrs* worth crores, and lakhs of men, should

Kora-Jahānābād, for the suppression of the *zamindar* Adārū (*First Two Nawabs*, 49–50). Sa'ādat Khān also intrigued constantly for the provinces of Agra and Allahabad (*Iqbāl*, 195–6, *Khujastah*, 118–19).

73 *J.A.S.B.*, 1878, 297–300.

74 Āshūb i, 558, *J.A.S.B.*, 1878, 283; *Iqbāl*, 162.

75 See pp. 223, 234 above.

76 Wārid, 24, *Iqbāl*, 168. Chhatrasāl had opened peace negotiations with M. Khān, and his sons had become so friendly with the Khan that a rumour had gained currency that an Afghan-Bundela pact had been formed.

join hands with other nobles and pay attention to the task (of driving out the Marāthās)—though he had sufficient means of his own not to depend on any one. The emperor himself should come to Agra. If this was done the mere handful of Marāthās could easily be checked and driven across the Narmada'. M. Khān Bangash also warned Jai Singh of the danger of the Marāthā-Bundela combine, adding that 'if they once take Agra, their boldness would increase beyond all bounds'.[77]

After the departure of Niẓām-ul-Mulk for the Deccan, two almost equally balanced groups emerged among the nobles at the court. One of these was led by the *wazīr*, Qamar-ud-Dīn Khān, and the other by the Chief *Bakhshī*, Khān-i-Daurān.

Qamar-ud-Dīn Khān was the son of M. Amīn Khān. He has been described as 'a munificent friend, a bountiful patron, and an enemy of oppression.' We are told that he perceived the dangers facing the empire better than any of his contemporaries. But he was a weak *wazīr*, wanting in activity and firmness, and rather too fond of pleasure. He was so negligent of business that he never attended any consultations, and sometimes absented himself from the court for long periods.[78] He had the complete trust and confidence of the emperor. Like his father, he, also, was a great patron of the Mughals, and it is said that he employed only Mughals and Turks in his service.[79]

The leader of the second group was *Bakhshī-ul-Mamālik* Khān-i-Daurān. He has been described as 'a learned man, and fond of the company of the learned.' His character in personal life was above reproach, and he was not personally corrupt or intent on private gain,[80] which was more than could be said of most of his

77 *Khujastah*, 281, 288, 208.

78 *Ḥikāyat* (A.S.B. Ms.), *Iqbāl*, 215, *M.U.*, 381, *Siyar*, 870.

79 Āshūb i, 230, 558, 562, ii, 102.

80 *Khazīnah-i-Āmirah*, 246, *M.U.* i, 836. Thus, when Ja'far Khān, the *ṣūbahdār* of Bengal, died and was succeeded by his son, Shuja'-ud-Daulah, the latter sent besides *peshkash* a large sum of money for Khān-i-Daurān. But the latter deposited this sum along with the *peshkash* in the Imperial Treasury.

In a letter to M. Khān Bangash in 1731, Khān-i-Daurān set forth his incorruptibility with great vehemence, and asserted that apart from an increment of one crore *dāms* he had not gained any additional *jāgīrs* since the accession of M. Shāh, or made any money out of transfers (*Khujastah*, 255–6).

contemporaries, for bribery was openly rampant in the court at the time under the guise of presents (*peshkash*), and even the emperor was said to share in it. Nor was Khān-i-Daurān wanting in understanding and loyalty to the ruling dynasty and the empire. He did not attempt to carve out a semi-independent principality for himself like many others. But he lacked the tenacity of purpose necessary for the fulfilment of any coherent policy in a faction-ridden court, and possessed little military capacity which made him shrink from war and place an excessive reliance on diplomacy.[81]

After the downfall of the Saiyids, Khān-i-Daurān was looked upon as the leader of the Hindustanis. Though his grandfather, Khwājah 'Abd'ul Mun'im had come to India from Bukhārā (Tūrān) at about the same time as Qamar-ud-Dīn's grand-uncle, 'Ālam Shaikh, the saintly life and calling of Khān-i-Daurān's family and his own co-mingling with ordinary soldiers early in his life had made him adopt the Indian manner of dress. He could not even speak Persian properly.[82] He had been loosely allied with the Rājpūt chieftain, Jai Singh, since 1715 and it was at his instance that Ajit Singh was paradoned and restored to the *ṣūbahdārī* of

81 *Siyar,* 464 says, 'Khān-i-Daurān, having fancied to himself that the evils that were undermining the Empire of Hindustan could be remedied by dint of policy, and lost countries recovered by art and cunning, expected to bring everything into order by a knack at negotiations and by tricks of leger de main... But in general, this minister was exceedingly unlucky. Every scheme which he projected turned out to the detriment and dishonour of the Empire.'

Āshūb (250) says that 'the *Amīr* was clever, gifted with judgement and discretion. He had dignity and maintained prestige, and he was endowed with charming manners and just feelings, and was a good commander... (though) he never even took the muster of his soldiers.... Excepting two defects, he was accomplished in all respects: he was very showy and proud of his parts but internally he was petty, and once the name of war reached him he would tremble.

'Secondly, his consideration for the infidel...'

82 *Risālah-i-Khān-i-Daurān* (I.O.L. Ms.), '*Imād,* 35, *Khazīnah,* 246, Yaḥyā 119b, Āshūb, 72.

Khān-i-Daurān was descended from a famous family of *Naqshbandīs*. His ancestor, Khān Bahā-ud-Dīn, had been the *Pīr* and *Murshid* of all Tūrān and Turkistan (Āshūb, 253). Khān-i-Daurān was one of five brothers, he and Muẓaffar Khān being from one mother, and the other three brothers from another.

Ajmer after the downfall of the Saiyids.[83] It is said that he employed only Hindustanis as soldiers. He was liberal in matters of faith: we are told that he practised *yoga*, and had attained considerable skill in holding breath (*ḥasb-i-dam*).[84]

Apart from these two leading nobles and their followers, there was a third group consisting of the personal favourites of the emperor, led by a woman of talent, Kūkī Jiū,[85] and the holy man. 'Abd'ul Ghafūr.[86] The part played by these two in bringing about the departure of Niẓām-ul-Mulk from the court has been already noted. Both Kūkī Jiū and Shāh 'Abd'ul Ghafūr continued to exercise considerable influence after the departure of Niẓām-ul-Mulk. 'Abd'ul Ghafūr, in particular, was said to be so influential that the emperor would do nothing in opposition to his wishes.[87] He

83 K.K., 938, *Siyar,* 453, *T. Muẓ,* 320

84 Āshūb, 250, *Siwānih-i-Khushgū* (O.P.L. Ms.) *f.* 140a–41b. His brother, Ja'far Khān, the holy man, was suspected of *Imāmite* tendencies (M.M., 53a–64a),

85 Daughter of geomancer, Jān M. Khān, who came into favour as result of some successful prophesies about Muḥammad Shāh. She was found useful by the queen mother in carrying messages to and fro. To give her a status, and facility of ingress and egress, it was given out that she was the foster-sister (*dū-gānā*) of the emperor (Wārid, 44, Āshūb, 161). It is doubtful that she ever became the mistress of the emperor, but she enjoyed great influence with him. K.K. (ii, 940) calls her 'a woman of great charm and intelligence.'

Four of her brothers held the rank of 5,000, and various other posts at the court. (Āshūb, 165–8, *T. Muẓ.*, 351).

86 It is said that he was a cotton-weaver. He claimed to know all sciences, and the art of controlling *jins* and spirits, and to see into the future. According to Shiv Dās (150), he was an obscure *faqīr* in Bahādur Shāh's time, and was presented to Farrukh Siyar by M. Amīn, and granted an allowance of Rs 500 per month and Sadarpur and Rohtas in *āl-ṭamghah.* He took part in the conspiracy against Ḥusain 'Alī, carrying messages to and from the palace, dressed as a milk-maid. He considered himself responsible for the downfall of the Saiyids and presumed accordingly (Āshūb, 229). During the *wizārat* of Niẓām-ul-Mulk, his power was so great that we are told revenue and administrative matters came to him before they came to Niẓām (*Iqbāl,* 150). Niẓām-ul-Mulk did not like this interference, but outwardly maintained good relations with him, due to his past connections with M. Amīn who had paid great deference to him (Āshūb, 229). After becoming the *wazīr,* Qamar-ud-Dīn kept good relations with him, and the latter posing as a friend, used to carry letters between him and the emperor (*Iqbāl,* 150, Āshūb, 229, Wārid, 58–71, *T. Muẓ.*, 350).

87 Wārid, 60.

interfered particularly in the revenue department. Neither Kūkī nor 'Abd'ul Ghafūr held any important posts, or high rank in the hierarchy of nobles. 'Abd'ul Ghafūr's influence seems to have rested largely on the superstitious belief of the emperor and his mother in his magical powers and ability to look into the future. The primary object of Kūkī and 'Abd'ul Ghafūr appears to have been personal enrichment. Since they enjoyed the confidence of the emperor, they were approached by governors and other needy people even from far-off places like Bengal, Thatta and Kashmīr. In return for their intercession with the emperor they received suitable presents, part of which found their way into the Imperial treasury by way of *peshkash*. Thus, the emperor was satisfied, while the two amassed a fortune of lakhs and crores.[88]

Two other personages were allied with Kūkī's gang from the very beginning: these were Khwājah Khidmatgār Khān, the *Nāẓir-i-Ḥaram*,[89] and Roshan-ud-Daulah Ẓafar Khān Pānīpatī, the third *Bakhshī*. Both were old employees of the state. Khwājah Khidmatgār had been trained under Aurangzīb and gave an impression of ability. It is said that he was averse to bribery and hence fell out with Kūkī Jiū.[90] Roshan-ud-Daulah was a supple courtier and had been associated with every group since 1713.[91] Like Khān-i-Daurān,

88 Āshūb, 170–2, 159, 228, Qāsim, 381–2 (Sarkar's Ms.).

89 His real name was Kh. Ambar. He had received training under Aurangzīb which gave him a superficial gloss of efficiency. He was in charge of all household affairs since the last days of Aurangzīb. In the early years of Muḥammad Shāh, he received the rank of 5,000/5,000 through Kūkī (Wārid, 44. Āshūb, 158 says 6,000/6,000), and a fringed *palki*—a distinction which till Bahādur Shāh's time, had been reserved for the princes.

90 Wārid, 47.

91 A Tūrānī who had long been settled in Panipat. His grand-father, Nāṣir Khān, had come to India in the time of Shāh Jahān and got a *manṣab* through Shuja'. (*M.U.* ii, 533, Āshūb, 57b, Wārid, 29, Irvine ii, 258). One of his brothers, Fakhr-ud-Daulah, was for long the Governor of Bihar, and subsequently, of Gujarāt which he attempted vainly to recover from the Marāthās. He had the reputation of being a brave officer (Āshūb, 193). Roshan-ud-Daulah had been found on every side during the *wizārat* of the Saiyids. He was related by marriage to Sher Afgan Khān, and, in 1730–1, also contracted a marriage alliance with Niẓām-ul-Mulk, by marrying his daughter to the latter's son Nāṣir Khān (*T. Muẓ*, 329). It is said that this made Muḥammad Shāh suspicious of him and his downfall began from that date.

Ẓafar Khān considered himself to be a Hindustani, and employed Indian Afghāns in his contingent.

The gang of favourites was not identified with any particular policy or group of nobles at the court. Hence, its political importance should not be over-rated. The influence of the favourites was erratic and fitful. They hindered the pursuance of any coherent state policy, and sometimes caused great resentment and annoyance to the ministers. Khān-i-Daurān openly inveighed against them on more than one occasion.[92] and it was due partly to his intrigues in conjunction with Sa'ādat Khān that 'Abd'ul Ghafūr and Kūkī Jiū fell from power in 1732–3.[93]

Thus, during the early phase of the Marāthā advance into Malwa and Gujarāt, the court and the leading nobles were paralysed by internal divisions, and by the domination of worthless favourites.

Khān-i-Daurān's policy was essentially one of balance of power. He desired that no noble or provincial governor should be allowed to become so strong as to create the danger of his establishing a personal domination, as had been done by the Saiyids and by M. Amīn Khān, and was apparently the aim of Niẓām-ul-Mulk. In particular, it implied that Niẓām-ul-Mulk, who was regarded as the source of all evil, should be carefully check-mated—if necessary, with the help of the Marāthās.

In pursuance of this policy, Khān-i-Daurān had refused to give any help to M. Khān Bangash against the Bundelas in 1728 by

---

Ashūb gives extravagant descriptions of his wealth. He dressed in gorgeous clothes of silver. Even his elephants and horses carried '*amāirs* and chains and saddles and trappings etc. all made of silver. Similarly, in his house, curtains and floors, the *mekh* and *tanā*, the walls and ceiling from the *naqqārah-khānah* to the *dīwān-khānah* and his *masnad* were full of rows upon rows of silver, Whenever he passed through the *bazars*, he scattered bag-fulls of silver, and all business came to a standstill (Āshūb, 170–2).

92 Āshūb, 190.

93 Most contemporary histories give lengthy details of the fall of these favourites (Wārid, 60–70, *Ibqāl,* 175–80. Āshūb, 225–48). The charge against all the three, 'Abd'ul Ghafūr, Kūkī Jiū and Roshan-ud-Daulah was misappropriation of money, which were brought to the Emperor's notice either by chance of by the contrivances of Khān-i-Daurān and Sa'ādat Khān. Kh. Khidmatgār died in 1732; 'Abd'ul Ghafūr was sent to the fort of Gwalior where he died. Roshan-ud-Daulah continued to be in disgrace for some time, but was rehabilitated through Khān-i-Daurān to whom he is alleged to have paid a bribe of one crore in cash (Āshūb, 190).

playing upon the fears of Muḥammad Shāh that a successful Afghān general would constitute a grave threat to the Timurid monarchy.

Again in 1725, Khān-i-Daurān strove to bring about an alliance of Jai Singh Sawai and Kanhoji Bhonsle to counteract the alliance of Niẓām-ul-Mulk and Baji Rao. Sarbuland Khān, Saif-ud-Dīn 'Alī Khān, Saiyid Ḥusain Khān the Governor of Ajmer, and a number of other nobles including the *ṣūbahdār* of Malwa were asked to help Jai Singh. A sum of fifty lakhs was allotted for the campaign from the royal treasury. Kānhoji Bhonsle, who had earlier helped Mubāriẓ Khān against Niẓām-ul-Mulk, deputed his brother Santāji Sawai to meet Jai Singh on the Narmada with 25,000 horse and 25,000 foot, and stated that Raja Sultānji Nimbālkar would join with 50,000 foot and 50,000 *jazā'il* as soon as a noble was appointed from the court. He even hinted that Shāhū was friendly.[94]

But the campaign never came off due to the luke-warm support of Jai Singh who had already established friendly contacts with the Marāthās, and disregarded the appeal of Khān-i-Daurān to come to the court 'if only for a day.'

It may be surmised that the court was not sorry to see Niẓām-ul-Mulk and Baji Rao fall out among themselves subsequently. The court hoped that this would give the empire a respite from Marāthā incursions. However, when Niẓām-ul-Mulk purchased a respite from the Marāthās at the cost of the empire, the nobles loudly accused Niẓām-ul-Mulk of treachery and collusion with the Marāthās. In October 1729, at the instance of Khān-i-Daurān, Jai Singh was appointed the Governor of Malwa and granted 13 lakhs of rupees to raise an army to drive out the Marāthās. He advocated peace with the Marāthās on certain conditions, as has been noted above. The emperor agreed at first, then changed his mind, and appointed M. Khān Bangash as the governor to implement a policy of stern resistance to the Marāthās.

Similarly, in Gujarāt, Sarbuland Khān, who had made a pact for *chauth* with the Marāthās, was replaced by Abhai Singh.[95]

The main reason for this sudden change of policy seems to have been the bombastic promises made by Niẓām-ul-Mulk. He had been attempting, once again, to organise an anti-Baji Rao coalition with the aid of the *senapati* and the *pratinidhi*. For a sum of 50 lakhs

94 *J.R.* (*Add. Pers.*, Vol. ii, 39, 40, 189, 118–22, v 92).
95 See 239, 243, 247 above.

from the court, he promised to clear the Marāthās from Malwa and Gujarāt.[96]

The offer of Niẕām-ul-Mulk was not accepted as the court continued to be deeply suspicious of his motives and actions. But M. Khān Bangash and Abhai Singh were ordered to co-operate with Niẕām-ul-Mulk in resisting the Marāthās. M. Khān Bangash hurried to the Narmada, and for 12 days conferred with Niẕām-ul-Mulk (about 26 March to 7 April). It was agreed to concert measures against the 'enemies of Islam', or rather, against Baji Rao and his party.[97] But the terms were not adhered to by M. Khān Bangash who attacked and razed to the ground the forts of Kākalī and Chikalatā belonging to Udāji Pawār who was said to be favourable to the anti-Baji Rao party.[98] Shortly afterwards, at Dabhoi, Baji Rao defeated Trimbakrao Dābhāde on whom Niẕām-ul-Mulk had built his hopes of destroying Baji Rao.[99] Niẕām-ul-Mulk now changed sides and concluded a pact with Baji Rao, a secret clause in which is said to have left the latter free to pursue his own schemes in the north.[100] This was followed by a secret meeting between Niẕām-ul-Mulk and Baji Rao at Rohe Rameshwar near the Moja river, near Ausa.[101]

The effect of this *volte face* on Niẕām-ul-Mulk's part was that the old suspicion between him and the court was revived, and any hopes of a joint front of the two against the Marāthās vanished for many years to come. The bitterness felt against Niẕām-ul-Mulk may be gauged from the fact that in 1732, Sa'ādat Khān

96 *Gulshan-i-Ajā'ib* (*Āṣaf Jāh*, 196),

In view of this, and the fact that M. Khān Bangash throughout kept the emperor informed of his projected meeting with Niẕām-ul-Mulk, it does not seem correct to regard the removal of M. Khān from the governorship of Malwa in 1731 due to his alleged collusion with the Niẕām (*Cf. T. Hindi*, 516, Irvine, *J.A.S.B.*, 1878, 328–34).

97 *Khujastah*, 328–36, *J.A.S.B.*, 1878, 311–13, *Aḥwāl*, 199–200. See also Irvine ii, 250–1.

98 *Khujastah*, 17–20, *J.A.S.B.*, 1878, 315–16.

98 See Dighe, 38–9.

100 *Khujastah*, 336–44.

101 *S.P.D.* xxx, 90, 91, 104, 105, 6, 83, Vad i, 55.

The dates of many of these papers are wrong. The meeting took place on *Pausha Vandya*, 2/20 *Rajab*/Wednesday 27 December 1732 (O.S., 6 January 1733 N.S.).

approached the Peshwa through the Bundela *wakil*, and, on behalf of the emperor, offered to accept the *peshwa*'s claim to nominate the *ṣūbahdārs* of the Deccan, and Malwa, and such other minor claims as he might present. But in return he stipulated that Niẓām-ul-Mulk must be 'taken care of'. To complete the negotiations, Sa'ādat Khān even offered to meet the *peshwa* in Malwa or Orchha, whichever place was suitable.[102]

The full effects of the new pact between Niẓām-ul-Mulk and the Peshwa were felt by the Mughals before long. In the campaigning season of 1731–2, the Marāthās invaded Malwa with more than 80,000 horse. M. Khān Bangash found his resources quite inadequate to the task of meeting this force, and sought a way out of his difficulties by forming a private pact with the Marāthās, agreeing to pay them one year's *chauth* for Malwa.[103] The principal demand for which the Marāthās had struggled for so long in Malwa was tacitly accepted by the Mughal governor in this way.

Thus, towards the end of 1731 and the beginning of 1732, the Mughal–Marāthā relations in Malwa entered a new phase.

102 *S.P.D.* xiv, 9
103 *Khujastah*, 139–43.

CHAPTER IX

Conquest of Malwa and Bundelkhand (1732–42)

THE PROGRESS OF MARĀTHĀ ARMIES

Soon after his verbal agreement with the Marāthās for the *chauth* of Malwa (1732), M. Khān Bangash was superseded as the governor of that province. Jai Singh Sawai was appointed in his place on condition that he maintained 30,000 horse and foot in equal numbers, two-third of the total income of the province from the land, tribute etc. being assigned to him for their expenses. But to impose a check upon him, it was stipulated that the *dīwān* of the province would maintain 18,000 horse and get one-third of the revenue which he was to collect through his own men. The raja's deputy was to remain in the province for at least six months in the year during the raja's absence.[1]

No governor had till then been given the resources which were placed at Jai Singh's disposal. He held the province of Agra in addition to Malwa, and could supplement the 48,000 horse and foot there by his own Jaipur contingent and the forces of the local rajas who were appointed to his army. In addition to the revenues from Malwa, he received a sum of 20 lakhs from the Emperor—13 lakhs as grant, and 7 lakhs as loan.[2]

In view of the raja's well known advocacy of a peaceful settlement with the Marāthās, it is hardly likely that he was appointed

1 *J.R.*, Aya Mal's Letter d. *Asauj Badi*, 13, 1789, 6 September 1732. (*Hindi Letters*, Vol. iii, Nos 28–9, pp. 48–51).

2 *Khujastah*, 314–15, *Vamsh*, 3212, Wārid, 115–16.

to Malwa to offer irreconcilable resistance to them. It rather seems that he was required to make a demonstration of strength before peace negotiations were undertaken.

Jai Singh reached Malwa in December 1732. The Marāthās swept into the province under Holkar who soon hemmed in the forces of Jai Singh at Mandsaur. News of an intended march by the emperor himself raised the spirits of the besieged who drove away Holkar 16 *kos* from Mandsaur. But the latter doubled back on his tracks, and Jaipur now lay open before him. In alarm, Jai Singh offered to make peace with the Marāthās. In March 1733, he agreed to pay 6 lakhs in cash (as indemnity), and to assign to the Peshwa 28 *parganas* in Malwa in lieu of *chauth*.[3]

This agreement marks a new stage in the Mughal-Marāthā struggle in Malwa. Hitherto, the Marāthās had been claiming *chauth* and *sardeshmukhi*, and urging its commutation into a lump annual sum of a *jāgīr*. Now, the ceding of certain *parganas* was demanded in lieu of *chauth*. Thus, all pretence of *chauth* being a payment in return for protection or refraining from plunder was dropped. The claim for *chauth* was revealed as merely an excuse for territorial aggrandizement. Henceforward, the demand for the *chauth* and *sardeshmukhī* of Malwa goes increasingly into the background, and the complete surrender of the province is demanded. Already, the Marāthās felt so secure in Malwa that in July 1732 the *peshwa* divided the province among his chief captains Sindhia, Holkar and the two Pawār brothers.[4]

No confirmation of Jai Singh's agreement was forthcoming, and next year (1733–4), the Marāthās raided Rājpūtānā on the one hand, and on the other, laid contributions on the states of Datia, Orchha, etc. The Marāthā armies were joined by the sons of Chhatrasāl Bundela who had formed an agreement with Appā in 1733, by which they were to help the Marāthās, and to share their conquests across the Jumna.[5]

The ever-extending sweep of the Marāthā depredations at last awakened the court to a sense of real danger, and between 1732 and 1735, three campaigns were undertaken to drive the Marāthās out of Malwa. In 1732–3, the *wazīr*, Qamar-ud-Dīn Khān, advanced

3 *S.P.D.* xiv, 2, 7, 9, xv, 6, xxx, pp. 310–11; *V.V.* ii, 1218–20.

4 *S.P.D.* xxii, 55, 82, R. Sinh, *Malwa*, 226.

5 *S.P.D.* xiv, 10, 13, 18 (the correct date of xiv, 13 is 9 April 1734).

upto the borders of Malwa with 80,000–90,000 men and camped in Gwalior district at Sheopuri. He sent A'ẓīmullāh Khān to chase the Marāthās who had been keeping a distance of 10–15 *kos* from the Imperial armies. A'ẓīmullāh caught up with Pilāji and, according to Shiv Dās, inflicted a defeat upon him, forcing the Marāthās to re-cross the Narmada. Content with this victory, A'ẓīmullāh then rejoined the *Wazīr.*[6] Meanwhile, the news of Jai Singh's defeat at Mandsaur was already known. No attempt was made to re-establish a defensive line on the Narmada in order to prevent future Marāthā incursions into Malwa. The rajas of Orchha and Rao Ram Chandra pressed the *Wazīr* to lead a campaign against the sons of Chhatrasāl who were in league with the Marāthās, and to crush them. The *wazīr* advanced upto the boundary of Raja Jagat Rai when he heard of a well-organized rebellion by a *zamindar,* Adārū, in his *jāgīr* in Ghāzīpur, and the death of his son-in-law, Niṣār Khān, at his hands. Greatly incensed, the *Wazīr* marched to that place and invested it. Shiv Dās was an eye-witness and has left a long account of the fight that followed. The defiance of the Imperial *Wazīr* by a petty *zamindar* graphically illustrates the decline of Imperial power and prestige.[7]

In 1733–4, the senseless proceeding of the previous year was repeated by Muẓaffar Khān, the brother of Khān-i-Daurān. Muẓaffar Khān advanced upto Sironj without encountering the Marāthās, and then returned without taking any steps for safeguarding Malwa from future Marāthā incursions.[8]

The climax of the Imperial efforts was reached in 1734–5 when two huge armies under the *Wazīr* Qamar-ud-Dīn Khān, and the *Bakhshī-ul-Mamālik* Khān-i-Daurān respectively were readied in order to drive the Marāthās beyond the Narmada. Khān-i-Daurān

6 *Iqbāl,* 183–4. No other source mentions any conflict between the forces of the *wazīr* and the Marāthās this year. According to the Marāthā sources, (*S.P.D.* xiv, 9), the Marāthās had collected their dues and retired before the *wazīr* reached Malwa.

7 *Iqbāl,* 194–6, *S.P.D.* xiv, 9.

8 *T. Hindī,* 525, *Siyar,* 467, Irvine ii, 279.

According to Āshūb (286–7), when Muẓaffar Khān reached Malwa, he dug trenches around his camp and waited for Malhār to attack. But Malhār refused to oblige him. Instead, he surrounded his camp and cut off his supplies. At length, with the approach of the rainy season, the Marāthās retired across the Narmada and Muẓaffar Khān returned to Delhi.

was joined by all the Rājpūt rajas, including Jai Singh, Abhai Singh and Durjan Sāl of Kotah. Holkar's raid into Rājpūtānā had opened their eyes, and in 1734, at the instance of Jai Singh, the rajas had met in a conference and taken a pledge of united resistance to the Marāthās.[9] The *Wazīr* commanded a force of 25,000, and Khān-i-Daurān upward of 50,000 men.[10] But this mighty host found itself helpless once more in the face of the Marāthā light cavalry. Khān-i-Daurān and Jai Singh were surrounded and cut off at Toda Tank, and Jaipur lay defenceless before the Marāthās. At last, at the instance of Jai Singh, Khān-i-Daurān opened negotiations and agreed to give 22 lakhs annually to the Marāthās as the *chauth* of Malwa.[11] Qamar-ud-Dīn Khān had a light skirmish with Pilāji Jādav near Narwar, but he could not inflict any serious damage on the Marāthā forces.[12]

These campaigns demonstrated once again the failure of the Mughals to find an answer to the Marāthā light cavalry tactics. This failure dated from the time of Malik Ambar and Shāhjī Bhonsle when Marāthā light-cavalry units had first made an organized appearance in the Deccan. Nor was an adequate answer to the Marāthā tactics to be found till the Rohillas adopted the quick-firing musket whose effectiveness was first demonstrated by Nādir Shāh at the battle of Panipat.[13] The Mughal armies, with their long baggage trains and heavy guns were more fit for positional warfare. Such a warfare, though presenting many difficulties, was still possible as long as the Marāthās had not crossed the line of the

9 *V.V.*, 1220–1.

10 *S.P.D.* xiv, 22, 23. The Marāthā *Wakīl* at Dhār, Nāro Sheodeo estimated the combined forces of Jai Singh, Khān-i-Daurān and Abhai Singh at 200,000 horse and innumerable foot. *Itihas Sangrah* (*Ait. Chariten,* Letter 68), places the number at 50,000 which seems more probable.

11 *S.P.D.* xiv, 21, 23, 24, 26, 27, 29, 57, xxii, 284; *T. Hindī*, 526–7. Irvine's account based on Āshūb is very confused. See Appendix 'A'.

Qāsim (Sarkar Ms., 385) makes out that the Marāthās had attacked at the instance of Jai Singh himself. Jai Singh accused the Niẓām of encouraging the Marāthās, and according to the author, persuaded Khān-i-Daurān to make peace with the Marāthās in order to prevent (recurring) Marāthā raids. Hence, 22 lakhs annually was granted, and Mahādeo Bhatt accompanied Khān-i-Daurān to Delhi.

12 *T. Hindī*, 528–9.

13 See Sarkar, *Fall of the Mughal Empire*, 30–1.

Narmada. With the final establishment of the Marāthās in south Malwa in 1732, the military problem for the imperialists changed entirely. They had now to fight a war of manoeuvre in the open plains where the Marāthā light cavalry was more formidable than ever, since it could hover round the Mughal armies outside the range of their heavy guns, and cut off their supplies and communications. Only after beating the Marāthās in a fight in the open plains could the Imperialists expel them from Malwa, and re-establish the line of the Narmada. The Mughals could devise no solution to this problem, and repeatedly found that the despatch of large armies against the Marāthās in Malwa failed to make any permanent impression on them, and left the *Dū'āb*, Rājpūtānā, and even Delhi dangerously exposed to Marātha raids.

THE 'PEACE' AND THE 'WAR' PARTIES AT THE COURT

In the circumstances, two groups representing different policies came to the fore at the court. One group, led by Khān-i-Daurān and Jai Singh, urged peace with the Marāthās; the other, led by Qamar-ud-Dīn Khān and Sa'ādat Khān favoured continued warfare with still greater preparations, and securing the support of the Niẕām for the purpose. M. Sarbuland Khān and Roshan-ud-Daulah supported the 'war' party.[14]

Three years of campaigning had only led to the reaffirmation of Jai Singh's agreement of 1733 for *chauth*. Sa'ādat Khān charged Jai Singh with treachery and accused him of collusion with his co-religionists. 'Jai Singh has ruined the empire by his secret support to the Marāthās', he declared. 'Give me only the governorship of Malwa and Agra. I do not ask for any monetary aid; Jai Singh may ask for crores but I do not need them. My treasury is full. The Niẕām is my friend. He will hinder the Marāthās from crossing the Narmada'.[15]

14 *S.P.D.* xx, 134. Sarbuland Khān had been forbidden the court for 1,000 days after his unauthorised fight with Abhai Singh who had replaced him as the governor of Gujarāt (*Sa'ādat-i-Jāwid* of Harnam Das, Elliot viii, 340). He was now back at the court.

15 *S.P.D.* xiv, 47. M. Khān Bangash revealed, however, that Sa'ādat Khān had asked for four *ṣūbahs* and the post of *Mīr Bakhshi*. The emperor was said to be willing to give two *ṣūbahs* and two crores (*S.P.D.* xxx, 134). Many other proposals were also made: that M. Khān should be given Agra or Malwa, and

When the emperor also joined in censuring Khān-i-Daurān and Jai Singh, Khān-i-Daurān replied, 'The Marāthās cannot be effectually subdued by fighting. By friendly negotiations, I shall induce either the Peshwa or his brother to come and meet Your Majesty. If his demands are accepted, there will be no disturbance in the Imperial domains in the near future. If, on the other hand, Sa'ādat Khān and the Niẓām combine, they will set up another monarch'.[16]

Khān-i-Daurān and Jai Singh were obviously of the opinion that it was not possible to fight the Marāthās successfully and that a policy of reconciliation with them was the only feasible policy. They played upon the emperor's fear that some of the powerful nobles might combine to set up a new monarch if they were placed at the head of large armies, and secured his consent for peace negotiations with the Marāthās. They also exploited the emperor's deep-seated suspicion of Niẓām-ul-Mulk's policies. In fact, it was difficult to follow the tortuous twists in the Niẓām's policy, and to place any confidence in his assurances. He had befriended the Marāthās in 1725 and 1728, and betrayed them both times. In 1731, he had proposed to M. Khān Bangash a joint campaign against the Marāthās and then concluded a treaty with Baji Rao in 1732. But, as before, he was prepared to betray this treaty also. In 1735, he moved upto Burhānpur to support the *wazīr's* campaign in Malwa, sending 5,000 horsemen to help him, and going so far as to ask Pilāji to withdraw.[17] All this was known at the court, but the Niẓām was still not trusted.[18] Sa'ādat Khān, who was in communication with him, also became suspect.

A long drawn out tussle ensued between the advocates of the two policies. At first, the emperor inclined in favour of the 'War' party. Abhai Singh was reconciled to the *wazīr*, and the Marāthā *wakīl* reported that the emperor proposed that Agra, Malwa and even Gujarāt should be given to Qamar-ud-Dīn Khān, and two grand

---

Sa'ādat Khān Patna; or that M. Khān should get Allahabad. Sa'ādat Khān himself was said to have offered a bribe of 15 lakhs to Khān-i-Daurān for being granted the *ṣūbah* of Allahabad (*S.P.D.* xiv, 39–42, *Khujastah,* 129–40).

16 *S.P.D.* xiv, 47.

17 *B.I.S.M. Quarterly* xii, 4, Dighe, 141.

18 *Cf.* the remarks of Rustam 'Alī: 'Niẓām-ul-Mulk, with the utmost hostility towards Islām, always held out encouragement to infidels and tyrants' (*T. Hindī,* 565).

armies sent out. If Jai Singh did not join, his country was to be plundered and his disloyalty punished. The emperor himself proposed to take the field as soon as the rivers became fordable. Jai Singh and Khān-i-Daurān were to be sent to the Deccan by way of Jaipur, while the *wazīr*, Abhai Singh and Sa'ādat Khān would march by way of Gwalior.[19] M. Khān Bangash, then living in retirement at Farrukhabad, had also been approached, and by promises of *jāgīrs* and other favours, induced to raise an army to guard the Jamuna fords from the Marāthās.[20]

To checkmate the 'war' party, the *peshwa* launched a diplomatic offensive in 1734–5. His mother went on a pilgrimage to northern India. She visited the capitals of all the great rajas, and the Marāthā *wakīls* utilized the opportunity to sound their opinions. Jai Singh was friendly, as also the Bundelas. The Maharana of Udaipur was hesitant, while the attitude of Abhai Singh was uncertain. Jai Singh invited the *peshwa* to northern India, offering to bear his expenses which came to Rs 5,000 a day, and to secure for him the *chauth* of Malwa, and to introduce him to the emperor (after assurances of safe custody) for the settlement of all his other claims.[21]

The action of Jai Singh in inviting Baji Rao to northern India has been regarded as traitorous by many writers, and it has been imagined that Jai Singh proposed a joint expedition against Delhi.[22] It is clear, however, that Jai Singh invited Baji Rao on a peace mission, for he asked him to come at he head of 5,000 horse only, telling the Marāthā *wakīl* that if the visit did not bear fruit, the *peshwa* would be free to pursue any other methods he chose, i.e. war.[23] Thus, it was a last desperate effort by Jai Singh to bring about peace before war was extended to the very heart of the

19 *S.P.D.* xiv, 39.

20 *Khujastah*, 228–30, 233, 256–9, 283–4, *J.A.S.B.*, 1878, 327–8.

21 *S.P.D.* xiv, 47, 51, xx, 134.

22 *Cf.* Sarkar (*Fall*, 263–4) who, relying on the doubtful authority of *Vamsh* (3239), declares that Jai Singh met Baji Rao at Bhambolao and told him that the time was not ripe for an invasion of Delhi. The Peshwa might come again next year etc.

But *S.P.D.* does not support this interpretation.

23 *S.P.D.* xiv, 47. The actual terms proposed by Jai Singh through his agent were: a cash indemnity of 20 lakhs, a *jāgīr* of 40 lakhs in Malwa (in lieu of *chauth*), and a *tankhwāh* on the territory of Dost M. Rohilla (*S.P.D.* xiv, 50).

empire. Jai Singh apparently felt that if the Peshwa came to northern India personally, it would be easier for him to arrive at a settlement with the Emperor than if he negotiated through intermediaries from Mahārāshtra.

Baji Rao's visit to north India in 1735–6 took place almost certainly with the knowledge, if not the consent of the court, *for the Imperialists undertook no campaigns against the Marāthās that year.*[24] From January 1736, as soon as the *peshwa* crossed the Narmada, money for the expenses of the Marāthā army was received from the Court through Khān-i-Daurān.[25] The *peshwa* left the Deccan in October 1735. By the end of November, he had crossed the Tapti at Nandarbār, and in January 1736, he reached Bānswārā on the border of Mewar. He reached Udaipur in the first week of February, and was met there by the *dīwān* and the agents of Raja Jai Singh. Peace envoys from the Imperial court also reached soon afterwards.[26] On 14 March, Jai Singh had his first meeting with the *peshwa* at Bhamolao, and remained with him for several days.[27] Jai Singh also had a personal motive in desiring a peace settlement with the Marāthās. He distrusted the 'Mughals', and felt that the only way of safeguarding his position in Malwa was to buttress it with the friendship of the *peshwa.* He keenly desired that the *ṣūbah*s of Malwa and Agra should be entrusted to him permanently.[28] He thus wanted to emulate Sa'ādat Khān and Niẓām-ul-Mulk in carving out a large territorial principality for himself.

24 See Appendix 'A'.

25 *S.P.D.* xxx, pp. 321–2. From February to April 1736, Rs 107,500 were received.

26 *S.P.D.* xxii, p. 168, xiv, 42, 50, xxx, 141; *Hingane Dafter,* No. 3, Dighe 124.

From Udaipur, Baji Rao wrote to his mother 'The Delhi situation seems to be more hopeful. Nijabat 'Alī is coming with campaigning funds from Khan-i-Dauran and Aya Mal from Jai Singh. The chief thing is that the Emperor desires our friendship' (*S.P.D.* xiv, 50).

27 *S.P.D.* xx, pp. 322–4 leaves no doubt of this. The *peshwa* remained with Jai Singh till 18th March. The date 8 *Rabī'* 1, 16 July 1736 given by Irvine (ii, 284) must, therefore, be rejected, as also the place of the meeting, Dholpur. There could have been no second meeting at Dholpur, for towards the end of May, the *peshwa* left for the Deccan after having stayed in Malwa for two months (*S.P.D.* xxii, No. 333, *Hingane Dafter,* 1, 2, 3).

28 *S.P.D.* xiv, 31, 47. He told the Marāthā *wakīl.* 'If the Turanis win over the Deccanis they will ignore me. Hence, in all matters, I will follow the wishes of the Peshwa.'

The Peace Negotiations of 1736

From February to June 1736, continuous negotiations took place between the emperor and the *peshwa* through Khān-i-Daurān and Jai Singh. It is not easy to follow the course of these complex negotiations which were carried on at three centres—Delhi, Jaipur, and the *peshwa*'s camp—through a host of intermediaries, and which ranged over a vast variety of topics. But all these long and complicated negotiations bore no fruit, due to the weak position of Jai Singh and Khān-i-Daurān at the court, the sustained opposition by the 'war' party, the intrigues of the Niẓām, and the *peshwa*'s extreme demands and his apparent unwillingness to come to the court personally and risk placing himself in the hands of the 'Mughals' (i.e. the 'War' party). The Marāthā *wakīl* warned Baji Rao. 'All the Mughals are on one side, Khān-i-Daurān and Jai Singh and some (other) chiefs are on the other. It seems that Sa'ādat Khān and Qamar-ud-Dīn will not let them carry through their decisions till they are defeated. The Mughals are untrustworthy, deceitful and faithless'.[29] Baji Bhivrao also wrote, 'In Delhi, the Mughals have made common cause. Khān-i-Daurān and Jai Singh are with the emperor. The spies of Niẓām come and go day and night. At the instance of Niẓām-ul-Mulk, Qamar-ud-Dīn, Roshan-ud-Daulah, Sa'ādat Khān and Abhai Singh have made common cause, and decided not to let you succeed. *You cannot go to Delhi trusting in them.* When Bālājī, the heaven departed, had gone (to Delhi), the Saiyids were trustworthy and Shankarāji was the intermediary. The Mughals were completely powerless, and the Niẓām was sitting in his house in retirement. Today they are in their splendour, with their forces mustered strong'.[30]

Bāji Rao presented his demands through his *wakīl*, Dhondo Mahādeo.[31] He asked for a hereditary state for himself under the crown, *manṣab*s and *jāgīr*s for himself and his chiefs,[32] cessation

29 *S.P.D.* xiv, 54.

30 *S.P.D.* xv, 89, 91.

31 The demands presented by Baji Rao at different times are contained in separate *yādī*s or memoranda along with the reply. Since these *yādī*s are not dated, their order can only be fixed on grounds of internal evidence.

32 Notice how Baji Rao gradually edges out Shāhū and his family from sharing in the concessions granted by the emperor. In 1730, the main demand had been for the grant of a *jāgīr* of 10 lakhs to Fateh Singh Bhonsle, the adopted son of Shāhū (See 239 above.)

of hostilities against his army, an indemnity of 13 lakhs to meet the war expenses,[33] and 20 lakhs as *chauth* for the current year.[34] He also demanded the *ṣūbahdārī* of Malwa and control of its entire territories excluding the forts held directly by the emperor, but including the lands of *jāgīrdārs*, old feudatories, grantees of rent-free lands and daily allowances, and the various *zamindars* who were to be maintained in their position only if they paid their dues to the Marāthās.[35] The *peshwa* was also to have the right to levy tribute on the chiefs of Bundelkhand. But the most important demand of all was for the grant of the hereditary office of the *sardeshpande* of the Deccan to the *peshwa*. The post was to carry with it five per cent of the revenues of the Deccan, and also, it would seem, some undefined administrative functions.[36]

All these demands were accepted. Yādgār Khān who is described as the 'key to Khān-i-Daurān's intelligence',[37] carried the royal patent granting the two provinces of Malwa and Gujarāt 'which Baji Rao already held by the tenure of the sword', and also authority to levy dues from the Rajas of Bundelkhand.[38]

Nevertheless, a final agreement could not be arrived at.[39] The

33 This was to be paid in three instalments (*S.P.D.* xv, 93). Later, in a separate *yādī*, 2 lakhs were demanded for Baji Rao's brother, Chimnaji (*Ibid*). Another *yādī* tells us that the emperor agreed to pay 15 lakhs to Baji Rao before, during and after his visit to the court (*S.P.D.* xv, pp. 94, 97). It would seem that this refers to the same demand for war expenses which had been previously agreed to.
34 *T. Hindī*, 530.
35 *S.P.D.* xv, pp. 92–3,
36 *S.P.D.* xv, pp. 92, 95, 96. The emperor agreed to this in return for a sum of 6 lakhs (Duff i, 433).
37 *Iqbāl*, 192.
38 *S.P.D.* xv, p. 94, *Siyar*, 468, 474, *Duff* (i, 432) says that Yādgār Khān, the envoy of Khān-i-Daurān, was sent from Delhi to negotiate with the *Peshwa*. He was secretly entrusted with *sanads* for the *chauth* and *sardeshmukhi* of Malwa, and the authority to levy tribute amounting to Rs 1,060,000 on the Rājpūt states beginning from Bundi and Kotah and extending upto Bhadāwar. The object was to create ill-will between the Marāthās and the Rājpūts. Yādgār Khān had been instructed not to produce these terms unless absolutely necessary. Unfortunately for the Mughals, the Marāthā agent of Baji Rao discovered what had been done and informed his master. Baji Rao, convinced that the emperor was at his mercy, raised his demands.
39 *S.P.D.* xx, 134 says Rs 20 lakhs in cash, and a *jāgīr* of 40 lakhs in Malwa

main reason may be sought in certain far-reaching demands regarding the Deccan which Baji Rao made at this time. The *peshwa* demanded a *jāgīr* of 50 lakhs in Khāndesh, Aurangabād and Bījāpur,[40] and the appointment of the crown-prince as the Viceroy of the Deccan with himself (Baji Rao) as the prince's deputy. All the administration was to be conducted through the latter, and any additional collections made in the Deccan were to be shared half and half.[41]

Thus, Baji Rao demanded the virtual ceding of the Deccan.[42] Other detailed demands about Malwa and Bundelkhand were also made in a separate *yādī*. These included the ejectment of Yār M. Khān from Bhopal, the handing over of the forts of Mandu, Dhar and Raisin, and the grant of the whole of Malwa including

---

and Bhopal in *tankhwāh* was agreed upon. Shiv Das (*Iqbāl*, 193) says that Baji Rao was granted Rs 7 lakhs per year in *tankhwāh* upon the Deccan, which were to be given when he reached the court and swore fidelity.

The *farmān* granting the *Nā'ib-ṣūbahdārī* of Malwa to Baji Rao was not issued till 29 September 1736 (xv, 86. The English date given by the Editor is wrong). It was also rumoured that the emperor had conferred the rank of 7,000 on Baji Rao and of 5,000 on Pilāji.

40 *S.P.D.* xv, p. 95. In a separate *Yādī* (pp. 95–6), 50 lakhs were demanded from the Bengal treasury to help the Peshwa to pay off his debts. It is not clear if this was a new demand or a slight variation of the above demand. Dighe (128) thinks that this was a disguised demand for the *chauth* of Bengal. But the demand does not seem to have been for a recurring sum, as would be the case if *chauth* was demanded. At the time of the battle of Bhopal (1738), a subvention of 50 lakhs was again demanded from the emperor, and agreed to by Niẓām-ul-Mulk (see p. 271 below).

41 *S.P.D.* xv, 94–5. These demands are contained in two separate *yādis*, the first of which is addressed to Niẓām-ul-Mulk. It is not clear when these demands were presented to Niẓām. The emperor's reply is not mentioned, but it may be presumed that they were rejected.

42 The demand for the right to nominate the Mughal Viceroy of the Deccan was raised by the Marāthās as early as 1724 at the time of the negotiations with Mubāriẓ Khān (*S.P.D.* x, 1). The *ṣūbahdārī* of Hyderabad and the ceding of several important forts had also been demanded. In 1733, the subject was reopened by Sa'ādat Khān who offered to accept the Marāthā right to nominate the *ṣūbahdārs* of the Deccan and Malwa, if they led a campaign against the Niẓām (*S.P.D.* xxiii, 9).

Viewed against this background, the demands of 1736 regarding the Deccan are not surprising.

the princely states as a *jāgīr.* The *peshwa* also asked for the holy cities of Prayag, Benares Gaya and Mathura in *jāgīr.* The emperor agreed to eject Yār M. Khān but was willing to grant only one fort for the safe-keeping of Baji Rao's family when he came to visit the emperor.[43]

These fresh demands placed the emperor in a quandry. He was prepared to give the Peshwa the right of *sardeshpande* over the Deccan, and thus inflame hostility between him and the Niẓām. But he was not prepared to hand over the entire Deccan to him. All this time, messages were being received by the emperor from Niẓām-ul-Mulk daily, asking him to stand firm, and offering help against the Marāthās.[44] Some lurking hope of saving Malwa and Gujarāt from the Marāthās may also have influenced the attitude to the emperor who was never long of one mind. Anyhow, the demands of Baji Rao were exhorbitant and threw the emperor into the arms of the 'war' party and Niẓām-ul-Mulk. Baji Rao waited in Malwa in vain till the end of May for a reply to his demands, and then left for Mahārāshtra with the determination of getting all his demands accepted next year, or carrying the war into the heart of the empire.[45]

Khān-i-Daurān was apparently keen that Baji Rao should visit the emperor and join his service, and he asked him to come again early in the next campaigning season. He promised that at Ujjain the first instalment of the five lakhs promised as expenses would be paid to him, and that at Agra he would be met by Amīr Khān and Jai Singh, who would conduct him to Delhi where he would meet the emperor during a ride (i.e. not in the court).[46] Jai Singh wrote expressing his friendship and requested the *peshwa* not to march the Marāthā armies over his country and Bundi.[47]

43 *S.P.D.* xv, pp. 95–6.
44 *S.P.D.* v, 89, 91, xxx, 196.
45 *S.P.D.* xxii, 33, *Hingane Daftar,* 3–6. The *peshwa* complained that at the time of Yādgār K.'s visit, it had been agreed that a reply to his demands would be sent within 20 days. He had waited in Malwa for two months, but no reply was forthcoming while he had been ruined by the expenses of maintaining an army (in camp).
46 *S.P.D.* xv, pp. 87–9, 94, 96.
47 *S.P.D.* xxx, 196.

The Marāthā Raid into the Dū'āb

Baji Rao was anxious not to annoy the emperor or to damage his prestige,[48] far less to replace the Mughal Emperor by a Hindu or a Marāthā King. Although the Marāthās often talked of a *Hindū-pad-pādshāhī*, the *peshwas* knew that they could not displace the Timurids from the throne and set up a Marāthā or even a Rājpūt prince in his place without uniting the rest if India against themselves.[49] Hence, the objective of the *peshwas* was to leave the Timurids on the throne of Delhi, and to utilize their prestige and the halo of their name to spread Marāthā authority over the whole of India.

The immediate aims of Baji Rao, it would appear, were to secure the emperor's recognition of the Marāthā conquest of Malwa and its neighbouring areas, and to completely dominate the Deccan with the emperor's sanction. There were other sundry demands, too, which had been put forward in 1736. A notable demand was for the grant of a large cash subsidy to enable the *peshwa* to clear his mounting debts. But these objectives could not be realized unless the 'war' party at the court had been defeated or thoroughly cowed down. With this object in view, the *peshwa* left the Deccan on the Dashera day in 1736, resolved to raid the *Dū'āb* and to show his invincible power to the emperor.

By February 1737, the *peshwa* had reached Agra. At Delhi, the 'War' party had made grand preparations. Two armies were to be sent out under Qamar-ud-Dīn Khān and Khān-i-Daurān. Sa'ādat Khān was to join at Agra, as also Abhai Singh. The combined army was then to proceed against the Marāthās. M. Khān Bangash had actually joined Khān-i-Daurān with 12,000 horse.[50]

The campaign began badly for the *peshwa*. A raid into the *Dū'āb* by Holkar was repelled by Sa'ādat Khān with serious losses to the

48 *Br. Ch.*, 27-Peshwa's letter to his brother Chimnaji. See H. N. Sinha, *Rise of the Peshwas*, 136–9, for an English translation.

49 The Marāthā *Wakīl* at Jaipur had sent a feeler in 1735, telling the *peshwa*, 'The Peshwa's power is so great that the time is suitable for the capture of the Delhi Empire and handing it over to the Chhatrapati' (*S.P.D.* xxx, 134). This seems to have evoked no response from Baji Rao.

Sardesai says, 'The dream of *Hindū-pad pādshāhī* was not territorial ambition but mainly limited to the religious field' (*New History of Marāthā People* ii, 35).

50 *S.P.D.* xxx, 196, *T. Hindī*, 539.

Marāthās. Two royal armies were converging on Agra, and Baji Rao had to move fast. Deciding to make a bold stroke, he slipped past the approaching Mughal armies and suddenly appeared before Delhi. His object was not to damage the prestige of the emperor or alienate him by sacking Delhi, but, as he himself says, 'to expose the boast of the "Turains" and to induce the emperor to make peace'. Hence, having made this demonstration of strength, and having held the emperor at his mercy for three days, the Peshwa retreated.[51]

Baji Rao succeeded in his objective of discrediting the 'war' party. The emperor was greatly incensed at Sa'ādat Khān, arguing that it was his haste in precipitating a fight with Holkar which had brought about the Delhi raid. Sa'ādat Khān's renewed offers to check the Marāthās if he was given Agra, Gujarāt, Malwa and Ajmer was brushed aside, and he was ordered to proceed to his charge without obtaining an audience with the emperor.[52] But Baji

51 *Br. Ch.*, 27. The Peṣhwa explained his conduct to Chimnaji thus: 'I was resolved to let the Emperor know the truth, to prove that I was still in Hindustan and to show him the Marāthās at the gates of the capital... Khan Dauran and Bangash reached Agra and met Sadat Khan who had already reached there with his army. My wakil Dhondo Pant was with Khan Dauran. Sadat Khan sent him a message that Baji Rao's army had been dispersed; that he had fled beyond the Chambal, and it was no longer necessary to honour his envoy; he should be dismissed forthwith. Dhondo Pant was therefore sent away and arrived in my camp... I now changed my plan of sacking the capital. I knew that the Emperor and Khan Dauran were inclined to grant my demands, but the Mughal faction was opposed to his conciliatory policy. I did not want to drive our friends to an extremity by committing sacrilege on the capital. I therefore sent letters assuring the Emperor....'

52 *S.P.D.* xv, 29. *T. Hindī*, 542. Āshūb, 125a says that after the raid, Khān-i-Daurān induced the Emperor to grant Baji Rao the *ṣūbahdārī* of Malwa, and 13 lakhs in cash were also promised.

Qāsim, 359 (Sarkar Ms.) says that after the raid the *wazīr* summoned Hingane for peace. The latter asked for the *chauth* of Malwa, Ujjain (Bundelkhand) and Gujarāt. *Siyar* also mentions that peace negotiations were opened.

On the other hand, the Marāthā *wakīl* wrote that his effort to open peace negotiations through Jai Singh had failed. The Niẓām was coming, everything would be settled on his arrival (*S.P.D.* xv, 33).

It is possible that exploratory talks were started, but broken off as soon as it became certain that the Niẓām was coming.

Rao failed to induce the emperor to make peace with him. His raid had inspired universal alarm. The emperor was now more prepared to listen to the overtures of Niẓām-ul-Mulk than to any peace offers, and *farmāns* were sent summoning the latter to the court.[53]

Thus Baji Rao was once again brought face to face with his old enemy, the Niẓām. Nothing could be decided till the issue between these two veterans had been settled, one way or the other.

The Battle of Bhopal

Niẓām-ul-Mulk had been closely following the progress of the Marāthā armies in northern India. He was desirous of evolving a balance of power between the Marāthās and the Delhi court, and was not averse to purchasing a respite for himself occasionally by conniving at Marāthā aggrandizement at the expense of the empire. But Niẓām-ul-Mulk had no wish to see the Marāthās establish a dominating position in the north. By 1735, the Marāthās had achieved such success that important areas of northern India seemed likely to come under their sway. Niẓām-ul-Mulk also felt uneasy at the negotiations of 1736, being afraid that the emperor would try to buy off the Marāthās at his expense. His apprehensions were correct, for the terms of 1736 had included a Marāthā demand for the appointment of the *peshwa* as the *Sardeshpande* and the deputy-viceroy of the six Deccan *ṣūbahs*. Hence, the Niẓām came to Delhi with two purposes, first and foremost, to safeguard his position in the Deccan, and second, to prevent the Marāthās from establishing a dominating influence in northern India and at the court. He might also have hoped to utilize the opportunity to gain further advantages for himself. If he could defeat the Marāthās with the help of the Imperial armies, he would be the real arbiter of India.

53 *S.P.D.* xv, 23, 26, 27, 33, x. Niẓām-ul-Mulk left for Delhi on 17 *Ẕilḥijjah*, 7 April 1737. The Marāthā *wakīl* wrote that he professed many friendly sentiments for Baji Rao, but his real intentions were different. He thinks, 'If Baji Rao goes to Delhi and meets the Emperor, what will happen to me? A new *subedar* (of the Deccan) will be appointed'. For this reason he has written to all the nobles and the emperor that he is coming. With the help of the Imperial treasure what difficulty can there be in beating the 'robbers' (*ghanīms*)! Upon this, His Majesty put off meeting Baji Rao, and sent a *nān* (piece of bread) to the Nizam (by way of invitation).'

Thus, the struggle between the Marāthās and Niẓām-ul-Mulk now was virtually a struggle for the domination of India—both northern and southern. Baji Rao was aware of the issues at stake. For him it was even more a battle for the domination of the Deccan than of northern India. 'Let every Marāthā join', he wrote to his brother, Chimnaji, on the eve of the battle of Bhopal in 1736, and one grand united push may make us masters of the Deccan. 'If the Nawab (Niẓām-ul-Mulk) is taken care of, the entire Deccan will be freed of danger', this phrase occurs repeatedly in his letters.[54]

Even before Niẓām-ul-Mulk reached Delhi, he was substantively appointed the *ṣūbahdār* of Agra and Malwa on the condition of driving out the Marāthās from there. It was reported that Allahabad, Gujarāt and Ajmer were also promised to his friends and nominees after the successful termination of the campaign against the Marāthās.[55] It was clear that the emperor could no longer avoid being dominated by one or the other of the protagonists, unless something unexpected supervened.

Niẓām-ul-Mulk reached Delhi on 12 July 1737, and was royally received. In August, he was formally appointed the Governor of Malwa in place of Baji Rao, and after the rains were over, he advanced into Malwa, determined 'to cure the Marāthā disease once for all'. He had 30,000 troops and detachments from all the prominant chiefs of Rājpūtānā and Bundelkhand who had joined him willy-nilly.[56] The *peshwa* encountered this with an army of 80,000 horse. The Niẓām was hoping for reinforcements from Sa'ādat Khān and from the Deccan. A contingent under Safdar Jang joined, but the Marāthās succeeded in preventing the Deccan

54 *Br. Ch.*, 33–5, *Riyasat*, 371–2. Thus, the view that by defeating Niẓām at Phalkhed in 1727, Baji Rao gained the supremacy of the Deccan would seem to be unhistorical. (*Cf.* Dighe, 20).

55 *S.P.D.* xv, 53.

56 *S.P.D.* x, 27, xv, 56–8, xxx, 207 (The correct date of x, 27 is 10 January 1737, and not 10 June 1724). It is stated that the number of his troops swelled to 70,000, but the *peshwa* in his letters places it at 35,000 (*Br. Ch.*, 134). We are told that a contingent from Sa'ādat Khān also joined at this time (xx, 207). Irvine (ii, 304), on the authority of Duff (i, 397), states that the contingent under Safdar Jang was intercepted and defeated by Malhar Holkar and Jaswant Pawār. But *S.P.D.* (xxx, 207) definitely states that the troops sent by Sa'ādat joined on 24 December (N.S.).

troops from joining him. Under the circumstances, the Niẓām's heavily armed and slow-moving troops were soon surrounded by the numerically superior Marāthās, and hemmed in at Bhopal. It was a repetition of the old tale of the slow-moving Imperial armies being unable to cope with the swift, lightly-armed Marāthā cavalry. The Niẓām's plight was worsened by his suspicion of his Rājpūt allies.[57] He could neither move, except at a snail's pace, nor come out and fight, and his provisions were running low. On the other hand, the Marāthās could not storm his camp due to his superior artillery. Therefore negotiations were set afoot, and after much hard bargaining, on 7 January 1739, Niẓām-ul-Mulk agreed to the following terms:

(i) Grant of the *ṣūbahdārī* of Malwa, and the whole of it in *jāgīr* (to the Peshwa),

57 Y. H. Khān (*Aṣaf Jāh*, 123) states that Niẓām-ul-Mulk could not take an offensive as 'he found that the Rājpūts and the Bundelas could not be trusted, in the event of general action. They were in fact secretly sending information to the enemy as to his plans and intentions.'

That the Niẓām and the Rājpūts were distrustful of each other is attested to by the Peshwa himself (*Br. Ch.*, 33). But there is nothing to prove that the Rājpūts were actually in secret collusion with the Marāthās. As a matter of fact, the Rājpūts bore the brunt of the fighting which took place, losing several hundred killed. (*Br. Ch.*, 33). The *peshwa*, who gives a detailed account of the fighting in his letters to Chimnaji, makes no mention of any help or information received from the Rājpūts. But when famine began in the camp of the Niẓām, everyone thought of getting away and many Rājpūts did likewise. (*Ibid.*).

Y. H. Khān further states (214), 'It is also quite probable that the Amiru'l Umara Samsamu'd Daulah who was jealous of Niẓām-ul-Mulk and desired his expedition against the Marāthās to fail, intrigued with the Rājpūts to thwart the Niẓām in this manner.'

The contemporary chroniclers, usually fertile in excuses, have not made any such suggestion. Rustam Ali (*T. Hindī*, 549–50), hints that the Niẓām himself was not serious about fighting the Marāthās. He observes—'As the crooked mind of Niẓām-ul-Mulk was bent towards such things as were contrary to what his name imports *viz.;* administration, he allowed disturbances to break out in the country and, with his eyes open, suffered for one or two days grain to be sold in his camp at one seer for a rupee. On account of the tumults and quarrels raised by him, many people were hastened to their graves with the stroke of starvation, and many Musalmans, by the tricks of that unprincipled man, fell into the hand of the enemy, and met with their destruction.'

(ii) Ceding of the complete sovereignty of the territory between the Narmada and the Chambal,

(iii) The Niẓām to obtain *sanads* of confirmation from the emperor for the above, and further,

(iv) to use every endeavour to procure the payment of 50 lakhs for war expenditure. The Niẓām promised to pay according to his circumstances, if the emperor did not agree to pay.[58]

Thus, by the Treaty of Bhopal, Baji Rao obtained confirmation of the most important of his demands presented to the emperor in 1736—except those relating to the Deccan. Malwa and Bundelkhand were practically ceded to him, and the 50 lakhs he had demanded from the Bengal treasury were to be paid by the Emperor from any source he liked. The Marāthā might have asked for more, but as Baji Rao wrote to Chimnaji, 'Fortified as the Niẓām was with strong artillery and with the Bundelas and Rajput rajas as his staunch allies, I accepted your advice and agreed to much lower terms than might have been exacted'.[59]

After the defeat of the most powerful general in the empire, it is more than probable that the emperor would have resigned himself to the loss of Malwa and Bundelkhand and confirmed the agreement made by Niẓām-ul-Mulk, especially as Jai Singh and Khān-i-Daurān had been urging such an agreement for a long time. It is not possible to visualize how the situation would have shaped after that. Baji Rao may have used Malwa as a base for advancing into the *Dū'āb*, or he might have maintained peace with the emperor and concentrated on the realization of his unfulfilled demands regarding the Deccan, i.e. the achievement of complete supremacy in the Deccan, including the transfer to him of the administration (*niẓāmat*) of the provinces.[60] Sooner or later, the whole of India seemed destined to come under Marāthā domination.

58 *Br. Ch.*, 35, 36, *S.P.D.* xv, p. 87.

59 *Br. Ch.*, 35, 36.

60 An extant paper sets out the following demands of Baji Rao which were presented to Niẓām-ul-Mulk: cede Chandawar which formed part of the old *swarajya* of Shivaji; help Peshwa who is burdened with debt and give him a *jāgīr* worth 50 lakhs in Khandesh, Bijapur and Aurangabad; give the post of *Sardeshpande* carrying a hereditary charge of 5 per cent on the revenue, the Deccan to be administered through the Peshwa; grant the fort of Shivner and certain villages in *in'ām* (*S.P.D.* xv, pp. 94–5). A verbal discussion is reported to have taken place.

This development was interrupted and given a new direction by the invasion of Nādir Shāh, which came as a bolt from the blue to most Indian observers, so used had they become to the safeguarding of the northwest passes by Mughal power.

For the Marāthās, the invasion of Nādir Shāh was an unpleasant intrusion by an outsider in a field which they had come to regard as their own. If Nādir Shāh was to stay in India and found a new dynasty subverting that of the *Chaghtāīs*—and reports spoke of his having declared himself Emperor of India and of his intention of marching south—it would be a big blow against Marāthā ambitions, and their new conquests beyond the Narmada would be imperilled. In the circumstances, a new approach became necessary. Shāhū instructed Baji Rao to hurry to the aid of the emperor 'in accordance with our undertaking to Aurangzeb that whenever the empire was in any difficulty, we would help'.[61] Prospects of a coalition of the forces of the Rājpūts and the Bundela princes with those of the Peshwa began to be discussed.[62] Nāṣir Jang was written to. But the Marāthā army was engaged in the siege of Bassein. Raghuji Bhonsle was engaged in his own projects; the Dābhāde was sulkily withholding co-operation, and without a large army Baji Rao refused to move.[63]

While the *peshwa*'s troops were still engaged in the siege of Bassein, Nādir Shāh turned back towards Īrān. He contended himself by sending a threatening letter to Baji Rao, bidding him to be loyal to the Mughal emperor else he would came back and punish him. Baji Rao replied in diplomatic terms and sent a *naẓr* of 101 *muhars*.[64]

Nādir Shāh's invasion did no more than reveal the real weakness of the Mughal empire to the whole world—the Marāthās had long been aware of it. But it brought home to the latter the danger of a foreign conquest of India. This called forth an interesting proposal from Baji Rao. He proposed that all the nobles, high and low, should join together with their armies in a kind of confederation as it were to reduce the affairs of the Timurid line

It is not clear when these demands could have been made. The Peshwa's letters make no mention of these demands in 1736.

61 *S.P.D.* xxx, 222.

62 *S.P.D.* xv, 72, 75, xx, p. 385, Dighe, 152.

63 Dighe, 152.

64 Sardesai, *Life of Baji Rao,* 335.

to a better order, and to oppose 'the enemy', i.e. the foreign invader.[65] M. Khān Bangash was one of the nobles to whom he broached this proposal. Baji Rao moved upto Malwa, and pretended that he had come to see the emperor. He also informed M. Khān that Jadu Rai had been sent to the emperor and awaited the *wazīr*'s reply to his proposals to end the difference among the nobles.[66]

While the proposals of Baji Rao did not meet with any success as was perhaps to be expected, they may be said to represent the beginning of a new political approach on the part of the Marāthās. Baji Rao, it would seem, had dimly begun to realize the need of enlisting the cooperation of the emperor and his ministers and of the leading 'powers' in north India to safeguard against the likely recurrence of foreign raids from the northwest. Carried to its logical conclusion, this new approach implied the establishment of a kind of a confederation under the overall direction and control of the *peshwa*, with considerable autonomy to the various 'powers' constituting it, and the retention of the Timurid monarchy as a symbol of unity and a rallying centre in case of foreign danger.[67] Thus, a new equilibrium was sought to be created between the age-old forces of unity and regional independence.

Final Ceding of Malwa and Bundelkhand

The invasion of Nādir Shāh resulted in far-reaching changes in the position and influence of the various groups at the court. Sa'ādat Khān, one of the pillars of the anti-Marāthā faction, died, while both Niẓām-ul-Mulk and Qamar-ud-Dīn Khān were discredited in the eyes of Muḥammad Shāh. Niẓām-ul-Mulk left the court, and reached an understanding with the Marāthās again.[68] In the

65 *Khujastah*, 219, 244, 376, *J.A.S.B.*, 1878, 333. Baji Rao wrote—

'*Dar-ān waqt waqt ast ki hamān sardārān-i-nāmdār wa nawīsān-i-ṣāhib-iqtidār bah ijtimā'-i-afwāj wa ittifāq-i-ham -dīgar pardākhtah musta'id u mutawajjih barāi muqāwamat-i-mukhālif bāshand.*'

66 *Khujastah*, 375–6.

67 *Cf.* the remark of Shāhū to Balaji Rao after Baji Rao's death. 'His (Baji Rao's) ambition was to guard the Mughal empire and the same time to conquer all Hindustan' (*Br. Ch.*, 117–20).

68 In 1740, the Niẓām met the Peshwa in Malwa and secured Marāthā aid against his son, Nāṣir Jang, who had rebelled (*S.P.D.* xxi).

opposite faction, Khān-i-Daurān also was killed. This left Jai Singh Sawai as the most influential of the old nobles. At his instance, peace was made with Marāthās in 1741. But this did not take place before the emperor had made one last effort to recover Malwa and Gujarāt, and was faced with the renewed threat of invasion by the new Peshwa, Bālājī Rao.[69]

The final terms negotiated with the Marāthās through Jai Singh were similar to those demanded by Baji Rao in 1736 and 1738. Malwa was ceded—though to save the prestige of the emperor, the Peshwa was only granted the *nā'ib-ṣūbahdārī* of the province, an Imperial prince remaining the formal governor. The grant to the *peshwa* included all *faujdārīs*, i.e. complete jurisdiction over the province including the states. The demand about the right of levying *chauth* on all states south of the Chambal seems also to have been accepted. In place of the cash demand of 50 lakhs by the *peshwa*, the *chauth* of Bengal, Bihar, and Orissa was ceded to him. No agreement seems to have been made about the Deccan, however, perhaps because Niẓām-ul-Mulk and the *peshwa* were on good terms again. Fifteen lakhs in cash were to be given to the *peshwa* in three instalments. In return, the *peshwa* gave a written undertaking, (i) to visit the emperor; (ii) to see that no Marāthās crossed the Narmada, holding himself responsible for the acts of any one who did cross; (iii) not to disturb any province except Malwa; (iv) not to ask in future for any money in addition to what was granted; (v) to depute one Marāthā general with 500 horse to serve the emperor; and (vi) to join the Imperial army with a contingent of 4,000 men whenever the imperialists undertook a campaign—any additional help to be paid for.[70]

These terms might be said to constitute a tacit alliance between the emperor and the Marāthās. The Marāthās were virtually left a free hand in the Deccan and, in return, promised not to molest the northern possessions of the emperor and to render him aid in case of need, i.e., in case of renewed foreign danger. Henceforth, an accredited Marāthā representative, Mahadev Bhatt Hingane, lived at the Delhi court, and became a powerful factor in Imperial politics.

69 Rajwade vi, 145, 149; *S.P.D.* xiii, 4, R. Sinh, *Malwa'*, 266–8, *T. Muẓ.*, 320.

70 *S.P.D.* xv, 86, pp. 97–8, Rajwade ii, pp. 91–5. These papers should be dated in 1741 [*S.P.D.* x, 186 should be 28 September 1741 (or 17 September old style), xv, p. 97, 15 July (or 4 July o.s.)].

The final ceding of Malwa and Bundelkhand to the Marāthās brings to an end a definite stage in Mughal–Marāthā relations, and marks the beginning of a new phase during which the Marāthās made a bid for supreme power in India, and closely influenced parties and politics at the court. However, a study of this phase lies outside the scope of the present work.

APPENDIX A

Was There an Imperial Campaign in the Year 1735–6?

Irvine (ii 283–4) speaks of an Imperial campaign in the eighteenth year of Muḥammad Shāh's reign (1735–6) after which the emperor accepted the proposal brought forward by Jai Singh that he should relinquish the government of Malwa in favour of Peshwa Baji Rao.

Sarkar (Fall' i 277–8) follows Irvine. Dr Raghubir Sinh (*Malwa* p. 239 fn. i) is doubtful if the campaign was continued after peace negotiations had begun in February 1736, but has left the issue undecided.

It is clear, however, that there could have been no campaign at all this year. The only authority which mentions the campaign is Āshūb. From internal and circumstantial evidence it is clear that Āshūb speaks, in fact, of the campaign of the seventeenth year (1734–5), but the details have been mixed up, either by the author himself or by some later copyist.

Āshūb speaks of two expeditions in the eighteenth year (1735–6), one of which was led by the *wazīr*, Qamar-ud-Dīn Khān, and proceeding by way of Mewar, fought several skirmishes with Pilāji Gaekwad (Āshūb, pp. 355–62). But this is impossible, as Pilāji was sick and did not come to north India at all that year. (*S.P.D.* xxii, 306–9, pp. 168–70, Dighe, fn. 9, p. 123). This is followed by a detailed account of the fight of Jai Singh and Khān-i-Daurān against Malhar Holkar at Tal Katora (Āshūb, pp. 363–74). This again, refers to the campaign of the previous year, because (i) a similar campaign was fought at the same place in 1734–5; (ii) there is no mention in Āshūb's account of any activity by *Baji Rao, who is mentioned as being busy in the Konkan;* (iii) we are told that after concluding a pact for *chauth* with Jai Singh, Malhar Rao returned to the Deccan (Āshūb, p. 374). But we know definitely that in April 1736 Malhar led a campaign into Marwar and remained camping at Malwa throughout the rains; (iv) In January, Hingane met Jai Singh at Jaipur (*S.P.D.* xiv, 50), in February, Khān-i-Daurān was at Delhi (xiv, 56), in March, Baji Rao, met Jai Singh (*S.P.D.* xxx, pp. 322–4). If so, when could the campaign have taken place?

Āshūb's dates relating to the Marāthā campaign are uncertain as he says (p. 249) that his papers got mixed up during a flood. The account of the seventeenth year (pp. 347–53, dated 1147 H., but wrongly placed under the eighteenth Regnal year) makes no mention of the activities of Qamar-ud-Dīn in Bundelkhand. The account relating to the activities of Khān-i-Daurān and Jai Singh also breaks off abruptly on page 363 (which is placed in the year 1148 H.)

It is clear that the account of Āshūb on pages 347–53 dated 1147 and on pages 355–75, dated 1148 *refer to the campaign of the same year,* i.e. 1147, 1734–5.

There was, thus, no Imperial campaign in 1735–6.

CHAPTER X

Mughal Politics and Nādir Shāh

THE NORTHWEST AND THE MUGHALS

The Great Mughals had kept a close and continuous watch on their northwest frontier which touched Īrān on the one hand, and the states of Tūrān on the other. In order to guard against the recurrent danger of invasion from these quarters, they had attempted:

(i) to prevent by diplomatic means the coming into being of a hostile combination of powers in West and Central Asia;

(ii) to maintain a strong administration in Kabul and to secure, if possible, Qandahār which was regarded as 'the gateway to Kabul'; and

(iii) to keep a contented population in Afghānistān and the tribal regions by providing economic assistance in various forms.

To implement this policy, some of the ablest nobles had been appointed as governors of Kabul with large armies at their disposal. A considerable amount had been spent from the central exchequer towards the maintenance of these armies, meeting the cost of administration, and also by way of subsidy for pacifying the war-like tribal population. In spite of foreign intrigues, a constant tussle with Īrān over the possession of Qandahār, and occasional unrest among the tribesmen, the Mughal policy had been successful in keeping prospective invaders at a safe distance from the frontiers of India.

From 1677 onwards the governor of Kabul was Amīr Khān, an extremely able noble who was greatly trusted by Aurangzīb. After his death in 1698, Shāh 'Ālam was appointed as the governor, with Nāṣir Khān as his deputy.[1] In 1700, Shāh 'Ālam was also appointed the governor of Lahore. The prince's eldest son, Jahāndār Shāh, remained in charge of Multan. Thus, the responsibility for safeguarding the northwest was placed in the hands of Prince Shāh 'Ālam. Aurangzīb himself kept the closest supervision over the affairs of these provinces,[2] while Shāh'Ālam, by his constant marches and counter-marches, kept good order in the region, and prevented the rebel Prince Akbar, who had taken shelter in Īrān, from attempting an invasion.[3]

After his accession to the throne, Bahādur Shāh appointed Ibrāhīm Khān, the son of 'Alī Mardān Khān, as the governor of Kabul. But the Khān failed to administer his charge in a proper manner. He was therefore superseded soon afterwards, and Nāṣir Khān was restored to his former post. Nāṣir Khān remained in charge of the province till his death in 1129 H, 1717, when he was succeeded by his son, who was also entitled Nāṣir Khān. As the mother of Nāṣir Khān II was an Afghān, he had good relations with the Afghāns. He made a proper settlement of the country, and kept the roads in good order.[4]

In 1719, Sarbuland Khān succeeded Nāṣir Khān at the instance of Saiyid 'Abdullāh Khān. The tribesmen were apparently disaffected. Sarbuland Khān's son, Khān A'ẓam Khān, while returning from Kabul to Peshawar after conducting operations, was surprised by the tribesmen and lost all his baggage and most of his men. After the overthrow of the Saiyids, Nāṣir Khān II was restored.[5]

Meanwhile, a great change was coming over the politics of West Asia due to the rapid decline of the Ṣafwīd empire. The decline of the Ṣafwīds gave an opportunity to the Ghilza'ī Afghāns

1 *M.A.*, 394. Amīr Khān was the son of the maternal aunt of Aurangzīb, and had married the daughter of Amīr-ul-Umarā 'Alī Mardān Khān. Among his great achievements was the regulation and settlement of the disturbed administration of the province (See also *Siyar*, 445).

2 See *Raqā'im ff.* 15a–17a, '*Anecdotes*' (Nos 12, 15) for some of the letters of Auragzīb to Shāh 'Ālam on this score.

3 See Sarkar, *Aurangzīb's Reign*, 113–18.

4 *M.U.* iii, 833–5.

5 Kāmwar, 481, *Siyar*, 455, 460.

inhabiting the Qandahār region to organize their power. In 1709, the Ghilza'ī chief, Mīr Wais, rose against the Persians, and seized the fort of Qandahār. But it was left to Maḥmūd, the son of Mīr Wais (d. 1715), to give the final blow to the Ṣafwīd empire. He forced Shāh Sulṭan Ḥusain Ṣafwī to surrender at Iṣfaḥān after a long siege (22nd October 1722). He then deposed the Ṣafwīd monarch, and had himself crowned.

The Delhi court was the silent spectator of these events. It failed to realize the incipient danger to Kabul of an independent Afghān state on the border. When Niẕām-ul-Mulk arrived at the court from the Deccan, he vaguely referred to an expedition to restore the Ṣafwīd, Shāh Ṭahmāsp, to Iṣfaḥān. But the court had neither the desire nor the power to do so. Instead, it sought to establish friendly relations with Maḥmūd by an exchange of letters.[6]

The victory of Maḥmūd at Iṣfaḥān was the signal for Russia and Turkey also to aggrandize themselves at the cost of Īrān.

Nādir Shāh gradually built up a position for himself by leading a Persian war of national resistance against all these encroachers. By 1730, Nādir had expelled the Ghilz'īs from the heart of Persia, and inflicted a signal defeat on the Abdālīs of Hīrāt. He then turned against the Ottomon Turks. In a series of protracted campaigns, Nādir drove out the Turks from the territory of the Ṣwafīd empire, but failed to take Baghdad. Finally, exhaustion compelled the two sides to conclude a truce in 1736.[7]

In the course of the struggle to drive out the Afghāns, Ottomon Turks and Russians from the former Ṣafwīd territory, Nādir had gathered together a band of faithful followers, and established his reputation as a bold and intrepid commander and leader of men. He had no difficulty in forcing Shāh Tahmāsp to abdicate in favour of his infant son in 1732, and finally, in ascending the throne himself in 1737.

RACIAL GROUPS AND PARTY POLITICS AT THE COURT (1728–37)

While these far-reaching changes were taking place across the border of India, the Mughal court was engrossed in factional

6 *Siyar*, 479.
7 Lockhart, *Nadir Shah*, 105–11.

politics and narrow self-seeking. We have noted in the previous chapter that the growing challenge of Marāthā invasion led to the emergence of a 'peace' and a 'war' party at the court, led by the Chief *Bakhshī*, Khān-i-Daurān, and the *Wazīr*, Qamar-ud-Dīn Khān, respectively. Simultaneously, relations between different ethnic and regional groups inside the nobility and the army tended to become strained. It is probable that the real cause of this was the shrinkage of employment opportunities consequent to the loss of large portions of the empire by conquest or by a process of open or concealed definace of Imperial authority by the provincial governors and others. Hence, there was acute rivalry for the appropriation of the remaining *jāgīr*s and the profitable posts at the court. In the face of the growing paralysis of the central authority, each noble sought to create a band of devoted followers by a careful distribution of patronage. The creation of such a group increasingly became not merely a devise for the capture of supreme power but a necessity for economic survival. Hence also the unusual degree of bitterness in the group politics of the period.

The two most important groups in the Mughal army at this time were the Mughals and the Afghāns. In addition to these, there were sizable numbers of Hindustanis in the army and the nobility. These consisted of both Muslims and Hindus. The struggle between the various nobles and their following during this period has often been interpreted as a struggle between different ethnic groups, or, more specifically, between the 'Mughals' and the 'Hindustanis'. However, most of the nobles had mixed contingents of Mughals, Afghāns, Hindustanis etc. The political affiliations of the nobles, too, cut across racial and religious groups. Nevertheless, the testimony of contemporary writers shows that there was a certain degree of ill-will and a sense of rivalry between the Mughals and non-Mughals, and that this sometimes led to an open conflict between them, and also affected relations between the nobles.

The *wazīr*, Qamar-ud-Dīn Khān, and Sa'ādat Khān, the governor of Awadh, were regarded as the two great patrons of the 'Mughals' at the court.[8] The following of Qamar-ud-Dīn Khān included 5,000 Tūrānīs, most of Sirhind being assigned to them for their

8 Āshūb, 562, ii, 102, 378; *Siyar*, 474.

pay. Sa'ādat Khān gave special preference to the Īrānīs.[9] On the other hand, the following of Roshan-ud-Daulah Ẕafar Khān, a noble of Tūrānian extraction, consisted almost exclusively of Afghāns and Hindustanis.[10] The following of Khān-i-Daurān, who was also of Tūrānian extraction, consisted largely of Hindustanis. Āshūb says that as a result of his patronage of Hindustanis, the descendents of the Īrānī and Tūrānī servants of M. A'ẓam Shāh received a set-back. The author further complains that he (Khān-i-Daurān) hated the name 'Mughal' and all it stood for, and that 'He confined his energies to the upkeep and maintenance of all that was Indian, whether Muslim or Hindu. Under him, infidel Rajas, Rājpūts, Jats and *zamindars*—whoever was Indian—were free of molestation'.[11]

The bitterness between the Mughals and the non-Mughals apparently increased during the period of Saiyid domination. Though not much in evidence during the period of Niẕām-ul-Mulk's *wīzārat*, it seems to have continued beneath the surface, and found dramatic expression in what is called the Shoe Sellers' Riot at Delhi in 1729. The riot arose out of a clash between one Subhkaran who was employed in the *Khān-i-Samān's* office and some Punjabi shoe-sellers on the occasion of the *Shab-i-Barāt* or festival of crackers. The shoe-sellers felt themselves the aggrieved party and vowed vengence. Subhkaran took shelter at the house of Sher Afgan Khān Pānīpatī,[12] his official superior and a friend and relation of Roshan-ud-Daulah Pānīpatī. As Sher Afgan refused to surrender Subhkaran, and the ministers could not make up their mind in the matter, the shoe-sellers refused to let the Friday prayers be conducted at the *Jāma' Masjid*—a common procedure of showing resentment. The *wazīr*, Qamar-ud-Dīn Khān, Roshan-ud-Daulah and Sher Afghan

9 Āshūb, 314–15, *Siyar*, 474. But Qamar-ud-Dīn's following also included Hindustanis. On one occasion, Sa'ādat Khān clashed with Muẓaffar Khān, the brother of Khān-i-Daurān. Sa'ādat Khān planned to raise 50,000 men from his *ṣūbah* of Awadh till Qamar-ud-Dīn came to his help, ostensibly on the ground that 'the honour of the Mughals. Īrānīs or Tūrānīs, is one,' but really on account of his rivalry with Khān-i-Daurān. (Most detailed account in Āshūb 373–9.) This incident took place in 1731–2.

10 Āshūb, 203–10, Wārid, 26–32, *Iqbāl*, 171–3.

11 Āshūb, 252–3.

12 He was the *Khān-i-Sāmān*, and was related to Roshan-ud-Daulah by marriage. His troops are described as Hindustani.

Khān came out with their following to maintain order. But their soldiers soon mingled with the crowd, and the riot became one between the Mughals on the one hand, and the Afghān and the Hindustani soldiers on the other.[13]

These events continued to excite popular imagination for a long time. But they can hardly be taken as proof that ethnic groups formed the main basis of the party conflict at the Mughal court. The real points at issue in the party politics were, as has been noted earlier, the question of the disposal of *jāgīrs* and high offices of state; the attitude to be taken towards the Marāthās, Rājpūts, and Jats.

Invasion of Nādir Shāh and the Attitude of the Nobles

The invasion of India by Nādir Shāh was not a sudden development. The possibility of a Persian invasion had long been discussed, and was, indeed, the topic of bazar gossip. For Nādir Shāh, the invasion of India was almost a logical step after the expulsion of the Ghilza'īs and Abdālīs from Persia and the stalemate in the war with the Turks. It was only from India that he could replenish his treasury for a renewal of the war against the Turks, while the example of Taimūr and Babar beckoned towards India as the land where territory and laurels might be gained without much difficulty. The weakness of the Mughal empire was also no secret—specially after the series of setbacks suffered by Mughals arms at the hands of the Marāthās. The necessary pretext for invasion was provided by the Delhi government's unwillingness or inability to prevent the influx of Ghilzā'ī refugees from across the Afghan border. As early as 1730, Nādir had sent 'Alī Mardān Khān Shāmlū to Muḥammad Shāh with a letter from Shāh Ṭahmāsp, announcing his intention to march on Qandahār and asking the emperor, in the common interest of his realm and that of Persia, and by reason of the old friendship between them, to close the frontier to all Afghan refugees once the operations had begun.[14] Muḥammad Shāh replied that the *ṣūbahdārs*

13 See Āshūb, 203–10, Wārid, 26–32, *Iqbāl*, 171–3, Irvine ii, 256–63.

14 Āshūb, 445–76 (text of Nādir's and Shāh Ṭahmāsp's letters), Lockhart 46–7.

of Kabul and Sindh were being instructed to comply, and that the Kabul army would be reinforced for the purpose.[15]

But Nādir Shāh became engrossed in the Turkish campaign and the Delhi court forgot all about the northwest once again. Khān-i-Daurān utilized the opportunity to bring to the Emperor's notice that Roshan-ud-Daulah Ẓafar Khān, who had been nominated to disburse the subsidy of 12 lakhs annually to the tribes of the North-West for keeping the passes open, had been regularly misappropriating half of it. This completed the ruin of Roshan-ud-Daulah who was also charged with peculating other sums. He was ordered to pay back two crores to the treasury, and lost his influence with the Emperor. The charge of disbursing the subsidy was transferred to Khān-i-Daurān.[16] Khān-i-Daurān, while not personally corrupt, was averse to the governor of Kabul, Nāṣir Khān, who had been appointed through Roshan-ud-Daulah. He connived at the peculation of the subsidy, so that none of it reached Nāṣir Khān who was, moreover, a pious man, and negligent of the affairs of administration. Thus, the efficiency of the Kabul army deteriorated, and the frontier tribes became disaffected.[17]

After the accession of Shāh 'Abbās III in 1732, Nādir Shāh sent a second messenger. The Delhi court excused itself on the ground of preoccupation against the 'Deccan infidels', and repeated the previous assurances.[18]

In 1737, when Nādir Shāh advanced against Qandahār, he sent further envoys.[19] The Mughal court's delay in sending a reply to Nādir Shāh and the detention of his envoy for more than

15 Āshūb, 476–81 (text of M. Shāh's reply). According to the author, at the time of his departure, the envoy was given three lakhs in cash and one lakh in goods by the emperor, while he and his companions received another three lakhs in cash and kind from the nobles.

16 *Siyar,* 479.

17 *Siyar,* 479, *M.U.* iii, 834–5.

18 Āshūb, 484–508 (text of Nādir Shāh's letter and the Emperor's reply).

19 Āshūb, 509–26, *Jahānkushā,* 331–2, *Siyar,* 480. According to the *Ḥikāyat-i-Fatḥ Nādirī* (Anon, ASB Cal. Ms., ff. 4b, 5a), Nādir reiterated the old demand for barring the passage of the Afghān refugees and demanded a sum of rupees one crore for failing to check depredations by the Afghāns in the past. The emperor was also reminded of the annuity which his ancestor (Humayun) had promised to pay (for Persian help).

a year[20] might have hardened Nādir Shāh's determination to invade India, but they can hardly be regarded as its primary causes. These, as has been noted, were both political and economic. However, Nādir Shāh kept up for a long time the pretence that his sole object was the destruction of the power of the Afghāns—the common enemies of Persia and India. Before entering India, Nādir Shāh is also to have declared that his major motive was to save the Mughal Emperor from the Marāthās.[21]

It was a common belief at the time in India that Nādir Shāh was also invited to invade the country by the 'Mughal party', and in particular, by Niẕām-ul-Mulk and Sa'ādat Khān.[22] The Marāthā *wakīl* at Delhi wrote, 'It is evident that it is all the Nizam's game'. Another contemporary observer noted, 'The *wazīr* and the *umarā* thought that the Marāthās have become very strong and the Emperor weak; Baji Rao over-runs the country upto Delhi, and Bhonsle had laid waste the country upto Bengal and Ayodhya. Therefore, the Īrānī Emperor should be called and a new empire established'.[23]

In the absence of any documentary proof, it cannot be definitely established that Nādir Shāh was invited by any section at the court—although such an invitation would have been quite understandable from the viewpoint of Niẕām-ul-Mulk and Sa'ādat Khān. It is true that Nādir Shāh did not stand in need of such an invitation. However, after the defeat of Niẕām-ul-Mulk at Bhopal, there remained no power in India capable of withstanding the Marāthās.

20 According to Āshūb (ii, 51), apart from the inability of the nobles to make up their minds, a second reason for the envoy's detention was his infatuation for a dancing girl.

21 Nādir Shāh is said to have written to the emperor 'My coming to Cabul and possessing myself thereof was purely out of zeal for Islam and friendship for you...my stay on this side of the Attock is with a view that when those infidels (the Marāthās) move towards Hindustan, I may send an army of the victorious Kizzilbash to drive them to the abyss of hell' (Fraeser, Nādir Shāh, 138. But no mention in Āshūb).

22 The following contemporary authorities repeat the charge against Niẕām; Jauhar f. 2b; *T. Hindi* (559) qualified by the words, 'some people thought' *Ḥālāt-i-Nādir, Nādir Var-Nijabat* (*Punjab Hist. Society*, 1916); Trilok Das (Hindi poem *J.A.S.B.*, 1897), Fraeser, 129–32; Hanway iv 142. *The Risālah-i-Muḥammad Shāh* holds Sa'ādat Khān responsible for inviting Nādir Shāh.

23 *Ait. Charchā*, 4, *Riyasat*, 367, 384.

Hence, certain elements at the court might have favourd an invasion by Nādir Shāh in the hope that he would destroy the Marāthā power in India, and leave the field clear for them.

The disaster which befell Mughal arms at Karnāl, was not the result of any organized treachery, but was due to the want of daring, imagination, and unity on the part of the Mughal nobles against one of the greatest generals of the age in Asia. No attempt was made by the Mughal court to aid and assist the Governor of Kabul to withstand Nādir Shāh. Nor were the passes into India defended. According to some writers, the Delhi court seems to have imagined that Nādir Shāh would turn back after the conquest of Kabul (June 1738). Khān-i-Daurān was among those who pooh-poohed most vigorously the alleged threat of a Persian invasion.[24] Perhaps, a more plausible explanation would be that the court was watching the outcome of the conflict between Niẕām-ul-Mulk and the Marāthās, and awaiting the return of Niẕām-ul-Mulk's armies to Delhi.

But once Nādir Shāh had crossed the Indus (c. 12 December 1738), and started moving on Lahore, the Persian threat could no longer be discountenanced. Niẕām-ul-Mulk had returned to the capital in April 1738. But he came only at the head of 5,000–6,000 horse, a small part of artillery and 2,000–3,000 foot-soldiers, having sent his best troops and artillery back to the Deccan.[25] The humiliating treaty that he had been forced to sign at Bhopal had also undermined his prestige, and revived old suspicions of a secret understanding between him and the Marāthās. Thus, the Mughal court found itself without any generally acceptable leader. At Khān-i-Daurān's instance, letters appealing for help were sent to Baji Rao and the Rājpūt princes. But the former was engaged in a campaign against Bassein, and no immediate response was forthcoming from the Rājpūt princes.[26] The only noble in the empire with his prestige unimpaired and large forces at his disposal was Sa'ādat Khān, the Governor of Awadh. Accordingly, at

24 *Siyar*, 481, *Bayān*.

25 Āshūb, 550–1. His idea is said to have been that if the nobles listened to him, the Imperial army would obey him and he could accomplish the task with its help. If, on the other hand, the nobles were hostile and attempted to ruin him, he would draw aside with his small army.

Perhaps, a more compelling reason for sending back the army was the fear of Marāthā incursions during his absence.

26 Rajwade vi, 130; *Siyar*, 482; Dighe, 151–2.

the suggestion of Niẕām-ul-Mulk, he was summoned from his *ṣūbah.*[27] The nobles failed to agree among themselves on the allocation of command, precedence etc.[28] Niẕām-ul-Mulk wanted, at first, that Prince Aḥmad Shāh should be nominated to the command of the armies. But Khān-i-Daurān opposed this scheme, and asked for the supreme command and unfettered powers for himself. Finally, all the nobles agreed that the emperor should be requested to lead the armies personally.[29]

Meanwhile, news arrived of the fall of Lahore (12 January 1739), and the submission of the governor, Zakariyah Khān, to Nādir Shāh. Hence, it was decided to entrench at Karnāl, and to await the arrival of Sa'ādat Khān.

Sa'ādat Khān started from Faizabad towards the end of January.[30] But he did not come by forced marches as might have been expected. According to some writers, this was out of a desire on his part to see Khān-i-Daurān defeated before his arrival. But others ascribe it to an abcess in his leg. Perhaps, Sa'ādat Khān wanted the Mughal court to feel its helplessness and its dependence on him, and hence deliberately approached slowly. More inexcusable was the conduct of his soldiers on the way. They ravaged the *chakla* of Etawah which was the *jāgīr* of Khān-i-Daurān, and heaped cruelties on women and children. On reaching Delhi, Sa'ādat Khān took a large sum of money from the treasury without permission, and distributed it among his soldiers.[31] But the court was in no position to protest against these high-handed proceedings.

At midnight on 12–13 February, Sa'ādat Khān reached the fortified Mughal camp at Karnāl, after covering the last 70 miles in four days. The Persian and the Indian armies had been lying face

27 A. L. Srivastava, *First Two Nawabs, loc. cit.* 62–3.

28 *Jauhar* (4b–5a), *Iqbāl* (215–17). *T. Hindi*, 560, Alī Hazīn (282–7), and *Siyar* (482–3) emphasize the rivalry and jealousy between Niẕām-ul-Mulk and Khān-i-Daurān so that the plan proposed by one was opposed by the other.

On the other hand, Āshūb, who is generally 'pro-Mughal' and opposed to Khān-i-Daurān, says that at the court, contrary to all his expectations. Niẕām-ul-Mulk was befriended by Khān-i-Daurān who daily conferred with him, and asked his advice as to how best to deal with Nādir Shāh (Āshūb, 554, 557).

29 *Iqbāl*, 215–17.

30 A. L. Srivastava, *loc. cit.* 63.

31 *Iqbāl*, 231.

to face for a couple of days. The following morning, Sa'ādat Khān waited upon the emperor, and, according to one writer, plans of operation were being discussed when news arrived that about 500 camels belonging to the baggage train of Sa'ādat Khān had been looted by the Persian forces.[32] Sa'ādat Khān immediately asked the emperor for permission to proceed against Nādir Shāh. What followed is not quite clear. According to some authorities. Niẓām-ul-Mulk counselled the delay of a few days as the Awadh armies were tired by incessant marching.[33] He is said to have remarked to Sa'ādat Khān that he only had experience of fighting *zamindars*, while this was a battle between kings and should only be fought after proper preparation by the artillery. By this time, the day was also well advanced.[34]

It seems that the emperor concurred with Niẓām-ul-Mulk, and that Khān-i-Daurān also supported his view. But Sa'ādat Khān was adamant, and rushed away, determined to fight a lone battle if necessary.[35] This placed the emperor and the nobles in a quandry. Khān-i-Daurān decided to risk battle along with Sa'ādat Khān rather than let him fight alone;[36] while the emperor and Niẓām-ul-Mulk also drew up their forces in battle array.[37]

By the time the Indian forces came out to fight, it was already past noon, or dark according to some others.[38] The Indian commanders had neither any plan of campaign, nor any co-ordination

32 Harcharandas, *Bayān*, 34, *T. Hindi*, 562.
33 *Bayān*, 34, Ānand, 27, *Siyar*, 483.
34 *Ḥikāyat*, 23a.
35 Bayān, 34, Ānand, 27, *Siyar*, 483.
36 *Iqbāl* (232)says that Khān-i-Daurān had planned to fight the following day, but he did not want to be left behind and to let Sa'ādat Khān get all the credit (for a victory).
Ānandram (27) says that Khān-i-Daurān objected to fighting that day, but that the Emperor overuled him.
The *Delhi Chronicle* (quoted by Sarkar, *Later Mughals*, ii, 343) and *Bayān*, 34 say that the Emperor ordered Khān-i-Daurān to attack the Persians.
37 *Iqbal*, 237, *Siyar*, 483, *Later Mughals*, 344.
38 *Bayān*, 34, and Ānand 27 say that there were only a few hours of daylight left; *Siyar*, 483 says that it was nearly three o'clock. But *Jahān-Kushā* (235) simply says that the sun had begun to decline from its meridian when the Indian armies were suddenly seen coming out for battle. According to the *Khiyāfat Nāmah-i-Himāyūn* (349), the battle started at one o'clock.

between their forces. The light screen of Persian horses retreated before them and having separated the forces of the two nobles from each other, led them into a trap which allowed full play to Nādir Shāh's deadly artillery. Thus, the Persians made short work of the Indian forces. Meanwhile, Niẓām-ul-Mulk calmly sat on an elephant at the head of his army, and sipped coffee.[39]

Sa'ādat Khān was certainly rash, to say the least, in risking battle with a seasoned commander like Nādir Shāh without adequate preparation and without coordinating his plans with and in opposition to the views of other prominent nobles. But once he had gone into battle, it would have been more appropriate for Niẓām-ul-Mulk to join with him in one concerted onslaught on Nādir Shāh, rather than staying aloof and facing the certainty of subsequent defeat.[40] As it was, Khān-i-Daurān was mortally wounded, and his younger brother, Muẓaffar Khān, and all three of his sons and many other relations and followers were killed, while Sa'ādat Khān was made captive after suffering severe losses. The only course left now for Niẓām-ul-Mulk was to negotiate with Nādir Shāh. From the beginning, the negotiations turned on the indemnity to be paid by the Delhi court. At first, Nādir Shāh stipulated with Niẓām-ul-Mulk for an indemnity of only 50 lakhs, out of which 20 lakhs were to be paid immediately, and the rest in instalments by the time Nādir Shāh reached Attock.[41] But it seems that later Nādir Shāh changed his mind, and decided to demand more, either because he had never been serious about the previous demand, or according to popular belief, because Sa'ādat Khān was enraged at the emperor's conferring the office of *mir bakhshī* which had been left vacant by the death of Khān-i-Daurān, on Niẓām-ul-Mulk, and decided to wreck the agreement made by the latter, suggesting to Nādir Shāh that he could get a much bigger sum by occupying Delhi.[42] Or, the same advice might have been given by others. It is significant that throughout the negotiations, Nādir Shāh closely invested the Indian encampment, and allowed no foodgrains to go

39 *Siyar,* 483. For details of the battle, see *Later Mughals,* 345–7, Lockhart 137–9.

40 Most contemporary authors are sharply critical of Niẓām-ul-Mulk for his failure to help Khān-i-Daurān and Sa'ādat Khān. Thus, see Bayān, *Jauhar,* and *T. Hindi,* 565. See also *S.P.D.* xv, 75 for the views of a Marāthā *wakīl.*

41 Harcharandas, *Later Mughals*, 354.

42 *T. Hindi,* 568. Harcharan.

inside.[43] Having reduced the Indian camp to sore straits, he summoned Niẕām-ul-Mulk, and demanded from him an indemnity of 20 crores. Since Niẕām-ul-Mulk could give no assurance that this staggering indemnity would be paid, he was placed in confinement.[44] Muḥammad Shāh was now deprived of his last means of resistance, and meekly surrendered.

Having thus secured the person of the emperor and made his leading nobles captives, Nādir Shāh, could enter Delhi without having to undertake a prolonged and costly siege. The story of the subsequent massacre and exactions is only too well known.[45] The populace of Delhi was assessed at two crores of rupees, and leading nobles like Niẕām-ul-Mulk, Sa'ādat Khān and Sarbuland Khān were forced to act as tax-collectors. In many cases, torture was applied. Apart from this, a vast sum was also collected in jewellery and goods. According to reliable estimates, the total value in cash and kind secured by Nādir Shāh came to about seventy crores.[46] Before his departure, Nādir Shāh also forced the emperor to sign a treaty making over to him the territories to the west of the river Indus, including 'the provinces of Thatta and the ports and fortresses belonging to them'.[47] To complete the humiliation of the emperor, he was also forced to agree to the marriage of one of the royal princesses to the son of the upstart, Nādir Shāh.[48]

The effects of Nādir Shāh's invasion continued to be felt long after his departure. The invasion proclaimed the real weakness of

43 Harcharan, *Jahānkushā*, 237, *Later Mughals*, 355, 357.

44 *Ibid. T. Hindi* (569) and the Marāthā *wakil* ascribe all this to the duplicity of Niẕām-ul-Mulk, and his attempt to carry favour with Nādir Shāh.

45 See Ānandram and *Ḥikāyat* (ff 37 a b) for some of the cruelties practised. A long dispatch from Jugal Kishore Sarwar, the *wakil* of Bengal, gives a graphic account of these extortions and the state of Delhi during the occupation of Nādir. We are told that Khush-hāl, *peshkār* of the *mīr bakhshī*, was made to pay Rs 257,000; and Sita Ram Khazānchī, 3 lakhs. Besides this, 2 crores and 12 lakhs were realized from Qamar-ud-Dīn, Sa'ādat Khān, Niẕām-ul-Mulk and the Qāẓīs etc. (Anglo-Arabic School, Patna, *doc.*)

46 For details, see *Later Mughals*, 370–3, Lockhart, 152–3.

47 *Jahānkushā*, 243, Āshūb.

48 Lockhart, 151. According to Jugal Kishore Sarwar (*loc. cit.*), three daughters of Muẕaffar Khān deceased (brother of Khān-i-Daurān), and 16 women from his *ḥaram* were forced by Nādir Shāh to enter his own *ḥaram.*

the Mughal empire to the entire world, particularly to the European adventurers who were gradually extending their commercial activities from the coastal regions of India and were watching the political situation in the country with keen interest.

The invasion of Nādir Shāh demonstrated forcefully that a new political situation had been created in north India. The loss of Kabul and the areas to the west of the Indus deprived India of an advance post for the country's defence and a vantage point for following West Asian affairs. All the Indian powers including the Marāthās were made painfully aware that a new force had arisen in West Asia and that India could no longer bank on the northwest regions being safe from recurrent foreign invasions. Whether these invasions would be in the nature of plundering raids only, or would aim also at the creation of a new dynastic empire remained to be seen.

The incipient threat of further invasions from the northwest led Baji Rao to postulate a new approach to the Mughal empire, visualizing a united front of all Indian powers under the aegis of the emperor, with the Marāthās playing the leading part in the coalition. The parties at the Mughal court were also affected by Nādir Shāh's invasion. Among the old leaders, Sa'ādat Khān and Khān-i-Daurān died, while Niẓam-ul-Mulk and Qamar-ud-Khān forfeited the confidence of the emperor for their sorry part in the battle of Karnāl. Niẓām-ul-Mulk decided once again to leave the Mughal Court to its devises and sought an agreement with Marāthās for maintaining his position in the Deccan. Ṣafdar Jang, Amīr Khān, and a number of other nobles gradually rose in the emperor's favour. The decline in the Imperial prestige led to a resumption of the old struggle for *wizārat*, with the important difference that the issue now was no longer one of revivifying the empire by internal reforms and new policies, but of preventing the emperor from falling under the domination of either one or another of the 'powers' contending for mastery in north India.

The wealth extorted by Nādir Shāh from the emperor, his nobles, the commercial classes, and the citizens of Delhi represented a big drain on the resources of the country. It not only dealt a crippling blow to the power and authority of the emperor who was left with no cash reserves for an emergency, but affected also the position of Delhi as one of the prime commercial marts of north India. The general impoverishment of the nobles led to a sharpening of the struggle for the possession of *jāgīrs*. Simultaneously, the tendency towards the rack-renting of the peasantry became more marked. The realization of land-revenue, never a peaceful affair, became more and more a kind of military operation in the course of which villages were devasted and large number of peasants were massacred.

Thus the various internal problems of the empire were intensified.

Nādir Shāh's invasion also led to the introduction of the quick-firing musket and improved light artillery in India. Characteristically, the Rohilla Afghāns were the first to adopt them, while the Marāthās adhered to their traditional mode of light-cavalry warfare—an omission for which they were to pay dearly.[49]

Finally, the rise of Nādir Shāh and his invasion of India ended the close cultural contact between India and Persia which had subsisted during the two preceding centuries. The Indian frontier no longer marched with Īrān and Tūrān so that the flow of adventurers from these countries into India finally stopped. While it is doubtful if this had any important bearing on the fate of the Mughal empire which was tottering to its death due to deep-seated problems to which no satisfactory solution was forthcoming, it had an indirect bearing on Indian social and cultural development. The Īrānī and Tūrānī immigrants who had settled down in India now found it even more difficult to stand aside as a separate cultural and social group, or to adopt an attitude of social and cultural superiority. Thus, the forces making for the creation of a composite culture and society in the country were strengthened in the long run.

49 The Rohilla infantry armed with muskets and light-artillery successfully defied the Marāthā lightly-armed cavalry before the battle of Panipat (1761). If the Marāthās had been able to overcome the Rohillas, the entire political situation in north India would have changed (see Sarkar, *Fall*, ii, 208–16).

Concluding Remarks

In the light of the preceding study, attention might be drawn towards some main points regarding the character and role of the nobility after the death of Aurangzīb and the trend of politics in the eighteenth century.

In the first place, the general assumption that parties and politics at the court of the later Mughals were based on ethnic or religious groupings among the nobility is not borne out. The groups which were formed at the court towards the end of Aurangzīb's reign were based on clan and family relationships, or personal affiliations and interests. Thus, Z̲u'lfiqār Khān, who was of Irānī extraction, was supported by a leading Tūrānī noble like 'Abduṣ-Ṣamad Khān, by an Afghan noble, Dā'ūd Khān Pannī, and by Hindus such as Rao Rām Singh Hāṛā and Dalpat Bundela. The Saiyids, who are said to have been the champions of the Hindustanis, attempted to secure the support of important Tūrānī nobles such as Niẓām-ul-Mulk, M. Amīn Khān and 'Abduṣ-Ṣamad Khān. But after Farrukh Siyar's deposition, when Niẓām-ul-Mulk made a bid for power, he raised the slogans of race and religion, urging that the struggle against the Saiyids was a struggle for the honour of all Mughals, whether Irānī or Tūrānī, and that the monarchy and Islam were in danger from the Saiyids and their Hindu allies. However, of the two leading Rajput Rajas, Jai Singh and Ajit Singh, the former was an inveterate enemy of the Saiyids. Chhabelā Ram Nāgar and Dayā Bahādur also resisted the Saiyid authority by force of arms. As for the Saiyid alliance with the Marāthās, the 'orthodox' Niẓām-ul-Mulk did not hesitate in 1724, and afterwards, from entering into an alliance with the Marāthās, whenever it suited his political purposes. In the subsequent period, the *wazīr* Qamar-ud-Dīn Khān, Sa'ādat Khān Burhān-ul-Mulk (the founder of the Nawabi of Awadh), M. Khān Bangash (an Afghān) and Raja Abhai Singh of Jodhpur formed one group, while Khān-i-Daurān (the descendent of a Tūrānī immigrant) and Raja Jai Singh remained on the other side along with some Afghān nobles. Hence, it would appear that slogans of race and religion were raised by individual nobles only to suit their convenience, and that the actual groupings cut across ethnic and religious divisions.

The background to the rise of parties at the court was the decline in the prestige of the monarchy as a result of Aurangzīb's failure to deal satisfactorily with the oppositional movements of the Marāthās, Jats, Rājpūts etc. The civil wars following the death of Aurangzīb further weakened the position of the monarchy, specially as no competent monarch emerged successful from them. Simultaneously, the crisis of the *jāgīrdārī* system which had been steadily worsening, led to inordinate delays in the allotment of *jāgīrs*, and even when a *jāgīr* was allotted there was sometimes a considerable gap between its paper and its real income. One reason for the growth of parties at the court was the scramble for the best and most easily manageable *jāgīrs*, the lion's share going to the more powerful political group. The struggle for *wizārat* was to some extent a struggle between such groups. Each group consisted of powerful individuals and their supporters who tried to win a leading position in the affairs of the state by securing control of the leading offices at the court, particularly the offices of the *wazīr* and the *mīr bakhshī*. Simultaneously, an attempt was made to dominate the emperor, and to restrict his freedom of intercourse with rival nobles in order to guard against intrigue. Hence, they also tried to secure control of the posts which gave access to the emperor.

The struggle for *wizārat* was not a struggle between the monarchy and the nobility as such, for the nobles, had no common bonds or interests. In fact, one of the few points of agreement among them was regarding the divine right of the Timurids to rule, since no group among the nobles felt strong enough to set up a new monarchy, and the Timurids still enjoyed considerable prestige.

But it would be wrong to see in the struggle for *wizārat* merely a fight between rival groups of nobles for office and power. Ẕu'lfiqār Khān and the Saiyid Brothers who enjoyed a dominating position in the state for some time, attempted to use their power to institute policies and measures aimed at giving a new lease of life to the Mughal empire. These nobles did not seek exclusive power for themselves. But their pre-eminent position aroused the jealousy of some nobles who intrigued to remove them from office and power.

The crisis might have been resolved if the *wazīrs* had enjoyed the confidence and support of the monarchs. In that case, the *wazīr* might have been able to carry through the reforms and policies necessary to revivify the empire. But since the *wazīrs* generally secured office due to their political and military strength, the monarchs were led to believe by interested sections that a capable and powerful *wazīr* would try to reduce the monarch to a nullity, and that he might even try to set up a new dynasty. The monarchs, instead of acting as a stabilizing force, became the focus of intrigue against their own *wazīrs*. This attitude towards the *wizārat* resulted in a series of violent internal crises which increasingly divided the whole court and the nobility into hostile factions struggling for supreme power. It was in this situation that the Saiyids were led to take the bold step of deposing the ruling monarch in order to place on the throne someone more amenable to their wishes, and gathering into their own hands the leading reins of authority. But the step defeated its own purpose, for it united powerful sections of the nobles in opposition to them, and ultimately led to their downfall.

Since the *wazīrs* could not secure the aid of the monarch, they tried to organize a bloc of supporters powerful enough to overawe all their rivals as well as the monarch. This created the danger that a successful *wazīr* might try to set up a new dynasty. However, no group inside the nobility was powerful enough to dominate the rest. Therefore, the question of setting up a new dynasty hardly arose, unless some powerful extraneous element intervened in the situation. But if the empire was not to be governed by a capable monarch or a competent *wazīr* exercising power with his backing, there was every danger that powerful and ambitious nobles would try to set up independent principalities, thus disintegrating the empire. Thus, the monarchs found that the only alternative to an all-powerful *wazīr* was the break-up of the empire.

Niẕām-ul-Mulk was faced with this situation after the overthrow of the Saiyids, whom he had denounced as traitors to the dynasty. He had to reckon with the opposition of a powerful group at the court and the underhand hostility of the emperor. Niẕām-ul-Mulk preferred to leave the court, and to carve out a principality for himself in the Deccan. His action was emulated by many other nobles who made themselves the masters of large tracts while paying nominal allegiance to the emperor.

Thus, the leading nobles who could have helped to institute policies and measures designed to consolidate and strengthen the Mughal empire, became themselves a prime factor in its disintegration.

A review of the struggle for *wizārat* suggests that a monarchical despotism such as that of the Mughal emperors was not capable of developing into a limited monarchy in which the king might only reign and be a symbol of unity, while the *wazīr* ruled as the real hub of power. The Mughal despotism could only be replaced by another monarchical despotism or by a series of states held together in a system of balance of power. The social forces which made the growth of a constitutional monarchy possible in England were far too weak and undeveloped in seventeenth century India, allowing full play to the forces of disintegration that were strong in a feudal society.

The struggle for *wizārat* also involved a struggle over policies. This conflict touched some of the most vital issues that had faced the Mughal empire since its inception and particularly during the long reign of Aurangzīb. Thus, such questions as the attitude to be adopted towards the Rājpūt states and individual Rājpūt Rajas, the status of the Hindus and the levying of cesses like the *jizyah*, the policy to be followed towards the Marāthās and such recalcitrant elements as the Jats—all these became issues of party politics. Basically, the question was whether the state ought to be based in the main on the Muslims, and rest on racist and religious foundations, or whether it should be broad-based on the support of both Muslims and Hindus, being essentially secular in spirit. Even in the time of Bahadūr Shāh, there was a trend towards a softer attitude towards the Rājpūts and the Jats, and a certain laxity was allowed in the collection of the *jizyah.* During Jahāndār Shāh's reign, Z̲u'lfiqār Khān abolished the *jizyah* and promised high *manṣabs* and posts to the Rājpūt rajas. He had earlier concluded a private pact with Shāhū for the payment to him of the *chauth* and *sardeshmukhi* of the Deccan. The policy of Z̲u'lfiqār Khān was taken up after his downfall by the Saiyid brothers. They once again attempted to broad-base the state on the support of the Hindus as well as the Muslims, and moved in the direction of a composite ruling class consisting of all sections of Muslims and of the Rājpūts as well as the Marāthās—even granting concessions to the Jat leaders (but not to the Sikhs). It is irrelevant for our purposes to argue that some of these concessions were made under the compulsion of events, and were the consequence of weakness rather than any well thought-out policy. Whatever the circumstances, they point to the working of certain definite forces within contemporary society. The new trend was not to the liking of certain sections in the nobility which opposed the Saiyids, and denounced their policies as pro-Hindu and as being against the best interests of the empire and the monarchy, as well as being opposed to the 'faith'. But the attempt of Niẓām-ul-Mulk who championed these sections to tread his way back to the policies of Aurangzīb met with the determined opposition of the large majority of the nobles and also of the subordinate officials among whom, we are told, Hindus and 'Hindustanis' predominated. This was followed by the withdrawal of Niẓām-ul-Mulk from the court, and the creation by him of a semi-independent principality in the Deccan.

Thus, the exclusionist policies associated with the name of Aurangzīb lasted only for a short time. In the 197 years of Mughal rule, from the foundation of the empire in 1526 to the invasion of Nādir Shāh in 1739, *jizyah* was collected only for 57 years. While this is not a true index of the attitude of the state towards the Hindus and of the position of the orthodox elements inside the empire during this period, it is at least a rough indicator. The forces which made for mutual toleration and understanding between the Hindus and the Muslims, and for the creation of a composite culture in which both Hindus and Muslims cooperated, had been silently at work for the past several centuries, and had gathered too much momentum to be lightly deflected by temporary political difficulties. The dominant picture of the eighteenth century is not of the Hindus and the Muslims forming mutually exclusive and antagonistic groups but of their cooperating in cultural affairs and social life, and of a remarkable absence of sectarian passions from political conflicts. Stray cases of communal passions, however, may be encountered here and there. Some religious divines sought to interpret the contemporary political tussle in religious terms. Thus, Shāh Walīullāh sought to rally the Muslims for the defence of Mughal empire, and dubbed the Marāthās as the enemies of the Muslim faith. He was not without his parallels among the Hindus, too, though it is not possible to point to any single dominant personality. But, on the whole, the Marāthā bid for political domination did not disturb the tenor of social life or unduly strain the relations of Hindus and Muslims in north India. Political alliances and shifts were decided primarily on political considerations. Thus, even Niẓām-ul-Mulk was quite prepared, when it suited him, to countenance Marāthā encroachments on the Mughal empire. The emperor and his advisers, on their part, were not loath to encourage Marāthā pretensions in the Deccan at the cost of Niẓām-ul-Mulk. The Rājpūt and Bundela princes initially attempted to block the Marāthā advance towards north India. Later, the Bundelas deemed it more profitable to enter into a defensive and offensive alliance with them, while Jai Singh Sawai attempted to play the peace-maker between them and the hapless Mughal court. On the other hand, the Rathor prince, Abhai Singh, continued to oppose the Marāthā invaders. Even Jai Singh never threw in his lot with the Marāthās as has been erroneously asserted on the basis of some crude forgeries. At a later date, both the Jats and the Nawab of Awadh befriended the Marāthās, only to abandon them on the eve of Panipat due to the endless rapacity of the latter. On their part, the Marāthās abandoned the ideal of a *Hindu-pad-pādshāhī*, aspiring only to rule the country in the name of the Emperor, and fully content to act and behave like other Mughal nobles. Thus, the basic trend of politics in the eighteenth century was secular. In the field of culture, too, there was a remarkable absence of narrow sectarian prejudices. The Marāthās adopted almost wholesale the Mughal court etiquette, and many social practices from north India found their way into Marāthā society.

The rapidity of the advance of the Marāthās towards north India during the second and third decades of the eighteenth century and the helplessness and inanity of the Mughal court in opposing them is partially responsible for the belief that the nobility of the Mughals, as a whole, had become decadent and effete. Various explanations have been advanced for this alleged decadence of the

Mughal nobility—excessive luxury including the practice of maintaining large *ḥarams*, the enervating climate of India, the religious policy of Aurangzīb which condemned the Muslims to the sterile profession of arms, the heterogenous character of the Mughal nobility, the drying up of the life-giving flow of recruits from Central Asian countries after the death of Aurangzīb etc. Most of these explanations are wide off the mark and have been put forward, singly or in conjunction, and in one form or another, to explain virtually every important turn in Medieval Indian history from the Ghorid invasion onwards. However, decadence must be considered an economic rather than a social phenomenon. There has been no historical period in which men of ability and character are wholly wanting. Moreover, judged by this test alone, the first half of the eighteenth century can scarcely be classified as a period of decadence. For during this period, we find a large number of capable administrators, generals, and men of learning and culture. This is the period during which the Saiyid brothers and Niẕām-ul-Mulk, 'Abduṣ-Ṣamad Khān and Ẕakariyah Khān, Sa'ādat Khān and Ṣafdar Jang, Murshid Qulī Khān and Jai Singh Sawai to name only a few of the most important ones come to the forefront. It is a different matter that the capacities and capabilities of these individuals were generally exercised not in advancing the interests of the empire, but in carving out their own principalities and in serving their own ends.[1]

In a historical sense, therefore, decadence has meaning if applied to a society which is no longer growing in an economic sense. Such a society has certain typical features—a deep-seated

1 As long as these nobles lived, the tasks of a civilized government were, on the whole, efficiently discharged within their principalities. The 'great anarchy' on which British historians like to dwell, and which has been put forward as a historical justification for the British conquest of India, was neither as widespread nor as prolonged as it has been made out to be. In the areas which had been brought under the control of one of the 'Nawabs', or had passed under the domination of the Marāthās, the old system of administration often continued without much change, specially at the district or *pargana* level, and passed over into the later British administration in many cases. The period of anarchy and misrule in most areas is really to be dated from the third battle of Panipat, and from the time the British and other foreign powers started actively intervening in the internal affairs of the Indian states.

financial crisis, pessimism and loss of faith in the future often leading to the growth of irrationalist and obscurantist ideas, the stagnation of science and technology etc. Many of these symptoms are to be found in Indian society during the second half of the seventeenth and the early part of the eighteenth century. It is beyond the scope of the present work to undertake a detailed survey of the economic trends in Indian society during this period in order to determine the causes or the actuality of economic stagnation and decline. Till the completion of such a task by scholars, many of our conclusions regarding political and cultural trends during the seventeenth and eighteenth centuries must remain somewhat tentative. However, it would not be far wrong to assert that the disintegration of the Mughal empire was not due to any absolute decline in the character or capabilities of the nobility of the Mughals. Nor was it due to the existence of diverse ethnic, national and religious elements in the nobility. The groups and factions which figure so largely in later Mughal politics were not organized along ethnic, or national or sectarian lines. In fact, the existence of diverse ethnic and religious elements made for tolerance and more liberal politics, and prevented a bid to establish an exclusive kind of domination by any one group which would have been no less disastrous to the empire, and would perhaps have entailed social consequences of a more harmful nature. The successful fusing together of these diverse elements into a group with a largely common outlook and common cultural values must be counted one of the lasting achievements of the Mughal emperors. The creation of such a ruling group had, in turn, a definite influence on contemporary Indian culture and society which acquired a broader, more assimilative and cosmopolitan outlook. This outlook did not come to and end with the reign of Aurangzīb, but is clearly seen at work during the eighteenth century.

The economic and financial crisis which forms an under-current to the seventeenth century, and which steadily worsened during the reign of Aurangzīb, assumed a particularly acute form during the eighteenth century. By the time Bahādūr Shāh died (1712), the accumulated treasures of previous generations had been exhausted. The *manṣabdārs* of lower ranks found it virtually impossible to make the two ends meet on the income from their *jāgīrs*, which was not a fraction of their paper value, and fluctuated greatly from year to year. Bahādūr Shāh's reckless generosity in granting *jāgīrs* and increments threatened either to make the *manṣabs* meaningless (since the means for maintaining the requisite quota were lacking), or to start the dangerous process of frittering away *khāliṣah* lands.

The process went much further during the reign of Jahāndār Shāh. Established rules of business were thrown to the winds, and the farming of even *khāliṣāh* lands became common. In the circumstances, sufficient attention could not be paid to the extension and improvement of cultivation. On the contrary, farming of the revenues seems to have led to rack-renting, and adversely affected the peasantry. Thus, actual revenues fell even further. The civil wars exhausted whatever financial reserves remained.

The Saiyids never showed much competence in administrative and revenue affairs. 'Abdullāh Khān left his affairs in the hands of Ratan Chand, who persisted in the practice of farming out *khāliṣah* lands. The division of the court into sharply opposed factions encouraged *zamindars* and recalcitrant elements everywhere who began to withhold revenue. In the Deccan, the Marāthās began to realize practically half the revenue, while the Jats and Sikhs created disturbances around Agra and Lahore.

After the overthrow of the Saiyids, Niẓām-ul-Mulk made a bold bid to institute an enquiry into the *jāgīrs* held by subordinate employees and nobles, and to abolish the practice of farming out *khāliṣah* lands. But he could not carry through his proposals and abandoned his attempt to reform the empire.

Thereafter, the process of the setting up of semi-independent principalities by provincial governors and powerful nobles, and of the withholding of revenue by *zamindars* became particularly marked. The effective control of the emperor was soon confined to a small principality around Delhi, his income being derived from it and from such tribute as his 'subordinate' rulers cared to seed him.

Thus, a financial and administrative crisis accompanied and accentuated the process of political disintegration.

In the light of developments during the period under review, it appears unhistorical to ascribe to Aurangzīb's religious policy a major responsibility for the downfall of the Mughal empire. However undesirable and retrogressive some features of Aurangzīb's religious policy might appear to a modern mind nurtured in the spirit of secularism, an objective approach to history demands that the line of distinction between cause and effect should not be blurred. *Jizyah* and other discriminatory practises (such as the ban on the use of 'Arabī and 'Irāqī horses by the Hindus, the ban on their use of *palkis* inside the *gulāl-bār* etc.) were abandoned barely half a dozen years after the death of Aurangzīb. Mughal forces were withdrawn from Jodhpur, and high *manṣabs* and *jāgīrs* were given once again to the Rājpūt rajas. In 1715, Jai Singh and the Bundelas joined together to inflict a crushing defeat on the Marāthās in Malwa. Both Jai Singh and Ajit Singh played a not inconsiderable role in Mughal court politics. In the case of the Marāthās, Shāhū was released from captivity and allowed to resume control of the territories in Shivaji's *swarajya*. By 1718, the Marāthās were also officially granted the *chauth* and *sardeshmukhi* of the Deccan. Nor are there any instances of the destruction of temples and only stray references of forced conversion during this period.

But even the wholesale abandonment of Aurangzīb's policies could not save the Mughal empire from disintegration. Many complex factors contributed to the break-up of the empire. Medieval Indian society lacked any essential basis of economic unity between the towns and the countryside. The economic atomism inherent in an economy based on largely self-sufficient village units encouraged atomism in the political sphere. The Mughals attempted to counter this fundamental atomism by a variety of devises, political economic and cultural. While these policies cannot be gone into in detail here, broadly speaking, the Mughals attempted to associate themselves with the culture of the country, not to interfere with the religious beliefs and customs of the people as far as possible, and to develop in the country a composite ruling class consisting of both Hindus and Muslims. With some setback in the time of Aurangzīb, this policy was generally pursued throughout the seventeenth century. The Mughals also strove to protect and extend agriculture, to protect and foster trade, and to stimulate production in various ways. The stimulus of economic development contributed to the growth of towns: Agra, Delhi, Lahore, Ahmadabad etc. developed to a size comparable to the greatest towns in the world at the time.[2] But these developments could not proceed sufficiently far to alter the fundamental character of the village-economy which

2 See Palseart, *Jahangir's India*, 7, 46; Thevenot, *Travels*, 44–6.

continued to rest on local self-sufficiency and subsistence farming, with only small exceptions in some areas. Hence, the peasant did not feel that he had any stake in a large, centralized empire, and in disturbed times tended to turn towards anyone who could offer him protection. Apart from the peasants, there was, as indicated earlier, the numerous and well-entrenched class of *zamindars* who were not interested in the creation and maintenance of a strong, centralized state. As against this, the classes that were directly interested in integration were comparatively weak, and numerically small. The traders and merchants who stood most in need of integration were economically too dependent on the feudal classes to aspire to an independent role. This made the role of the nobility crucial. As long as the nobility cooperated with the monarchy in preserving law and order, and administered the state with due regard to the promotion of trade and industry and the development of agriculture, they could enjoy the goodwill of the peasants and the cooperation of the business community: the support of these broad sections was a definite factor in helping them to keep in check the separatist and disruptionist tendencies of the *zamindars*, rajas and other chiefs of various types. But when mutual trust and cooperation between the nobles and the monarchs came to an end, and the nobles could no longer realize their ambitions in the service of the state, the highly centralized, bureaucratic system of administration built up by the Mughals collapsed rapidly.

We have attempted to investigate in the present work some of the causes which were responsible for the conversion of the Mughal nobility from an instrument of integration into an instrument of the disintegration of the empire. Opinions might vary about the respective share of the nobility and the elements represented by the Marāthās, Rājpūts, Jats etc. in the break up of the empire. But few will deny that the nobility had no mean share in it. It is difficult to set a precise date when the nobles ceased to find in the service of the empire an adequate outlet for the fulfilment of their ambitions. We have seen that the crisis of the *jāgīdārī* system became manifest by the middle of the seventeenth century, and steadily worsened during the long reign of Aurangzīb. By the beginning of the eighteenth century, it had reached the state of acute crisis, foreshadowing a complete breakdown or a total re-organization. But even a total re-organization would have only postponed for some time a final breakdown unless ways and means were found of overcoming the economic and technological stagnation of contemporary Indian society.

Thus, the roots of the disintegration of the Mughal empire may be found in the Medieval Indian economy; the stagnation of trade, industry and scientific development within the limits of that economy; the growing financial crisis which took the form of a crisis of the *jāgīrdārī* system and effected every branch of state activity; the inability of the nobility to realize in the circumstances their ambitions in the service of the state and, consequently, the struggle of factions and the bid of ambitious nobles for independent dominion; the inability of the Mughal emperors to accommodate the Marāthās and to adjust their claims within the framework of the Mughal empire, and the consequent break-down of the attempt to create a composite ruling class in India; and the impact of all these developments on politics at the court and in the country, and upon the security of the northwestern passes. Individual failings and faults of character also played their due role but they have necessarily to be seen against the background of these deeper, more impersonal factors.

Document to Illustrate the Early Relations of the Saiyids and the Rājpūts

Text of Pancholi Jagjiwan Das's report to Jai Singh regarding negotiations with the Saiyid brothers in 1713 preceding Ḥusain 'Alī's invasion of Marwar:

(p. 155) سری مهاراجه دهراج مرزا راجه سوای
جےسنگه جیومد ظله العالی

عرضداشت فدوی خانه زاد پنچولی جگ جیونداس قواعد تسلیمات و مراسم کورنشات که شیوه خانه زادان درست اعتقاد است بتقدیم رسا نیده بعزعرض فیض اندوزان حضور لامع النور صاحب و قبله خدائیگان فیض بخش دو جهان میرساند (p. 156) که قبل ازین حقیقت رسیدن عثمان خان قراول و اظهار حقایق زبانی مشارالیه مفصل معروض داشته بعرض عالی رسیده با شد سری مهاراج سلامت منی آسوج سدی نومی نواب امیرالامرا بهادر حقایق اظهار زبانی عثمان خان بعرض حضرت ظل سبحانی رسا نیدند حضرت شیندہ بسیار برهم و مستاسل شدند نواب قطب الملک و خاندوران بهادر و میر جمله را طلبیده خلوت فرمودند حضرت فرمودند که ما می دانستم که مرزا راجه سوای جےسنگه دراعتقاد بندگی صادق است از اظهار عثمان خان صریح معلوم می شود که در اتفاق مهاراجه اجیت سنگه است تا این مدت بحکمت عملی دفع‌الوقت نموده برای صوبه داری گجرات و مالوه یا مالوه و برهانپور که التماس نموده این ممکن شدنی نیست که ما هردو را به یک طرف بفریسم در صورت پذیرائی این التماس باعث برهم‌زدگی سلطنت است (p. 157) به نواب امیر الامرا بهادر فرمودند که الحال در کوچ شما تاخیر چیست چنانچه حضرت برای کوچ نواب امیر الامرا بهادر را تاکید بسیار فرمودند تفصیل طومار فوج همراهی نواب امیر الامرا بهادر از فرد جدا گانه بعرض خواهد رسید - سری مهاراجه سلامت - برای کوچ نواب امیر الامرا بهادر از

پیش گاہ خلافت تاکید بسیار است یقین که بعد رمضان کوچ میشود خانه زاد را
نواب صاحب طابیده بمعرفت ببیا تولا رام این تمامی حقایق را گفتند و فرمودند که
بمضمونے بر نگارد که اصلاح زبانی تا معلوم نشود و این ممکن نیست که هر
دو صاحبان را صوبه داری یک طرف بشود از راه خیراندیشی و دولت خواهی
التماس دارد که (p 158) اگر مرضی مبارک باشد و ارشاد گردد براے صوبه داری
لاهور یا اوده یا اله اباد یا بنارس ازین صوبه ها یک صوبه بنام مهاراجه اجیت
سنگه جیو و صوبه‌داری مالوه یا برهانپور بنام آن خداوند بعرض نواب صاحب
رسانیده شود اما التماس اینست که هرگز ظهار فدوی منکشف نشود- سری مهاراجه
سلامت - صورت حال اینجا بدین منوال است هرچه مرضی مبارک باشد بزودی
ارشاد شود و پروانجات هر یک مطلب جداگانه مرحمت میکرده باشد که بروقت
کاربرجسته از نظر نواب صاحب گذرانیده آید نواب صاحب می فرمودند که ما می
دانستم که انچه درمیان ما و میرزا راجه جیو قرارشده دران تفاوت نیست بقول همون
که قول مردمان جان دارد اما از اظهار زبانی عثمان خان اصلاح ازین معنی عشر
عشیر بظهور نیامد - سری مهاراجه سلامت - سری رانا جیو و سری مهاراجه
اجیت سنگه جیو (p.159) به و کلائے خود نوشته‌اند که همراه فوج نواب صاحب
بیایند - بموجبے که بخانه زاد ارشاد شود بعمل آرد و خانه زاد دهرام از دربار خبردار
خواهد بود برائے روانه شدن چون (؟) حضرت بسیار بسیار تاکید فرموده‌اند عنقریب
روانه می شود زیاده جرأت حدبندگان نیست - الهی آفتاب دولت و جاه ابد
الدهر از مطالع اقبال و اجلال تابان و درخشان باد برب العباد بتاریخ هفتم رمضان
سنه ۲ تحریر یافت فقط -

تفصیل امرایان عظام - (p. 160)

نواب امیر الامرا بهادر- خاندوران بهادر - غازی الدین خان بهادر - افراسیاب
خان بهادر بخشی سوم - راجه راج بهادر- راجه پرتاب سنگه - مهاراجه
بهیم سنگه - راجه مهاسنگه ولد محکم سنگه -

میر مشرف صوبه دار الهآباد - پسران و برادران روح الله خان مرحوم - سردار خان
و ناهر خان و غیره میواتیان - فتح الله خان وغیره -

فوج قطب الملک - بدهائے والاشاهی - فوج روهله -

تفصیل فوج هندی همراهی نواب امیر الامرا بهادر -

سوار	برقنداز	سرب	باروت	بان
(؟) ۲۵۹۵۳ نفر	۲۰۰۰ نفر	۴۰۰ من	۴۰۰ من	۴۰۰۰

توپ کلان	رهکله
۱۰ ضرب	۲۰۰ ضرب

(*Jaipur Records*, Sarkar's Collection, vol. ii, Sitamau transcript).

APPENDIX C

Documents Concerning the Early Relations of the Rājpūts and the Marāthās

(a) *Yād-dāsht* submitted by an announymous agent, d. S. 1783, *Śāwan Sudi* 11, 29 July 1726, proposing to settle the Marāthā claim for the *chauth* of Malwa and Gujārāt by assigning them a *jāgīr* worth 20 lakhs a year in the two *ṣūbahs* (see Chapter VIII p. 238 above):

श्री रामो जयति

श्री एकलिंग जी

याददास्त

उप्र कागद २ राजरां आया सो कागद १ पहला मोहे समाचार लिख्या था। तारो मतलब तो म्हें अठा थी याददास्त माँहे लिखे। लिखया पहली ही राज हजूर मोकल्यो है। सो व्यौरो मालुम हुवो है गो ने जठा पाछे कागद १ पाछा थी आयो ती माँहे लिख्यो थो सो तो नी तराय हैं। उठे भोकत्यो है सो वे अठे आया थी समाचार सारा सांमलों ने पाछो जावसी ताब लिखावांगा। और राजा साहूजीए समाचार लिख्या वा वास्ते हुक्म हुओ सो ऐ समाचार तो जादुराय अठे थी जदी ही ऊणी नेंरे लीखया है न राजरो पण भलो आदमी उठे गयो है। ती हे पण लिखावारो हुकम है। पण सुरत या है सो दशराना पछे अठे फोज बंदी होगी। ने राज पण पधारोगा सो ईणी तरफ है पधारया पछे राजा साहुजी थी रद बदल करांवांगा सो राज पधारया पछे ज्या ही बात करोगा सो ही कबुल करेगा। पहली ही बात करावांगा तो वे जाणेगा सो म्हांथी दब्या थका

बात करे है। सो आपे तो ऊणाए वीस लाष रूपयारी दौई सुबा माँहे जागीर देबारी है। सो दोई सुबा माहे रूपया लाख ५० पचासरी पैदायस है। सो या बात किस भांत रेवेगी। तेथो राज अठे पधारया ही ज्या बात वणेगी सो वणेगी पण पहली ही या बात पेस न पोहचेगी राज ने तरदुद कीयो है सो अवल कीयो है सो श्रीजी[1] रां प्रताप थी राजरां बोलबाला ही होगी ने आगे बड़ा महाराजा श्री जयसिंहजी दिखण्या ऊपे विदा हुआ था जदी सीवेजी ८४ चोरासी गंठारी कूंची आणे मेढ आगे नाखी थी। सो ऊसा तो ऐन है ने ऊणरा तो घर माँहे हु लेवो हे सो एक राज थी तीरा दोय राज हुआ है सो ईणी वातरी तो राज घणी खुश्याली ही रखावसी। या बात पेस ही पोहँचेगी ने इतरो किया वगर पण या बात थाल पड़ेगी नही। ने ईणाए च्यार दिनने हर मिल्या है तो दिन दिन सिर जोर हैगा। तीथो ही बारूं थी काची वेदम तोड नाखजे सो राज तो दोई जान हो सो ज्या वात करोगा सो अवल ही करोगा ने ही वांरूरी ज्या तरेनीजर आयी है सो तो राज है लिखी है ने उठारी पातशाह तरफरी कवीश कहै सो। अंजु महकम करे योगाजी और नबाब निजामल मुलकजी है सो अठा थी कीधी पण अवल है सो इणी बात उप्रे ऊणारां मनरी वगी सो ये पण कहेगा संवत् १७८३ वष सावण शुदि ११ गुरौ।

(*Jaipur Records*, Hindi Letters, v, 85–6).

1 Srināthji, the patron diety of the house of Mewar, situated in the village of Sihad.

(b) Jai Singh's memorandum to the Emperor in October 1729 after being appointed the governor of Malwa, setting out the reasons for his advocacy of a peace settlement with the Marāthās (see p. 241 above):

فدوی درگاه والا برائی تنبیه مرهته صوبهٔ مالوه مامور شده به فضل اله و اقبال بادشاه به تنبیه انها خواهد پرداخت - تعلق این جماعه از مدت درین صوبه خجسته بنیاد (؟) اند این سال اگر بسبب فوج سنگین دخل نه یافتند یا به تنبیه بر سیدند هر سال صرف دین همه مبلغ خطیر معلوم - لهذا امید وار است راجه سا هو را که از عهد خلد مکان به شرف بندگی مفاخرت اندوز است به عطای جاگیر ده لک روپیه بنام کشن سنگه پسرش به شرط عدم شورش در صوبهٔ مالوه و بودن جمعیت کمکی همراه ناظم آن‌جا عطا شود که درین‌صورت ملک بادشاه محفوظ و مامون خواهد ما ذد - و هر کفایت در اخراجات فوج کشی خواهد شد و اگر با وجود آن انحراف خواهد ورزید به سزا خواهد رسید - امید وار است که اگر با حال قدری کم یا زیاده مقرر شود منظور گردد و به گفتهٔ ار باب عرض نوع دیگر نه شود -

The Emperor wrote in his own hand.

البته منظور خواهد شد به خاطر تجویز نماید

Select Bibliography

SOURCES: PERSIAN

I. Chronicles: Mss.

'Aẕam-ul-Ḥarb.—by Kām Rāj; Rieu iii, 937a, and Sitamau. transcript. Account of A'ẕam's reign.

Bahādur Shāh Nāmah—by Ni'mat Khān 'Āli; Rampur Library. Official history of first two years of Bahādhur Shāh reign.

Taẕkirah or Tārīkh-i-Mubārak Shāhī—by Irādat Khān (Mirza Mubārakullāh); Bankipur vii 579. Completed in 1126Ḥ, 1714.

Jahāndār Nāmah—by Nūr-ud-Ḍīn Fārūqī Balkhī Deḥlavī Multanī., I.O. 3988. A gossipy account of Jahāndār's reign, completed in 1127Ḥ, 1715, or 1131, 1718–19.

Tārīkh-i-Farrukh Siyar—by M. Aḥsan Ījād; Rieu i 273a. Account of Farrukh Siyar's minority till accession on 25 *Ṣafar* 1125, 23 March 1712. Āshūb (i 8), however, says the account was continued till the 4th year of the reign.

'Ibrat Nāmah—by Mirza Muḥammad Ḥārisī; Bankipur vii 623. A very useful account upto the deposition of Farrukh Siyar in 1719.

Tārīkh-i-Muḥammadī—by the same author, Bankipur. Chronicle of important events, deaths etc. till 1190, 1777.

Tārīkh-i-Shāhanshāhī—by Khwājah Khalīl; National Library, Calcutta. An account upto 1715 by a contemporary observer; used for the first time by the present author.

Aḥwāl-ul-Khawāqīn—by M. Qāsim Aurangābādī; Rieu i 276b. A history of Aurangzīb's successors upto 1151, 1738–9.

Chahār Gulshan—by Chhatarman Rai; Sarkar's Lib. Partly translated by Sarkar in *'India of Aurangzeb'*.

'Ibrat Nāmah—by M. Qāsim Lāhorī; Sarkar's Library and Bankipur. Account of Timurids upto the fall of the Saiyids, written in 1135Ḥ,1722–3.

'Ibrat Maqāl; Punjab University Library (Bankipur transcript); another version of the above upto the 3rd year of Muḥammad Shāh's reign, with the pro-Saiyid portions deleted.

Tazkirat-us-Salāṭīn-i-Chaghtā—by M. Hādī Kāmwar Khān, Sitamau transcript from V.U.L., Udaipur, also Lucknow Pub. Lib., (entitled *Tārīkh-i-Mughaliyah*). Account of Timurids upto 6th year of Muḥammad Shāh's reign—mostly official appointments, transfers etc.

'Ibrat Nāmah—by Kāmrāj son of Nain Singh; Ethe 391. General account from 1707 to 1719.

Mir'āt-i-Waidāt or *Tārīkh-i-Chārightā'ī*—by Shafi Wārid Tehrānī. General account upto 1734. Bankipur vii, 580—part relating to M. Shāh's reign.

Nādir-uz-Zamānī—by Khush-ḥāl Rai, Khalsa College, Amritsar, transcript of Hyderabad Ms., general history upto 17th year of Muḥammad Shāh's reign (1734–5).

Tārīkh-i-Hindī—by Rustam 'Alī Shāhabādī. A General history upto 1153, 1740, written in 1154Ḥ. Rieu iii 909, Or. 1628.

Tazkirat-ul-Mulūk—by Yahyā Khān; Ethe 409. A general history upto 1149, 1736–7.

Shāhnāmah-i-Munawwar-Kalām—by Shiv Dās Lakhnavī, B.M. (Rieu i 274, iii, 939–8), A.S.B. (Ivanow 25 1/33). Detached historical narratives and Court news relating to Farrukh Siyar's reign and the first four years of Muḥammad Shāh reign; completed on 2 *Muḥarram* 1209Ḥ, 30 July 1794.

Iqbālnāmah: author anon. But probably same as above. Author claims to be eye witness of events in 1734; Rampur Library. A connected history from the beginning of Farrukh Siyar's reign upto the 25th year of Muḥammad Shāh's reign; with three separate pieces appended at the end:

I. An account of the rise of the *sardar*s of Amber and Jaipur—upto 1227H, 1814;

II. An account of the war between Ḥusain 'Alī and Dā'ūd Khān in 1715;

III. The battle between the Marāthās and Aḥmad Shāh at Panipat in 1761.

Tārīkh-i-Shahādat-i-Farrukh Siyar wa Julūs-i-Muḥammad Shāhī—by Muḥammad Bakhsh 'Āshūb'; Sarkar's Lib., written in 1196H, 1782. Valuable but chronologically unprecise.

Bayān-i-Wāqi'—by 'Abdul Karīm Kashmīrī; Sarkar's Lib.

Chahār Gulzār-i-Shujā'ī—by Harcharan Dās, Khalsa College, Amritsar.

Ḥikāyat-i-Fatḥ Nādirī, Anon., A.S.B. Lib.

Jauhar-i-Ṣamṣām—by M. Khān Bijnori; Ivanow 2nd Supp. 929. Account of Nādir Shāh's invasion and the fight of Khān-i-Daurān.

Tārīkh-i-Fatḥiyah—by Yūsuf M. Khān, Daftar-i-Diwani, Hyderabad. Account of Āṣaf Jāh I in verse.

Tārīkh-i-Muẓaffarī—by M. 'Alī Khān Muẓaffarī, Allahabad University Library, written in c. 1800.

Taẕkirah—by Shākir Khān, Sarkar's Ms.

PRINTED WORKS

Muntakhab-ul-Lubāb—by Khāfī Khān; Bib. Ind. Series.

Ma'āṣir-ul-Umarā—by Shāhnawāz Khān; Bib. Ind.

Mir'āt-i-Aḥmadī—by M. 'Alī Khān; Bib. Ind.

Tārīkh-i-Jahāhkushā-i-Nādirī—by Mirza M. Mahdi; Litho. Tihran Edition.

Siyar-ul-Muta'khkhirīn—by Ghulam Husain; Litho. Lucknow Edition.

Hadīqat-ul-Muta'akhkhirīn—by Mīr 'Ālam, Litho. Haiderabad Edition.

II. Documents, Letters etc.—Mss.

Jaipur Records (Sitamau, Transcripts); classified as *Akhbārāt* (Daily Court Reports); Misc. memoranda, reports, *farmāns* etc. bound as *'Miscellaneous Papers'* (4 vols), *'Additional Persian Papers'* (5 vols) *'Sarkar's Collection'* (14 vols), *'Hindi Letters'* (3 vols). The *Akhbārāt* virtually end with the deposition of Farrukh Siyar.

Aurangzīb's Letters: *Ruqqa'āt-i-Ināyat Khānī* (Sarkar's Library), *Raqā'm-i-Karā'im*—Letters of 'Abdullah Khān, mostly relating to 1712; I.O.L.

Bālmukand Nāmah—Letters of 'Abdullāh Khān, mostly relating to 1719–20. Mr S. A. Askari's Ms, Patna, and my copy. Used for the first time by the present author. A very valuable and rare Ms.

Khujastah Kalām, Letters of Muḥammad Khān Bangash, ed. by Sahib Rai; I.O.L. (Sitamau transcript).

Inshā-i-Gharīb, ed. by Lala Ujāgar Chand 'Ulfat', Research Society, Patna.

Safīnah-i-Khushgū, Life of poets etc. Bankipur viii, 85–115.

Nigār Nāmah-i-Munshī, Aligarh University.

Waqā'i' Sarkar Ranthambor wa Ajmīr, transcript from Asafiya Jib., Hyderabad, Fan-i-Tarīkh 2242, Aligarh University.

Printed in Litho.

Inshā-i-Madho Ram ed. by Madho Ram, Litho., Nawal Kishore.

Khazīnah-i-'Āmirah—by Ghulam 'Alī Āzād, Bib. Ind.; lives of poets etc.

Marathi

Aithihasik Patra Vyavahār	Ed. by S. G. Sardesai (2nd ed.)
Brahmendra Swāmichen Charitra	Ed. by Parasnis
Chhratrapati Shāhū Mahārāj	Chitnis
Hingane Daftar (vol. I)	Ed. by Sardesai
Kavyetihās Sangraha Patren Yādi	Ed. by Sadesai and others, 1930 ed.
Marāthi Itihāsānchi Sādhanen (vols II, III, IV, VI only)	Ed. by Rajwade
Maratha Wakils	
Selections from the Peshwas Daftar (vols 3, 7–17, 22, 28, 31, 33, 34)	Ed. by S. G. Sardesai

Hindi

Vamsh Bhāskar	by Suraj Mal Mishran In verse. Historically valueless
Vir Vinod vol. iii	by Kaviraj Shyamal Das, Useful for documents from documents from Udaipur museum

English

Diary of E. Conrad Graaf — (Abridged English trans. in of the U.P. Hist. Soc. x pt. i)

Early Annals of the English in Bengal (2 vols) — Ed. by C. R. Wilson, Calcutta, 1911

Madras in the Olden Times (vol. ii) — Ed. by J. Talboys Wheeler, Madras, 1861

SECONDARY WORKS

Aziz. A. — The Manasabdari System, Lahore, 1945

Baji Rao Peshwa (Marathi) — S. G. Sardesai, Bombay, 1946

Banerjee, I. B. — Evolution of the Khalsa, vol. ii, Calcutta, 1947

Duff, J. G. — History of the Marathas (vol. I), London 1912 ed.

Dighe, Dr V. G. — Baji Rao I and Maratha Expansion, Bombay, 1944

Elliot & Dowson — History of India (vols VII and VIII)

Faruki, M. — Aurangzib and his Times, Bombay, 1935

Gribbli, J. D. B. — History of the Deccan, (vol. III), London, 1896

Irvine, Sir William — Later Mughals (2 vols.), Calcutta, 1922

Irvine, Sir William — The Army of the Indian Mughals, London, 1903

Joshi, V. V. — Clash of Three Empires, 1941

Khan, Dr Yusuf Husain — Nizamu'l Mulk Asaf Jah I, Mangalore, 1936

Keena, H. G. — The Fall of the Moghul Empire, London, 1876

Kincaid, C. A. & Parasnis, Rai Sahib, D. B. — A History of the Maratha People, vols ii, iii, 1922

Khosla, R. P. — Mughal Kingship and Nobility, Allahabad 1934

Kosminski — Studies in the Agrarian History of England, Oxford, 1956

Lockhart, L.	Nadir Shah, London, 1938
Macauliffe M. A.	Sikh Religion, 1909, vols IV, V
Marwar ka Itihas (Hindi)	Pt. V. S. Reu, (2 vols)
Marathi Riyasat (Marathi)	S. G. Sardesai
Owen, S. G.	The Fall of the Moghul Empire, London, 1912
Qanungo, Dr K.	History of the Jats, Calcutta, 1925
Ranade, M. G.	Rise of the Maratha Power, Bombay, 1900
Rajputana ka Itihas (Hindi)	G. S. Ojha
Sardesai, Rai Sahib, S. G.	New History of the Maratha People, vol. i, Bombay, 1946, ii, 1948
Sarkar, Sir J. N.	History of Aurangzeb (vols iii–v), Calcutta, 1924
Sarkar, Sir J. N.	House of Shivaji, 1940
Sarkar, Sir J. N.	Shivaji and His Times, 4th ed. 1948
Sarkar, Sir J. N.	Mughal Administration, 1935
Sarkar, Sir J. N.	Fall of the Mughal Empire, (vol. i), 1932
Sarkar, Sir J. N.	History of Jaipur (unpublished Ms)
Scott, Jonathan	History of Deccan
Singh, Prof Ganda	Banda Singh Bahadur
Sen, S. N.	Administrative System of the Marathas, Calcutta, 1928
Sinh, Dr Raghubir	Malwa in Transition, 1936
Sinha, H. N.	Rise of the Peshwas, Allahabad, 1931
Spears, P.	Twilight of the Moghuls, Cambridge, 1951
Srivastava, Dr A. L.	First two Nawabs of Oudh, 1936
Tarikh-i-Sadat Baraha (Urdu Ms)	Muzaffar Ali Khan, K. B. Jansath, 1910
Tod, Col James	Annals of Rajasthan, Calcutta, 1916 ed.
Tara Chand, Dr	Influence of Islam on Indian Culture, Allahabad, 1946

Tripathi, Dr R. P. — Some Aspects of Muslim Administration, Allahabad, 1936

Select Articles

Journal of the Asiatic Society of Bengal

1878 — Bengal Nawabs of Farrukhabad by Sir William Irvine, pp. 259–383

1897 — Hindi Poem by Trilok Das-Text and Translation by Irvine

1900 — Jangnamah of Sri Dhar Murli, Text and Translation by Sir William Irvine, pp. 1–30

Journal of Indian History

Vol. xii — Ajit Singh by V. Reu, pp. 85–9

Journal of the Bombay Branch of the Royal Asiatic Society

Vol. XXII — Shivaji's Swarjya by Purushotam Vikram Mawji, pp. 30–42 (Based on the Persian and Marathi Ms 'Jabita Swarajya')

Journal of the UP Historical Society

1941, 1942 — Economic History of India 1600–1800 by Radhakamal Mukerji, pp. 49–69

Indian Culture

1934–5 — History of Abhai Singh of Gujarat from 1730 by his own Letters by Pt. V. S. Reu, p. 239

1935–6 — Sawai Jai Singh by D. C. Sircar, p. 376

Islamic Culture

1941 — Two Historical Letters by Asaf Jah I-Text and translation by Sir J. N. Sarkar, p. 341

1944	The Mughal Empire and the Middle Class—a Hypothesis by W. C. Smith, pp. 349–63
1946	Lower Class Risings in the Mughal Empire by W. C. Smith, pp. 21–40
1949	Dhulfiqār Khan Nusrat Jang by Satish Chandra, pp. 151–61

Asiatic Miscellany

1885	Letter of Nizam-ul-Mulk to M. Shah after his victory over Mubariz-ul-Mulk—translation by W. Irvine, pp. 482–93

Proceedings of the Indian History Congress

1938	Mansabdari under Jahangir by Dr B. P. Saxena, pp. 388–90
1939	Two letters of Abhai Singh by Pt. V. S. Reu, pp. 112–14
1941	Bihar in the First Quarter of the 18th Century by Prof. S. H. Askari, pp. 394–405
1946	Jizyah in the Post-Aurangzib by Satish Chandra
1948	Raja Jai Singh Sawai's Contribution to Imperial Politics by Satish Chandra, pp. 181–7

Proceedings of the Indian Historical Records Commission

1937, '38, '39, '40	Letters of Abhai Singh by V. S. Reu and 1942
1940	Some Documents bearing on Imperial Mughal Grants to Raja Shahu (1717–24) by Dr A. G. Powar, pp. 204–15
1942	'The Death of Aurangzib and After-Two Important Letters' by Dr A. G. Powar, pp. 336–40

Sardesai Commemoration Volume

The Marathas in Malwa 1707–19 by Dr R. Sinh, pp. 59–72

Bharat Itihas Sanshodhak Mandal Quarterly

Vol. xii — Article on Pilaji Jadhav's Campaign in Bundelkhand in 1735

Medieval India Quarterly

1957 — Early Relations of Farrukh Siyar and the Saiyid Brothers by Satish Chandra, pp. 135–46

Chronology

(ENGLISH DATES ACCORDING TO THE REFORMED GREGORIAN CALENDAR)

1707	3 March, 28 *Ẕīqa'dah* 1118	Aurangzīb's death
	17 March	A'ẕam leaves for N. India
	22 March, 18 *Ẕilḥijjah*	Bahādur Shāh crowned at Jamrud
	8 May	Shāhū leaves A'ẕam's camp
	18 June, 18 *Rabī'* 1119	A'ẕam defeated at Jājū
	12 November	Bahādur Shāh leaves for Rājpūtānā
1708	22 January	Shahu crowned King
	26 February	Ajit Singh submits to Bahādur Shāh
	30 April	Ajit Singh and Jai Singh flee from royal camp
	17 May	Bahādur Shāh crosses Narmada into Deccan
	6 October	Ajit Singh and Jai Singh restored to their *manṣab*s
	end of year	Sikh uprising under Banda
1709	13 January, 3 *Ẕīqa'dah*	Kām Bakhsh defeated and killed

	25 December	Bahādur Shāh re-crosses Narmada into N. India
1710	10 March	Governor of Burhānpur killed by Marāthās
	22 May	Wazīr K. *faujdar* of Sirhind, defeated and killed by Sikhs
	22 June	Rajput Rajas granted interview, peace made
	10 December	Mughal capture Lohgarh, Banda escapes
1711	28 February	Mun'im Khān, *wazīr*, dies
	August	Chadrasen Jadhav joins Mughals
	2 October	*Khuṭbah* riot at Lahore
1712	27 February, 20 *Muḥarram*	Bahādur Shāh dies at Lahore
	29 March, 21 *Ṣafar*	Jahāndār Shāh crowned after defeating all rivals
	6 April, 29 *Ṣafar*	Farrukh Siyar crowned at Patna
	7 April	Jahāndār abolishes *jizyah*
	22 June	Jahāndār enters Delhi
	22 September	Farrukh Siyar leaves Patna
	24 November	Prince 'Azz-ud-Dīn defeated at Khanwah by Saiyid Brothers
1713	11 January	Jahāndār Shāh defeated at Agra
	16 January	*Jizyah* abolished by Farrukh Siyar
	12 February	Farrukh Siyar enters Delhi
	2 March	Niẓam-ul-Mulk appointed Governor of the Deccan
	25 October	Jai Singh appointed governor of Malwa
1714	6 January	Ḥusain 'Alī leaves for Marwar campaign

	March	Ḥusain 'Alī concludes treaty with Ajit Singh
	April–May	Mīr Jumlah made (absentee) Governor of Bengal
	16 July	Ḥusain 'Alī returns to the Court
	20 September	Ḥusain 'Alī appointed to Deccan in place of Niẕām-ul-Mulk
	16 December	Mīr Jumlah leaves the Court
	29 December	Ajit Singh appointed Governor of Gujārāt
1715	20 May	Ḥusain 'Alī departs for the Deccan
	23 May	Jai Singh defeats the Marāthās in Malwa
	13 July	Niẕām-ul-Mulk reaches Delhi
	6 September	Ḥusain 'Alī defeats and kills Dā'ūd K. at Burhānpur
	17 December	Sikhs surrender at Gurdāspur
1716	16 January	Mīr Jumlah returns from Bihar
	4 June	Jai Singh reaches the Court
	25 September	Jai Singh appointed to lead expedition against Jats
1717	April	*Jizyah* re-imposed
	July	Ajit Singh dismissed from Gujārāt
	July–August	Ḥusain 'Alī begins negotiations with the Marāthās
	November	M. Amīn K. appointed to Malwa in place of Jai Singh

1718	10 February	Ḥusain 'Alī signs agreement with Marāthās
	19 April	Churāman Jat presented at the Court, peace made
	July	Farrukh Siyar summons Ajit Singh, Sarbuland K. and Niẕām-ul-Mulk
	14 December	Ḥusain 'Alī leaves Burhānpur for N. India
1719	7 January	Ajit Singh appointed Governor of Gujarat (2nd governorship)
	7 February	Niẕam-ul-Mulk appointed Governor of Bihar
	16 February	Ḥusain 'Alī arrives near Delhi
	28 February, 9 *Rabī'* II 1131	Farrukh Siyar deposed
	March	*Jizyah* abolished
	March	Marāthā troops leave for the Deccan
	15 March	Niẕam-ul-Mulk leaves
	18 May	Neku Siyar proclaimed Emperor at Agra
	6 June, 19 *Rajab*	Rafi'-ud-Daulah succeeds Rafi'-ud-Darjāt as Emperor
	8 July	Siege of Agra commences
	12 August	Agra surrenders
	August	Girdhar Bahādur rebels at Allahabad
	28 September, 15 *Ẕīqa'dah*	Muḥammad Shāh succeeds Rafi'-ud-Dullah
	5 November	Ajit Singh appointed Governor of Ajmer in addition to Gujārāt
1720	April	Bālāji Vishwanath dies, Baji Rao appointed Peshwa
	8 May	Niẕām-ul-Mulk crosses

		Narmada into the Deccan, begins rebellion
	11 May	Girdhar Bahādur evacuates Allahabad
	19 June	Niẓam-ul-Mulk defeats ʻĀlam ʻAlī Khān
	8 October	Ḥusain ʻAlī assassinated
	13 November	ʻAbdullāh Khān defeated
	3 December, 2 *Ṣafar*	Niẓam-ul-Mulk issues *sanad* for *chauth* and *sardeshmukhi* of Deccan
	25 December	M. Amīn K.'s attempt to revive *jizyah* fails
1721	14 January	Niẓām-ul-Mulk meets Baji Rao at Chikhalthan
	27 January	M. Amīn K., *wazīr*, dies
	May	Ajit Singh removed from Gujārāt and Ajmer—first uprising
	21 October	Niẓām-ul-Mulk leaves Aurangabad for Delhi
1722	January	Ajit Singh withdraws from Ajmer
	29 January	Niẓām-ul-Mulk reaches Delhi
	21 March	Envoys of Ajit reach Delhi for submission
	1 April	Ḥaider Qulī leaves for Gujārāt
	19 April	Jai Singh appointed for expedition against Jats
	1 September	Saʻādat Khān appointed Governor of Awadh
	November–April 1723	Baji Rao raids Malwa
	11 November	Niẓām-ul-Mulk leaves for Gujārāt
	18 November	Fall of Jat stronghold, Thūn
1723	6 January	Ajit Singh commences second uprising

	March	News received of fall of Iṣfaḥān to Gilzaīs on 22 October
	23 February–1 March	Niẓām meets Baji Rao at Bolasha near Jhabua
	May	Niẓam assumes charge of Malwa also
	3 July	Niẓām returns to Delhi
	August	Ajit Singh submits again
	December	Niẓām departs from Delhi
1724	January	Baji Rao enters Malwa again
	3 February	Mubāriz Khān appointed to Deccan in place of Niẓām
	28 May	Niẓām meets Baji Rao at Nalcha
	May–June	Niẓām reaches Burhānpur
	7 June	Abhai Singh succeeds Ajit Singh
	22 July	Qamar-ud-Dīn Khān appointed *wazīr*
	11 October, 23 *Muḥarram* 1137	Niẓām defeats Mubāriz Khān at Shakar Khera
1725	June	Girdhar Bahādur appointed to Malwa
	20 June	Niẓām pardoned, granted title of Āṣaf Jāh
	November–May 1726	Baji Rao's first expedition into Karnatak
1726	3 May, 1 *Ramāẓan* 1138	Sarbuland agrees to *chauth* and *sardeshmukhi* of Gujārāt for the year
	November–April 1727	Baji Rao's second expedition into Karnātak
1727	February	M. Khān Bangash invades Bundelkhand
	2 March	Sarbuland signs pact for *chauth* of Gujārāt with Chimnaji

	August–February 1728	War between Niẓām and the Marāthās
1728	6 March	Niẓām signs treaty with Baji Rao at Mungi Shivagaon
	June	M. Khān Bangash besieges Chhatrasāl at Jaitpur
	October–May 1729	Chimnaji invades Malwa and Bundelkhand
	9 December	Girdhar Bahādur and Daya Bahādur killed at Amjhara
1729	March	Shoe Sellers' Riot at Delhi
	March–June	Baji Rao meets Chhatrasāl, M. Khān Bangash besieged
	October	Jai Singh appointed to Malwa (2nd governorship)
1730	2 April	Sarbuland signs pact for *chauth* of Gujārāt
	May	Abhai Singh appointed Governor of Gujārāt
	29 September	M. Khān Bangash replaces Jai Singh in Malwa
	October	Niẓām approaches Dābhāde for joint action against Baji Rao
1731	February	Abhai Singh meets Baji Rao, signs pact for *chauth*
	end of March	Niẓām and M. Khān Bangash confer
	11 April	Baji Rao defeats Dābhāde at Dabhoi
	24 December	Chhatrasāl Bundela dies
1732	2 April	Abhai Singh slays Pilaji Gaekwad
	July	Peshwa divides Malwa

		between Sindhia, Holkar and Pawar
	Early half	Fall of royal favourites at the court
	8 October	Jai Singh appointed Governor of Malwa (3rd governorship)
	October	Bundelas assign *jāgīr* to Marāthās, sign offensive and defensive pact
	November—May 1733	First Imperial campaign to clear Malwa
	December	Niẓām and Baji Rao meet at Rohe Rameshwar
1733	Early part	Chimnaji in North India
	February	Umabai besieges Aḥmadabād, Abhai Singh withdrawn from Gujārāt
	March	Jai Singh besieged at Mandsaur, gives *chauth* for the year
	October–May 1734	Holkar invades Rājpūtānā, Pilaji levies *chauth* in Bundelkhand
	October	Muẓaffar Khān advances upto Sironj
1734	October–May 1735	Sindhia and Holkar raid Malwa, Pilaji in Bundelkhand
	October–May 1735	Grand Imperial effort to oust Marāthās
1735	3 April	Khān-i-Daurān signs pact for *chauth* with Holkar
	October	Peshwa leaves for N. India
1736	26 February	Nādir ascends throne of Persia
	14 March	Peshwa meets Jai Singh in Rājpūtānā

	March–May 1737	Peace negotiations with Baji Rao
	May	Peshwa returns to Deccan
	October	Peshwa leaves for N. India again
1737	3 March	Nādir Shāh invests Qandahar
	12 March	Sa'ādat Khān repulses Holkar's raid into Dū'āb
	9 April	Baji Rao appears at the gate of Delhi
	17 April	Niẓām leaves Burhānpur for N. India
	12 July	Niẓām reaches Delhi
	16 December	Niẓām besieged at Bhopal
1738	7 January	Niẓām accepts Baji Rao's terms
	12 March	Fall of Qandahar
	19 June	Fall of Kabul
	12 December	Nādir Shāh crosses Indus
1739	12 January	Fall of Lahore
	13 February	Battle of Karnāl
	3 March	Nādir Shāh enters Delhi
	1 May	Nādir Shāh leaves Delhi

Index

'Abdul Ghafūr Bohra, question of escheat of the property of 203n, 208
'Abdul Ghafūr (Shāh), a faqir, joins plot against Hussain 'Alī, interferes in administration 248–9; fall from power 250
'Abdul Ḥaī Bohra, son of 'Abdul Ghafūr 208
'Abdullāh Khān Saiyid Miyān father of 'Abdullāh Khān 127
'Abdullāh Khān, Saiyid (Qutb-ul-Mulk), antecedents and early career 126–8; appointed deputy governor of Allahabad 129; seizes convoy of treasure, removed from post, joins Farrukh Siyar 134–5; claims post of *wazīr* 134–5; attempts to conciliate old nobles, especially M. Amin K., Nizam-ul-Mulk 135–8; abolishes *jizyah* 138n; attitude to Rājpūts 140; writes to Husain 'Ali regarding emperor's intrigues 140; opposed by personal favourites of King, resents their interference, role of Ratan Chand 142–8; prepares for showdown 150n; position after departure of Husain 'Ali for Deccan and of Mir'Jumlah for Bihar 154–5; continues to face opposition of emperor and of M. Amin K., and Nizam, the force at his disposal 156–7; return of Mir Jumlah, recommends his case 158; grants *diwani* of Bengal etc. to English 159; opposes Jat campaign of Jai Singh 163; peace concluded with Jats at his instance 164; neglects administration, opposes re-imposition of *jizyah* and other reforms of 'Inayatullah K. 165–6; emperor's attempt to imprison, recruits fresh troops 172–4; wins over Nizam-ul-Mulk Sarbuland K., Ajit Singh and M. Amin K. 174–6, 202; asks Husain 'Ali to return to Delhi 177; attitude to Farrukh Siyar—opposes deposition 176;

imprisons Farrukh Siyar, 179, 201; blames Husain 'Ali for deposition 182; favours proposal to accept Neku Siyar as emperor 184; his political difficulties—attempt to consolidate alliance of Rājpūts, Marāthās and old nobles 186–9; struggle for power with Husain 'Ali 189; differences over attitude to old nobles and Nizam-ul-Mulk 190; M. Amin Khan spared at his instance 196–7; favours accommodation with Nizam-ul-Mulk 197, 198; raises Ibrahim K. to throne after assassination of Husain 'Ali, defeated and taken prisoner 199, 200; character and administration 202–3; significance of his *wizārat* 202–4; concluding remarks 293–7

'Abd-un-Nābī Khān, fights Marāthās 88

'Abduṣ-Samad Khān, early career 108n; appointed *Sadr* with the rank of 7,000 68; intercedes with Asad Khan on behalf of Chīn Qulīch Khan 116–17; Saiyids give him rank of 7,000/7,000 and governorship of Lahore 137; opposes Saiyids along with Nizam-ul-Mulk and M. Amin Khan 153; retains the governorship of Lahore after downfall of Saiyids 205; opposes Nizam-ul-Mulk's scheme to reimpose *jizyah* 212, 220; death, succeeded by son, Zakariyah K., 221

Abhai Singh (son of Ajit Singh), sent to court with Husain 'Ali (1714) 141; raids Imperial territory 217; sent to court after peace in 1724–5, 218; succeeds Ajit Singh with rank of 7,000/7,000 and title of Rajah-i-Rajeshwar 218; desires to carve out independent principality 222–3n; appointed governor of Gujarat 242, 251; agreement with Baji Rao for *chauth* and *sardeshmukhi*, opposes policy of alliance with Nizam 233, 242–3; withdraws to Jodhpur 242; arrives at court, befriends the Wazir, Qamar-ud-Din K., 259; joins him and others in resisting Marāthās 259, 261, 266

Abwāb (illegal cesses, see also *rahdāri*) 121n, pilgrim tax 138, 170n, in Gujarat 176n

Adaru, Zamindar, fight of Sa'ādat K. and Qamar-ud-Dīn with 245n, 250

Afghans position in nobility xix, 2; growth of power 223, 245; and Nadir Shah 279–80, 283–4

Afẓal Khān, tutor of Farrukh Siyar, dispute regarding his appointment 142–3

Agra, occupied by 'Azīm-ush-Shān 54; battle between Jahandar Shah and Farrukh Siyar 123; Neku Siyar's rebellion at and siege of by Saiyids 183–4

Aḥmad Khān, Mīr, Governor of Burhampur, killed fighting Marāthās, 88

Ahmad Sa'īd (Hussain K.) Bāraha, appointed *faujdār* of Amber, 68, 69, 74

Aḥmad Shāh, Prince 287

Ajit Singh, promised *manṣab* and *raj* by Aurangzīb 23; given title of Maharaja, *manṣab* of

7,000/7,000 and governorship of Gujarat by A'zam Shah 59, 67, 113; reoccupies Jodhpur 67; Bahadur Shah's expedition against 66–7; peace made, given *manṣab* of 3,500/3,000 and title of Maharaja, but Jodhpur reoccupied, kept under semi-captivity 69–72; escapes, and renews war 71–3; peace concluded, *manṣab* and homeland restored 75; dissatisfied, wants *subahdari* of Gujarat and high *manṣab* 77, serves against Sikhs, granted *faujdāri* of Sorath, returns home 77–8

Raised to *manṣab* of 7,000/7,000, granted *ṣūbahdāri* of Gujarat by Z̲u'lfiqār K. 114; summoned for help against Farrukh Siyar 123n; submits to Farrukh Siyar 138; granted rank of 7,000/7,000 and governorship of Thatta, asks for Gujarat, emperor decides on war 139–40; Husain 'Ali's campaign, Farrukh Siyar's secret letter, secret pact with Husain 'Ali, 140–1; daughter married to Farrukh Siyar 141; Farrukh Siyar opposes the pact, delays appointment to Gujarat 149; recalled to court, attempt of Farrukh Siyar to enlist against Saiyids 172–3, 173n; dismissed from Gujarat for oppression 175n, 216; advises deposition of Farrukh Siyar 177, 179; pelted with stones by Delhi populace 202n; appointed governor of Gujarat and Ajmer after deposition, his influence 186–7; attempts to mediate between Jai Singh and Saiyids 186–7, 196n; does not help Saiyids 186–7, 196n; does not help Sayids in their hour of need 204; shelters Mukham Singh Jat 215, removed from Gujarat after fall of Saiyids, but allowed to retain Ajmer 216, court discusses plan of campaign against 216–18; murders newly appointed *dīwan* of Ajmer, Imperial campaign against 218; submits 218; murdered 218

Ajit Singh, son of Guru Govind 115

Akbar (Emperor) attitude to *zamindars* 9, 7; to regional sentiments 10-11; his organization of the nobility 4–7; Rājpūt policy 8

Akbar (prince) 50n, 62, 279

Akbar (fictitious prince) 175

Aku Ghorpādē, raids Karnaṭak 88

'Alam 'Alī, Saiyid, deputy of Husain 'Ali in the Deccan 188, 189, 190, 195, 197, 198, 198, 203

'Ālamgīr—see under Aurangzīb

'Ālam Shaikh, grandfather of Ghāzī-ud-Dīn Fīrūz Jang 46

Alāwal Khān, nephew of Dā'ūd Khān Pannī 87

'Alī Mardān Khān Shāmlū, agent of Nādir Shāh to Delhi 283

'Alī Tabār, son of 'Aẓīm-ush-Shān 109

Allahabad, governorship of 'Abdullāh K. 133–4; of Sarbuland K. 173n; rebellion of Chhabelā Ram and siege of by Saiyids 184–6

Amānat K., diwan of the Deccan 83n
Amar Singh II (Rana of Udaipur) alleged secret treaty with Bahadur Shah in 1681 for abolition of *jizyah* etc. 70, 71n; cooperates with Jai Singh 68; averts threatened invasion of his country by sending his brother to wait upon Bahadur Shah 70, agreement with Ajit Singh and Jai Singh to fight Mughals 72; Imperial grant of *pālkīs* and 'Arabi and 'Iraqi horses to 95n
Amīn-un-Dīn Sambhalī, imprisoned after accession of Jahandar 118n; advises Farrukh Siyar to resist Saiyids 178n; his property etc. confiscated after the deposition of Farukh Siyar 182
Amīr-definition 6 (see under nobility)
Amīr Khān, governor of Kabul 279
Amīr Khān, ('Ālamgirī) 118n, 182
Amīr Khān, M. Shāh's favourite 265
Amjad Khān, Saiyid, promised post of *Sadr* by 'Abdullah K. 142
Anup Singh, *dīwan* of Ajit Singh 207n
Anwar Khān, Saiyid, adviser of S. Husain 'Ali 169
Anwārullāh K., joins Niẓām-ul-Mulk 195
Asadūllāh Khān, S. uncle of Abdullah K. 152n
Asad Khān, *Wazīr-al-Māmalik*: ancestry 40; made *wazīr* by Aurangzib 41; recommended to sons 41; proceeds to Jinji 42; favours A'zam 50, 51; not keen to take part in civil war 51; left at Gwalior with ladies etc. 55; Bahadur Shah sends letter of reassurance 62; arrives at court, claims *wizarat* 63, made *Wakil-i-Mutlaq* 63–4; leaves for Delhi 65; ordered to repress Rājpūt uprising 63, negotiates with Rājpūts 74–5; ordered to march against Sikhs 90; revival of claim for *wazīr*'s office 93; position under Jahandar Shah 107–8; *jizyah* abolished at his instance 113; helps Chin Qulich 117; disgraced by Farrukh Siyar 136–7, 145
Āṣaf Khān (Yamīn-ud-Daullah) 64, 135n
Āṣaf Jāh (see under Niẓām-ul-Mulk)
Aurangzīb (also 'Ālamgīr) and Jats 19–20; Satnamis 20, 21; and Sikhs 21; and Marāthās 23–6, and Deccan problem 23–6; financial reforms 27; situation of empire at death 26–7, 53, 57n, 148; attitude towards Shi'ism and Iranis 13, 129; parties among nobles towards the end of reign 40–9; attitude towards sons and grandsons 49–50, 54, 61, 94n, 104; scheme of partition of empire 50, 63, 79–80; death 51; position of *wazīr* under 101–2; opinion regarding Baraha Saiyids 126–7; gradual abandonment of his Rājpūt, Marāthā and Hindu policies, by Bahadur Shah 79, 88, 95–6, by Z̲u'lfiqār Khān 59, 114, 124 and by the Saiyid brothers 137–40, 167–8; attempt of Nizam-ul-Mulk to revive partially 202, 211, fails 212; lessons 220

Ayā Mal, Maratha *wakīl*, 115, 261n
A'ẓam Khān, brother of Kokaltāsh Khān, 109
A'ẓam Shāh, at siege of Bijapur 46; wins over Asad and Zu'lfiqar Khan 50; clashes with Kam Bakhsh 50; ascends throne after death of Aurangzīb, prepares for civil war 51–2; attitude of leading nobles 51–2; suspected of Shi'ite tendencies 52n; financial and other difficulties 53–4; battle of Jaju 55–6; makes large concessions to Rājpūt and Marāthās at instance of Zu'lfiqar Khan 57–60
'Azīmullah Khāṇ, fights Marāthās 256–7
'Azīm-ush-Shān, second son of Bahādūr Shāh, sovereignty forecast for him while governor of Bengal 130; recalled by Aurangzīb from Patna before his death 55; reaches Agra first 55; Jai Singh and Ajit Singh seek his mediation 74; pace restored at his instance 75–6; becomes centre of all affairs 77; offered Viceroyalty of Deccan after defeat of Kam Bakhsh, prefers Bengal, Bihar, Orissa and Allahabad 81n, 82, 128; appoints Husain 'Ali his deputy in Bihar, and 'Abdullah Khan in Allahabad 129; influence of Mir Jumlah over 144; attitude towards question of *wizarat* after death of Mun'im Khan 92–3; rift with Z̲u'lfiqār Khān 94; other princes organize against him 104; his wealth 99–100, 119n; rejects Z̲u'lfiqār's attempt at compromise regarding succession 105; attitude towards Z̲u'lfiqār's scheme of partition of empire 107; civil war at Lahore, stands on defensive in expectation of reinforcements, defeated 106–7; uprising of his son, Farrukh Siyar (q.v.), against Jahandar Shah 104, 131
A'zz-ud-Dīn (prince) leads army against Farrukh Siyar 115–16; his flight from Khanwah 123

Badan Singh (Jat) succeeds Churaman, growth of Jat power under 215.
Bahādūr Khān (Ranmast Khan), uncle of Dā'ūd Khān Pannī, 45
Bahramand Khān, *mīr bakhshī* of Aurangzīb, 43
Bahādūr Shāh (Prince Mu'aẓẓam, Shāh 'Ālam), early life 49n–50n, 61–2n; released and appointed governor of Kabul 61, 279–80; prepares for civil war 54–5, 61; war with A'zam 54–5; appointments etc. 62–6; Rājpūt policy of 67–79; war with Kam Bakhsh 80–1; administrative arrangements for Deccan 82–3 Marāthā relations of 84–8; criticism 88; operations against Sikhs 89–92; controversy regarding appointment of *wazīr* after death of Mun'im Khan 93–4; general policy and administration—cautious departure from policies of Aurangzīb, breach with orthodox elements, *jizyah* etc. enforced 95–6; neglect of

administration 96; deterioration of financial situation, worsening of crisis of *jāgīrdāri* system 96–100; estimate 99; position of *wazīr* under 102–3; civil war among sons 104–8

Baji Rao (*Peshwa*), helps 'Alam 'Alī against Niẓām-ul-Mulk 197; his advice rejected by 'Alam 'Ali 199n, 204; first meeting with Nizam (1721) 205, invades Malwa, second meeting with Nizam, 209–10; helps Nizam against Mubariz K. 214; appointed *Peshwa* 225; controversy with *Pratinidhi* regarding Marāthā expansion and north India 225–8; war with Nizam-ul-Mulk, treaty of Shivgaon (1728) 227–31; organizes systematic raids into Malwa and Gujarat, and demands *chauth* 231–4; defeats Girdhar Bahadur at Amjhara, raids Bundelkhand 234; early relations with Jai Singh Sawai 236–40; treaty with Abhai Singh for *chauth* of Gujarat 242–4; agreement with Bundelas 244–5; renewed hostility of Nizam (1729) 231, 242n, 251–2; third secret meeting with Nizam 252; sounds Northern powers regarding peace, invited by Jai Singh for peace talks 260, 276–7; arrives in Rajputana, meets Jai Singh 261; peace negotiations (1736) 262–5; returns to Deccan due to failure of negotiations 229; raids *Du'ab* and Delhi 266–8; renewed struggle with Nizam, battle of Bhopal 268–73; prepares to resist Nadir Shah instructed to help emperor 272, sends *nazr* to Nadir Shah 272; proposes united front of Indian powers under emperor to oppose foreigners 272; nature of his ambitions 227–8, 266, 272, 273n

Bakht Singh, brother of Rana of Mewar, sent to Bahādūr Shāh 70

Bakht Singh, kills his father, Ajit Singh 242

Baji Bhivrao, presents demands of Baji Rao to emperor 262

Balaji Baji Rao—raids Malwa, peace made by emperor, Malwa and Gujarat ceded 274

Balaji Vishwanath (Peshwa) 87, helps Ḥusain 'Alī 170, 177, 236; demands *chauth* of Malwa and Gujarat 177; 231; Saiyids ask for help against Nizam 197; settlement of *chauth* etc. 225

Banda, the false *guru*, uprising under 76, 78; founds first Sikh state, its character 89–92; suppressed 137

Bāqī Khān, commandant of Agra fort, submits to Shah 'Alam 54, 55

Bhajja (father of Churaman Jat) 161

Bhimsen, historian 56n

Bhim Singh Hara (son of Ram Singh) granted Bundi by Husain Ali 160, displaced to placate Jai Singh 163, advises deposition of Farrukh Siyar 177, restored to Bundi 178

Bhopal, battle and treaty of 269–72; Bidar Bakhi (Prince) 8, 15, 17, 20, 200

Bidar Bakht (Prince) 47, 54, 56, 59, 235

Bihari Das, Jaipur *wakīl*, advises

'Abdūllah Khān to abolish *jizyah* 138n
Bijai Singh, see Vijai Singh
Budh Singh Hara—displaced from *zamindari* of Bundi (1706) 44, 69n; sides with Bahadur Shah at Jaju, granted 54 forts including Kotah 160; sent to Jodhpur to reassure Ajit Singh 70; alienates Saiyids, removed from Bundi 160; seeks intercession of Jai Singh 161; comes to court with Jai Singh, restored to Bundi 162, 163; defeated by Bhim Singh and displaced from Bundi 178
Buland Akhtar, Prince 170
Burhān-ul-Mulk, see Sa'ādat Khān

Chhabelā Ram Nagar, antecedents and early career 143n; *jizyah* abolished by Farrukh Siyar at his instance 48n; appointed *diwan-i-khalisah walan* 143, appointed governor of Agra 143; fails in campaign against Jats 162; remains hostile to Saiyids after deposition of Farrukh Siyar 183; uprising at Allahabad 185; negotiations with Saiyids 184; dies 185
Chauth: origin 25; attitude of Aurangzīb towards 25, 26; did A'ẓam concede *chauth* of Deccan? 57–9; Shahu's petition for *chauth* of Deccan rejected by Bahadur Shah 84–5; Da'ud's pact for *chauth* of Deccan 87, 88; Husain 'Ali's pact 169–70; confirmed by emperor 187; nature of *chauth* under Peshwas 228–9, 231–4 (see also under Marāthās)
Chandrasen Jādhav 86–7; joins Mughals 87, 115n; fights Marāthās 168
Chhatrasal Bundela: remains a royal feudatory during reign of Bahadur Shah, asked to join Prince A'zz-ud-din in campaign against Farrukh Siyar 115; serves Jai Singh against Marāthās in Malwa, summoned to court by Farrukh Siyar (Sept. 1715) 162; attacked by M. Khan Bangash 245; summons Marāthās to his help, agrees to annual tribute 244; active alliance with Marāthās till death (1731) 244
Chimnaji Appa, brother of Baji Rao, 255, 263n, 266n, 266, 269, 269n, 271
Chīn Qulīch K. (Niẓam-ul-Mulk), antecedents and early career 47; raised to 5,000/5,000 (1705) 47; rivalry with Ẕu'lfiqār K. 49; raised to 7,000/7,000 and made governor of Khandesh by A'ẓam Shah, abandons him 51; plunders near Aurangabad 52; invited to court by Bahadur Shah 62; raised to 6,000/6,000, and made governor of Awadh, resigns, raised to 7,000/7,000 'Azim-ush-Shan 116; Ẕu'lfiqār desires to crush him, 'Abdus-Samad K. intervenes 115–17; granted rank of 5,000 and *sūbahdāri* of Malwa, resigns 116; insulted by La'l Kunwar, Ẕu'lfiqār K. helps him 116; re-employed and given *manṣab* of 7,000, asked to help in checking Farrukh Siyar 117; remains neutral in battle with

Farrukh Siyar 123 (see under Nizam-ul-Mulk) for later career)
Churman Jat, obtains the rank of 1,500/500, sides with 'Azim-ush-Shan at the battle of Lahore, takes part in Sikh campaign promises to help Jahandar against Farrukh Siyar, loots both sides during the battle 116, 160–2; tacit support by Saiyids, gradually falls out of royal favour, Jai Singh's campaign against 162–3; peace made through Asadullah Khan; further concessions by Saiyids after deposition of Farrukh Siyar 196n; helps Saiyids in battle of Hasanpur 198, 214; defeats and kills deputy of Sa'adat Khan 215; dies 215

Dabhade (Trimbakrao) Senapati 234, 243, 252, 272
Dalpat Rao Bundela, lieutenant of Z̲u'lfiqār K. 43–5, 45n, 51, 57
Dānishmand Khān (Ni'mat Khān 'Alī), historian 56n, 81n
Dārā (prince) 51, 12, 56
Dā'ūd Khān Pannī, a Deccani Afghān, son of a merchant, chief lieutenant of Z̲u'lfiqār Khān 44; raised to the rank of 6,000/6,000 in 1704 45; said to favour Hindus and to keep Hindu idol in house 45; opposes Kam Bakhsh in Karnaṭak 81; appointed deputy to Z̲u'lfiqār Khān as Viceroy of the Deccan with rank of 7,000/5,000 and the governorship of Bijapur, Berar and Aurangabad 82; Hiraman his deputy 87, 104; makes private pact with Shahu for *chauth* of Deccan 87–8, 114; leaves all power in the hands of Deccani Brahmins 121; transferred to Gujarat by Farrukh Siyar 137; appointed his deputy in the Deccan by Husain Ali 149; instructed by emperor to oppose Husain 'Ali defeated and killed 153; Nizam not responsible for his appointment 153n
Dayā Ram, killed with Girdhar Bahādūr at Amjhara 234
Dhānājī Jādav 42, 43
Dilāwar 'Alī Khān, *bakhshi* of S. Husain 'Alī 184b, 194, 197, 198
Diler Khān, fights Marāthās in Karnaṭak 88
Diyānat Khān Khwāfī, (son of Amānat K., entitled Amānat K.) *dīwan* of Z̲u'lfiqār K. in the Deccan, 83n, dies 172
Diyānat Khān (or Dī'ānat K.) son of the above. Appointed deputy to his father 83n; warns Nizam-ul-Mulk about Saiyid intentions, 195; a well-wisher of the Saiyids 198
Dost M. Khan, *Nawab* of Bhopal 210
Durgadas 70, 162
Durjan Sal of Kotah 257

Fakhr-ud-Daulah, brother of Roshan-ud-Daulah, 234n, 249n
Farrukh Siyar, early life 129; proclaims 'Azīm-ush-Shān as King 90; early relations with Husain 'Ali 130–2; abolishes *jizyah* while in Bihar 133; joined by 'Abdullah Khan 134; continued suspicion of Saiyids

135; defeats prince A'zz-ud-Din 122–3, defeats Jahandar Shah 123; appointments etc. 135–8; imprisons Asad K. and executes Zu'lfiqār K. against advice of Saiyids 136; confirm abolition of *jizyah* 138; attitude towards Rājpūts 138–41; intrigues with Ajit Singh against Saiyids 141; causes of conflict with Saiyids 140; causes of conflict with Saiyids—struggle for power, divergent outlook regarding role of *wazīr*, administrative incompetence of Saiyids, role of favourites 141–9; first trial of strength, its results 150–3; instructs Da'ud Khan to oppose Husain 'Ali 153; continues intrigues against 'Abdullah Khan 156; disgraces Mir Jumlah on his return to Delhi, 157–8; attempts to use Jai Singh to oppose Saiyids and to crush Jats 160, 162, 163; forced to conclude peace with Jats—further straining of relations with the Saiyids 164; attempts to rally old nobles, appoints 'Inayatullah K., re-imposes *jizyah* 166; intrigues against Husain 'Ali in Deccan 168; opposes Husain 'Ali's pact with Marāthās 171; attempts to check Husain 'Ali from marching to Delhi 170–3; attempts to arrest 'Abdullah Khan, summons Nizam, Sarbuland and Ajit Singh 172, 173; his isolation 174–5; events leading to his deposition 176–80; killed 180; the deposition discussed 201–3

Fazlullāh Khān, *bakhshi* of Burhanpur 172

Fīrūz Jang (see Ghāzī-ud-Dīn Fīrūz Jang)

Ganga, a Marāthā *sardar* dismissed by Fīrūz Jang, creates distrubances in Burhandpur and Malwa 87

Gaj Singh, at the siege of Thūn 163

Ghairat Khān, Saiyid, appointed governor of Agra 183n

Ghāzī-ud-Dīn Khān Ahmad Beg, earliest supporter of Farrukh Siyar, 131, 133, 135, 182, 199

Ghāzī-ud-Dīn Fīrūz Jang: power and influence of his group towards the end of Aurangzīb's reign 46–9; raised to 7,000/7,000 and made *Sipah Salar* 46; his artillery 46–7; partronizes Turanis 48–9; becomes blind 49; his strained relations with son, Chīn Qulīch 49; refuses to march with A'zam in civil war, appointed viceroy of Deccan 51–2; appointed governor of Gujarat by Bahadur Shah, afraid of coming to the court 65; ordered to repress Rājpūts, dies 75

Ghorpade, Aku, raids Karnaṭak 88

Ghorpade, Santaji 42, 87

Girdhar Bahādūr—nephew of Chabelā Ram, continues rebellion against Saiyids at Allahabad 185; appointed governor of Awadh 185; opposes move of M. Amin Khan to reimpose *jizyah* 206; succeeds Nizam-ul-Mulk as governor of Malwa (1722) 209; removed by Nizam 210; with

Jai Singh in Jat campaign, proceeds against Ajit Singh 218; appointed governor of Malwa again (1725), fights Marāthās 233–4; defeated and killed at Amjhara 234
Gulab Chand *Karori Saïr*, 176n
Guru Govind, dies 89, 91, 92
Gūjar Mal, *diwan-i-khalisah*, dies 213

Hāfiẓ Ādam, follower of Sh. Ahmad Sirhindī, helps Sikhs
Haibat Rao Nimbālkar, Maratha *sardar*, invades Bījapūr 87
Haider Qulī Khān, early career 207–8; 207n, 146n, 150n, 197, 199, 205; raised to rank of 8,000/7,000 and appointed (absentee) governor of Gujarat for his part in fall of Saiyids 208; Nizam-ul-Mulk resents his interference, sent to assume personal charge of Gujarat, accused of violating royal privileges, expedition of Nizam against 209–10; appointed to lead campaign against Ajit Singh 216, 217
Hakīm-ul-Mulk, chief adviser of Jahān Shāh, imprisoned 118n
Hāmid Khān Bahādūr, brother of Nizam-ul-Mulk, 46, 47, 48n, 49, 211, 222n
Hamid-ud-Dīn Khān ('Alamgiri) 56, 80n, 118n
Hamilton, Dr 159
Hanumant, a Marāthā *sardar*, 128
Hāshim 'Ali Khān, adviser of Husain 'Ali, favours deposition of Farrukh Siyar 179
Hidāyat Kesh, *Wāqa' Nigār Kul*, imprisoned 118n, 146
Hidāyatullāh Khān, (see Sa'dullāh K.)
Himmat Khān Bāraha, Saiyid, appointed *ataliq* of emperor 186
Hindu-Pad-padshahi—and Marāthās 240, 266, 298
Hindustanis—definitions 15, 16; character of 19; soldiers 157n, 247, 313; in the administrative services, oppose *jizyah*, 166–7; and Saiyids 191; relations with Mughals etc. during the period, 280–3
Hiraman, deputy of Dā'ūd Khān in the Deccan 87–8
Hirdesa, son of Chhatrasal Budela, 244
Holkar (Yashwantrao), lieutenant of Bāji Rao 255, 256, 266, 267, 269–70n
Husain Khān, Saiyid, governor of Ajmer, 251
Husain 'Alī, Saiyid (*Amīr-ul-Umarā*, *mīr bakhshī*), antecedents 126–7; early career 127, 128, 122; appointed deputy governor of Allahabad by 'Azim-ush-Shan 129; strained relations with Farrukh Siyar in Bihar 129–30; opposes proclamation of 'Azim-ush-Shan as King 130; motives for joining Farrukh Siyar 131–2; mutual suspicions continue 132–5; abolishes *jizyah* 133; joins attempt to conciliate old nobles 136–8; Rājpūt policy of 137–40; leads expedition against Ajit Singh, private pact with him 140–1; causes of differences with Farrukh Siyar 141–8; obtains Viceroyalty of Deccan, desires to govern it through a deputy 149; opposed by Farrukh Siyar, agrees to assume personal charge on certain conditions 150–3; fights

and defeats Da'ud Khān Panni 153; relations with Marāthās 167–8, forms pact with Shahu through Shankaraji 170–1; attempt of Farrukh Siyar to check 171–2, 174–5; marches to Delhi, deposes Farrukh Siyar 177; general policy after deposition of Farrukh Siyar 185–9; differences with 'Abdullah K. over sharing of power 189; his character 177, 190, 196, 203n; his attitude towards old nobles and Nizam-ul-Mulk 190–1, plan of partition of empire 193; attempt to remove Nizam from Malwa 194; plan to assassinate M. Amin Khan 196–7; his plan of action against Nizam 197, 198; rejects 'Abdullah Khan's idea of a compromise with Nizam 198; marches to the Deccan, assassinated 199; his policy etc. discussed 201–3

Ibrāhīm Khān, son of 'Alī Mardān Khān, appointed governor of Kabul 279

Ijārah (revenue-farming) 121, 148, 155, 202–3, 211

Ikhlās Khān, *'arẓ-i-mukarrar* 96–7, 165, 179

'Ināyatullāh Khān, Mīr Munshī of Aurangzīb, 164–7

Inder Singh, 114; sons assassinated by Ajit Singh 140

Iqtā', iqtādār 3, 7, 36

Irādat Khān, historian, 66n, 105, 107, 118, 120, 79, 81

Īrānīs (see also Mughals)—position in the nobility 13–16; and Shi'ism 18; Aurangzīb's attitude towards 43n, 47–8

'Isā Khān Main, favourite of Jahāndār Shāh, 128

Islām Khān, Mīr Ātish, 118n

I'tiqād Khān (see M. Murād)

I'tiṣām Khān, *dīwān-i-khāliṣah,* 126n

'Izz-ud-Daulah Khān-i-Jahān 'Alamgirī 35; appointed governor of Orissa 89n, 132

Jadu Rai, Maratha agent, 238, 273

jāgīr, jāgīrdārī: character and nature of 3, 10–11; crisis of *jāgīrdārī* in seventeenth century, attempt at reform by Bahadur Shah 96–9, by Ẕu'lfiqār K. 119–21, by Inayatullah K. under Farrukh Siyar 166, by Nizam-ul-Mulk 211–12
  Interference of provincial governors etc. with 162, 175–6n, 185, 210, 222, 270–1; summary 301–4

Jahāngir 61n, 87, 138

Jahāndār Shāh (Bahāḍūr Shāh's son), governor of Multan at the time of Aurangzīb's death 54; succeeds in civil war due to the support of Ẕu'lfiqār Khān 104–7; relations with Asad and Ẕu'lfiqār Khān after accession 107–9; personal favourites 109–10; La'l Kunwar, her political influence exaggerated, widens breach between Jahandar and Ẕu'lfiqār Khān 110–13; high price of grain causes popular discontent 121; financial difficulties and extravagance of 121–2

Jahān Shāh, son of Bahādūr Shāh, supports claim of Asad Khan for *wizarat* 63; joins league against 'Azim-ush-Shan for partition of the empire 104,

105, 106; early relations with Saiyids 128; his son, M. Shah, succeeds to throne 181, 216

Jai Singh Sawal, early career 82; raised to 7,000/7,000 and appointed governor of Malwa by A'zam Shah 59, 113; deserts A'zam in battle of Jeju 69; deprived of Amber by Bahadur Shah, and replaced by Vijai Singh 67–70; escapes from royal camp, agreement with Rana and Ajit Singh for joint campaign against Mughals, recovers Amber 74; restored to *manṣab,* peace made 74–5; serves against the Sikh Guru, appointed *faujdār* of Chitrakut,' demand for governorship rejected, returns home 77–8

Raised to 7,000/7,000 and appointed governor of Malwa by Jahandar Shah 114; asked to help against Farrukh Siyar, his alliance with Ajit Singh disapproved, raised to 7,000/7,000 and appointed governor of Malwa 138–9; persuades Ajit Singh to end war with Husain 'Ali 141; wins crushing victory against Marāthās in Malwa 160; early relations with Saiyids 160–2; summoned to court by Farrukh Siyar, appointed to lead expedition against Jats 162–3; fails due to secret opposition of Saiyids, difficulties of terrain etc. 162–3; Farrukh Siyar's letter to regarding *jizyah* 165n; removed from Malwa 171; banished from court at Husain 'Ali's instance, his country ravaged 174–6, 177–8n, 178; withdraws to Amber, shelters opponents of Saiyids 183, 186; Saiyids try to win him over 186–7; also approached by Nizam-ul-Mulk 192; opposes proposed re-imposition of *jizyah* by M. Amin K. 206; attempt made through him to enlist Marāthās against Nizam 214; second Jat expedition of 215; asked to assist in expedition against Ajit Singh 218; personal friendship with Khan-i-Dauran, appointed governor of Agra and then of Malwa through him 218–19; ambition of establishing a hegemony upto Narmada 254–5; relations with the Marāthās 240–3; appointed governor Malwa (1729), then replaced 240–1; clash of interests with Sa'adat K. over *du'ab* 244–5; warned by M. Khan Bangash regarding Marāthās 245; appointed governor of Malwa for third time (1732), agrees to pay *chauth* 251–2, 254–5; his policy discussed 258–9; invites *Peshwa* to Delhi for peace negotiations 260; meets Baji Rao 261, 266; emperor negotiates with Marāthās through him and Kahn-i-Dauran 262; *Du'ab* raid and Jai Singh 265–6, 267–8n; final agreement for ceding Malwa and

Bundelkhand made through him (1741) 274–5
Jaju, battle of, 54–7
Jagannāth, Marāthā *sardar,* raids Bijapur 86–7
Jalāl-ud-Dīn K., nominated *dīwan* of Burhanpur by Farrukh Siyar, 171, 172–3n
Janoji, nephew of Hanumant, converted to Islam 128
Jaswant Singh, Maharaja, 46–7, 70
Jats—Aurangzib's conflict with 19–20; Jai Singh's first expedition against 160–4; second expedition 214–15
jizyah—secret treaties signed by sons of Aurangzīb for remission of 59n, 61–2; levied by Bahadur Shah 71; gradually falls into disuse 96; abolished by Jahandar at instance of Asad Khan, 114, 124; abolished by Farrukh Siyar in Bihar at instance of Husain 'Ali 133; order confirmed after accession 137; revived at instance of 'Inayatullah Khan, opposed by 'Abdullah Khan 165; abolished again after deposition of Farrukh Siyar 186; 196; M. Amin Khan's attempt to revive; attempt of Nizam-ul-Mulk to revive fails due to general opposition 206, 219–20

Kām Bakshh, Muḥammad (Prince), son of Aurangzīb, Shahu transferred to his camp; in Jinji campaign 42; appointed governor of Haiderabad 45; conflict with A'zam 49–50; deserted by M. Amin Khan 52; Bahadur Shah's offer regarding partitioning of empire 62, 79–80; defeat and death 81–2; Rājpūt relations 72n
Kanhoji Bhonsle, approached for help against Nizam-ul-Mulk, instructed by Shahu to remain neutral 214, 229n, 251
Kantha Kadam, Lieutenant of Dabhade in Gujarat, 233, 234, 243
Karnal, battle of 287–9
Khāfī Khān, historian 52, 61, 71, 96, 97, 99, 110, 115, 186, 195
khāliṣah and *zamindārs*, used as Court of Wards 163; its frittering away and farming-out 99, 119, 148
Khān A'ẕam Khān, son of Sarbuland K., killed in northwest 279
Khande Rai, agent of Jai Singh, 223
Khāndū Dābhdē, defeats *mīr bakhshī* of Husain 'Ali 168
(Khwājah 'Aṣim) Khān-i-Daurān (Ṣamṣam-ud-Daulah), early career 145–6, 247n; joins Farrukh Siyar in Bihar, attempts to remove suspicion against Husain 'Ali 133, 135; joins with Mir Jumlah in opposing Saiyids 145, 148, 150; appointed deputy of Husain 'Ali, secretly promises not to oppose Saiyids 152–3; his influence over-estimated by English embassy 159; appointed governor of Agra, his policy of peace with Jats 162; alienated due to rise of new royal favourite, advises deposition of Farrukh Siyar 175–6, 179; supports 'Abdullah K.'s proposal for compromise with Nizam-ul-Mulk 197

Remains chief *bakhshi* after fall of Saiyids 205; opposes Nizam-ul-Mulk 208; favours conciliation of Ajit Singh and of Rājpūts generally 216–19, 242n; leader of a group at the court, opposes royal favourites 247, 283; his character and general policies 246–8, 246n, 250–1; favours peace with Marāthās 256–7, 257–62; Baji Rao negotiates with emperor through him 262–4, 276–7; attitude after failure of negotiations 266, 267n, 271, as a patron of Hindustanis 247, 281–2; connives at peculation of subsidy to northwest tribes 284; minimizes Persian danger 285–6; relations with Nizam-ul-Mulk before battle of Karnal 286–7; writes to Rājpūts and Marāthās for help 286; killed in battle with Nadir Shah 288–9

Khān-i-Jahān, uncle of S. 'Abdullāh Khān and Husain 'Ali 164, 172–3n

Khān-i-Zamān, son of Mun'im Khān 64, 70, 93, 118n

Khaṣūṣ K., brother of La'l Kunwar 112n

Khūsh-hāl K., brother of La'l Kunwar 111, 112n

Khūsh-ḥāl K., historian 156

Khushal Singh, adopted son of Shahu 241

Khwājah 'Abdullāh, appointed *Sadr* by Aurangzīb, dies 48

Khwājah 'Abid, grandfather of Nizam-ul-Mulk 7, 8

Khwājah Anwār, brother of Khān-i-Daurān 144

Khwājah Hasan Khān-i-Daurān, brother-in-law of Kokaltāsh Khān, raised to 8,000/8,000 109; appointed *atalīq* of Prince A'zzud-Dīn 110, 122

Khwājah Ja'far, a faqir of Imamite tendencies, brother of Khan-i-Dauran 105n, 114n, 211n

Khwājah Khidmatgār, a *khwājah sarai*, joins Kūkī's gang 208, 249, 250n

Kokaltāsh Khān, an old favourite of Jahāndar Shāh, resents appointment against Z̲u'lfiqār K. 108–13, 120; appointed *mir bakhshi*, intrigues against Z̲u'lfiqār K. 108–13, 120, 174n; responsibility for executions etc. after accession of Jahandar 119; at battle of Agra against Farrukh Siyar 123

Kūkī Jiū Jiū, one of the favourites of Muḥammad Shāh, extent of her influence 120, 208; leads to increase in corruption and bribery 211; her supporters 248–50; opposed by Khan-i-Dauram, fall from power (1732–3) 248–9

La'l Kunwar, mistress and Queen of Jahandar Shah, antecedents 110; accorded regal state, rise of relations causes dissatisfaction among nobles, Jahandar neglects business and decencies of conduct due to her influence 111–12; political influence exaggerated 112; conflict with Nizam-ul-Mulk 117; Rustam 'Ali executed for raising hand against her 119n;

Prince A'zz-ud-Din's dislike of 122; fondness for celebrations 123
Lashkar Khān 410
Lutfullāh Khān Ṣadiq, antecedents 143n; appointed *dīwan* of Prince A'zz-ud-Din, deserts to Farrukh Siyar 122; dispute over his appointment as *diwan-i-khalisah* 142–3; helps Saiyids against Farrukh Siyar; gives cash salary to lower *manṣabdārs* 156

Mahābat Khān, son of Mun'im Khān 64, 92, 118n
Māhī-marātib (fish-standard) 46, 50n
Mahmūd, son of Mīr Wais, deposes Ṣafawid monarch 243
manṣabdārs 5-6 (also see under *jāgīrdārs*)
Marāthās, and Aurangzib 23–6, 294; position of at death of Aurangzib 34; attempt of A'zam to conciliate 56–9; and Bahadur Shah 83–8; and Jahandar Shah 114–15; and the Saiyids 168–71, 177, 187–9, 197–8, 203, 293, 296; and M. Amin Khan 206; and Nizam-ul-Mulk 167, 207, 209, 210, 228–31, 240–1n, 250–3, 259, 267–72; and Rājpūts 235–45; and Nadir Shah 236–7; and Muhammad Shah 218–32, 273–4; conquest of Malwa and Gujarat by 224–8, 231–4, 273–5
Maratha *wakīls* 114, 232n, 234, 238–9, 241, 236–7n, 261n, 262, 263, 272
Marḥamat Khān, dismissed qila'dar of Mandu, employed by Nizam-ul-Mulk 192
merchants, effect of revenue-farming on 156; treatment of 'Abdul Ghafur Bohra 147n, 208
Mīr Jumlah, early career 143–4; upholds principle of personal rule of monarch 145; accused of plotting to destroy old nobility 146; gains great influence with Farrukh Siyar, opposes Saiyids and interferes in administration 146, 146–8; appointed (absentee) governor of Bengal 148–9; struggle with Saiyids, ordered to leave for Bihar 150, 151; returns to Delhi, disgraced by Farrukh Siyar, helped by 'Abdullah K. 157–8; recalled from Lahore 177; appointed *Sadr* after deposition of Farrukh Siyar 182; part in assassination of Husain 'Ali 199; continues as *Sadr* 205
Mīr Wais, captures Qandāhār 280
Mitr Sen, proclaims Nekū Siyar at Agra 183, 184
Mu'aẓẓam, Muḥammad (see under Bahādūr Shāh)
Mubāriz Khān, deputy of Niẓām-ul-Mulk in Deccan, repudiates Nizam's agreement for *chauth* 209; Nizam tries to remove from Deccan 212–13, appointed Viceroy of Deccan, defeated and killed by Nizam 214; his attempt to get help of Marāthās 59, 229
Mughal (see also Irani and Turani): definition of xi; Mughal nobles allowed to maintain contingent exclusively of Mughals xv, xvi; not foreigners xix; their arrogant attitude xviii; averse to sharing

power with others 67, 191, 196; role in party politics of the time 280–3, 293–4

Mughal Khān, son of Niẕām-ul-Mulk, sent to Jai Singh 191, 192

Muḥammad 'Ali K., *bakhshi* of Jahān Shāh, imprisoned 118n

Muḥāmmad Amīn Khān Chīr (I'timād-ud-Daulah), ancestry 46, 47; appointed *Sadr* by Aurangzīb 47; petitions for *bakhshi-giri* 48; a patron of Turanis 49; ordered to join Kām Bakhsh 50; abandons him and joins A'zam 51; summoned to the court by Bahadur Shah after accession 62; given rank of 5,000 and *faujdāri* of Moradabad 65; remains in background due to alleged ill-will of Mun'im Khan 66; ordered to march against Rajputs 74; marches against Banda 90, 91; leaves his post to take part in civil war at Lahore 92; appointed against Banda again by Z̲u'lfiqār Khān 115, 116; remains neutral in battle against Farrukh Siyar 117, 124, 144

Appointed 2nd *bakhshi* and given high rank by Saiyid brothers 137, bid to displace Saiyids from position 150, 153; forms a powerful group in opposition to 'Abdullah Khan 153–4; attempt of Farrukh Siyar to win him over 155; attitude of Saiyids 166–7; posted to Malwa to check Husain 'Ali 172, 236; negotiates with Jai Singh 172; rumour of his invading the Deccan, precautions of Hussain 'Ali 174; leaves Malwa and returns to the court 175; dismissed from *manṣab* etc. by Farrukh Siyar, won over by 'Abdullah Khan 177; advises deposition of Farrukh Siyar 179, remains 2nd *bakhshi* after the deposition 182; clash of interests with the Saiyids 189; warns Nizam-ul-Mulk against Saiyids 195; Husain 'Ali's scheme to assassinate him opposed by 'Abdullah Khan 196; idea abandoned 197; offers to negotiate with Nizam-ul-Mulk on behalf of Saiyids 198; his part in the assassination of Husain 'Ali 199; fights 'Abdullah Khan 199–200; assessment of his role in relation to the Saiyids 200, 202

Appointed *wazīr* by M. Shah, his powers and position 205; his general policy was *wazīr* 206, 219; fails in attempt to revive *jizyah* 206; removes Ajit Singh from Gujarat 207; dies 207

Muhammad Ghauṣ Muftī, sent to re-establish Islam in Jodhpur, 70

Muḥammad Khān Bangash, antecedents and early life 245; joins battle against 'Abdullah Khan 199; establishes an Afghān centre at Farrukhabad 223; invades Budelkhand (in 1728) 244; besieged at Jaitpur by Baji Rao and forced to relinquish all his conquests in

Bundelkhand 234; jealousy of Sa'ādat Khān for him 245; his policy and ambitions 245; attitude of Muhammad Shah and Khan-i-Dauran towards 251; appointed governor of Malwa 242; agrees to pay *chauth* for Malwa 253; replaced by Jai Singh 254; fights Marāthās in *du'ab* 260, 266; approached by Baji Rao with proposal for building a united front against foreign invaders 272

Muḥammad Murād Kāshmīrī, a favourite of Farrukh Siyar, antecedents and early life 174; his rise alienates Khan-i-Dauran and others 174; his *manṣab* and property confiscated after the deposition of Farrukh Siyar 182; sides with 'Abdullah Khan in battle against Muhammad Shah 199

Muhammad Shāh, accession 181; his position during the Saiyid hegemony 203n; secret appeals to Nizam-ul-Mulk against Saiyids 195; proceeds to Deccan with Husain 'Ali, 'Ali, after assassination of Husain 'Ali fights and defeats 'Abdullah K. 199–200; his position during the *wizarat* of M. Amin Khan 205; character, neglects government, ruled by favourites 160, 208, 248, 249, 251; attitude to Nizam-ul-Mulk 212; rejects his proposals 213; Jat and Rājpūt affairs under 214–20; Marāthā affairs 231–3; and Nadir Shah 283–90

Muḥammad Sulṭān, son of Aurangzīb, 49n

Mukham Singh, son of Churaman Jat, 214

Mukham Singh, son of Inder Singh, assassinated 140

Mukham Singh, *Wāqa'-Nigār Kul* under Bahādur Shāh 139; *dīwan* of Husain 'Ali in the Deccan 168; at the battle of Hasanpur 199n

Mungi Shivgaon, battle of, 231.

Mun'im Khān (Khān-i-Khanan), early career 54; his part in success of Bahadur Shāh in the War of Succession 54, appointed *wazīr* 64; resentment of Asad and Z̲u'lfiqār Khān, and their rivalry with him 63–5, 66; attitude towards old nobles 62n, 64–5, 66; favours cautions compromise—Rājpūt policy 72, 75, 77; opposes grant of wide powers to Z̲u'lfiqār Khān in the Deccan 83; presents petition of Tara Bai for *sardeshmukhi* 84; blamed for escape of Banda 91; death 92; controversy between his sons and Z̲u'lfiqār Khān for *wizarat* 92–3; his administration 96–9; *Sufi* inclinations 66, 95; relations as *wazīr* with Bahadur Shah 101–3

Muqṭī'—see *iqṭā'dār*

Murshid Quli Khan, governor of Bengal 83n, 132, 221

Mu'tamad Khān, appointed *diwan-i-khalisah* 143

Muẓaffar Khān, brother of Khan-i-Dauran, 144n, 256n; appointed governor of Ajmer 179, 180; quarrels with Sa'ādat K. 185, 245n; killed 253

Nādir Shāh: Marāthā attitude to 271–3; rise of 280; envoys to

Mughal court 283–4; was he invited by the Mughals? 285; begins invasion of India 286–7; battle of Karnal 287–9; for occupation of Delhi 290; impact on Indian politics and society 291–2

Nāhar Khān, *nāib* of Ajit Singh in Gujarat 207n; murdered by Ajit Singh 218

Najābat 'Alī Khān, Saiyid, brother of S. 'Abdullah K. 92, 135, 183n

Nāmdār Khān, brother of La'l Kunwar 112n

Nāṣir Jung, son of Niẓām-ul-Mulk 273n

Nāṣir Khān I, governor of Kabul 278, 279

Nāṣir Khān II, governor of Kabul 279, 284

Nekū Siyar, proclaimed emperor at Agra 183, 184, 193

Netaji 24

Nīlkanth Nāgar, deputy of Sa'ādat K. 214

Nīmājī Sindhia, Marāthā *sardar* 47, 86n, joins Mughals 84, 127, 168

Niṣār Khān, son-in-law of Qamar-ud-Din K. 256

Niẓām-ul-Mulk (see under Chīn Qulīch Khān for early life). Given title of Niẓām-ul-Mulk, and appointed Viceroy of Deccan with wide powers by Saiyids 137; Abdullah Khan's regard for 137; his powers in the Deccan—sends back the *dīwan* 146n; replaced in Deccan by Husain 'Ali, joins Farrukh Siyar against Saiyids 149, 153, 154; summoned from Moradabad by Farrukh Siyar 172; alienated due to removal from *faujdāri* of Moradabad 175; 176; remains neutral during deposition of Farrukh Siyar, Saiyid suspicion of and attempt to conciliate 183, 188, 189; appointed governor of Malwa, but mutual ill-will continues 190–1; approaches Jai Singh for joint action against Saiyids 187; revolt against the Saiyids 187; revolt against the Saiyids, causes and issues involved 192–204. Retains charge of Deccan—first meeting with Baji Rao, confirms grant of *chauth* and *sardeshmukhi* 205, 206; appointed *wazīr,* his difficulties at the court 207–10; campaign against Haider Quli, meets Baji Rao again, his general policies 209–11; scheme for reforms and for re-imposition of *jizyah* rejected, leaves for Deccan 211–14, 220; defeats Mubariz Khan 214, 219; relations with Marāthās upto 1728, treaty of Mungi Ṣhivgaon 228–31; relations with Khan-i-Dauran and Delhi court 243, 250, 251, 252, 253; secret treaty giving Baji Rao free hand in north India 251; accused by Jai Singh of helping Marāthās 257n; alliance of Sa'ādat Khan with, concern at negotiations of Baji Rao and emperor 258, 259, 263–4n arrival at the court, battle of Bhopal 268–71, did he invite Nadir Shah? 285: sends back army to Deccan from Bhopal, summons Sa'ādat K. 286; takes no part in battle of

Karnal 288; imprisoned by Nadir Shah 289; acts as tax-collector for Nadir Shah 290; discredited in the eyes of emperor 273, 291; his role in party politics 293, 296–7, 298

nobility (see also *jāgīrdārs*) character, composition and organization 11–19; growth of features of a bureaucracy, but remain essentially an elite ruling group 12–13; position of ethnic and regional groups during seventeenth century 13–19; effect of political stresses and crisis of *jāgīrdāri* on 29–33

Groups towards end of Aurangzīb's reign 40–9; groups at Bahadur Shah's court, and their policies 63–7, 83–4; groups at Jahandar's court, dissatisfaction of old nobles 107–13, 116–17; parties under Farrukh Siyar, destruction of many old families, attempt of Saiyids to ally with old nobles and Hindus 143–8, 150–4, 166–8, 182; failure of Saiyid attempt to ally with old nobles 188–96, 202–3; 'Peace' and 'War' parties at the court, their attitude to Marāthās and to Nizam-ul-Mulk 246–53, 258–9; effect of ethnic groups on party politics 280–6; role of nobility in disintegration of empire 287–99

Nūr Jahān 112, 112–13n

Nūr-ud-Dīn 'Ali Khān, Saiyid, killed at Jājū 128

Nūrullāh Khān, joins Niẓām 195

Nuṣrat Yār K., Bāṛaha 184n; fights Abdullah K. 199n; appointed governor of Ajmer 217

Paimā Rāj Sindhia, joins Mughals 87

Parsoji Bhonsle, conquests of 193

Pawār (Yashwantrao) in Malwa 255, 269n

Pidiā Nāyak, escapes from Wakindhara 44

Pilājī Gaekwar, in Gujarat 233, 243, 255, 259, 228

Pijājī Jādhav, fights Qamar-ud-Dīn 257, 276

Pratinidhi (Shrīpat Rao) dispute with Baji Rao 226–7; Nizam's alliance with 229–30, 232, 240, 252

Qudratullāh Shaikh, favourite of 'Azīm-ush-Shān, 64; executed 146n

Quṭb-ul-Mulk, see 'Abdullāh Khān

Qamar-ud-Dīn Khān, son of M. Amīn Khān, made *Darogah* of the *ahadis* 98; granted the rank of 7,000 and *faujdāri* of Moradabad after the fall of Saiyids 205; offered *subahdāri* of Ajmer shrinks from cost and the difficulty of campaign against Ajit Singh 217; Haidar Quli Khan appointed governor of Ajmer at his instance 218; as *wazīr* of M. Shah—his character and policy 246, 247; joined by Abhai Singh 244; his campaigns against the Marāthās 255; deals with rebellion of Adaru 256, 257; leader of 'War' party at the court, tussle with Khan-i-Dauran

and Ajit Singh 258–61; opposes peace negotiations with Baji Rao 262, leads campaign against Marāthās in 1737 266; as a patron of Mughals 281–3; forfeits confidence of M. Shah due to role in battle of Karnal 291; character of his group 293
Qāẓī Qāẓī Khān, sent to re-establish Islam in Jodhpur, 70

Rafī-ud-Daulah, raised to throne by Saiyids 180
Rafī-ud-Darjāt, raised to throne after deposition of Farrukh Siyar 180, 181
Rafī-ush-Shān, son of Bahādur Shān, fights war of succession at Lahore 64, 65
Raghuji Bhonsle, does not cooperate with Bajī Rao, 272
Rāhḍārī, 123, 131
Raḥīm-ud-Dīn K., half brother of Niẓām-ul-Mulk 47, 48n
Rai Rāyān, resigns post of *diwan-i-khalisah* 165*n*
Rājārām 26–8, 42, 43
Rājārām Jat 161
Rājpūts, and Akbar 11; and *manṣabdari* 11, and tribalism 14; Aurangzīb's relations with 19–29; attempt of A'zam to conciliate 59; and Bahadur Shah, cautious conciliation 67–79, 296; large concessions under Jahandar Shah 113–14; and Farrukh Siyar, war against Ajit Singh 139–41; and Saiyids 185–8, 203, 293, 296; and M. Shah 215–19; desire for aggrandizement after departure of Nizam-ul-Mulk, 222–4; and Marāthā expansionism 235–45, 255–7, 262; at battle of Bhopal 269; appeal to for help against Nadir Shah 286
Rāj Singh, restored to Rupnagar, 114. (Rao) Rambhā Nimbālkar, joins Mughals 87, 115n; sides with Nizam in rebellion 195n
(Rao) Rām Singh Hārā, lieutenant of Ẕu'lfiqār K., 44, 45n, 51, killed at Jājū 57
Rana of Mewār 22, 62, 68–9, 70
Ratan Chand, *dīwan* of 'Abdullāh Khān, antecedents 147n; 'Abdullah Khan, leaves all affairs in his hands, opposed by Mir Jumlah and Farrukh Siyar for bribery and revenue-farming 146–8; continues these practices, influences even appointment of *qazis*, accused of neglecting old nobles 155–6; attempt of 'Inayatullah to reduce his authority 165–6; opposes re-imposition of *jizyah* etc. 166; Girdhar Bahadur submits to Saiyids through him 185; brings about agreement between 'Abdullah K. and Husain 'Ali 189; supports 'Abdullah Khan's proposal for compromise with Nizam 197; supports Haider Quli 208; blamed for un-popularity of Saiyids 196n, 202, 301
Riāyāt Khān, captures Rohtas fort 130
Roshan-ud-Daulah Ẓafar Khān Pānī-patī, a Turani, appointed 3rd *bakhshi* by Saiyids 182; sides with Kuki 248–9n, 250n; supports 'war' party 258, 262; in shoe-sellers' riot 282, 283, downfall 283
Rustam Dil Khān at Jājū 56; fights Sikhs 81n, 90–1, 92

Rustam Khān Bījāpūrī, punished for failure against Marāthās 86, 87

Sa'ādat Khān (Burhān-ul-Mulk) joins in plot against Husain 'Ali 199; appointed governor of Awadh 206; harried by Jats in march against Ajit Singh 216; his deputy in Agra, Nilkanth, defeated and killed by Jats 214; takes possession of *jāgīrs* in Awadh, defies imperial orders transferring him from Awadh 221; clash of interests with Jai Singh and M. Khan Bangash regarding *du'ab*, advocates resistance to Marāthās 245; joins Khan-i-Dauran in intrigues against royal favourites 250; tries to enlist Baji Rao against Nizam 252–3, 264n; opposes Marāthā policy of Khan-i-Dauran and Jai Singh 258–60, 261; fights Baji Rao in *du'ab* 266; emperor's annoyance, sent to his province 268; helps Nizam at battle of Bhopal 269–70; a patron of Iranis 281; suspected of inviting Nadir Shah 285; summoned for help by Nizam 286; at battle of Karnal 287–8; acts as tax-collector 290; dies 291

Sa'ādat Khān, relation of Farrukh Siyar, 182

Sabha Chand, *dīwān* of Z̲u'lfiqār K., 108, 72

Sa'd-ud-Dīn Khān, *Khān-i-Samān*, 207n

Sa'dullāh Khān (Hidāyatullāh Khān) *diwan-i-tan-o-khalisah* under Bahadur Shah 92, 93, 96; opposes Z̲u'lfiqār K. 109; executed by Farrukh Siyar 146n, 164

Safdar Jang, reinforces Niẓām-ul-Mulk at Bhopal, 269–70

Saif Khān 72n

Salābat Khān, Saiyid, appointed *mir atish* 183n

Samṣām-ud-Daulah, see Khān-i-Daurān

Santaji Sawai, deputed to meet Jai Singh for campaign against Nizam, 251

Santoji Bhonsle, joins Husain 'Ali on behalf of Shahu 171

Sarbuland Khān (Mubāriz-ul-Mulk) antecedents 175n, appointed governor of Gujarat 110; replaces Mir Jumlah as governor of Bihar 157; his stern dealing with *zamindars* 173n; summoned by Farrukh Siyar for ousting Saiyids 173; removed from Bihar, appointed to Kabul at 'Abdullah's instance 174–5; neutral in deposition of Farrukh Siyar 176, 202; son, A'zam K., killed by tribesmen while returning from Kabul to Peshawar 279; as governor of Gujarat, concludes pact, for *chauth* with Baji Rao 233; removed from Gujarat, attempts independence 222n; 233, 239n, 242, 251, 258n supports 'War' party at Delhi 258; acts as tax-collector for Nadir Shah in Delhi 290

Sardeshmukhi origin 25; Shivaji's demand for 25; and Tara Bai 27; Aurangzib's willingness to concede; conceded by A'zam, 57–9; granted by Bahadur Shah to Tara bai and Shahu 84–5;

Da'ud Khan's pact for 87, 88
Husain 'Ali's pact for 169–71; confirmed 187
Sardeshpande, post of 263, 265, 268
Satnamis 20–1
Senapati (see Dabhade).
Shāh 'Ālam—see under Bahādur Shāh
Shāh 'Ali Khan Bāraha, Saiyid, appointed governor of Allaḥabad 183n, 185
Shāh Jahān 55, 101–2, 105, 135n, 249n
Shahji Bhonsle 257
Shah Tahmasp Safavi, Nizam's desire to restore 211n, 280–1; abdicates 283
Shāh Waliullāh, Muslim divine, 298
Shāhū, granted *manṣab* of 7,000, Zu'lfiqār Khān's personal interest in 44, 45; allowed to escape 57–9; Bahadur Shah's refusal to grant *chauth* to and to recognize as Maratha King 85; creates disturbance in Deccan 85–6; private pact with Da'ud Khan Panni for *chauth* and *sardeshmukhi* of Deccan 87–8; struggle with Tara Bai 115; Da'ud Khan's pact revoked by Nizam-ul-Mulk, renewed hostilities with the Mughals 169; urged by Farrukh Siyar to oppose Husain 'Ali 169; pact with Husain 'Ali 169–70; his family sent from Delhi by Husain 'Ali after Farrukh Siyar's deposition 188; cordial relations with Husain 'Ali, demand for *chauth* of Gujarat and Malwa 193, 194, 231–2; requested by Saiyids to assist 'Alam Ali against Nizam-ul-Mulk 197, 197n; Nizam-ul-Mulk's agreement with for *chauth* and *sardeshmukhi* 206n, 210; Nizam's deputy, Mubariz K. repudites pact 122; approached by Muhammad Shah to helping Mubariz Khan against Nizam-ul-Mulk 214; division of revenues between him and *sardars* 224–5; appoints Baji Rao as Peshwa 225; Karnaṭak expeditions 230–1n; assigns *chauth* of Gujarat to Pratinidhi, contested by Baji Rao 233; patches up agreement between them 233; Girdhar Bahadur disregards his representation regarding Malwa 234; Jai Singh's proposal for settlement with 240–1, 298; favours moderation in dealing with the Mughals 240; attitude towards Nizam-ul-Mulk 251; gradually edged out of power by Baji Rao 262n; instructs Baji Rao to aid the emperor against Nadir Shah 272; attitude towards Baji Rao's proposal for building a united front against future invasion from north 273
Saif-ud-Dīn 'Ali Khān, Saiyid, brother of S. 'Abdullah K. 183n, 199n, 251
Shankarāji Malhar, adviser of Saiyids in the Deccan 169, 188, 262
Sharf-ud-Daulah 218
Shā'istah Khān, relation of Farrukh Siyar, property confiscated 182; sheltered by Jai Singh 184
Sher Afkan Khan, brother of Roshan-ud-Daulah 249n, 282

Shiv Singh, son of Dhir, *zamindar* 199n
Shambhaji, Kolhapur Raja, 230
Shī'ism, Aurangzīb's dislike of 18, 19n, Shī'ism and Iranis 18, 48; and A'ẕam 52; and Bahadur Shah 60–1, 95; in the time of Farrukh Siyar 145
Shivaji rise 23, treaty of Purandar with Jai Singh 23–5, subsequent relations with Mughals 25–6, claim for *chauth* 25–7, of Malwa and Gujarat 231
Shivaji II, son of Rājārām 84, 114
Shujā'at Khān Bāraha, Saiyid, displaced from Ajmer 74, 76n, 129
Shujā 'Khān, recognized as governor of Bengal 221
Siddhishta Nārāyan, *zamindar* of Bhojpur 133
Sidi of Janjira 226, 237
Sīdī Qāsim, the *kotwāl* 146.
Sikhs—clash with Aurangzīb 21–2, with Bahadur Shah and his successors 89–92
Sipah Sālār, post of 47, 50n, 52
Ṣūfī Bāyazīd of Burdhwan, hails Farrukh Siyar as king 130n
Sultān Ḥusain Ṣafwī, defeated and deposed by Mahmūd 280
Sultanji Nimbalkar, deputed to help Jai Singh against Niẓām 251
Surman, John, English factor 159, 165n
Swarajya (of Shivaji), 57, 169–70

Tāhir Khān—governor of Asirgarh, joins Niẓām 195
Taqarrub Khān, executed by Kām Bakhsh 82
Taqarrub Khān, a personal follower of Farrukh Siyar 136n, sheltered by Jai Singh 184
Tārā Bāi, widow of Rajaram 27, 84, 114, 193
Tarbiyat Khān, *mīr ātish* 51
Thakurs (see *zamindars*)
Tulsi Bai 88
Tūrānīs (see under Mughals)

Udāji Pawār, lieutenant of Baji Rao, 234, 252
Umabai Dabhade 234

Vijai Singh, brother of Jai Singh, appointed to Amber in place of Jai Singh 67, 68, 69; his later life 69n

Wazīr Khān, *faujdār* of Sirhind 76, 89
wizārat evolution under successors of Akbar, military aspect emphasized 101–2, position of Mun'im Khan as *wazīr* 101–2, Ẕu'lfiqār Khān's concept of *wizārat*, significance of his *wizārat* 94, 104, 107–13, 124; Saiyid concept of 'new' *wizārat* 135, 136; not accepted by emperor and his favourites 142–4, 145; 'new' *wizārat* becomes identified with liberal politics 165, 166–7; significance of Saiyid *wizārat* 200–4; Saiyid concepts and M. Amin Khan and Nizam-ul-Mulk 213–14, 219–20, general summary 294–8

Yādgār Khān, negotiates with Baji Rao on emperor's behalf 263, 263n, 264n
Yār M. Khān, *nawab* of Bhopal, 264

Ẓafar Khān, brother of Kokaltāsh K., 109n
Ẓafar Khān Panīpatī, see Roshan-ud-Daulah
Ẕakariyah Khān, son of 'Abduṣ Ṣamad Khān, 205, 225, 287, 299
zamindars—their position compared to *iqta'dars* and *jāgīrdārs* 7, 7–11; relations with Sultans of Delhi and Mughal emperors; tolerated, but attempts made to reduce their power 8–11: promote regional sentiments, position of petty-assignees (holders of *waqf, in'am, milk, maddad-i-mu'ash*) in relation to 10; admitted to *manṣabs* in limited number by Akbar 10, 11; Rājpūt *zamindars* and Akbar 14; support oppositional movements, *zamindars* and *khalisah* 20–1; conflict of governors with *zamindars* in Bihar 133, 157, 173n, 190; in Awadh and Allahabad 172–3n, 244; in Karnaṭak 88, 169–70; in Narnol 217; general growth in power of 202, 223, 256
Zīnat-un-Nisā Begum 65
Ziyá-ud-Dīn Khān, appointed *dīwan* of Deccan by Farrukh Siyar, Husain 'Ali's treatment of 172
Zuhrah, a friend of La'l Kunwar, her influence in time of Muhammad Shah, 111, 116
Ẕu'lfiqār 'Alī Khān, *mīr bakhshi* of Ḥusain 'Alī killed 168
Ẕu'lfiqār Khān (Itiqād Khān), antecedents and early career 27, 29, 41–4, 128; his supporters, character of group, its power and influence 45–6, 47, 48, 49; relations with A'zam 49–52; flees from Jājū 55–7n; Shahu escapes at his instance, concessions to Rājpūt rajas 57–9
Summoned by Bahadur Shah, appointed *mīr bakhshī* 62, 63; appointed deputy to his father 65; conflict for power and regarding policies with Mun'im K. 64, 66, 74, 82, 84; appointed (absentee) Viceroy of the Deccan with wide powers 82–4; *jāgīrs* looted by Marāthās 86; pact for *chauth* made by his deputy 66; alienated from 'Azim-ush-Shan, organizes other princes against him 92–4, 104–7; Jahandar succeeds with his support, power and position as his *wazīr* 107–8; opposition of royal favourites and La'l Kunwar 108–13; attitude towards Rājpūts, Marāthās etc. and Hindus 113–16; relations with M. Amin K. and Chīn Qulīch 115–17; fails to rally old nobility 117, 120; charge of oppression and miserliness 117–19; his administration 119–21, 296, 301; leaves affairs in hands of subordinates 120–1, 165n; defeated by Saiyids, and executed 121–3, 135–6, 138–9, 145–6; significance of his *wizarat* 124, 142, 149, 219–20, 293
Ẕu'lfiqār Khān Qarāmāulu, father of Asad Khān 40